EMPLOYABILITY AND MOBILITY OF BACHELOR GRADUATES IN EUROPE

Employability and Mobility of Bachelor Graduates in Europe

Key Results of the Bologna Process

Edited by

Harald Schomburg
International Centre for Higher Education Research (INCHER-Kassel),
University of Kassel, Germany

and

Ulrich Teichler
International Centre for Higher Education Research (INCHER-Kassel),
University of Kassel, Germany

SENSE PUBLISHERS
ROTTERDAM / BOSTON / TAIPEI

A C.I.P. record for this book is available from the Library of Congress.

ISBN 978-94-6091-568-0 (paperback)
ISBN 978-94-6091-569-7 (hardback)
ISBN 978-94-6091-570-3 (e-book)

Published by: Sense Publishers,
P.O. Box 21858, 3001 AW Rotterdam, The Netherlands
www.sensepublishers.com

Printed on acid-free paper

All rights reserved © 2011 Sense Publishers

No part of this work may be reproduced, stored in a retrieval system, or transmitted in any form or by any means, electronic, mechanical, photocopying, microfilming, recording or otherwise, without written permission from the Publisher, with the exception of any material supplied specifically for the purpose of being entered and executed on a computer system, for exclusive use by the purchaser of the work.

CONTENTS

Preface
Harald Schomburg and Ulrich Teichler   1

Bologna – Motor or Stumbling Block for the Mobility
and Employability of Graduates?
Ulrich Teichler   3

Moving to the Bologna Structure:
Facing Challenges in the Austrian Higher Education System
Helmut Guggenberger, Maria Keplinger and Martin Unger   43

Professional Success due to Scarcity?
Bachelor Graduates in the Czech Republic
Radim Ryška and Martin Zelenka   69

Bachelor Graduates in Germany:
Internationally Mobile, Smooth Transition and Professional Success
Harald Schomburg   89

The Vocationalisation of University Programmes in France:
Its Consequences for Employability and Mobility
Jean-François Giret, Christine Guégnard and Claire Michot   111

Bachelor Graduates in Hungary in the Transitional Period of
Higher Education System
László Kiss and Zsuzsanna Veroszta   129

Mixed Outcomes of the Bologna Process in Italy
*Andrea Cammelli, Gilberto Antonelli, Angelo di Francia,
Giancarlo Gasperoni and Matteo Sgarzi*   143

Employability and Mobility of Bachelor Graduates in the Netherlands
Jim Allen and Johan Coenen   171

Employability and Mobility of Norwegian Graduates Post Bologna
Liv Anne Støren, Jannecke Wiers-Jenssen and Clara Åse Arnesen   185

CONTENTS

The Employability and Mobility of Bachelor Graduates in Poland
Gabriela Grotkowska   209

The UK Bachelors Degree – A Sound Basis for Flexible
Engagement with an Unregulated Labour Market?
Brenda Little   229

Employability and Mobility of Bachelor Graduates:
The Findings of Graduate Surveys in Ten European Countries
on the Assessment of the Impact of the Bologna Reform
Harald Schomburg   253

The Authors   275

PREFACE

Since the late 1990s, cooperation among European countries has substantially intensified in undertaking similar higher education reforms. The efforts to establish a convergent system of a cycle-structure of study programmes and degrees has captured the minds of actors and experts and have led to a lively debate about the desirability and feasibility of the reform programme. The public debate is lively and controversial because it is not just a matter of quantitative and structural changes. Rather, very ambitious aims are pursued with the restructuring of the higher education system. It was emphasised from the outset of this reform programme that the new Bachelor-Master system and various accompanying measures should help to increase student mobility. In the subsequent years of the "Bologna Process" a second aim became relevant: the structural and the curricular elements of the reform should contribute to a closer relationship between higher education and subsequent employment, often called "employability".

The public debate addresses the rationales of the reform as such: What type of higher education do we want? What should be the future role of student mobility? What kind of links between higher education and the world of work are desirable and questionable? But over the years, the discourse changed and questions concerning implementation and impact have gained momentum: To what extent and how has a cycle-structure of study programmes been established? What relationships between study and subsequent employment have emerged? Can both developments be seen to be in tune with the objectives of the Bologna reform?

The information base on the developments of student mobility and on employment in the framework of the Bologna Process is quite limited. The discussions as to whether the Bologna Reform is a motor or stumbling block for increasing mobility and desirable "employability" cannot draw from a wealth of empirical findings.

This book aims to show what information can be drawn from graduate surveys which are periodically undertaken in various European countries as regards the implementation and the results of the Bologna process. Those responsible for national graduate surveys were asked to concentrate on the findings of the most recent surveys and to present information that can answer three major questions:

- What share of Bachelor students and all students have international experience in the course of their study?
- How many Bachelor graduates, possibly sub-divided into Bachelors from universities and from other higher education institutions and programmes, opt for employment and how many for further study?
- How is the employment situation of Bachelor graduates – in general and notably of university Bachelor graduates? How much do their income and their positions differ from those of graduates from Master programmes or from – old or new – long single-cycle study programmes? How different or similar are the contractual relationships with their employers and the links between level of degree and level of position and the links between the substance of study and their work tasks? Finally, are Bachelor graduates satisfied with their employment situation compared to other graduates?

H. Schomburg and U. Teichler (eds.), Employability and Mobility of Bachelor Graduates in Europe, 1–2.
© 2011 *Sense Publishers. All rights reserved.*

HARALD SCHOMBURG AND ULRICH TEICHLER

Researchers at the International Centre for Higher Education Research of the University of Kassel (INCHER-Kassel – Internationales Zentrum für Hochschulforschung), Germany, asked colleagues from nine other countries to contribute to this volume. Countries were chosen where the Bologna Process has sufficiently progressed to undertake a meaningful interim account and where national graduate surveys are conducted periodically: Austria, the Czech Republic, France, Hungary, Italy, the Netherlands, Norway, Poland and the United Kingdom, as well as Germany, the country where this comparative study was initiated.

The authors first presented their findings at an international conference arranged for this purpose. The conference on "Employability and Mobility of Bachelor Graduates" was held in Berlin from 30 September to 1 October 2010. Organised by INCHER-Kassel, it was sponsored by the German Federal Ministry of Education and Research (BMBF – Bundesministerium für Bildung und Forschung) and supported by the German Rectors' Conference (HRK – Hochschulrektorenkonferenz). The conference also helped to explore opportunities for future cooperation in analysing the findings of graduate surveys. The conference was viewed as an eye-opener to see how findings could be organised and presented in a more fruitful way as meaningful evidence for the policy discourse on higher education reforms.

The editors of this volume are grateful to the authors of the country chapters for their readiness to structure and interpret their findings along the lines of the questions above. Also, their willingness to take on such a task within a relatively short period is highly appreciated. The editors also wish to express their gratitude to the sponsor and to the official supporter of the conference. The BMBF did not only provide generous financial support, but also – together with the HRK – helped sharpen the focus of this dialogue between actors and researchers. This was also true of many persons contributing to the discussion.

Finally, the editors are indebted to the many persons who supported the organisation of the conference, the analysis of the German case, and the comparative analysis, and the preparation of this volume. Our gratitude goes to the team at INCHER-Kassel and more especially to Lutz Heidemann, Katharina Benderoth, Constanze Engel, Susanne Steinke, Vera Wolf, Pia Wagner, Florian Löwenstein, René Kooij, Martin Guist and Christiane Rittgerott, as well as to the students who supported the team. The editors thank Roman Schmidt, Wibke Gröschner and Vasileia Skrimpa for their tireless efforts before and during the conference. Paul Greim, Christina Keyes and the staff from B.Effective were reliable partners in publishing this volume and organising the international conference in Berlin.

We expect that further analyses of the impact of European cooperation in higher education reforms on graduate employment will be undertaken in the future. Other issues are salient. Some themes can be analysed in a better way once the implementation of the reform has progressed. And graduate surveys may become more elaborate and comparable in the future and, thus, provide more relevant evidence for the respective public debates.

Kassel, January 2011
Harald Schomburg and Ulrich Teichler

ULRICH TEICHLER

BOLOGNA – MOTOR OR STUMBLING BLOCK FOR THE MOBILITY AND EMPLOYABILITY OF GRADUATES?

INTRODUCTION

A decade of European reforms

The first decade of the 21st century is characterised by a lively debate about the future of higher education and by collaborative efforts to change the national systems of higher education in Europe in a similar direction. In the "Bologna Process", structural changes are the focal operational arena of higher education reform. Steps have been taken since the late 1990s to replace or complement the variety of national patterns of higher education systems by a convergent cycle-model, often called the Bachelor-Master model.

When the Bologna Declaration was signed in 1999 by the ministers in charge of higher education in most European countries, increase and improvement of student mobility was underscored as the major rationale for this structural reform approach. Notably, it was assumed that the new model could make higher education in Europe more attractive for students from other regions of the world and facilitate intra-European mobility.

In the course of the Bologna Process, a second rationale has been emphasised the structural reform and various other measures should contribute to closer relationships between higher education and the world of work. It was obvious from the outset that the new structures and study programmes and degrees challenges established relationships in this domain and that quantitative-structural changes in higher education had to be accompanied by curricular reforms. The recent debates and activities – often summarised in the catchphrase "employability" – indicate that a major movement has been triggered of reconsideration and reshaping the way higher education addresses the subsequent employment of the graduates, i.e. beyond the needs of the structural reform.

When the Bologna Process was launched, one expected that most of the reforms were likely to be implemented within a decade. This was symbolically stressed by calling 2010 the year of the start of the "European Higher Education Area". Even though most actors and experts agreed that such a substantial reform agenda needed a longer period of decision-making and implementation, 2010 was often taken as a kairos for interim accounts of the Bologna Process.

Structural change: the operational aim

As regards the changing patterns of the higher education systems in Europe we note a varying speed in the implementation of the Bachelor-Master structure. Indi-

H. Schomburg and U. Teichler (eds.), Employability and Mobility of Bachelor Graduates in Europe, 3–41.
© 2011 *Sense Publishers. All rights reserved.*

vidual countries varied more than was expected in determining the length of the study programmes, the conditions of progression from the first to the second cycle, the role of the various types of higher education in the provision of first-cycle and second-cycle programmes and the fields of studies excluded from this cycle-model. Of course, questions emerged concerning how such a structural change of study programmes up to a Master-level was linked to the overall quantitative and structural development in higher education, for example to changes in access and admission and to practices of regulating the conditions for the transition from the Bachelor stage to the Master stage. Furthermore, doctoral training was declared as a third stage in the mean time, though no convergent steps are advocated as to how to shape such a third cycle and how to link it to the preceding cycles. Finally, a controversial debate emerged about the changing functions of higher education in the process of such a structural change. Many academics called into question the desirability of short university programmes as an entry qualification to the labour market.

Enhancing student mobility: the core objective of the Bologna Process

As regards the enhancement of student mobility, increasing mobility at the time when the Bologna Declaration was signed was greatly appreciated, and the increase in student mobility could be seen as an uncontroversial goal that was high on the political agenda. But there was a need to specify the directions of mobility: should only inward mobility of students from other parts of the world be stimulated, or should outward mobility of students from European countries to other parts of the world also be stimulated? What role should "diploma mobility" (i.e. studying for the whole programme in another country) play vis-à-vis temporary mobility in the course of study? How varied should the flow patterns between countries be, and is a there a virtue in reciprocal flows? Moreover, the conditions of mobility were constantly being debated: What modes of funding are desirable? What are the opportunities and limitations in the encouragement of the recognition of study abroad? Last but not least, the real trends of student mobility and the underlying causes became an issue of debate.

Available data suggest that the number of students from outside Europe choosing European countries has increased and the increase beyond the general trend of worldwide student mobility suggests that higher education in European countries has become attractive for students from other regions of the world. But the public debates focused on the question as to whether intra-European student mobility was really increasing substantially and whether higher education reforms in Europe had really served to facilitate intra-European student mobility or on the contrary turned out to be stumbling blocks . Those supporting the latter view argue that the shorter study programme up to a first degree and that the accompanying measure of introducing or spreading a credit system as well as various activities towards a detailed structuring of the Bachelor programmes have undermined the readiness of students to study abroad for a period and have reduced their chances of having their study achievements abroad recognised upon return.

Enhancing "employability": the increasingly relevant additional objective

As regards employment, it was clear from the outset that the introduction of a convergent cycle-structure of study programmes and degrees would provoke the established links between higher education and the world of work most strongly in one respect: What would be the role of Bachelor programmes as regards preparation for the world of work in countries, fields of study and occupational areas and higher education agenda where no study programmes of a similar length existed previously? One could not be surprised if employers were uncertain whether and in what areas they should employ graduates. One could expect controversial debates in universities that traditionally offered only long study programmes leading to Master-equivalent degrees: Obviously, uncertainty prevailed in how to develop professionally relevant short study programmes and how one should strike the balance between their functions to lay the foundation for professional work and advanced study. Finally, one could not be surprised that students were uncertain as to how to handle these new options. These challenges were anticipated in the Bologna Declaration of 1999 in the often quoted sentence "The degree awarded after the first cycle shall also be relevant to the European labour market."

Over the years, however, "employability" was constantly extended in the process of the Bologna Process. Universities were called upon to reflect more strongly on the "learning outcomes", the "competences" to be enhanced through the study provisions and conditions and the impact of study programmes on graduate employment and to draw conclusions for the design of curricula. "Qualifications frameworks" were developed in the Bologna Process at the European, national and disciplinary levels in order to ensure a certain similarity of curricular thrusts and strengthen the perspectives of "learning outcomes", "competences" and "employability". This triggered a lively debate not only about the suitability of these kinds of operations and concepts, but also about fundamental issues of the teaching function of higher education: To what extent should study programmes aim to serve specialised and professional knowledge and to what extent should "generic skills" or "key qualifications" be promoted? To what extent should curricula, teaching and learning be designed to prepare for employment or be geared to employers' expectations, or to what extent should they emphasise other aims, i.e. academic quality and pursuit of knowledge for its own sake, cultural enhancement and civic responsibility, or the ability to address expectations critically and innovatively in order to become agents of change. This debate was often polarised by calls that higher education should adapt to the presumed demands of the "knowledge economy" and by calls to resist a sell-out of the university to instrumental pressures and thereby uphold the principles of the European university of being both driven by rationales of academic reasoning and professional relevance and to learn to act professionally and question the existing professional, economic and societal settings.

ULRICH TEICHLER

Limited information about structural change, mobility and graduate employment

In the public discourse about the process of the Bologna reform and the changes occurring in the key areas of this reform endeavour, we observe an enormous variety of statements about the facts. With all due respect to the interesting arguments that are presented, one can argue that the Bologna discourse is not very evidence-based. For example, we hear that the countries have established similar Bachelor-Master models or have gone in quite divergent directions. We are told that student mobility has substantially grown in the Bologna Process or that the Bologna Process hampers mobility. We hear claims that the new pattern of degrees is widely accepted on the labour market or that university Bachelor graduates face extreme difficulties in finding employment.

Many evaluation studies have been commissioned at the European level and in the individual countries and many scholars have taken initiative to analyse this reform process and its consequence for higher education. But many of these studies merely collect the views of actors and experts who present sophisticated guesses rather than reliable information. Also, many studies analyse statistics, surveys and other empirical sources which are not designed in such a way as to give convincing answers to the questions which must be posed in the Bologna Process. To take a well-known example: The currently available student statistics for Europe do not provide figures about the number of Bachelor and Master students and do not tell us how many students study in another European country for a semester or a year.

A secondary analysis of national graduate surveys

Enormous efforts will be needed in the future to ensure that reform efforts in higher education such as the Bologna reform can work as evidence-based policies: that a basis will be created for regular stock-taking and that the information thus provided and the analysis thus enabled will contribute to a reflection on the preceding aims, processes and result and to a creative revision of future aims and activities. First, more systematic collection of information will be needed. Second, more efforts will be needed to harmonise national data collection in order to improve the opportunities of creating Europe-wide databases or to undertake comparative studies on the basis of comparable sources. Third, the principles and details of information collection must be updated more quickly in order to get responses to new questions or gain relevance in the reform processes. To take an example: The stimulation of temporary mobility in Europe is seen as one of the most important and successful policy initiatives for more than two decades, but we still have to guess whether we have about 300,000 or 600,000 temporarily mobile students in Europe this year.

The establishment of a proper information base across Europe for each of the major themes addressed here could take a decade or more, once the view that a good information basis should be established has been widely accepted. Therefore, it remains important to examine existing sources of information to see whether they can provide a better quality of information than the type of information and analysis which seems to have currently the strongest influence on public discourse.

This volume is the result of the collaboration of researchers in various European countries who are active in undertaking graduate surveys. They have tried to identify the potentials of surveys on the employment of former higher education students in order to respond to some key questions raised in the stock-taking concerning what higher education looks like after some years of the Bologna reform.

As will be shown below, graduate surveys are not only a suitable source for taking up questions which arise in the context of the "employability" debate. They can also comprise information on mobility. Various graduate surveys ask retrospectively about experiences in the course of study and, thus, are in the position to establish how many graduates have spent a study period in another country. Moreover, various graduate surveys provide information about international mobility after graduation – an issue that is not directly addressed in the discourse about the Bologna reform, but that is certainly an indicator for the potential impact of student mobility.

The aim of this chapter

The aim of the introductory chapter of this volume is two-fold. First, an account of the Bologna Process is presented to identify salient issues which must be taken into consideration when analysing the potentials of graduate surveys to provide meaningful information for the Bologna Process and in this framework notably information on the employment of Bachelor graduates. Second, a review is undertaken of available sources of information, and notably of graduate surveys, in order to identify their value in enhancing the information base as regards the Bologna Process.

THE BOLOGNA THRUST

The Bologna Declaration

On the occasion of an anniversary of the Sorbonne University in Paris in 1998, the ministers of education of France, Germany, Italy and the United Kingdom declared that they would establish a "harmonised" structure of study programmes and degrees. As the signing of the *"Sorbonne Declaration"* was criticised as an isolated attempt of a few European countries, but the concept found widespread support in other European countries as a great leap forward, efforts were made to establish a broader basis for further action.

In Bologna (Italy) in June 1999, the ministers of 29 European countries signed the *"Bologna Declaration"*, according to which a cycle structure of programmes and degrees should be established and a "European higher education area" should be implemented by the year 2010. Subsequent ministerial *follow-up conferences* to monitor, specify and stimulate this process were held in Prague (Czech Republic) in 2001, Berlin (Germany) in 2003, Bergen (Norway) in 2005, London (United Kingdom) in 2007, Leuven (Belgium) in 2009, this time jointly prepared by the governments of the Netherlands, Belgium and Luxembourg, and Vienna (Austria) and Budapest (Hungary) in 2010. In the meantime, 47 countries joined this cooperation venture.

The major supra-national actor of the "Bologna Process", in contrast to that of the process to establish a European Research Area, is not the European Union; rather, the ministers of individual countries jointly promote this process. The European Commission, the governmental body of the European Union, was caught by surprise in 1998 because the four ministers who signed the Sorbonne Declaration advocated exactly what they had forbidden the European Commission to do in the past: to challenge the variety of higher education systems in Europe.

Major aims and operational objectives

The Bologna Declaration, in its core, calls for the establishment of a *cycle system of study programmes and degrees* all over Europe: a first study programme leading a degree which is called Bachelor in the Anglo-Saxon World, and a second leading to a Master.

The ministers of the European countries involved in the Bologna Process *never agreed on a common model as regards length of the study programmes*. As will be pointed out below, three-year Bachelor and two-year Master programmes were established most frequently, and five years of study up a Master is the most widespread model, but room for manoeuvre remained for other options (see Reichert & Tauch, 2003, 2005).

Over the years, the Communiqués signed by the ministers in the follow-up conferences emphasised that *doctoral studies* should be seen as the third stage of the Bologna model. However, no concrete agreements were reached as regards its nature, the status of doctoral candidates or similar salient issues.

The Bologna Declaration also suggested *accompanying measures* to reinforce the possible impact of the structural convergence of higher education systems in the European countries. First, a *credit system* should be introduced everywhere in order to measure study achievements cumulatively and to have a common "currency" for decisions to recognise the study achievements abroad upon return of the temporarily mobile students. Secondly, a *"diploma supplement"* should be awarded to all students upon graduation in order to provide easily readable and internationally understandable information on the national higher education system, the study programme and the individual students' achievements. Thirdly, close cooperation between the European countries was advocated in evaluation activities, in this context often called *"quality assurance"* (cf. Cavalli, 2007).

In the Bologna Declaration, this structural reform and the accompanying measures are called for to serve the major aim of *contributing to student mobility* which is:
– to increase the attractiveness of higher education in Europe for students from other parts of the world, and
– to facilitate intra-European mobility.

Without explicitly stating so, the Bologna Process aims primarily to increase the following modes of student mobility: (a) inbound mobility for the whole degree programmes from other parts of the world, and (b) temporary (between three months and a year) inbound and outbound mobility between the European countries (see Teichler, 2009b; Wächter, 2008).

It is also clear that the Bologna reform programme considers the cycle system of degrees as a virtue for the options of the students and for a better articulation between the provisions of the higher education system and the needs of society. *Short study programmes should be made more attractive*, and students should have more *flexibility in the course of their study career* whereby study could be more easily stretched over the life course ("lifelong learning").

In the course of the years, the *Bologna agenda seems to have broadened*. As the Bologna Process turned out to be a motor of change in higher education in many European countries, many actors aim to widen the agenda either by suggesting that the European governments add new themes to the Communiqués of the follow-up conferences or, less officially, to the official conferences held under the auspices of the Bologna Follow-up Group (BFUG, the coordination group between the ministerial conferences), or by just reinterpreting the Bologna discourse as including their preferred themes. For example, the European Commission published various papers in which it claimed that the philosophy underlying the Lisbon Process was more or less identical to that underlying the Bologna Process (cf. European Commission, 2010).

There is no doubt, however, that another major theme of the Bologna Process emerged and grew over time in addition to the structural theme (the stage structure of study programmes and degrees) and the theme of student mobility: that of the *substance of the study programmes*, notably the major curricular thrusts and the relationships between study and subsequent graduate employment. "Qualifications frameworks" and "employability" became the most frequent terms referred to in order to underscore the relevance of this second major theme (see Haug, 2005).

The debates and policies in the framework or the context of the Bologna Process spread beyond those themes. Joint activities of *"quality assurance"* extended beyond the initially envisaged objectives. Various themes were added to the list: *widened access* to higher education and permeability between the vocational training system and higher education, as well as the *"social dimension"* of higher education, notably in terms of widened access and equality of opportunity, but also of the financial conditions for study and the actual study conditions.

Preceding developments and policies

The Bologna Process is a clear step forward towards closer cooperation on selected issues of higher education. But it was not completely new: neither in terms of joint action between different countries in higher education nor in terms of the themes addressed. Rather, repeated activities have been undertaken since the end of World War II in the various European countries to counteract the idiosyncrasies and the relative isolation of national systems of higher education. Such policies were promoted by different *supra-national actors* as a quick glance on the five most influential activities within four stages of development (see Teichler, 2010).

In the first stage, efforts were made to increase the *mutual understanding* between the various European countries. In this framework, activities to *facilitate student mobility* played a dominant role in the hope that more detailed knowledge of other countries would dilute prejudices and increase sympathy for other ways of life and thinking. In Western Europe, the *Council of Europe* has been active since the early 1950s in facilitating mobility through conventions signed and ratified by individual countries for the *recognition of study* – more precisely for the recognition of prior education as entry qualification to higher education, of periods of study for mobile students during the course of study, and of degrees for mobile graduates. Similar activities have been undertaken by Eastern European countries since the 1970s for all European countries through cooperation between the Council of Europe and UNESCO, and in 1997 through the Lisbon Convention for the recognition of studies initiated again by the Council of Europe and UNESCO, this time in cooperation with the European Commission (see Teichler, 2003).

In the second stage, since the 1960s, most Western European countries and market-oriented economically advanced countries outside Europe have collaborated in the search for the best ways to stimulate and accommodate the *quantitative expansion of student enrolment* in higher education, thereby both aiming to *contribute to economic growth and to the reduction inequalities of educational opportunity*. The OECD (Organization of Economic Co-operation and Development), a think tank for mutual economic and social advice of these countries, suggested expanding the enrolment capacity of higher education through *the upgrading and the extension of relatively short study programmes* in institutions where there was no close link between teaching and research. Hence, diversification in higher education by types began to play a major role in many European countries.

The third stage was characterised by greater *cooperation, mobility* and the search for concerted *European dimensions* of higher education. This was initially put forward in the political "club" named European Union since the 1990s. The *ERASMUS programme,* inaugurated in 1987 to promote short-term student mobility within Europe, is the most prominent example of this stage.

In the fourth stage, the *individual European countries jointly* aimed *to pursue similar higher education policies and to strive for a system convergence*. In the Bologna Declaration of 1999, ministers in charge of higher education of almost 30 European countries expressed their intention to establish a common stage structure of study programmes and degrees. Subsequently, in the Lisbon Declaration in 2000, the European Council, i.e. the assembly of the heads of governments of the countries of the *European Union*, agreed to cooperate and take joint measures to invest in research and development and establish a "European Research Area" by 2010. Notably, public and private expenditures for research and development should be increased on average to three per cent of the Gross Domestic Product, thus helping to make Europe "the most competitive and dynamic knowledge-based economy of the world".

Obviously, the efforts to change higher education in Europe in the framework of the "Bologna Process" are by no means isolated. They could be seen as the most ambitious activities to increase the common characteristics of national higher education systems in Europe.

In looking at the themes of the Bologna Process, we also note that they were not totally new at the time when the Bologna Declaration was signed. The views vary, however, among experts as regards the major *factors that triggered the decision* to advocate a convergent system of study programmes and degrees in Europe (see Witte, 2006). One can argue that three factors were frequently cited by experts exploring this issue. First, since the 1960s there have been debates in various European countries about the most desirable patterns of the higher education system and a need was felt to *make relatively short study programmes more attractive* in the wake of the expansion of higher education. Second, the ERASMUS programme inaugurated by the European Commission in 1987 was seen as such a "success story" that it stimulated debates on how *temporary student mobility within Europe* could be spread further. Thirdly, many politicians and other actors became concerned since about the mid-1990s that study in non-English-speaking European countries seemed to lose *attractiveness for students from other parts of the world*; the introduction of a Bachelor-Master structure of study programmes was considered to be a major vehicle to increase this attractiveness. These views spread rapidly, notably in France and Germany. In Germany, the Framework Act for Higher Education was already revised early in 1998 in order to facilitate the establishment of stages of study programmes and degrees, before joint declarations were signed across Europe.

It should be noted that *the basic assumptions that triggered the Bologna Process were not well founded statistically*. The number of students worldwide who were studying abroad and who opted for study in the non-English-speaking European countries was not really on the decline, as it was often claimed (see Teichler, 1999). Moreover, it is not certain whether measures of structural convergence are the most important to make higher education in Europe more attractive to students from other parts of the world: The language issue, the scarcity of highly organised doctoral programmes or the deficiencies regarding individual academic and administrative support for the students in some European countries could have been more salient factors. But, clearly, beliefs are also facts: The belief spread in Europe around the year 2000 that the structural similarities of the European higher education systems would make them more attractive for persons from outside Europe.

Also, a second assumption underlying the Bologna Process is questionable. The Bologna Declaration stressed that similar programmes and degrees in Europe would also serve intra-European student mobility. But temporary student mobility in Europe worked quite well beforehand in the framework of ERASMUS, and if problems of recognition did occur, they were seldom attributed to the structural variety of higher education across Europe. Intra-European student mobility could work better, if programmes and degrees were similar, but one could conclude that European countries would not have revamped the programmes and degrees in Europe, for a moderate increase in student mobility within Europe.

ULRICH TEICHLER

Reviewing the processes and results of the Bologna Process

The Bologna Process was accompanied by many *evaluation activities*:
- For the preparation of each ministerial follow-up conference, the individual countries were asked to write *progress reports*, and every time a working group synthesised these in an overall *"stocktaking" report*.
- The European University Association (EUA) or individual experts were commissioned regularly to undertake *"trend"surveys at higher education institutions* on the implementation of the Bologna Process (Haug & Tauch, 2001; Reichert & Tauch, 2003, 2005; Crosier, Purser & Smidt, 2007; Sursock & Smidt, 2010).
- On various occasions, *higher education researchers* were asked to assess the overall development of the Bologna Process (see Alesi, Bürger, Kehm & Teichler, 2005; Kehm, Huisman & Stensaker, 2009; Center for Higher Education Policy Studies, International Centre for Higher Education Research Kassel & ECOTEC, 2010).
- Several studies were commissioned on *specific themes*, such as statistics and developments of student mobility (Kelo, Teichler & Wächter, 2006; Center for Higher Education Policy Studies, International Centre for Higher Education Research Kassel & ECOTEC, 2008; Teichler, Wächter & Lungu, 2011), the opinions of academic staff (Gallup Organization, 2007) or student statistics and surveys in general (EUROSTAT & EUROSTUDENT, 2009).
- Moreover, various studies were commissioned *in individual countries* or undertaken by various agencies and scholars on their own initiative.

Yet, most actors and experts discussing the implementation and results of the Bologna Process come to the conclusion that *the information base achieved is deficient*. Available *statistics* are often not suited to measure Bologna-relevant phenomena. There are few valuable *surveys* that cover all the European countries. Information provided by actors is often highly politicised. Many reports focus on how far actors comply to the official *operational objectives* without any discussion of salient effects and possibly unintended effects (see Reichert, 2010). Many reports are characterised by *pre-mature expectations*. They aim to measure and assess the results at a time when only the first steps of change are underway: For example, reports on the acceptance of the new Bachelors in the labour market were often undertaken and presented as valid findings before one tenth of the graduates had studied in the new degree system. Last but not least, the exciting and controversial reform climate created by the Bologna Process led to many *emotionally coloured reports* on its processes and impact.

A provisional account of the results of ten years of the Bologna Process

The analyses of the Bologna Process and the changes occurring in the process cannot be easily and comprehensively summarised. Yet, the author of this chapter claims that the following account covers the main messages of available analyses.

Speed of implementation: The operational objectives of the Bologna Process were implemented at very varying speed in the individual European countries. In some countries, the new degree structures and most of the accompanying measures were already introduced by 2002. In others, implementation started early but lasted many years. In other countries, the first years were characterised by debates on whether the new structures should be introduced, and it was only after a few years of discussion about the "if" of the reform that the "how" became the focus of the debate. In other countries, not much has happened after a decade since the Bologna Declaration (see Alesi et al., 2005; Sursock & Smidt, 2010).

The introduction of the Bachelor-Master structure: Surveys undertaken on behalf of the European University Association (see Sursock & Smidt, 2010) suggest that a Bachelor-Master structure of study programmes and degrees was implemented by 2010 in most higher education institutions in the Bologna countries. Accordingly, 53 per cent had implemented a cycle – Bachelor, Master and possibly doctor – structure in 2003. This share rose to 82 per cent in 2007 and to 95 per cent in 2010.

It can be added here that the "accompanying measures" to the structural change seem to have been carried out to a similar extent. 96 per cent of the higher education institutions responding in the EUA survey 2010 stated that they had a *credit accumulation system* for all Bachelor and Master programmes. Hence, 88 per cent make use of the ECTS system (60 credits as a normal nominal work load for one academic year). Also, the *Diploma Supplement* spreads quickly. According to the surveys named, 48 per cent of the higher education institutions in 2007 and 66 per cent in 2010 issued it to all graduating students and a further 14 per cent of institutions upon request.

The survey results are reported here, even though only 15 per cent of the higher education institutions had provided information. Certainly, institutions are more likely to respond to such a survey if they have implemented the changes addressed in the survey. Thus, the figures exaggerate the actual degree of implementation. Yet, most experts are convinced that the formal implementation of the Bologna mechanisms has progressed considerably.

Variation by field of study: However, the Bachelor-Master structure was not introduced to the same degree across all fields of study. As one might expect, it remained a minority phenomenon according to the EUA 2010 survey in most medical fields (veterinary medicine 16 per cent, dentistry 21 per cent, pharmacy 27 per cent, medicine 28 per cent, midwifery 36 per cent and nursing 46 per cent). But the introduction of the cycle-structure also remained incomplete in other fields, notably: architecture (46 per cent), law (61 per cent), teacher training (68 per cent) and engineering (73 per cent).

The Bachelor degree – a terminal or transitional degree: The Bachelor programmes at universities seem to function predominantly as an interim stage towards a Master degree. 85 per cent of the university representatives and 55 per cent of those from other higher education institutions responding to the 2010 EUA survey expect that most Bachelor graduates will not enter the labour market directly.

Length of study programmes: Although common goals and operational objectives were emphasised, the individual countries varied substantially in their interpretation of the goals and operational activities. Even the most obvious possible measure of European coordination within the new system of study programme, namely a standardisation of the length of the study programmes, has never been achieved. 18 countries consistently introduced 3-year Bachelor and 2-year Master programmes. Six have a 4+2 system, and four countries 4-year Bachelor programmes and Master programmes comprising one or 1½ years. The other countries have varied models (Eurydice, 2010).

Concurrent curricular reforms: Most higher education institutions responding to the 2010 EUA survey claim that curricular reconsiderations have taken place along structural changes. Among those introducing a Bachelor-Master structure, 77 per cent reported that this had been on the agenda in all departments.

Thematic range of the Bologna Process: As already pointed out, the thematic range of the Bologna Process widened substantially over time. As the Bologna Declaration was successful in triggering intensive discussions and efforts to change higher education, efforts were frequently made add issues to the Bologna agenda. Some observers consider this as steps towards a comprehensive reform of higher education in Europe, while others view this as a dilution of the reform programme.

In some countries, the introduction of the cycle system of study programmes and degrees was accompanied by intensive activities of *reconsideration and change of curricula*, while in others operational changes were implemented with few curricular considerations. In the course of the ministerial follow-up conferences, greater emphasis was placed on substantive matters of the new study programmes. This could be seen as an indication of disappointment that the initial aim to strive for structural convergence of the higher education system across Europe was a less powerful instrument for an overall reform than initially envisaged. In contrast, one could have assumed from the outset that a structural reform had to be accompanied by major curricular reforms. Most observers believe that the curricular debates on a stronger awareness of the results of study ("competences", "learning outcomes"), on feedback of experiences for the improvement of teaching and learning ("quality assurance"), on the levels of competences to be reached at the end of the various stages of study ("qualifications frameworks"), on the links between study and subsequent employment ("employability") and on the role of higher education programmes in the life course ("lifelong learning") indicate the need for improvements as well as successful changes (cf. Teichler, 2009c). But nobody dares to assess the extent to which changes in those directions have taken place. The aims of such reforms remain controversial. And it has remained an open question to know how far a paradigmatic shift towards a curricular convergence across Europe has taken place in recent years or how far the initial aim of preserving curricular variety amidst structural convergence has been upheld.

Involvement of actors: Many assessments of the Bologna Process point out that the *governmental actors* have been the strongest advocates of the key reforms from the outset. *Leaders of higher education institutions* followed quickly, while many *academics* continued to consider the Bologna programme as an undesirable imposition from "above". And protests by *students* were not infrequent. There were widespread critiques that a university Bachelor was not a sufficient level of academically-based study, and many university teachers and students see the university Bachelor as a transition stage to the Master. The learning processes are often viewed as over-regulated in the short Bachelor programmes that are shaped by frequent examinations as a consequence of the implementation of a credit system. There are concerns that the strong drive towards "employability" undermines academic quality and students' critical and innovative reasoning.

General acceptance: As the debates about the strengths and weaknesses of the Bologna agenda are highly emotional and as we note many "eulogies and protests" (Reichert, 2010), it is very difficult to establish *how far the major reform trend is accepted or refuted.* In a survey of academic staff in 31 European countries conducted in 2007, about one third agreed to the statement "It would have been better if the old single-tier system (without a split in Bachelor and Master) was kept", while almost six out of ten disagreed (Gallup Organization, 2007). Disapproval of the Bachelor-Master system was most frequent on the part of academics in Germany (53 per cent), followed by those in Estonia (46 per cent), Hungary and Italy (42 per cent each).

Protracted process towards a European Higher Education Area: The Bologna Declaration of 1999 called for a "European Higher Education Area" by 2010. Actors and observers agree that major changes have taken place since 1999, but that a comprehensive reform has not taken place so far. The ministers of the European countries involved in the Bologna Process indicated in the their Communiqué of 2009 and 2010 that they saw another decade of the Bologna Process shaped by further steps of implementation of the initial goals, necessary revisions and efforts to reach even more ambitious goals.

Heterogeneous national approaches of "Bologna": Finally, it became clear that higher education in the various European countries, despite efforts for increased similarity and cooperation, has remained quite heterogeneous (cf. Eurydice, 2010). This is mirrored in the enormous differences, in the length of study programmes and curricular approaches. But it also affects the frequency of student mobility across Europe, as well as key issues of the relationships between higher education and the world of work touched upon in the Bologna reforms.

THE STRUCTURE OF STUDY PROGRAMMES AND DEGREES

"Convergence" and "comparability"

As already pointed out, the major operational objective of the 1999 Bologna Declaration was to encourage all countries to introduce a cycle system of study programmes and degrees. The aim was not to create a homogeneous structure. The term "harmonization" employed in the Sorbonne Declaration was replaced by the term *"convergence"* in the Bologna Process, but obviously a high degree of similarity was intended in order to achieve the aims of this structural reform.

ULRICH TEICHLER

The introduction of a convergent Bachelor-Master structure (the individual countries, of course, are free to name the degrees and titles as they like) was envisaged in order to reach a *"greater compatibility and comparability of the systems of higher education"*. This was expected to help to increase the recognition of study of students who were during their course of study and make the study programmes and degree more transparent for the students, graduates and employers,.

Length of study programmes

Prior to the Bologna Declaration, the *years of study* were viewed as the most important, though not only, criteria to compare study programmes and degrees. For example, reference to the years of study was a major point in facilitating student exchange and recognition in the framework of the ERASMUS programme. A high degree of "comparability" could be reached if the European countries agreed on a standard length of both Bachelor and Master programmes. This would imply a substantial change, for an analysis undertaken in the late 1980s had shown that the length of first study programmes in European universities had varied between three and six years and those, in other higher education institutions between one and four years, and among them those at least equivalent to a Bachelor between three and four years (Teichler, 1988).

Therefore, great efforts were made in the early stages of the Bologna Process to reach an agreement on the standard length of study. But these efforts failed. As already pointed out, the length of Bachelor programmes is 3-4 years, that of Master programmes 1-2 years and the overall length up to a Master degree 4-6 years. Hence the length of study is often formulated in terms of credits (60 ECTS credits equal one year of full-time study). However, the 3+2 structure became the most common. The 4+2 structure prevailed in the U.S. and the 3+1 structure in England and Wales. Yet, it is premature to assess whether the degree or the years of study are the dominant "exchange rate", if a comparison between programmes and degrees based on different lengths must be undertaken concerning mobility and employment. In any event, the lack of standard periods impedes "comparability".

Types of study programmes

A further issue as regards the extent of homogeneity or variety of the Bachelor structure is the *typology of the various Bachelor and Master programmes and degrees*. Different types of Bachelor programmes and degrees might exist de facto or de jure if there is not only a formal diversity of higher education programmes according to the study cycles, but also according to types of higher education institutions and study programmes already existing prior to the Bologna Declaration (for example in Austria, Germany and the Netherlands among the countries addressed in this comparative study). Also, a division of Bachelor programmes according to types may have been established in the Bologna Process (for example, the vocational Bachelor programme in French universities along the general Bachelor programme which corresponds to the traditional licence). Furthermore,

Bachelor programmes could be introduced in some countries in some tertiary education institutions that are not considered as higher education institutions (ISCED 5b), while in other countries these programmes are neither called Bachelor nor considered equivalent to Bachelor programmes.

Moreover, some countries opted for different types of Master programmes – varying, for example, according to whether they have an academic or professional emphasis, whether they are a sequel to a Bachelor in a certain discipline or can be a second cycle for Bachelor graduates from different disciplines, whether they cover the range of the respective discipline or are more highly specialised, whether they are studied, as a rule, immediately after the award of the Bachelor or whether a time span between the Bachelor award and the start of the Master programme is customary or even mandatory (in the case Master programmes for continuing professional training) (cf. Davies, 2009).

Opportunities of entry and transition

A further possible variation is worth noting. There may be differences within countries and between countries in the regulations and practices as regards *entry to Bachelor study* and the *transition from Bachelor to Master study*. For example, entry requirements to study programmes of different types or to study programmes in different types of higher education institutions may vary. And Bachelor graduates from different programme or institutional types may face more problems than others in being admitted to certain Master programmes. Even if there is no distinction as regards the Bachelor awards, Master programmes may vary between countries and within countries as regards entry conditions: They may offer open access for all Bachelor graduates, those from certain institutional types, those from their own institution or they may set restricted admissions for all students. The selection criteria and processes may be determined supra-institutionally, by the individual higher education institutions or by those responsible for the individual study programmes. Hence, the selection criteria and processes may be closely linked to prior study (e.g. according to grades obtained in Bachelor studies) or be based on specific selective admission systems.

There may also be a considerable diversity of Bachelor and Master programmes on the basis of *formal elements of diversity* in higher education. And many of the formal elements of diversity did not emerge in the Bologna Processes, but are carryovers from the previously existing formal diversity of higher education. Experts agree that the difference between types of institutions was the most salient element of formal diversity prior to the Bologna process in many European countries (cf. the overview in Teichler, 2007a, 2008), and this element did not become marginal when the Bologna reform aimed to make the cycle structure the single most important element of formal diversity in European higher education.

ULRICH TEICHLER

Transition from traditional to new structural types

In analysing the ten European countries addressed in the comparative study of this volume we note *five different types of structural changes or structural continuity of study programmes* possibly linked differently to types of higher education institutions:
- Substitution of a more or less unitary system (only universities, almost only long study programmes) by a two-cycle system within a single institutional type: Italy.
- Substitution of a two-institution type system with single-cycle study programmes (longer programmes at universities and shorter programmes at other higher education institutions) by a two-cycle system with Master programmes at both institutional types: Austria, Germany and Hungary and the Czech Republic, where first steps towards a two-cycle structure were already undertaken prior to the Bologna Declaration.
- Substitution of some models above (two-institution type system by single-cycle study programmes of different lengths) by a two-cycle (Bachelor-Master) system with Master programmes at one type of institution (the universities) and only Bachelor programmes at other higher education institutions: the Netherlands.
- Substitution of a system of long study programmes at universities in a broad range of fields and short study programmes at universities as well as in a limited number of fields by a two-cycle system in a broad range of fields: France, Norway and Poland. In the case of France, a new vocational Bachelor degree was established where most students move after the award of a two-year diploma programme to a third-year vocational Bachelor programme. In Norway, two types of short study programmes existed previously: programmes for select fields of study (notably humanities and natural sciences) at universities and study programmes in most fields provided by other higher education institutions.
- Continuation of a traditional two-cycle structure: United Kingdom.

As a consequence of both varied structures prior to the Bologna Declaration and varied approaches within the Bologna Process, we note a *variety of patterns of study programmes and degrees*:
- As regards (first-cycle) *Bachelor programmes*, a single type of Bachelor graduates seems to have emerged de jure or de facto in Italy, Poland and the United Kingdom. In contrast, two types of Bachelor graduates have been created de jure or de facto in Austria, the Czech Republic, France, Germany, Hungary, the Netherlands and Norway. Hence, the university Bachelor graduates are seen as a partly new or completely new type of graduates, while the other Bachelor graduates are seen as the successors of those from the previously existing short study programmes at other higher education institutions.
- As regards (second-cycle) *Master programmes*, the country reports on Austria and Germany present a divide by institutional type, even though more refined and cross-institutional types overlapping typologies of Master programmes exist in these countries.

– As regards *long single-cycle programmes*, we note that the two-cycle structure has not been established in all fields of study. There are single-cycle long study programmes in all countries in which the two-cycle structure was introduced as the dominant pattern in the framework of the Bologna Process. In some instances, traditional programmes persist which are expected to be phased out over time. But in all countries efforts often led to decisions to keep single-cycle programmes in selected fields, most frequently in medical fields, but also in some other fields, as pointed out above. Most country reports do not delineate traditional and new single-cycle programmes, and no clear distinction is made between the terms "traditional study programmes" and "single-cycle programmes".

Obviously, the transition from the formal diversity preceding the Bologna process to the new formal diversity, primarily based on cycles of study programmes, can be achieved more easily if (a) some short programmes had already existed previously and/or if (b) there is no clear divide between university Bachelor programmes and Bachelor programmes from other types of higher education institutions.

Informal diversity

The "comparability" of study programmes and degrees is not only challenged by elements of formal diversity in higher education, but also by *informal diversity*. Concurrently to the Bologna Process, greater attention is paid in the public to the informal vertical diversity, i.e. differences between individual higher education institutions as far as reputation and "quality" are concerned. *"Rankings"* of "world-class universities" (see the controversial debates in Sadlak & Liu, 2007; Usher & Savino, 2006; Marginson, 2008; Kehm & Stensaker, 2009; Shin, Toutkoushian & Teichler, 2011) became extremely popular and are believed by experts to reinforce an even more steeply stratified system. In contrast, *informal "horizontal" diversity* in terms of specific "profiles" of the individual higher education institutions is advocated here and there, but does not gain the same momentum or is even undermined by the trend towards imitation of the thrust of the top universities. This competition for informal vertical ranks seems to counteract the vision of the Bologna Process according to which student mobility is facilitated between large numbers of institutions and according to which formal degree levels are viewed as important for "comparability". In response to "ranking" pressures to increase vertical diversity, the European Commission supports a project aimed at establishing a multi-dimensional "classification" of higher education institutions (van Vught, Kaiser, Bohmert, File & van der Wende, 2008). But this project is also driven by the view that maximal diversification is desirable and that multi-dimensional rankings should be pursued and, thus, does not match the vision of the Bologna Process of facilitating mobility and increasing comparability through new formal degree structures – a vision which requires that many institutions mutually trust each other as far as the similarity of the quality level is concerned.

ULRICH TEICHLER

Bachelor graduates: Transition to the world of work or further study?

The introduction of the Bachelor-Master structure is also expected to make the Bachelor programmes more attractive as a basis for subsequent employment. This will require efforts on the part of the universities to organise curricula in such a way that they cannot be understood as merely the first stage of a Master programme and acceptance on the part of the students and employers for whom short study programmes at universities are a new phenomenon. Therefore, the Bologna Declaration stated that: "The degree awarded after the first cycle shall also be relevant to the European labour market".

Formal vertical diversification in various European countries has been pursued since the 1960s by establishing – alongside universities – other higher education institutions with a vocational emphasis, concentrating on the teaching function and relatively short study programmes. It is taken for granted that a large number of graduates from the other higher education institutions would be employed in associate professional positions, while most university graduates would be employed in managerial and professional positions. This was viewed as normal in the wake of higher education expansion, even though the successful careers of some graduates from other higher education institutions in a professional and managerial position were viewed as helping to stabilise the reputation of these institutions and their study programmes.

As the Bologna Process aims to make the Bachelor-Master structure the most important dimension of formal vertical diversity, one could expect that the Bachelor-Master distinction would play a similar role in the labour market as the other higher education institutions-universities distinction had played: Most Bachelor graduates could be expected to be employed in associate professional positions, whilst most Master graduates would be absorbed in professional and managerial positions. Similarly, one can expect that Master graduates will have a somewhat higher average income than Bachelor graduates from the same field of study who are employed after the award of the Bachelor degree.

Conclusions for the analysis of graduate surveys

An account of the structural-quantitative changes occurring in the Bologna Process makes clear that the introduction of a convergent system of study programmes and degrees across Europe as such does not automatically create a "greater compatibility and comparability of the systems of higher education". Many specifications, such as the length of the study programmes, the possible creation of different types of Bachelor and Master programmes, and regulations and practices as regards entry to Bachelor programmes and progression from Bachelor to Master programmes are handled differently in the European countries. Graduate surveys – as they are designed – cannot reveal the diversity in those respects, but they can show how far professional success varies between Bachelor graduates from universities and Bachelor graduates from other higher education institutions.

Moreover, one must point out that the promotion of a cycle structure of study programmes and degrees can only be viewed as successful if a sizeable proportion of Bachelor graduates opt for employment after the award of the degree. Graduate surveys are the most suitable tool to measure rates of Bachelor graduates embarking on employment and those who continue their studies. They can serve this purpose if they do not exclude Bachelor graduates who continue study, and they can serve this purpose even better if they are undertaken not too soon after graduation.

Finally, graduate surveys can help to assess the functioning of the cycle structure of study programmes and degrees by measuring how close or how different the "professional value" of the Bachelor degree is compared to that of the Master degree. This will be the major theme of the subsequent chapters.

Here also the question is asked: How many Bachelor graduates continue their studies? But either this share cannot be compared with respective shares of other Bachelor graduates because such a comparison group does not exist, or the difference between the professional success of university Bachelor graduates and other Bachelor graduates is likely to be smaller because there was a tradition of transfer to employment on the part of university short-programme graduates prior to the Bologna Process. Therefore, more or at least the same degree of attention is paid to the second question: How far does the professional success of university Bachelor graduates differ from that of Master graduates?

THE BOLOGNA PROCESS AND STUDENT MOBILITY

The initial objectives

The Bologna Declaration of 1999 set the enhancement of student mobility as the major strategic objective of the reform. From the outset, the key operational objective was to establish a cycle structure of study programmes and degrees, and the increase of student mobility was the single most important strategic objective. Other strategic objectives gained momentum in the Bologna Process over time, but increasing mobility remained an undisputed priority.

As already pointed out, two aspects of mobility were emphasised at the beginning: The structural reform and the accompanying measures should help (a) to increase the attractiveness of higher education in Europe for students from other parts of the world, and (b) to facilitate intra-European mobility.

Categories of mobility

The region of origin or destination (or specifically the country of origin and destination) of student mobility already addressed at the outset of the Bologna Process is only one of the relevant categories in the analysis of mobility in Europe. The following other categories are also employed frequently in policy discourses as well as in analytical studies, as a methodological study on the quantitative measurement of student mobility has pointed out (Kelo, Teichler & Wächter, 2006):

Many actors and experts refer to the *nationality* (or "citizenship") of the students and its relation to the country of study. In contrast, other analyses measure *genuine mobility*, i.e. border-crossing for the purpose of study.

All analyses make a distinction between the directions of mobility. If citizenship is referred to, a distinction is made between "foreign students" and "study abroad", and if mobility is addressed, the respective terms are *"inward mobile students"* and *"outbound mobile students"*.

As a rule, mobile students are foreigners; in contrast, many foreign students have lived and learned in the host country prior to study: they are foreign but not mobile for the purpose of study. As a consequence, figures of foreign students are higher as a rule than those of mobile students. However, not all students are foreigners, but persons may have lived and learned abroad prior to study and opt to study in the country of the nationality. Therefore, a distinction can be made between *"foreign mobile students"* and *"home country mobile students"*.

Some students go to another country in order to study and are awarded a degree or any other certificate or diploma that testify the successful completion of the study programme in that country. Other students go to another country for a period of study, often for a semester or an academic year. In the methodological study quoted above, a distinction is made between *"diploma mobility"* and *"credit mobility"*. Terms such as "degree mobility" and "temporary mobility", "short-term mobility", etc. are also employed.

A short-term *sojourn may serve different activities*. Students may study regularly or make short visits, take language courses, participate in an internship or work abroad, where the work may be linked to the field of study and the prospective vocational area. Activities other than study are not addressed, as a rule, in educational statistics (unless students doing other activities are regularly enrolled), but some surveys make distinctions between various activities: in the latter case, these may be described as either "study" or "(other) study-related activities"; some surveys use various categories of study-related activities.

A further distinction is sometimes made between mobility that is funded or arranged by the institution on the one hand and mobility outside such institutional frameworks on the other, i.e. choice of the partner institution outside institutional exchange arrangements and funding by other means than support schemes for student mobility. Terms such as *"programme mobility"* and *"exchange students"* are used on the one hand and *"individual mobility"* and *"free movers"* on the other. Hence, these terms are not used consistently: "Free movers", for example, in some texts are understood as students who are mobile outside support programmes and in others as students who spend the period abroad at a higher education institution which is not linked to the home institution through any partnership arrangement.

Finally, the methodological study above underscores the difference between *"vertical"* and *"horizontal" student mobility*. Students of the former type move to a higher education institution with greater academic quality than at the home institution or t home country, whence the higher academic quality in the host country is often combined with a more favourable economic situation. In contrast, the latter students go to a country and institution where the academic quality is similar to that at home. Such a distinction cannot be made consistently on the basis of available statistics and is often as informal distinction, but it is very important, as far as the students' motives for mobility, their conditions of learning in another country and the typical outcome of study in another country are concerned. Vertically mobile students expect a major quality leap forward, and for that purpose they have adapted to the conditions at the host institution; they are more likely to study for the whole programme abroad, and they have a great need of academic support on the part of the host institution. Horizontally mobile students are more likely to learn from contrasts of profile rather from a higher level or quality in the host country; many are temporarily mobile and need less academic and administrative support than vertically mobile students.

In the early years of the Bologna Process, the discourse about student mobility often remained vague concerning the terms employed and the underlying concept. Also, no strong need was felt to set common priorities for student mobility along those categories. For example, many actors and experts quoted available statistics of foreign students and study abroad as if they were not aware of the difference between foreign nationality and mobility for the purpose of study abroad, while others accepted statistics on foreign students as the best available "proxies" for student mobility.

Lack of statistical data on student mobility

International educational statistics are jointly collected and compiled by UNESCO, OECD and EUROSTAT[1] (*UOE*) which are delivered to them by the respective national statistical agencies. Until recently, the UOE statistics informed solely on foreign students and study abroad (if some countries collected data on genuine mobility, these were presented in statistics on foreign students and study abroad without any respective explanation). In the light of the information needs of the Bologna process, we observe further weaknesses of the available international statistics:
- Many countries include temporarily mobile students – the most frequent mode of intra-European student mobility – only partially or not at all in their student statistics. Some countries even count temporarily outbound mobile students as home students during the study period abroad.
- The available international statistics do not make any distinction between "degree-mobile" or "diploma-mobile" students, i.e. those intending to study a whole study programme abroad, and "temporarily mobile", "short-term mobile" or "credit-mobile" students, i.e. those intending to study abroad for one semester or a somewhat longer period within a study programme.
- There is no distinction in the international statistics according to citizenship or mobility according to Bachelor and Master programmes.

---

[1] The statistical agency of the European Union.

- The statistics present student numbers in a given year (in most cases an academic year). Thus, they are not suitable to establish how many students have studied in another country during their course of study – either for the whole programme or for some period during the course of study.

The gradual move towards genuine mobility data

The methodological study on student mobility data pointed out that nine European countries had statistical data on genuine student mobility – most of them in addition to nationality data, but some instead of nationality data. Students were counted as mobile if the country of prior education was different from the country of study or if the country of residence was different from the country of study (Kelo, Teichler & Wächter, 2006). Therefore, it was possible to show how statistics of foreign students differed from statistics of inward mobile students for some countries. This can be illustrated for Austria – the only country of the ten countries addressed in this comparative for which detailed data were available both for 2002/03 and for 2006/07 (see Teichler, Wächter & Lungu, 2011). In 2002/03, 11 per cent of all higher education students in Austria were foreign mobile students and 1 per cent were home country mobile students, thus adding up to 12 per cent all mobile students, while 3 per cent were foreign non-mobile students and thus 13 per cent of foreign students. From 2002/03 to 2006/07, the proportion of foreign mobile students – the most important of the available statistical data for the Bologna Process – increased from 11 per cent to 12 per cent.

The methodological study triggered efforts on the part of various European countries to also collect data on genuine student mobility; in the meantime, most European countries collected data on both foreign and mobile students. However, the number of countries that collects data on mobility is still too limited to calculate outbound mobility with the help of data on inward mobility. Moreover, the international data collectors recommend that national agencies exclude short-term mobile students; many countries follow this recommendation, while others include foreign and possible foreign mobile students for a short period.

Hence, data are now available now on foreign students and students studying abroad which most likely include all diploma-mobile and possibly half the short-term mobile students. Clear distinctions can neither be made between diploma-mobile and short-term mobile nor between Bachelor and Master students: Data are available on foreign inward mobile students in a selected number of European countries without a corresponding calculation of foreign outbound mobile students. No international statistical data set at all on short-term mobile students.

Three other data sources for student mobility can be taken into consideration and are used in some instances:
- *Administrative data*: Agencies promoting student mobility set up their own administrative data. Obviously, the data collection of student mobility in the framework of the ERASMUS programme is the largest of its kind. In the absence of statistical data on temporary student mobility, ERASMUS data are taken in some analyses as a proxy for temporary student mobility in Europe (e.g.

EUROSTAT & EUROSTUDENT, 2009), though one does not know whether ERASMUS mobility comprises half, a third or even less of temporary student mobility in Europe.
- *Student surveys:* A student survey called EUROSTUDENT, periodically undertaken in various European countries, provides information about the proportion of students having been temporarily abroad prior to the time of survey (see Orr, 2008). This survey is bound to undercount temporary mobility, because the students surveyed may study abroad temporarily in the remaining period of study.
- *Graduate surveys:* The two major European comparative graduate surveys undertaken hitherto (graduation cohorts 1994/95 and 1999/2000) asked the graduates to provide information on mobility prior to study, during the course of study and in the early years after graduation (cf. Schomburg & Teichler, 2008).

In the meantime, various national governments, the ministers cooperating in the Bologna Process and the European Commission have moved towards declaring targets of mobility. The authors of a second methodological study on student mobility data, in analysing respective policy documents, came to the conclusion that measures of two modes of mobility are now most indicative of the prevailing mobility policies (see Wächter, 2011):
- the current share of inward mobile students from other parts of the world to European countries, and
- the outbound mobility among European students, i.e. the quota of European students who had studied in another country (in or outside Europe, short-term or all the study period, once or more frequently) during the course of their studies.

As regards the latter, the ministers in charge of higher education stated in the Leuven Communiqué in 2009 that a quota of outbound mobility (for study and practical periods) of 20 per cent should be reached by 2020. They did not provide any further definition of the quota.

Trends in study abroad and mobility

For the development in first decade of the Bologna Process, only data on foreign students from countries outside Europe can be referred to because most European countries have not collected genuine mobility data for the whole period. A recent statistical analysis (Teichler, Wächter & Lungu, 2011) shows that the number of foreign students from outside Europe (and unknown nationality), who were enrolled in tertiary education institutions in the 32 European countries addressed in this study (ERASMUS-eligible countries and Switzerland), almost doubled from slightly more than 400,000 in 1999 to about 800,000 in 2007. The rate among all students in these countries grew from 2 to 4 per cent during this period. The increase in foreign students from outside Europe in Europe was also clearly higher than the growth of worldwide study abroad; while the former figure doubled, the latter increased by about 50 per cent (see United Nations Educational, Scientific and Cultural Organization: Institute for Statistics, 2009). This finding suggests that higher education in European countries has become more attractive for students from other parts of the world in the course of the Bologna Process. And the fact, reported by various European countries that foreign students from other part of the world make up a relatively high proportion of Master students indicates that the Bologna reform of establishing a cycle structure of study programmes and degrees made study in European countries more attractive where a single-cycle structure had existed previously.

It could be added here that the respective proportion of foreign student is smaller if all the signatory countries of the Bologna Process are taken into consideration (see CHEPS, INCHER Kassel & ECOTEC, 2010). This is primarily due to the inclusion of Russia – characterised by a large absolute number of students and a low percentage of foreign students. But these data also confirm an increase in the share of foreign students.

According to the statistics for the 32 European countries, the number of foreign students who are citizens of other European countries increased from 3 per cent in 1999 to 3.3 per cent in 2007. According to the same source, however, the available statistics of students studying abroad from these 32 countries slightly declined from 3.3 per cent in 1999 to 2.8 per cent in 2007 in Western Europe. The respective figures for the 10 countries addressed in this comparative study are presented in table 1: We note an increase of student mobility in five of ten countries.

Table 1. Ratio of Students with Home Nationality Enrolled Abroad to Resident Students with Home Nationality (per cent)

Country	Ratio 1998/99	Ratio 2002/03	Ratio 2006/07	Change* of ratio	Change* of absolute numbers
AT Austria	5.1	6.4	6.0	+18	+14
CZ Czech Republic	1.7	2.5	2.5	+47	+119
DE Germany	•	3.1	4.3	(+39)**	(+69)
FR France	2.4	2.8	3.2	+33	+38
HU Hungary	2.4	2.2	2.1	-13	+34
IT Italy	2.4	2.3	2.3	-4	+4
NL The Netherlands	2.8	2.5	2.6	-7	+13
NO Norway	7.1	7.7	6.8	-4	+7
PL Poland	1.1	1.3	2.0	+82	+169
UK United Kingdom	1.4	1.4	1.2	-14	-10

* Increase/decrease from 1998/99 to 2006/07
** Change 2002/03-2006/07

Source: Based on Teichler, Wächter and Lungu (2011)

As these figures comprise only some short-term mobile students, we can estimate that about 2 per cent of the students from the 32 European countries who are mobile within Europe study in the other country for the whole study period and that this rate has not changed substantially in recent years. Table 1, however, suggests that this share varies dramatically between the ten countries addressed in this comparative study: in 2006/07 just little over one per cent of British students to almost 7 per cent of Norwegian students.

Despite the weaknesses of the available data, we can infer that of the two strategic aims of the Bologna Declaration as regards student mobility, one was successful: Students from other parts of the world came to Europe in larger numbers than one could have expected from trends in worldwide mobility increase. The other was not successful: Student mobility within Europe seems to have increased at a slow pace – slower than in the 1990s during the first decade of the 21st century.

Future measures of mobility

In considering the past weaknesses and the steps underway for improvement, we can expect that the number of students from outside Europe studying at a certain moment in time in European countries will continue to be provided through official national statistics and compiled by UNESCO, OECD and EUROSTAT. Therefore, data on foreign students and study abroad will be increasingly supplemented by data on foreign mobile students.

Second, we can expect that the fact of having studied in another country during the course of study will be measured with the help of two sources. Educational statistics compiled by UNESCO, OECD and EUROSTAT will show what proportion of students from the various European countries study for a degree in another country. And graduate surveys will be referred to as the most suitable instrument of measuring the – share of outbound mobile students.

THE BOLOGNA PROCESS AND "EMPLOYABILITY"

The role of the link between study and employment in the Bologna Process

As already pointed out, the relationships between study and subsequent employment have emerged in the Bologna Process as a second major strategic objective. The debates and statements on that theme, however, have not led to clear targets and measurable results in the same way as those on mobility.

The Bologna Declaration of ministers from 29 countries in 1999 does not comprise any recommendation to strengthen the employment orientation of higher education. Their quote for a labour "relevance" of "the degree awarded after the first cycle" was not a call for a stronger professional emphasis of study programmes in general, but rather for some degree of professional emphasis across all levels of study programmes.

Except for the issue above, nothing is said about possible curricular implications, and no call is made for curricular convergence. Also, the accompanying measures of spreading the practice of handing out an internationally readable "Diploma Supplement" to all students upon graduation is not based on the aim to change curricula, but rather to document the existing curricula and the individual study achievements.

However, the term "Bologna Process" is not used just to observe the implementation of the Bologna Declaration of 1999, but to describe a continuous process of policy formulation, implementation, stock-taking of results, and policy reformulation. As a rule, the communiqués published at the end of the follow-up conferences of the ministers are viewed as officially documenting such policy reformulations. And the communiqués of the theme-specific conferences of actors and experts organised by the Bologna Follow-up Group (BFUG), such as the first conference on employability held in Swansea in 2006[2], are viewed as quasi-official specifications of the Bologna policies. Hence, we can say that the process of policy reformulation is not limited to experienced-led modification of the thrusts of the Bologna Declaration, but that the changing policy formulation reflects the changing Zeitgeist of higher education in general as well as possible interests of actors involved to increase the political relevance of their objectives through incorporation in the above named communiqués.

While a structural approach dominated at the beginning, *the Bologna Process gradually moved towards curricular matters.* The terms "quality assurance", "employability" and "qualifications frameworks" signal this shift of emphasis. Certainly, this shift was to some extent determined by the logic of the initial structural approach. Structural convergence in terms of a cycle system of study programmes and degrees *necessarily calls for some curricular reflections and measures:*
– the issue of curricular relevance of a university Bachelor,
– the issue of distinct levels of competences typical for a Bachelor and for a Master, and
– the issues of "international education" and the "European dimension" of higher education which became more relevant due to increasing mobility.

The second issue plays a stronger role in the Bologna Process. A need was felt to disentangle the level of competences and knowledge strived for up to a Bachelor and to a Master degree. The national ministers approved the formulation of *"qualifications frameworks"* in their communiqué of 2005 which could be formulated for Europe as a whole or within national settings and disciplinary settings. For example, Bachelor graduates should be able to "apply their knowledge/understanding in a manner that indicates a professional approach", while Master graduates should be able to "apply their knowledge/understanding and problem solving abilities in new and unfamiliar environments within broader contexts".

Undoubtedly, however, the subsequent debates and policy statements were not merely driven by the necessary specification of the structural reform envisaged in the Bologna Declaration. Rather, the scope of these debates widened and developed their own dynamic. The Bologna Process is so open and controversially interpreted that nobody can claim to know for sure what are its "employability" objectives and targets. The author of this article, however, had argued that the "employability" thrust in the Bologna Process can be characterised by four aspects (see Teichler, 2009a, 2009c): (a) a discussion centred around a misleading term, (b) a

---

[2] For further information see http://www.bolognaconference.swansea.ac.uk/ (retrieved January 25, 2011)

growing "output and outcome awareness" in higher education, (c) a growing emphasis on abilities not straightforwardly enhanced in the acquisition of academic knowledge, e.g. general competences and practice-oriented learning, and (d) a growing pressure on higher education to strengthen the utility of study for the subsequent work of graduates. This will be explained briefly.

The term "employability"

The term "employability" is frequently used when the relationships between study and subsequent employment are addressed. The term as such is misleading in two respects:
- First, "employability" is a well established term of labour market research and policy addressing problems of *"youth at risk"*, notably problems of finding employment. In contrast, "employability" in the context of the Bologna Process addresses the question of how a very privileged group on the labour market might enhance its career prospects even further.
- Second, the term "employment" refers to the "exchange dimension" of the world of work, i.e. to salaries, positions, envisaged duration of employment in the contract, holidays, and social benefits linked to employment. In contrast, the respective debates in the Bologna Process focus on the quality and relevance of curricula for subsequent work assignments.

In looking at the debates on the "employability" of higher education graduates, we note that a broad range of goals is advocated, for example: The higher education institutions should do what they can to enhance the professional success of their graduates; students should strive to enhance the exchange value of their studies, i.e. choosing the university which promises the highest credential value, choosing a subject leading to well-paid occupations, etc.; a closer link should be established between the substance of study programmes and of work tasks; more emphasis should be placed on learning to transfer academic knowledge to action in the world of work, e.g. an applied emphasis, fostering problem-solving abilities; more should be undertaken to enhance competences which are not closely linked to the academic subject matter, but are highly appreciated in the employment system (e.g. socio-communicative skills); higher education institutions should assist their students and graduates in the job search process (information and advice as regards occupational choice, help to get in touch with employers, coaching for employment interviews, etc.).

Many actors and experts involved in the Bologna Process believe that the term "employability" has a normative undercurrent of subordinating study to the prevailing demands of the world of work; this is the cause of highly controversial debates. The author of this article is convinced that the thrust of this debate would be expressed in a better way if the term "professional relevance" was used: Higher education institutions are challenged to take into consideration when shaping their curricula what learning and enhancement of competences will mean for subsequent work. This holds true, irrespective of whether fields of study are traditionally closely linked to certain occupational areas or not, whether a more theoretical or a more applied curricular emphasis is preferred and whether one wants to adapt students to the prevailing job requirements or strengthen their potentials of being agents of change.

Output and outcome awareness

The Bologna Declaration does not call for "employability". However, the "outcome awareness", which has been growing for about two decades in Europe, is likely to affect debates on the changing educational function taking place in the Bologna Process.

Since the 1980s, various activities have spread in Europe to evaluate teaching and learning, research and administration of higher education (see the overview in Cavalli, 2007). *Evaluation* – undertaken in various institutional settings such as accreditation or in the achievement-oriented remuneration of academics, competitive research funding, output indicator-based institutional funding, etc. – is understood as activities of periodic, systematic and comprehensive analyses and assessments of the aims, processes and results of the core activities of higher education. In a mixture of mechanisms that both stimulate the reflection and control the action of key actors in the higher education system, these key actors are expected to concentrate their attention not only on their major activities, but also on a meta-level of observation and assessment: Why and how are activities undertaken? What results are envisaged and achieved? The basic underlying assumption of the many evaluation activities is that the key actors must constantly reflect on the rationales, processes and effects of their activities in order to achieve improvement and that they are able to find appropriate means for improvement.

It has recently become more popular to ask those responsible for study programmes and examinations at higher education institutions not to consider teaching, learning and examination in terms of knowledge, knowledge transmission and knowledge acquisition, but rather in terms of abilities that have been shaped by higher education and could be useful to cope with work and other life tasks after graduation. *"Learning outcome"* is a general term that is used in this context, and *"competences"* refer to potentially useful abilities which have been shaped, but not exclusively, by higher education. This is reflected in various communiqués of the ministers in charge of the Bologna Process, notably in recommendations concerning the establishment of "qualifications frameworks".

Beyond acquisition of knowledge: general competences and practice-oriented learning

There is no comprehensive analysis of the major curricular thrusts which have emerged in the process of curricular reforms that accompany the introduction of a convergent cycle system of study programmes and degrees in the various European countries. Most available documents suggest that two curricular thrusts that are linked to the frequently used term "competences" (see the overviews of concepts in Bennet, Dunne & Carrée, 2000; Knight & Yorke, 2002, 2003) have gained momentum. Both have in common that *competences are not merely viewed as based on knowledge and cognition*, but are also affective-motivational and to a certain extent sensu-motorical dimensions, and second, that these competences must be enhanced by a *broader range of measures than just classroom instruction and related learning.*

The first thrust aims to enhance competences that are not related to specific subject matters. Terms such as *"generic skills" and "key skills"* are used to characterise these competences (see Villa Sànchez & Poblete Ruiz, 2008). Some actors and experts believe that these can be enhanced in the courses that are closely linked to specific subjects, whilst others advocate the introduction and extension of non-subject related courses, e.g. foreign languages, rhetoric, logic of science, paper writing, etc.

The second thrust, often called *practice-oriented learning*, aims to strengthen the links between academic learning and the anticipation of future professional tasks. Frequent approaches are internships, project-based learning, involvement of practitioners as part-time teachers, etc.

Long lists of competences are often put forward to underscore the broad mandate of higher education institutions to enhance competences. The classifications vary, but the overall range of themes addressed is quite similar. As an example, the author of this paper presents a classification he has suggested (Teichler, 2009a): (a) *general cognitive competences*, i.e. emphasis on generic skills and broad knowledge, on theories and methods instead of knowledge areas, learning to learn, etc., (b) w*orking styles*, e.g. working under time constraints and perseverance, (c) *general occupationally-linked values*, e.g. loyalty, curiosity and achievement orientation, (d) *specific professionally related values*, e.g. entrepreneurial spirit, service orientation, (e) *transfer competences*, e.g. problem-solving ability, (f) *socio-communicative skills*, e.g. leadership, team work, rhetoric, (g) *supplementary knowledge areas*, e.g. foreign languages, ICT, (h) *ability to organise one's own life*, (i) *ability to handle the labour market*, e.g. job search relevant knowledge, promising self-presentation to employers, and (k) *international competences*; e.g. knowledge and understanding of foreign cultures, comparative analysis, coping with unknown persons.

One must admit, though, that the debate about competences to be enhanced by higher education is often fuzzy, because the various themes addressed tend to be defined according to three dimensions. First, some areas of competences are defined according to the *knowledge* dimension, e.g. knowing and understanding theories, methods and knowledge of academic disciplines (e.g. mathematics); in that case, it is clear what should be enhanced, but it is not really clear what it means for the competence of the persons and successful utilisation. Second, other competences are defined according to the *personal ability* dimension, e.g. "wise" or "smart"; in this case, how this competence could be fostered and translated into professional action remains vague. Third, some competences are defined according the *functional dimension*, i.e. the ability to achieve something on the job or in other life spheres, for example the "problem-solving ability"; in that case, the use of competences is clear, but how such competences are enhanced in higher education remains a "black box".

ULRICH TEICHLER

Strengthening the utility of study?

Learning in higher education can be described as both academic and professional. In some fields, an academic approach may prevail, whilst in others a professional approach may prevail. In universities, understanding academic knowledge tends to be viewed as more important than in other higher education institutions which may have an "applied" emphasis.

Leaving aside nuances, we find a *far-reaching consensus* in economically advanced countries about the *key educational functions of higher education*. Higher education is expected to:
- teach students to understand and Master academic theories, methods and knowledge domains,
- contribute to cultural enhancement and personality development,
- prepare students for subsequent work and other life spheres through relevant knowledge and help them to understand and acquire the typical "rules and tools" needed in their professional life,
- foster the ability to challenge prevailing practices. Graduates must be sceptical and critical, be able to cope with indeterminate work tasks and be able to contribute to innovation.

In the Bologna Process, a controversial debate developed about the functions of higher education. The discourse on "knowledge society" and "knowledge economy" underscores that higher education is becoming increasingly more important for technology, economy, society and culture and that, as a consequence, it is increasingly under pressure to provide evidence that it is useful for society. Extreme voices are frequently heard. On the one hand, we hear that higher education should have a close "match" to the current visible "demands" formulated by employers or inferred from the trends on the labour market. On the other, there are arguments that the Bologna Process in its emphasis on "employability" and the "professional relevance of Bachelor programmes" is an instrument of destruction of the traditional values of higher education, according to which a certain distance between knowledge and its use and certain discrepancies between job requirements and the enhancement of competences through higher education are creative for the knowledge system and for the world of work.

Obviously, the term "employability", as it is used in the Bologna Process, creates the impression that higher education should subordinate itself to the currently presumed "demands" of the employment system. The author of this article, in contrast, has argued that it would be preferable to use the term "professional relevance" because it suggests that in the "knowledge society", higher education is bound to reflect on the outcomes of its activities for the world of work and draw conclusions from that. But this reflection leaves open a broad range of options whereby the subordination to the presumed labour market needs may not be the most creative way for higher education to serve society (see Teichler, 2009a).

As a consequence of this controversial debate, one could assume that graduate surveys would serve the Bologna Process best if they measured "professional success" according to broad range of objectives which play a role in the public debates and according to the graduates' values and intentions. Graduate surveys must take care that their design does not only shed light on a limited range of views on how the relationships between higher education and subsequent employment should be shaped.

THE POTENTIALS OF GRADUATE SURVEYS IN THE FRAMEWORK OF THE BOLOGNA PROCESS

Potentials for the analysis of mobility

The comparative study presented in this volume is based on the conviction that graduate surveys can be a valuable tool for assessing the processes and results of the Bologna reform (cf. the approaches of comparative graduates surveys demonstrated in Teichler, 2006; Schomburg, 2007; Mora, 2008). This – according to the authors of this volume – holds true for both major strategic objectives: to increase student mobility and to enhance the "employability of graduates".

As regards mobility, graduate surveys are the best tool to measure the *frequency of mobility,* i.e. how many students have spent a period in another country during the course of their studies for the purpose of study or for various study-related activities. Graduate surveys have this potential because they can collect information retrospectively on activities in the course of study up to graduation. Therefore, respective information is provided in the subsequent chapters.

We should bear in mind, though, that national and internationally comparative graduate surveys are only suitable to measure short-term mobility. Information on the much smaller number of students from the respective country or countries who have spent the whole study period up to a degree in another country can be measured with the help of international education statistics which also comprise data on the number of graduates.

Graduate surveys are also potentially suitable instruments to provide an overview of the frequency of *other study-related activities* undertaken during the course of study, e.g. internships, employment related to the field of study or the prospective future professional area, summer schools, language courses, etc. Both the gathering of information on study and on other study-related activities with the help of student or graduate questionnaire surveys, however, only works if the categories of responses provided in the questionnaires are clearly formulated. For example, the graduates surveyed in the comparative REFLEX-study had responded affirmatively to the question of whether they had studied abroad so frequently that we can infer by taking into account various other sources that they included brief visits, summer schools, languages courses, etc. (see the report of the responses in Schomburg & Teichler, 2008). Obviously, a distinction must be made in the questionnaire between study for at least a term or semester on the one hand and short study and various other study-related activities on the other.

In this comparative study, information on study abroad during the course of studies is presented only for the most recent graduates. A *time series study* could be undertaken if graduate surveys were undertaken periodically and if the same or similar questions were asked.

Graduate surveys also provide the opportunity of analysing border-crossing *mobility during the first years after graduation*. In this comparative study, the authors of country chapters also report about employment after graduation. The analysis is more refined in some country studies and can be more refined in future comparative analysis if a clear distinction is made between international activities between graduation and the time of the survey on the one hand and international activities at the time of the survey on the other. Moreover, one could address mobility in the framework of further study as well as professional mobility in terms of being sent abroad by the home country employer.

Finally, graduate surveys can contribute to the analysis of factors triggering student mobility and the impact of mobility in the course of study on subsequent employment. This type of analysis has been undertaken in the past in surveys that focus on the employment of mobile graduates (see Janson, Schomburg & Teichler, 2009). General graduate surveys provide the opportunity to measure the impact of student mobility in a more sophisticated way by comparing employment between formerly mobile and formerly non-mobile students (ibid.; see also Jahr & Teichler, 2007).

Potentials for the analysis of the functioning of the cycle structure

As regards the functioning of the cycle-structure of study programmes and degrees, graduate surveys can provide information about Bachelor graduates' whereabouts some time after graduation. It is a crucial for the Bologna Process that actors and experts know how many Bachelor graduates continue their studies, both study and work, are employed, are unemployed or undertake other activities. Graduate surveys cannot only provide this information, but they can also specify the profile of graduates who opt for employment compared to that of graduates who opt for further study (for example the type of higher education institution, the field of study, the socio-biographic background of study achievement in the framework of the Bachelor programme). Again, periodic surveys could help to establish a time-series of the whereabouts of graduates.

We must bear in mind, though, that graduate surveys undertaken shortly after graduation can only present an incomplete picture of the number of persons who pursue their professional career with a Bachelor or a Master degree, because some Bachelor graduates may be employed initially and begin Master studies some years later. But starting Master studies does not guarantee successful completion; hence, some of those who opt for it may eventually settle with a career at Bachelor level.

Data on the whereabouts of Bachelor graduates are crucial for the assessment of the functioning of the cycle structure of study programmes and degrees. However, the interpretation of the facts may vary dramatically: Some actors and experts are convinced that this new structure is reasonably implemented if a minority of Bachelor graduates transfers to Master programmes, whilst others consider the transition of the majority to employment as normal. Some consider the cycle structure as a success if professional careers of Bachelor graduates are very similar to those of

Master graduates, whilst others consider a certain gap of professional rewards between the two levels as normal within an educational meritocracy.

Potentials for the analysis of "employability"

As regards "employability", graduate surveys have a much wider range of options to analyse graduate employment and the relationships between study and subsequent employment.

First, graduate surveys can describe the early career of Bachelor graduates – again in comparison to that of Master graduates – in terms of conventional descriptors of professional success, e.g. occupational group, remuneration, full-time employment, permanent employment, etc.

Second, it became customary in graduate surveys that graduates were asked to rate how closely their professional situation – both vertically and horizontally – is linked to their studies.

Third, graduate surveys may try to explore the extent to which graduate employment is linked to the graduates' values and intentions: How a good job in their view could be characterised and how close their situation is to this view and how satisfied they are in their professional situation.

These three aspects are taken up in the comparative analysis in this volume because a larger number of the national surveys reported here had asked questions in that domain. Future comparative studies on issues of "employability" in the framework of the Bologna Process could make use of a wider potential of graduate surveys. We know from prior examples of national surveys and multi-country surveys that three steps towards a complex analysis can be viewed as feasible.

Fourth, graduate studies may undertake multi-variate analyses to explore the weight of various factors in explaining the varying professional success of graduates. Questions such as the following can be taken up: To what extent can professional success be attributed to the various elements of the study provisions and conditions that the graduates believe to have experienced as compared to characteristic features of their socio-economic background? To what extent does the reputation of the university, the graduates or the areas of specialisation during the course of study play a role for the graduates' early career? (cf. Teichler, 2007a, 2007c). Do we note differences in the weight of these factors with regard to graduates from Bachelor programmes with an academic emphasis as compared to a vocational emphasis, or differences in those respects between Bachelor and Master graduates (see Allen & Van der Velden, 2007)?

Such complex analyses are needed because professional success is not the same as "output" of higher education. Rather, other "intervening variables" may explain success, notably different socio-biographic preconditions of students of certain institution types, institutions and programmes, differences according to learning prior to and outside higher education, differences in the study behaviour during the course of study in higher education, processes of recruitment and job search, regional labour markets, and disciplinary labour markets. Many outcome-based university rankings or similar assessments neglect the power of these variables.

Hence, some universities are "rewarded" and others are penalised for something which is out of their reach.

Fifth, information from other sources can be taken into consideration in order to interpret differences between countries in employment of Bachelor graduates. This can be illustrated for the countries addressed in this comparative study with two examples.

We could assume that Bachelor graduates are more likely to opt for employment after graduation in countries with a high graduation rate. Table 2 shows that the graduation rate has increased on average in the eight countries for which information is available from 26 per cent in 2000 to 36 per cent in 2008. Hence, the rate varies between 25 per cent in Austria and Germany on the lower end and 51 per cent in Poland on the higher end.

Table 2. Rate of First-time Higher Education Graduates of the Corresponding Age Group in Ten European Countries (ISCED 5A, per cent)

	1995	2000	2001	2002	2003	2004	2005	2006	2007	2008
AT Austria	10	15	17	18	19	20	20	21	22	25
CZ Czech Republic	13	14	14	15	17	20	25	29	35	36
FR France	m	m	m	m	m	m	m	m	m	m
DE Germany	14	18	18	18	18	19	20	21	23	25
HU Hungary	m	m	m	m	m	29	36	30	29	30
IT Italy	m	19	21	25	m	36	41	39	35	33
NL The Netherlands	29	35	35	37	38	40	42	43	43	41
NO Norway	26	37	40	38	39	45	41	43	43	41
PL Poland	m	34	40	43	44	45	45	47	49	50
UK United Kingdom	m	37	37	37	38	39	39	39	39	35
OECD average	20	28	30	31	33	35	36	37	39	38

Source: OECD, Education at a Glance, 2010

We could also assume that the availability of jobs requiring a Bachelor-level or a Master-level degree may have an impact on the Bachelor graduates' decision to find employment after graduation; for example, they may have a better chance of being employed as managers or professionals in those countries where the proportion of these groups among the employed is very high. Table 3 shows that the share of persons in managerial and professional occupations ranges in the 10 European countries addressed in the comparative analysis from less than 20 per cent in Austria, the Czech Republic and Italy to 30 per cent and more in the Netherlands and the United Kingdom.

Table 3. Proportion of Persons Employed in Managerial/Professional Occupations and Technicians'/Associate Professional Occupation among Employed Persons in 10 European Countries 2009 (according to ISCO-88, per cent)

	Managers or professionals (ISCO 1 or 2)	Technicians and associate professionals (ISCO 3)	Other (ISCO 0, 4-9)	Total
AT Austria	17	20	62	100
CZ Czech Republic	18	24	58	100
DE Gernany	21	22	58	100
FR France	22	19	59	100
HU Hungary	22	14	64	100
IT Italy	18	20	61	100
NL The Netherlands	31	18	52	100
NO Norway	20	25	55	100
PL Poland	22	11	66	100
UK United Kingdom	30	13	57	100
EU 27	23	16	61	100

Source: EUROSTAT, LFS database[3]

Sixth, graduate surveys could try to establish the extent to which certain *profiles of competences are relevant for the professional success of Bachelor graduates*. It would not be possible to undertake competence testing in the framework of graduate surveys; in some surveys, however, graduates were asked to rate their competences upon graduation and the job requirements they perceived at the time of the survey (for example in the CHEERS study; see Schomburg & Teichler, 2006): This also provides information about the dimensions of competences where graduates seem to be already close to the job requirements at the time of graduation as compared to dimensions where catching up through learning on the job and initial training is on the agenda.

Seventh, graduate surveys could be relevant to assess the extent to which certain curricular profiles of Bachelor programmes have an impact on the subsequent employment of their graduates. If a large number of graduates from individual higher education institutions and study programmes are surveyed and if questions of the questionnaire refer to the specific profile of the institution or the study programmes, graduate surveys can be a valuable feedback for the respective Bachelor or Master programmes (see Alberding & Janson, 2007).

---

[3] Retrieved January 22, 2011

ULRICH TEICHLER

The need for complex and comparable graduate surveys

Graduate surveys can provide a meaningful feedback for the Bologna Process and notably for the impact of the various national strategies chosen in the implementation if they are relative complex and conceptually ambitious and if the surveys in the different countries are quite similar. The comparative analysis presented in this volume shows that a certain extent of complexity and similarity has been reached across some countries, but that further efforts are needed.

The first national graduate surveys were undertaken in some countries several decades ago. The initial surveys only collected information about a few socio-biographic elements, the field of study and the higher education institutions, the whereabouts of graduates some months after graduation, the economic sector, the occupational groups and possibly income and the location of employment. Valuable as this range of information may be, it led to over-exaggerated interpretations of the value of having studied at certain institutions and in certain fields, as well as to exaggerated conclusions as regards "over-education", i.e. graduates not employed in "appropriate" occupations. Further research showed that many graduates who were not employed in high positions noted close relevance of their studies for their work. More attention was paid to the fact that educational and professional motives are quite diverse and do not necessarily resemble those of a "homo oeconomicus"; therefore more attention was paid in graduate surveys to job orientation and job satisfaction. One noted that a link between the university from which a person graduated and professional success was not necessarily the result of the competences fostered by that university but of a credentialist recruitment policy of employers; therefore, graduate surveys began to examine the links between study provisions and conditions, competences upon graduation, job requirements and professional success. Only if those responsible for graduate surveys believe that attention should be paid to such issues when taking into account the length of a questionnaire that is acceptable for potential respondents can such a valuable thematic range be covered.

The national graduate surveys addressed in this study comprise various similar questions. But the subsequent analysis will show that there gaps as far as comparability is concerned. Identical or similar national surveys can be ambitious if a joint international graduate survey project is undertaken. Many of the countries addressed in this comparative analysis were included in the two major international graduate studies undertaken hitherto (both supported by the European Commission and various national sources). In the CHEERS study ("Careers after Higher Education: A European Research Study"), those who graduated in the academic year 1994/95 were surveyed somewhat less than four years after graduation; about 40,000 graduates from 11 European countries and Japan, i.e. about 40 per cent of those contacted responded to quite a long questionnaire – about 600 variables (see the results in Schomburg & Teichler, 2006; Teichler, 2007). In the REFLEX study ("The Flexible Professional in the Knowledge Society"), those who graduated during the academic year 1999/2000 were surveyed about five years after graduation; more than 40,000 graduates from 15 European countries and Japan, i.e. about

35 per cent of those contacted responded to a questionnaire which was about two-third of the length of the CHEERS questionnaire (see Allen & van der Velden, 2007).

These two international surveys provide a relevant account of the employment of generations of graduates who had studied in various countries prior to the Bologna cycle-structure. Thereafter, however, no similar studies have been undertaken which could be taken as an information base to assess the impact of the Bologna reform. This is because there is a readiness in various countries to continue or start to sponsor nationally representative graduate surveys. In contrast, surveys such as CHEERS and REFLEX, which had been initiated by scholars, have not been undertaken recently, and no policy initiative has been successful to create a European system of surveying graduates periodically.

If national graduate surveys will continue to be undertaken in individual European countries and no European-wide system of graduate surveys is established in the near future, the quality of the feedback of these studies for the Bologna Process will depend on a high degree of comparability of national graduate surveys. The initiators of this comparative study hope that the cooperation between those responsible for national graduate surveys will be intensified and will lead to further sophistication and greater comparability of these surveys.

REFERENCES

Alberding, R. & Janson, K. (Eds.) (2007). *Potentiale von Absolventenstudien für die Hochschulentwicklung* [Potentials of graduate surveys for higher education policy and practice] (Beiträge zur Hochschulpolitik, No. 4/2007). Bonn: Hochschulrektorenkonferenz.

Alesi, B., Bürger, S., Kehm, B.K. & Teichler, U. (Eds.) (2005). *Bachelor and Master courses in selected countries compared with Germany*. Bonn, Berlin: Federal Ministry of Education and Research.

Allen, J. & van der Velden, R. (Eds.) (2007). *The flexible professional in the Knowledge Society: General results of the Reflex project*. Maastricht: Research Centre for Education and the Labour market.

Bennet, N., Dunne, E. & Carré, C. (2000). *Skills development in higher education and employment*. Buckingham: SRHE & Open University Press.

Cavalli, A. (Ed.) (2007). *Quality assessment for higher education in Europe*. London: Portland Press.

Center for Higher Education Policy Studies, International Centre for Higher Education Research Kassel & ECOTEC (2008). *ERASMUS and quality, openess and internationalisation in higher education in Europe*. Enschede: Twente University, CHEPS (unpublished).

Center for Higher Education Policy Studies, International Centre for Higher Education Research Kassel & ECOTEC (2010). *The first decade of working on the European higher education area: The Bologna Process independent assessment. Volume 1*. Enschede: Twente University, CHEPS (unpublished).

Crosier, D., Purser, L. & Smidt, H. (2007). *Trends V: Universities shaping the European higher education area. En EUA report*. Brussels: European University Assocation.

Davies, H. (2009). *Survey of Master degrees in Europe*. Brussels: European University Association.

European Commission (2010). *The EU contribution to the European higher education area*. Luxembourg: Office for Official Publications of the European Communities.

EUROSTAT & EUROSTUDENT (2009). *The Bologna Process in higher education in Europe: Key Indicators on the Social Dimension and Mobility*. Luxembourg: Sogeti.

Eurydice (Ed.) (2010). *Focus on higher education in Europe 2010 – The impact of the Bologna Process*. Brussels: Eurydice.

Gallup Organization (2007). *Perceptions of Higher Education Reforms: Survey among teaching professsionals in higher education institutions, in the 27 Member States, and Croatia, Iceland, Norway and Turkey* (Flash Eurobarometer 198). Brussels: European Commission.

Haug, G. (2005). The public responsibility of higher education: Preparing for labour market. In L. Weber & S. Bergan (Eds.), *The public responsibility for higher education and research* (pp. 203-209). Strasbourg: Council of Europe.

Haug, G. & Tauch, C. (2001). *Trends in learning structures in higher education (II): Follow-up report prepared for the Salamanca and Prague Conferences of March / May 2001*. Bonn: HRK.

Jahr, V. & Teichler, U. (2002). Employment and work of former mobile students. In U. Teichler (Ed.), *ERASMUS in the SOCRATES programme: Findings of an evaluation study* (pp. 117-135). Bonn: Lemmens.

Janson, K., Schomburg, H. & Teichler, U. (2009). *The professional value of ERASMUS mobility*. Bonn: Lemmens.

Kehm, B.M., Huisman, J. & Stensaker, B. (Eds.) (2009). *The European higher education area: Perspectives on a moving target*. Rotterdam: Sense Publishers.

Kehm, B.M. & Stensaker, B. (Eds.) (2009). *University rankings, diversity and the landscape of higher education*. Rotterdam: Sense Publishers.

Kelo, M., Teichler, U. & Wächter, B. (Eds.) (2006). *EURODATA: Student mobility in European higher education*. Bonn: Lemmens.

Knight, P.T. & Yorke, M. (2002). Employability through the curriculum. *Tertiary Education and Management, 8*, 261-276.

Knight, P.T. & Yorke, M. (2003). *Learning, curriculum, and employability in higher education*. London: RoutledgeFalmer.

Marginson, S. (2008). *The new world order in higher education: Research rankings, outcome measures and institutional classifications*. Victoria: University of Melbourne, Centre for the Study of Higher Education.

Mora, J.-G. (Ed.) (2008). The labour market of European higher education graduates: Some analytical approaches. *European Journal of Education, 42*(1) (special issue).

Organisation for Economic Co-operation and Development (2010). *Education at a glance: OECD Education Indicators 2010*. Paris: OECD.

Orr, D. (Ed.) (2008). *Social and economic conditions of student life in Europe*. Bielefeld: Bertelsmann.

Reichert, S. (2010). The intended and unintended effects of the Bologna reforms. *Higher Education Management and Policy, 22*(1), 99-118.

Reichert, S. & Tauch, C. (2003). *Trends in learning structures in European higher education III: Bologna four years after: Steps sustainable reform if higher education in Europe*. Brussels: European University Association.

Reichert, S. & Tauch, C. (2005). *Trends IV: European universities implementing Bologna*. Brussels: European University Association.

Sadlak, J. & Liu, N.C. (Eds.) (2007). *The world-class university and ranking: Aiming beyond status*. Cluj: Cluj University Press.

Schomburg, H. (2007). The professional success of higher education graduates. *European Journal of Education, 42*(1), 35-47.

Schomburg, H. & Teichler, U. (2006). *Higher education and graduate employment in Europe: Results of Graduates Surveys from 12 Countries*. Dordrecht: Springer.

Schomburg, H. & Teichler, U. (2008). Mobilité international des étudiants et débuts de vie active [International students mobility and early career]. *Formation emploi, 103*, 41-55.

Shin, J.C., Toutkoushian, R.K. & Teichler, U. (Eds.) (2011). *University rankings: Theoretical basis, methodology, and impact on global higher education*. Dordrecht: Springer (in press).

Sursock, A. & Smidt, H. (2010). *Trends 2010: A decade of change in European higher education*. Brussels: European University Association.

Teichler, U. (1988). *Convergence or growing variety: The changing organisation of study*. Strasbourg: Council of Europe.

Teichler, U. *(1999)*. *Internationalisation as a challenge to higher education in Europe*. Tertiary Education and Management, *5(1), 5-23*.

Teichler, U. *(2003)*. *Mutual recognition and credit transfer in Europe: Experiences and problems*. Higher Education Forum, 1, 33-53.

Teichler, U. (2004). The changing debate on internationalisation of higher education. *Higher Education*, *48*(1), 5-26.

Teichler, U. (Ed.) (2007a). *Careers of university graduates: Views and experiences in comparative perspective*. Dordrecht: Springer

Teichler, U. (2007b). *Higher education systems*. Rotterdam: Sense Publishers.

Teichler, U. (2007c). Higher education and the European labour market. In E. Froment, J. Kohler, L. Purser & L. Wilson (Eds.), *EUA Bologna handbook – Making Bologna work (*pp. 1-34). Berlin: Raabe.

Teichler, U. (2009a). *Higher education and the world of work: Conceptual framework, comparative perspectives, empirical findings*. Rotterdam: Sense Publishers.

Teichler, U. (2009b). Student mobility and staff mobility in the European higher education area beyond 2010. In B.M. Kehm, J. Huisman & B. Stensaker (Eds.), *The European higher education area: Perspectives on a moving target* (pp. 183-201). Rotterdam: Sense Publishers.

Teichler, U. (2009c). The professional relevance of study. In G. Pusztai & M. Rébay (Eds.), *Kié az oktátaskutatás? Tanulmányok Kozma Tamás 70. Születésnapjára* [Whose interest is educational research: Festschrift for Tamás Kozma's 70th birthday) (pp. 256-267). Debrecem: Csokonai Könyvkiadó.

Teichler, U. (2010). Europäisierung der Hochschulpolitik [Europeanisation of higher education policy]. In D. Simon, A. Knie & S. Hornbostel (Eds.), *Handbuch Wissenschaftspolitik*. (pp. 51-70). Wiesbaden: VS.

Teichler, U., Wächter, B. & Lungu, I. (Eds.) (2011). *Mapping mobility in higher education*. Brussels: European Commission.

United Nations Educational, Scientific and Cultural Organization: Institute for Statistics (2009). *Global Education Digest 2009*. Montreal: UIS.

Usher, A. & Savino, M. (2006). *A world of difference: A global survey of university league tables*. Toronto: Educational Policy Institute.

van Vught, F., Kaiser, F., Bohmert, D., File, J. & van der Wende, M. (2008). *Mapping diversity: Developing a European classification of higher education institutions*. Enschede: University of Twente, Center for Higher Education Policy Studies.

Villa Sànchez, A. & Poblete Ruiz, M. (Eds.) (2008). *Competence-based learning: A proposal for the assessment of generic competences*. Bilbao: University of Deusto.

Wächter, B. (2008). Mobility and internationalisation in the European higher education area. In M. Kelo. (Ed.), *Beyond 2010: Priorities and challenges for higher education in the next decade* (pp. 13-42). Bonn: Lemmens.

Wächter, B. (2011). National policies on mobility in higher education. In U. Teichler, B. Wächter & I. Lungu (Eds.), *Mapping mobility in higher education*. Brussels: European Commission.

Witte, J. (2006) *Change of degrees and degrees of change: Comparing adaptations of European higher education systems in the context of the Bologna process*. Enschede: CHEPS/UT.

Wolf, A. (2002). *Does education matter? Myths about education and economic growth*. London: Penguin Books.

HELMUT GUGGENBERGER, MARIA KEPLINGER
AND MARTIN UNGER

MOVING TO THE BOLOGNA STRUCTURE: FACING CHALLENGES IN THE AUSTRIAN HIGHER EDUCATION SYSTEM

THE STUDY STRUCTURE IN AUSTRIA[1]

The higher education system in Austria[2] consists of universities (22 public, of which 6 are general and specialised in specific disciplinary areas, and 12 are private), 20 universities of applied sciences (UAS, *Fachhochschulen/FH*) and (since 2007) 14 university colleges (and additionally three private courses) of teacher education (*Pädagogische Hochschulen*) providing ISCED 5A education as well as other institutions offering ISCED 5B tertiary education programmes.[3] The objectives of the universities are (among others) to offer scientific or artistic education in preparation for a profession. UAS, in contrast, provide vocationally-oriented education at tertiary level. Hence, UAS also offer specialised programmes for working students and often include compulsory work placements in the study programmes. The UAS sector was set up in 1994 and is still developing today. It started with a focus on courses in economics and engineering, but has widened its scope since then to programmes in art, tourism, social work and health care. The number of available study places is expanding every year, as is the number of students.

Access to university studies is generally open. Only in a few fields (medicine, dentistry, veterinary medicine, psychology, art and music) are study places limited and admission tests required. For some studies, applicants must demonstrate their artistic talents, practical skills, or physical aptitude in addition to the matriculation examination. Students are selected through entrance examinations for UAS programmes.

---

[1] Author of this chapter is Maria Keplinger
[2] See Eurydice country report in the Eurybase databank, retrieved August 13, 2010 from www.eurydice.org/portal/page/portal/Eurydice/DB_Eurybase_Home and www.bmwf.gv.at
[3] Master craftsmen/ foreman courses, technical and vocational education colleges, post-secondary colleges for medical services, and university courses.

H. Schomburg and U. Teichler (eds.), Employability and Mobility of Bachelor Graduates in Europe, 43–67.
© 2011 *Sense Publishers. All rights reserved.*

In the 1990s, the Austrian higher education system was characterised by a two-type structure, i.e. universities and UAS. Bachelor and Master programmes were introduced at public universities in 1999 and at UAS in 2002 through the University Act 2002 (*Universitätsgesetz 2002,* Bundesministerium für Wissenschaft und Forschung [bmwf], 2009a). Figures 1 and 2 illustrate the development of study programmes at universities and UAS following the three-tier Bologna structure as from 2000.

Figure 1. Development of Study Programmes at Public Universities in Austria, Winter Term 2000 to 2009 (absolute numbers)

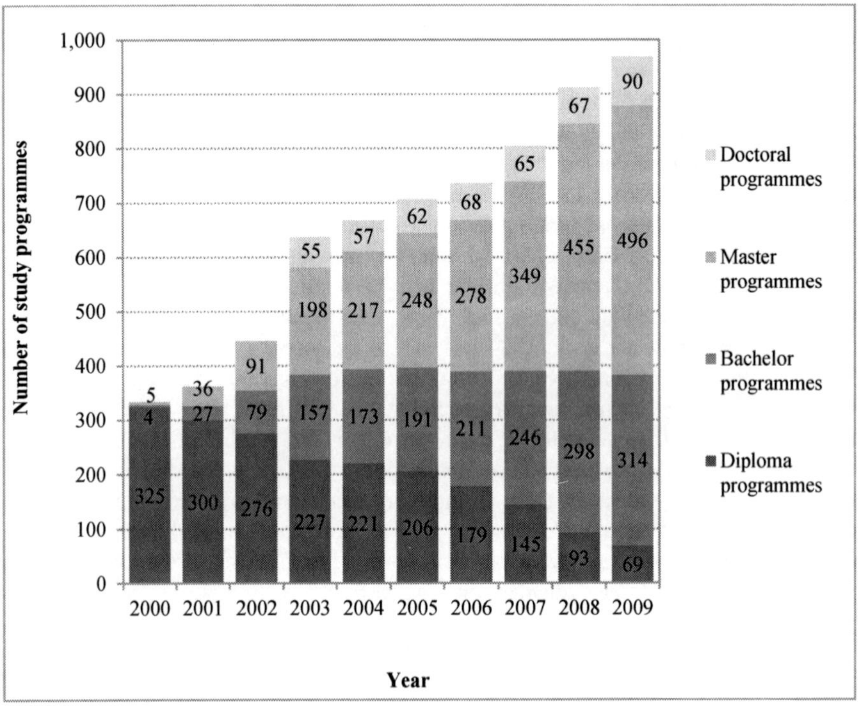

Source: bmwf (Federal Ministry of Science and Research)

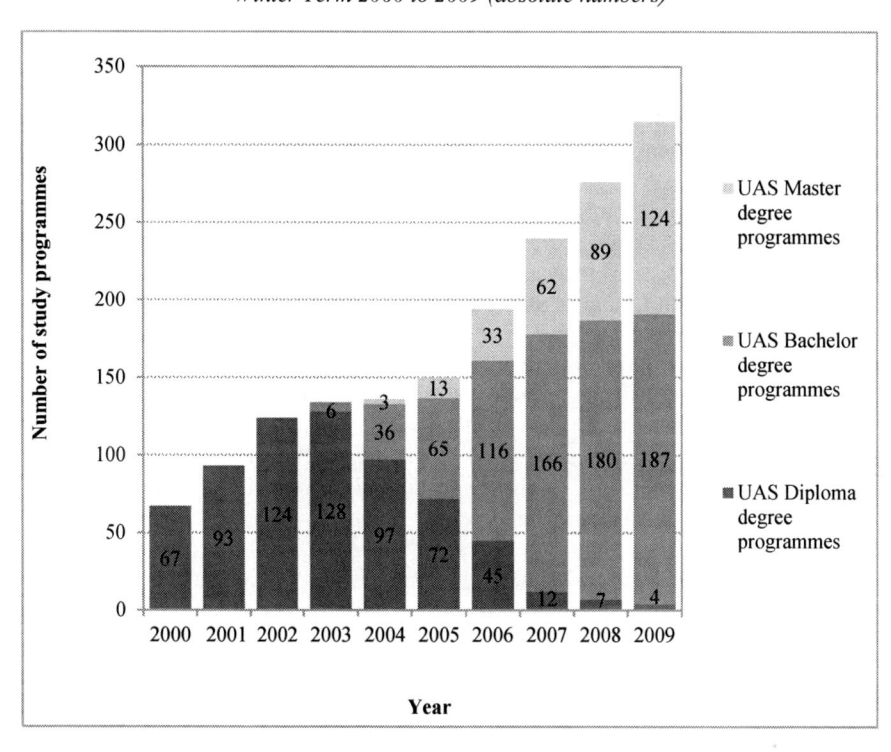

Figure 2. Development of Study Programmes at Universities of Applied Sciences in Austria, Winter Term 2000 to 2009 (absolute numbers)

[Bar chart showing number of study programmes by year 2000-2009, stacked by UAS Diploma degree programmes, UAS Bachelor degree programmes, and UAS Master degree programmes.

- 2000: Diploma 67
- 2001: Diploma 93
- 2002: Diploma 124
- 2003: Diploma 128, Bachelor 6
- 2004: Diploma 97, Bachelor 36, Master 3
- 2005: Diploma 72, Bachelor 65, Master 13
- 2006: Diploma 45, Bachelor 116, Master 33
- 2007: Diploma 12, Bachelor 166, Master 62
- 2008: Diploma 7, Bachelor 180, Master 89
- 2009: Diploma 4, Bachelor 187, Master 124]

Source: Fachhochschulrat (*Council of Universities of Applied Sciences*)

As of winter term 2009, 84 per cent of all study programmes at universities followed the Bachelor/Master structure. Many universities have already completed their course-conversion but medicine is still excluded. Teacher training for upper secondary education was changed with the 2009 amendment to the University Act 2002, which provides for the option of a 4-year Bachelor for certain fields.

At the UAS, 98 per cent follow the Bachelor/Master two-cycle structure and almost all private universities follow it. University colleges of teacher education have fully converted to Bachelor programmes (66 study programmes in winter term 2009) in a major reorganisation which became effective in September 2007.

Almost all new entrant students at the UAS and three quarters of those at the universities chose Bachelor study programmes in winter term 2009. At public universities, the number of students in the traditional single-cycle programmes is still relatively high (50 per cent of students are enrolled in diploma programmes). As the consequence of the gradual conversion of study programmes, a minority is awarded degrees according to the new two-cycle system.

In the recent *Studierenden-Sozialerhebung 2009* (student social survey, Unger et al., 2010), an online survey among all students at higher education institutions with a special focus on their social situation and study conditions, 75 per cent of Bachelor students in Austria responded that they intended to enter a Master programme, and one third intended to study in the Master programme while concurrently entering the job market. Only 8 per cent wanted to engage exclusively in employment upon the award of the Bachelor degree. When asked about their study motives, 69 per cent of students in Master programmes stated that they regarded the Bachelor degree as not sufficient, although only 22 per cent said their Bachelor degree had failed to help them find an adequate job.

In order improve the recognition of the Bachelor degree in terms of its employability on the labour market and its value as academic study by the students and graduates themselves, awareness measures have been launched (for example in cooperation with the Austrian Chamber of Commerce).[4] Current discussions like the *"Dialog Hochschulpartnerschaft"* (i.e. five working groups consisting of stakeholders in higher education)[5] have also focused on the employability of Bachelor graduates. The aim of these working groups is to find a common understanding or definition of "employability" of Bachelors. The conclusion was that, in the context of higher education, it not only aims at employability in the short run, but at the acquisition of competences which enable sustainable personal and professional development, because this is the only way that graduates will be able to handle future challenges on the labour market. Job-descriptions and possibilities for professional developments should be included in the curricula in order to raise the acceptance of this "new" degree.

GRADUATE SURVEYS USED FOR THE ANALYSIS[6]

Arbeitssituation von Universitäts- und FachhochschulabsolventInnen

The recent survey *"Arbeitssituation von Universitäts- und FachhochschulabsolventInnen (ARUFA)"* (in English: The working situation of graduates from universities and UAS) is the most comprehensive graduate survey ever undertaken in Austria. Graduates from Austrian public universities and from UAS were surveyed from December 2009 to February 2010. The survey addressed the five graduation cohorts from the academic year 2003/04 to the academic year 2007/08. It was designed as a total population survey undertaken through internet with the help on an online questionnaire. The study, which was commissioned by the Austrian Federal Ministry of Education, was undertaken by the International Centre for Higher Education Research of the University of Kassel (Germany) (INCHER-Kassel) – under the direction of Harald Schomburg – in cooperation with the Department of Soci-

---

[4] Booklet "Bachelor welcome!" (Wirtschaftskammer Österreich & Bundesministerium für Wissenschaft und Forschung, 2010)

[5] A series of discussion events held during the first half of 2010 in 5 working groups with stakeholders representing the university and UAS area (Retrieved August 13, 2010 from http://www.bmwf.gv.at/startseite/dialog_hochschulpartnerschaft_ergebnisse/)

[6] Authors of this chapter are Helmut Guggenberger and Martin Unger

ology (IfS) at the Alpen-Adria University of Klagenfurt and was coordinated by Helmut Guggenberger. The graduates from all 21 universities (as defined according to the University Act 2002) were contacted using the Universities' Data Network run in Vienna by the *Bundesrechenzentrum* (*BRZ*; federal computing centre of Austria). Graduates from the UAS were contacted in most cases by the Department of Sociology at Klagenfurt, which was provided with graduate address details by the individual organisations in charge of the UAS; in total, 15 UAS took part.

The ARUFA study yielded 25,669 responses with a response rate of 25 per cent. This can be viewed as highly satisfactory given the typical problems of online surveys and the declining willingness to participate in surveys, and as representative. In order to ensure a better similarity to the other country reports, the following analysis is based only on the graduates of the academic years 2006/07 and 2007/08 who responded; thus responses which had been provided between about 1½ and 2½ years after graduation are treated. Of the approximately 9,600 respondents included in the analysis, 17 per cent are Bachelor graduates from universities and 6 per cent from universities of applied science. Graduates from traditional study programmes prevail: 62 per cent from universities and 15 per cent from UAS. Master graduates are not included because their number is marginal among the respondents as a consequence of the gradual conversion of the study programmes to the Bachelor-Master structure.

Studierenden-Sozialerhebung 2009

The *"Studierenden-Sozialerhebung 2009"* is an online survey covering all students at public higher education institutions in Austria. All students at those institutions were invited in May/June 2009 via e-mail to participate, and more than 42,000 (out of approx. 265,000) did so. The *Sozialerhebung* covers a wide range of topics. In 2009, questions were added asking students in Master programmes about their experiences on the labour market as Bachelor graduates. The subsequent analysis will only comprise those Bachelor graduates who are named here "consecutive Master students".

SOCIO-BIOGRAPHIC BACKGROUND AND COURSE OF STUDY[7]

58 per cent of the recent graduates participating in the ARUFA study are female. As can be seen in table 1, women comprise more than 60 per cent of those who studied at universities, but less than half of those who studied at UAS.

More than one third of the graduates have parents (father and/or mother) with higher education. Among the graduates of traditional programmes, this share was by far higher amongst university graduates (41 per cent) than of those from UAS (23 per cent). The respective difference is clearly smaller among Bachelor graduates (37 per cent as compared to 29 per cent).

---

[7] Author of this chapter is Helmut Guggenberger

91 per cent are Austrian citizens. 7 per cent had not acquired their *higher education entrance qualification* in Austria (more than one third in Italy, almost one third in Germany and about one sixth in East European countries). The share of foreign graduates and of those having been educated abroad prior to study is about twice as many at universities as at UAS (see table 1).

Table 1: Socio-biographical Background and Course of Study of 2007 and 2008 Graduates from Higher Education Institutions in Austria (per cent)

	Bachelor graduates			Trad. graduates			Total		
	Univ.	UAS	All	Univ.	UAS	All	Univ.	UAS	All
Female graduates	57	44	54	63	47	60	61	46	58
A-typical entry qualification	52	69	57	43	66	48	45	67	50
Father and/or mother with an HE degree	37	29	35	41	23	37	40	25	37
Foreign graduates	12	5	10	10	5	9	10	5	9
Entry qualification abroad	9	3	8	7	3	7	8	3	7
Vocational training before HE	37	52	41	30	53	34	31	52	36
Total years of study in HE									
arithmetic mean	4.1	2.9	3.7	6.8	4.0	6.3	6.2	3.6	5.7
median	3.6	2.8	3.3	6.2	3.9	5.7	5.8	3.8	5.1
Age at time of graduation									
arithmetic mean	25.5	26.1	25.7	28.0	27.4	27.9	27.5	27.0	27.4
median	24.0	24.0	24.0	26.0	25.0	26.0	26.0	25.0	26.0
N	1,624	625	2,249	5,959	1,415	7,374	7,697	2,063	9,851

Source: INCHER-Kassel, Austrian Graduate Survey 2010 (ARUFA)

More than half had taken a "traditional" route to higher education, i.e. first attending a general secondary school (AHS), and almost one third had gone to a secondary vocational school (BHS) (30 per cent); only 4 per cent had followed a "non-traditional" access path (higher education entrance examination or similar). One third had completed their *vocational education* prior to study (e.g. apprenticeship or secondary vocational school), and seven out of ten had gained previous professional experience (full-time or part-time work; during or after secondary education, in any case before enrolment in higher education); hence, both vocational training and professional experience were more common among those from UAS than among those from universities.

The *period of study leading to the first degree* lasted on average 5.7 years for graduates from the academic years 2006/07 and 2007/08. In the cases of Bachelor graduates from UAS, the average period of study (2.9 years) was not longer than the required period of study, while university Bachelor graduates studied on average 4.1 years. The graduates from traditional study programmes not only studied longer (4.0 years and 6.8 years of study), but also prolonged their study beyond the required length of study more often.

For about two-thirds, study had been the *main activity* (this proportion was slightly higher among Bachelors). More than eight out of ten had taken part in a *study-related work placement*: about half completed a *compulsory internship* (almost half in the case of Bachelors).

The average age at the time of the graduation was 25.5 years among university Bachelor graduates and 26.1 per cent among graduates from universities of applied science. The average among graduates from traditional programmes was 28.0 and 27.4 years respectively, as is seen in table 1. One must bear in mind that student at UAS are older on average when they enrol for the first time, since a higher proportion is active in vocational training and gainful employment than among university students.

As regards their life situation, three quarters of the respondents in the Austrian ARUFA study reported a partnership at the time of the survey (partner 53 per cent, married 21 per cent and registered partnership 1 per cent). 19 per cent had one child or more living with them. Daytime childcare is most frequently provided by the partner (61 per cent), followed by parents or relatives (34 per cent), kindergarten/crèche or similar (35 per cent), and less often (24 per cent) by the respondents themselves.

INTERNATIONAL MOBILITY[8]

Like in other countries, international student mobility is perceived as a challenge posed by the Bologna Process, and there is a declared target that 50 per cent of students in Austria should acquire overseas experience by 2020 (see Bundesminsterium für Wissenschaft und Forschung [bmwf], 2008a, pp. 290f.; Bundesminsterium für Wissenschaft und Forschung [bmwf], 2008b, p. 6; Bundesminsterium für Wissenschaft und Forschung [bmwf], 2009b, pp. 54-59; Bundesminsterium für Wissenschaft und Forschung [bmwf], 2010, p. 26). There are arguments that student mobility may even drop in the new two-cycle structure of study programmes (see e.g. Kellermann, Boni & Meyer-Renschhausen, 2009; Heissenberger, Mark, Schramm, Sniesko & Süss, 2010). What do the data of the Austrian study reveal in this regard?

Study abroad

According to the *Sozialerhebung 2009*, 13 per cent of all Bachelor students in Austria already have study-related experiences in a foreign country; most studied for at least a semester abroad, did an internship or attended a language class. Among Master students, this ratio is 35 per cent. Nearly every fifth Master student

---

[8] Authors of this chapter are Helmut Guggenberger and Martin Unger

studied at least partially in a foreign country, namely during the Bachelor or the Master programme. 13 per cent did an internship, 6 per cent participated in a summer school, 6 per cent followed a language course and 5 per cent did research. One must bear in mind that the *Sozialerhebung* comprises students of various years of study (from beginners to students close to graduation); therefore the data do not show what proportion of students will be mobile up to graduation. Yet, they allow one to infer that temporary mobility is more likely to happen during the Master programme than during the Bachelor programmes.

Table 2. *International Mobility during the Course of Study and after Graduation of 2007 and 2008 Graduates from Higher Education Institutions in Austria (per cent)*

	Bachelor graduates			Trad. graduates			Total		
	Univ.	UAS	All	Univ.	UAS	All	Univ.	UAS	All
a. During the course of study									
Study abroad and/or short study-related activities abroad	24	33	27	37	40	37	34	38	35
... Temporary study abroad	16	22	18	24	24	24	22	23	22
... Short study related activities abroad	14	19	15	23	26	23	21	24	22
b. After graduation									
Study and/or practical training abroad after graduation	25	17	23	13	7	12	15	9	14
Employment abroad after graduation	12	12	12	20	22	20	18	19	18
... At present employed abroad	9	9	9	11	8	11	11	8	11

Source: INCHER-Kassel, Austrian Graduate Survey 2010 (ARUFA)

According to the ARUFA survey, more than one fifth of the graduates from Austrian universities had spent a study period abroad: 16 per cent of the university Bachelor graduates, 22 per cent of the Bachelor graduates from UAS and about 22 per cent from traditional programmes at both types of higher education institutions (see table 2). It does not come as a surprise to note that somewhat more university graduates from traditional programmes have studied abroad than university Bachelor graduates. This does not mean, however, that the new Bologna two-cycle structure has led to a decline in student mobility, because most Bachelor graduates continue to Master study and may be mobile in the second cycle. Thus, the actual frequency of study abroad up to graduation in the new two-cycle system will only be known when sufficient information is available on graduates from the Master programmes. It is exceptional in Austria, though, that students from other type of higher education study abroad in larger numbers than university students. However, the Bachelor graduates from UAS have spent on average a shorter period abroad (7 months as compared to 8 months).

Students who do not study abroad often give as a reason for not studying their concern that study abroad may prolong the overall study period. Other concerns are, according to the student surveys above, separation from family/friends, costs incurred to keep their accommodation in Austria and costs related to the sojourn abroad. Students having studied abroad most frequently see the costs of the sojourn abroad as the major barrier.

Employment abroad after graduation

12 per cent of the university Bachelor graduates and of those from universities of applied science were employed abroad after graduation for some period. These rates were somewhat lower than among the graduates from traditional single-cycle programmes, as table 2 shows. At the time of the survey, the proportion of those employed abroad was slightly higher at universities than at universities of applied sciences: 11 per cent as compared to 8 per cent among graduates from traditional programmes.

The choice of host country can be an indication of the purpose of mobility. For instance, some of student mobility between Germany and Austria is linked to the delicate issue of "numerus clausus refugees"; mobility from and to some countries may be interpreted as "brain drain" or "brain gain". Most of the mobile graduates from Austria are employed in Germany and Italy (together about 60 per cent of the professionally mobile graduates).

Other questions posed in the questionnaire show that graduates consider international competences and foreign language proficiency as not ranking highly among the employers' recruitment criteria. But about 40 per cent believe that their company or other employing institutions is active in an international sphere.

EMPLOYMENT AND FURTHER STUDY OF BACHELOR GRADUATES[9]

Whereabouts after graduation

More than two-thirds (68 per cent) of Bachelor graduates of the academic year 2007/08 from universities in Austria stated, when asked about their whereabouts one-and-a-half year after graduation, that they continued their studies. This share was lower amongst graduates from UAS: yet, a majority of them (54 per cent) also opted for further study, as table 3 shows. About four out of five Bachelor graduates who continue their studies were enrolled in Master programmes.

---

[9] Authors of this chapter are Helmut Guggenberger and Martin Unger

Table 3. Whereabouts of 2008 Graduates from Higher Education Institutions in Austria (per cent)

	Bachelor graduates			Trad. graduates			Total		
	Univ.	UAS	All	Univ.	UAS	All	Univ.	UAS	All
Employed (only)	26	42	31	62	83	66	54	69	57
Professional training	1	1	1	5	2	4	4	2	3
Study and employment	28	23	26	14	7	13	17	12	16
Study (only)	40	31	37	10	3	9	17	13	16
Search for job (without employment)	2	1	2	3	3	3	3	2	3
Family, children, etc.	1	1	1	2	1	2	2	1	2
Other	1	2	1	4	1	3	3	1	3
Total	100	100	100	100	100	100	100	100	100
Count	790	359	1,149	2,678	669	3,347	3,522	1,035	4,590

Source: INCHER-Kassel, Austrian Graduate Survey 2010 (ARUFA)

However, many of those who continued their studies did this in conjunction with employment: 28 per cent and 23 per cent respectively. A further one per cent was in professional training for public service – an arrangement which can also be viewed as combining employment and further learning.

26 per cent of Bachelor graduates from universities solely opted for employment. As one might expect, this proportion was higher among graduates from UAS (42 per cent). As about a quarter of the Bachelor graduates continues study whilst being employed, the overall proportion of employed Bachelor graduates (i.e. including those studying concurrently) was 55 per cent among university Bachelor graduates and 66 per cent among graduates from UAS. As one does not know whether the option of both study and employment will lead to an advanced degree or if it is just a temporary arrangement which delays the decision for either direction, a genuine rate of transition from Bachelor study to employment can only be established a few years later.

Very few Bachelor graduates reported that they neither studied nor were employed one and a half years after graduation (4 per cent each). Among them, only 2 per cent of the Bachelor graduates from universities and 1 per cent of those from UAS were unemployed.

In this context, the reported *motives for studying* are rather interesting. The following aspects were of particular significance for the decision about the choice of course of study leading to the first degree: "Personal development; professional interest in the course content; inclination/talent", as well as "Working on an interesting topic" – in other words, aspects relating to character or to the degree courses themselves. Professional aspects were quoted somewhat less frequently: "Having a wide range of career opportunities", "A particular career aspiration, "Good opportunities on the labour market", as well as the "Opportunity to achieve a secure professional position". In contrast, "Recommendations by parents/relatives" as well as the desire to "maintain the student status" hardly played any role.

As regards *professionally oriented motives*, almost two-thirds of the Bachelor graduates reported that they wanted to specialise in a particular area of expertise. About half each quoted "Particular professional aspiration", "Good labour market opportunities" and "Secure professional position". The latter two motives were more frequently voiced by Bachelor graduates from UAS than by those from universities.

It is interesting in this context to note that graduates report in retrospect a high degree of *satisfaction* with their study: about three-quarters of Bachelor graduates from UAS and about two-thirds of Bachelor graduates from universities stated that they were "very satisfied" or "satisfied" with their study programme overall (see table 4). And about seven out of ten stated that they would choose the same programme again. In sum, the widespread simplistic argument often put forward in the public discourse on the Bologna study reform is not supported by the results of this survey: The arguments that Bachelor graduates opt for continued study because of lack of "employability".

Table 4. Satisfaction with the Course of Study of 2008 Graduates from Higher Education Institutions in Austria (per cent)

	Bachelor graduates			Trad. graduates			Total		
	Univ.	UAS	All	Univ.	UAS	All	Univ.	UAS	All
1 Very satisfied	19	25	21	19	29	21	19	28	21
2	47	50	48	48	51	49	48	51	48
3	23	20	22	24	15	22	24	17	22
4	10	5	8	7	4	7	8	4	7
5 Very dissatisfied	2	0	1	2	1	2	2	1	2
Total	100	100	100	100	100	100	100	100	100
N	830	373	1,203	2,778	686	3,464	3,665	1,066	4,767
Combined values									
Satisfaction (1 and 2)	66	75	69	67	80	70	67	79	69
3	23	20	22	24	15	22	24	17	22
Dissatisfaction (4 and 5)	11	5	9	9	5	8	9	5	8
Arithmetic mean	2.3	2.0	2.2	2.2	2.0	2.2	2.3	2.0	2.2

Question D8: How satisfied are you with your studies in general?

Source: INCHER-Kassel, Austrian Graduate Survey 2010 (ARUFA)

In the *Studierenden-Sozialerhebung 2009*, Master students were asked about their *reasons for the continuation of study after the award of the Bachelor degree*. More than half of the "consecutive" Master students stated that they never planned to enter the labour market after finishing their Bachelor studies. Notably, a large proportion of Master students in the Natural Sciences stated this, and in various disciplines more women than men reported that they never planned to embark on employment after the award of the Bachelor degree.

Among Master students at UAS the answer pattern is quite different.

UAS offer two different types of programmes: On the one hand full-time programmes and on the other programmes for working students where lectures are given in the evenings, at weekends and during holidays. Both types of programmes provide 60 ECTS per year, hence programmes for working students are not part-time by nature, because they comprise the same amount of lectures per year as full-time programmes. Nevertheless, both types of programmes attract very different types of students, as seen for example in the fact that students in programmes for working students are on average six years older (namely around 30 years) than their colleagues in full-time programmes.

Even though, we see a higher transition rate from Bachelor to Master studies among graduates from programmes for working students than among those from full-time programmes, far more graduates from programmes for working students looked for a job: half the graduates in Business Administration and 40 per cent of the Engineers compared to 7 per cent of graduates in Business Administration and 27 per cent of Engineers from full-time programmes. On the other hand, only about 5 per cent of the graduates from programmes for working students stated they had never thought about looking for a job after graduation. Among Master students in full-time programmes, this ratio differs between 58 per cent in Engineering studies and 84 per cent – the highest ratio of all student groups – in Business Administration.

Hence, not surprisingly, students in programmes for working students want to continue studying alongside their work. However, we suppose their transition rate to Master programmes to be higher, because a Bachelor is of less value than their already accomplished years of vocational experience. Only a Master provides them with a comparative advantage for their future career. Hence the situation for (mainly young) graduates from full-time programmes at UAS: They have chosen an applied education programme because they wanted to enter the labour market quickly and with more practical experience than from a Scientific University. Hence, it is rational for many of them to leave the education system at least temporarily. That seems especially true in Engineering studies, where the labour market has a great demand for graduates.

Almost half of all students in consecutive Master programmes had the impression that there were no adequate jobs in their field of study available for Bachelor graduates. This is far more often stated by female Master students than by male Master students. As regards fields of study, we note that many students in natural sciences and in the humanities perceive such a lack of suitable employment opportunities. Similarly, only a quarter of the Master students see the Bachelor degree as a sufficient entry qualification for a career. Altogether, three quarters of the Master students believe that a Bachelor graduate is not regarded (and paid) as a higher education graduate in the Austrian labour market. On this point, both genders, students of all ages and in most fields of study agree to the same extent. It does not come as a surprise to note that Bachelor graduates who had opted for employment see the employment opportunities of Bachelor graduates more favourably. But even then most of them state that Bachelor graduates are not treated in the labour market as really being graduates.

JOB SEARCH[10]

The most common routes taken during the search for employment (often multiple answers) were "Applying for advertised jobs" as well as "Direct contact to employers or clients/blind applications, unsolicited applications". "Assistance from friends, acquaintances or fellow students" as well as "Internships during the course of studies" were quoted much less often. Asked about the success of the methods employed, four out of ten said "Applying for advertised jobs", almost two out of ten stated "Direct contact to employers or clients/blind applications, unsolicited applications" and one out of ten "Assistance from friends, acquaintances or fellow students". Only one per cent reported that they found their job with the help of the employment service or company contact fairs.

"Employability", the second keyword in the Bologna Process in addition to "mobility", is seen in Austria as a very important challenge. The Ministry in charge calls it "Förderung der Beschäftigungsfähigkeit von Absolventinnen und Absolventen mit Bachelorabschluss, auch im öffentlichen Dienst" (in English: "Promoting the employability of graduates with a Bachelor's degree, including public service", see bmwf, 2009b, p. 40). Critique as regards this target is often voiced (see e.g. Liessmann, 2006; Prisching, 2008). It might be premature to assess the link between Bachelor studies and employment (see the arguments in Campbell & Brechelmacher; 2007, Schneeberger, Petanovitsch & Nowak, 2010). At present, we note that many students perceive their studies as being "complete" only upon graduation from a Master programme (see Schneeberger & Petanovitsch, 2010a), even though the Bachelor degree is supposed to be a "complete" qualification according to the Bologna rationales.

In the ARUFA survey, graduates were also asked to report the duration of the *search period* for employment. Among those who were seeking for a job, Bachelor graduates from universities reported 4.9 months of search on average, while search took less long for Bachelor graduates from UAS: 3.2 months on average (see table 5).

---

[10] Author of this chapter is Helmut Guggenberger

Table 5. Duration of Job Search and Time from Graduation to First Employment of 2008 Graduates from Higher Education Institutions in Austria (means)

	Bachelor graduates			Trad. graduates			Total
	Univ.	UAS	Total	Univ.	UAS	Total	
a. Job search duration							
Arithmetic mean	4.9	3.2	4.3	4.6	3.9	4.4	4.4
Median	3.0	2.0	3.0	3.0	3.0	3.0	3.0
N	154	92	246	1,119	321	1,440	1,686
b. Time from graduation to first employment							
Arithmetic mean	4.9	2.3	4.0	3.2	2.1	3.0	3.1
Median	.0	.0	.0	1.0	.5	1.0	1.0
N	322	187	509	2,035	490	2,525	3,034

Source: INCHER-Kassel, Austrian Graduate Survey (ARUFA) 2010

PROFESSIONAL SUCCESS[11]

The tasks of higher education institutions and the measurement of professional success

The Universities' Act of 2002 (§ 3) specifies the various tasks of Austrian universities, among them: "3. Scientific, artistic, artistic-pedagogical and artistic-scientific pre-professional education, qualification for professional activities that require the application of scientific knowledge and methods, as well as the development of artistic and scientific skills up to the highest level" (bmwf, 2009a, p. 16). (This is followed by "4. Training and encouragement of young scholars and artists" and "5. Further education, particularly of graduates" (ibid., p. 16-17). The Studies Act for UAS states the tasks of these institutions as follows in § 3: "1) Degree programmes offered at UAS are programmes at university level expected to provide scientifically-based vocational training. The primary goals are: 1. To ensure practical training at university level; 2. To impart the ability to solve the tasks faced by the respective professional field in accordance with current scientific knowledge and with practical requirements; 3. To promote the permeability of the educational system and the professional flexibility of graduates" (Fachhochschul-Studiengesetz, 2010).

The laws clearly expected study programmes of UAS to be more closely geared to the preparation for future occupations than those of universities. No specific reference is made to sectors, e.g. the (decreasing) public and (increasing) private sector, or to employment status, e.g. employed vs. self-employed: The latter is quite large among graduates from Austrian universities, as the CHEERS survey

---

[11] Author of this chapter is Helmut Guggenberger

had shown for graduates from the mid-1990s (8 per cent; see Guggenberger, Kellermann & Sagmeister, 2001, p. 6) and the REFLEX survey for those graduating around 2000 (11 per cent of university and UAS graduates; see Guggenberger, Kellermann, Sagmeister & Steingruber, 2007, p. 25).

It is not difficult to provide information about various dimensions of employment. It is not clear from the outset, though, how one can measure what to describe the vocational routes of graduates from different institutions of the tertiary sector using statistical criteria. How should one measure something called "professional success"? In the framework of this publication, the authors agreed to examine the share of graduates employed full-time and employed permanently, the income, the adequacy of level of educational attainment and position as well as the use of knowledge, and finally job satisfaction.

In the subsequent analysis, those Bachelor graduates are compared to those from traditional programmes who are solely employed. This choice was made because the employment situation of graduates who work and study can be viewed as atypical for graduates' career prospects. Often, jobs which help to fund studies are chosen deliberately, although they are not considered as matching the level of educational attainment. Moreover, it should be stated that the comparison of income according to type of study programme or higher education institution is only undertaken for full-time employed graduates.

Employment conditions

When employed for the first time, about six out of ten Bachelor graduates were employed full-time, and about the same proportion had a permanent contract. The findings presented in table 6 refer to the time when the survey was conducted, i.e. between about 1½ years after graduation. At that moment in their career, full-time employment of Bachelor graduates had progressed further: 65 per cent of university Bachelor graduates and 83 per cent of Bachelor graduates from UAS. These rates are lower than the respective rates among graduates from traditional programmes (79 per cent and 91 per cent respectively). But these findings certainly do not confirm frequent claims that graduates face a high risk of ending up in precarious employment.

This can be underscored as well with data about the rate of permanent employment at the time of the surveys. 80 per cent of university Bachelor graduates and 86 per cent of Bachelor graduates from UAS were permanently employed when this survey was conducted. The rates did not differ much from the respective rates of graduates from traditional programmes.

Table 6. Aspects of Professional Success of 2008 Graduates from Higher Education Institutions in Austria who are only Employed One and a Half Years after Graduation (per cent)

	Bachelor graduates			Trad. graduates			Total		
	Univ.	UAS	All	Univ.	UAS	All	Univ.	UAS	All
Full-time employed	65	83	73	79	91	82	78	89	81
Unlimited term contract	80	86	82	77	90	80	78	89	80
Vertical match	77	83	80	86	88	87	85	87	86
Horizontal match	48	51	49	47	54	49	48	53	49
Job satisfaction	71	73	72	73	78	74	73	77	74
N	371	248	619	3,086	938	4,024	3,505	1,202	4,744

Source: INCHER-Kassel, Austrian Graduate Survey (ARUFA) 2010

It is interesting to note that there are substantial differences by field of study as far as full-time employment is concerned: Only 46 per cent of university Bachelor graduates from the humanities and social sciences were employed full-time when the survey was conducted, as compared to 83 per cent of those from economic fields. In contrast, the proportion of those who are permanently employed varied by groups of fields of study between 77 per cent and 82 per cent.

Income

The average *gross monthly income* of full-time employed Bachelor graduates from universities was about 2,358 € about 1½ years after graduation, as compared to 2,641 € for those from traditional university programmes. Thus, Bachelor graduates from universities earn only 11 per cent less than graduates from the long university programmes.

It is worth mentioning that the average income of graduates from universities of the applied sciences is even higher than that of university graduates. This can be explained to a certain extent by the different composition according to fields of study and related occupational areas and is influenced by the fact that the former more often have already been professionally active than the latter. This notwithstanding the formers' income is impressive. Bachelor graduates from UAS have on average an even higher income (2,748 €) than those from traditional university programmes (2,614 €), and their income is only 5 per cent less than that of graduates from traditional programmes of the UAS.

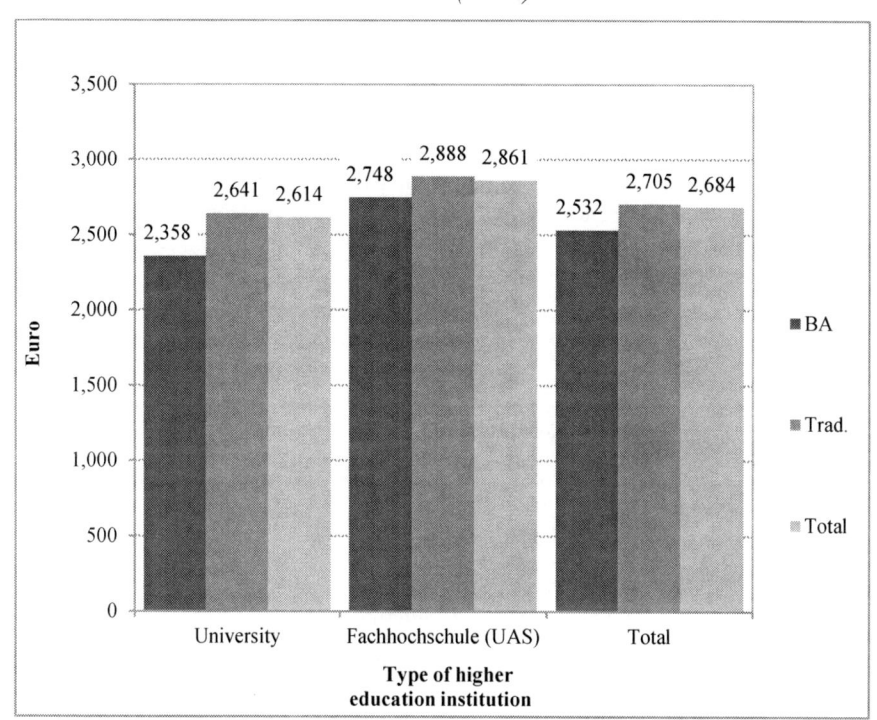

Figure 3. Gross Monthly Income of 2008 Graduates from Higher Education Institutions in Austria (means)

[Bar chart showing gross monthly income in Euro by type of higher education institution:
- University: BA 2,358; Trad. 2,641; Total 2,614
- Fachhochschule (UAS): BA 2,748; Trad. 2,888; Total 2,861
- Total: BA 2,532; Trad. 2,705; Total 2,684]

Question F5: What is your gross monthly income? (incl. special payments and overtime)

Source: INCHER-Kassel, Austrian Graduate Survey (ARUFA) 2010

As one might expect, the average income varies substantially by groups of field of study: University Bachelor graduates from the humanities and social sciences (1,801 €) earn only about seven-tenth as much as those from engineering (2,644 €), and graduates from UAS in mathematics and natural sciences (2,126 €) have a similar income disadvantage to those from engineering (2,960 €). These differences by field among the Bachelor graduates, however, are not greater than those by field among graduates from traditional study programmes.

Links between study and employment/work

The *vertical relationships between study and employment* was addressed in the ARUFA survey with the help of the question "In your opinion, what is the most appropriate academic level for your current occupation?". In table 6, the responses "My degree level" and as well the few responses "A higher degree level" are classified as a vertical match, whereas the responses "A lower degree level" and "No degree required" are viewed as not matching (see also table 7).

As table 6 shows, six out of seven graduates surveyed consider that their occupation requires at least their level of degrees. As can be seen in table 7, among university Bachelors, the proportion of those who believed that a lower level of educational attainment would have been appropriate (34 per cent) was 3 per cent higher than among Bachelor graduates from UAS (31 per cent). This proportion was lower among graduates from traditional programmes (24 per cent and 21 per cent respectively). It is difficult to say whether such a difference can be explained as being so high that it is likely to cause decisions on the part of the university Bachelor graduates to opt for further study rather than for employment after the award of their degree.

Table 7. Link between Level of Education and Present Job Perceived by 2008 Graduates from Higher Education Institutions in Austria being solely Employed One and a Half Years after Graduation (per cent)

	Bachelor graduates			Trad. graduates			Total		
	Univ.	UAS	All	Univ.	UAS	All	Univ.	UAS	All
A higher academic degree	9	11	10	6	5	6	6	6	6
My academic degree	57	59	58	70	74	71	69	71	70
A lower academic degree	11	14	12	10	9	10	10	10	10
No academic degree necessary	23	17	20	14	12	13	15	13	14
Total	100	100	100	100	100	100	100	100	100
N	368	242	610	3,059	936	3,995	3,474	1,193	4,701

Question H3: In your opinion, which academic degree is best suited for your current job?

Source: INCHER-Kassel, Austrian Graduate Survey (ARUFA) 2010

The ratings of a vertical match are exceptionally low in two cases: 61 per cent of the university Bachelor graduates from the humanities and social sciences and 69 per cent of those from mathematics and natural sciences. In all other categories of institutional types, programme types and disciplinary groups, the respective ratio varies between about three-quarters and almost all respondents.

The *horizontal match* presented in table 6 is measured by asking the graduates about the extent to which the knowledge they had acquired in the course of study was used on the job. As can be seen in table 6 and 8, the responses vary only moderately according to type of degree and type of higher education institution. About half each of Bachelor graduates from both types of institutions stated that they used their competences to a high extent; the same holds true for graduates from traditional study programmes.

Table 8. Utilisation of Knowledge and Skills Acquired during the Course of Study in Current Job Perceived by 2008 Graduates from Higher Education Institutions in Austria who are solely Employed One and a Half Years after Graduation (per cent)

	Bachelor graduates			Trad. graduates			Total		
	Univ.	UAS	All	Univ.	UAS	All	Univ.	UAS	All
1 To a very high extent	14	17	16	15	12	14	15	14	14
2	34	33	33	33	41	35	33	40	35
3	28	34	30	33	35	34	33	34	33
4	17	13	16	16	11	15	16	11	15
5 Not at all	6	2	5	3	1	3	4	1	3
Total	100	100	100	100	100	100	100	100	100
N	373	241	614	3,063	928	3,991	3,483	1,184	4,702
Combined values									
High extent (1 and 2)	48	51	49	47	54	49	48	53	49
3	28	34	30	33	35	34	33	34	33
Low extent (4 and 5)	24	16	21	19	12	18	20	12	18
	2.7	2.5	2.6	2.6	2.5	2.6	2.6	2.5	2.6

Question H1: If you take into consideration your current work tasks altogether: To what extent do you use the knowledge and skills acquired in the course of study?

Source: INCHER-Kassel, Austrian Graduate Survey (ARUFA) 2010

It can be added that less than one-third of Bachelor graduates, but slightly more than one-third of graduates from traditional programmes considered their chosen field of study as "the only possible/by far the best" to fulfil their professional tasks (see table 9). A higher proportion, among them more Bachelor graduates than graduates from traditional programmes agreed to the statement "some other fields could prepare for the area of work as well". About a quarter of the graduates opted for one of the two remaining categories which indicate a low horizontal match: "another field would have been more useful" and "the field of study does not matter very much", among them a slightly higher proportion of Bachelor graduates than of graduates from traditional programmes.

Table 9. Link between Field of Study and Work Tasks Perceived by 2008 Graduates from Higher Education Institutions in Austria who are solely Employed One and a Half Years after Graduation (per cent)

	Bachelor graduates			Trad. graduates			Total		
	Univ.	UAS	All	Univ.	UAS	All	Univ.	UAS	All
My field of study is the only possible/by far the best field for my present work tasks	28	26	27	40	22	36	39	23	35
Some other fields could prepare for the area of work as well	41	48	44	37	57	42	38	55	42
Another field would have been more useful for my present work tasks	11	7	10	10	9	10	10	9	9
In my present work the field of study does not matter very much	20	19	20	13	12	13	14	13	14
Total	100	100	100	100	100	100	100	100	100
N	369	241	610	3,056	935	3,991	3,472	1,191	4,697

Question H2: How would you characterise the relationship between your field of study and your area of work?

Source: INCHER-Kassel, Austrian Graduate Survey (ARUFA) 2010

Asked to take into consideration "all aspects of their professional situation (status, position, income, scope of duties etc.) related to their current occupation" and to rate on that basis the extent to which their occupation is commensurate to their training, about 60 per cent of the respondents noted a clear link between study and work. This was stated by Bachelor graduates slightly less frequently than by graduates from traditional programmes.

Those who accepted a job that was not linked clearly to their study were asked why they opted for this job. About a quarter each of the Bachelor graduates gave the following two reasons: "This job represents an interim stage, as the respondent is still in the process of occupational orientation" and "the job allows for activities that are flexible in time". Less than one fifth each agreed to the following response categories "this job makes it possible to work in a desired location" and "the current occupation offers greater security. Only slightly more than one tenth stated that they had not yet found a suitable occupation.

In response to the question whether their professional situation corresponded to their expectation at the start of their study almost half of the graduates – both Bachelor graduates and graduates from traditional study programmes stated that their current professional situation was "much better" or "better than expected". Only one sixth of the Bachelor graduates and even slightly fewer of the graduates from traditional programmes considered their professional situation as "worse" or even "far worse than expected".

Job satisfaction

In response to the question about the extent to which they are *satisfied overall with their professional situation*, graduates from the different types of study programmes and institutional types reacted in a similar way: Around three quarters stated that they were "very satisfied" or "satisfied" (see table 4 and 10). The previous comparative studies – CHEERS and REFLEX – had already shown that the average job satisfaction of graduates from Austrian institutions of higher education was among the highest of the European countries surveyed.

Table 10. Job Satisfaction of 2008 Graduates from Institutions of Higher Education in Austria (per cent)

	Bachelor graduates			Trad. graduates			Total		
	Univ.	UAS	All	Univ.	UAS	All	Univ.	UAS	All
1 Very satisfied	30	35	32	29	28	29	29	29	29
2	42	38	40	44	50	46	44	48	45
3	18	17	17	18	14	17	18	15	17
4	8	8	8	7	5	6	7	6	6
5 Very dissatisfied	3	2	2	3	3	3	3	2	3
Total	100	100	100	100	100	100	100	100	100
N	371	248	619	3,086	938	4,024	3,505	1,202	4,744
Combined values									
Satisfied (1 and 2)	71	73	72	73	78	74	73	77	74
3	18	17	17	18	14	17	18	15	17
Dissatisfied (4 and 5)	11	10	11	9	8	9	9	8	9
Arithmetic mean	2.1	2.0	2.1	2.1	2.0	2.1	2.1	2.0	2.1

Question G5: How satisfied are you with your current job?

Source: INCHER-Kassel, Austrian Graduate Survey (ARUFA) 2010

There are some variations by field of study. Less than 70 per cent among university graduates from humanities and social sciences expressed a high degree of satisfaction- both those with a Bachelor (63 per cent) and those with a traditional degree (66 per cent). The same held true for university Bachelor graduates in mathematics and natural sciences (65 per cent) and for graduates from the UAS in engineering (69 per cent).

CONCLUSIONS

Two recent headlines can serve to illustrate aspects of the public discourse on academic degrees in Austria: "Increasingly precarious working conditions for academics" (Austria Presse Agentur, 2010); "Rising unemployment among academics despite positive trend" (derstandard.at, 2010). These and similarly striking phrases point to two reasons for public concern: There is "poor" (here: precarious) occupation or "unemployment" (i.e. no occupation) for university graduates. While the first information is based on a study conducted by the Austrian Institute for Research on Vocational Training[12] (see Schneeberger & Petanovitsch, 2010b), the second rests on the labour market statistics that are continuously produced by the AMS (Labour Market Service) – however, neither of these sources suggests such sensational headlines. The results of the project "The Working Situation of Graduates from Universities and Universities of Applied Sciences" can contribute to a factual and data-based discussion about the employability and professional relevance of graduates from higher education institutions in Austria.

In the winter semester of 2008/09 Austrian universities offered a total of 298 Bachelor, 455 Master and 93 Diploma degrees for enrolment; in 2003/04 the relation was still 157 to 198 and 227 (bmwf, 2008a, p. 137). At the time, some universities had already stopped any new enrolments to Diploma degrees (ibid., p. 136). Because the Diploma degrees can be completed within an appropriate timeframe, in addition to having the option to transfer from an initiated Diploma degree to a newly established Bachelor degree course, a certain kind of duality is expected to continue for some time, between graduates from "old", or traditional degree courses and those from "new" degree courses, which comply with the three-tiered Bologna structure.

Moreover, there will continue to be a range of combinations of studying and working: Bachelor, Master and doctoral degrees completed back-to-back; alternating phases of either exclusively studying or working; various manifestations of "students who are gainfully employed" or "gainfully employed persons who study". No doubt, the heterogeneity of forms of studying and of transitional forms will provide a number of challenges for the institutions in the tertiary educational sector – keyword "job-accompanying courses of study", but also new forms of "blended learning" and "e-learning".

In order to identify key features of the new academic degrees, as well as distinctions with the traditional degrees, selected results were presented in this paper – for the most part from the perspective of a comparison of the new Bachelor degree at universities and universites of applied science with the traditional degrees (*Magister*, *Diplom* and *Dipl.-Ing.*) of these types of higher education institution. In some instances, this comparison revealed fewer differences between types of degree than between types of instution.

Two prominent objectives of the Bologna Process, namely the encouragement of international student mobility and the promotion of employability, are the focus of this presentation.

---

[12] Institut für berufliche Weiterbildung (ibw)

What promotes and what impedes student mobility? Some of the newly established degrees or degree programmes include periods abroad for study or training purposes to a greater extent (see Wirtschaftskammer Österreich & Bundesministerium für Wissenschaft und Forschung, 2010, p. 4), and at the individual universities special units provide relevant support to students. The European Credit Transfer System should ensure that the mutual recognition of academic performance (comparability of *workload* or *grades*) gradually becomes less of an issue. However, experience shows that there is still room for improvement and – as our data illustrate – study-related periods abroad are still more of an exception than the rule.

What promotes and what impedes employability, at least after the first cycle (Bachelor level)? On the whole, the Austrian university graduates involved in the ARUFA study seem satisfied with their studies and the associated conditions; a few aspects (such as under-developed job-related elements in the degree, or a lack of awareness about course content) appear to justify criticism. Job satisfaction also appears to be very high – however, we are not in a position to establish a truly "objective" picture based on a survey of students or graduates (it is also possible that respondents have few expectations or a low level of requirements). As far as horizontal (usefulness of qualification) and vertical (adequacy of degree) fit are concerned, no significant problems were revealed; only to a limited extent are Bachelor graduates worse off here with regard to other criteria relating to (emerging) professional success.

Measured against the expectations aroused by the public discourse we find relatively few differences between "traditional" (*Magister, Dipl.-Ing.*) and "new" (Bachelor) degrees, nor do we find disadvantages for the latter – depending on the anticipatory attitude, this result may either disappoint or satisfy. We do, however, identify clear differences between the types of higher education institution – which may be largely due to the divergent tasks with which they are endowed (greater scientific or basic research orientation at the universities versus a more pronounced practice and application orientation at UAS) and which may also be ascribed to varying conditions ("open admission to higher education", in part "mass studies" or "admission", "university place management").

Further analyses, for example grouped by fields of study or by strongly represented single degrees or degree programmes, appear to be an obvious next step, and can very well be conducted with the data at hand. A greater level of differentiation by year of graduation would be meaningful in this context. Certainly, the different cohorts face somewhat changed conditions in the (academic) labour market; and certain aspects of gainful employment only become visible in the system of organised occupation after a certain lapse of time.

REFERENCES

Austria Presse Agentur (2010). *Immer mehr prekäre Arbeitsverhältnisse bei Akademikern* [Increasingly precarious working conditions for academics]. Retrieved March 22, 2010, from http://www.zukunftwissen.apa.at/cms/zukunft-wissen/schule-und-bildung/meldung.html?id=ZUK_20100322_ZUK0046

Bundesministerium für Wissenschaft und Forschung (2008a). *Universitätsbericht 2008. 2., korrigierte Auflage* [University report 2008. 2nd rev. edition].Wien: bmw_f²

Bundesministerium für Wissenschaft und Forschung (2008b). *Zukunftsbotschaften des Forschungsministers: Strategische Handlungsfelder für Österreichs Frontrunner Strategie 2020* [Messages for the future by the Minister of Research: Strategic spheres of activity for Austria's Frontrunner Strategy 2020]. Retrieved August 13, 2010, from http://www.bmwf.gv.at/fileadmin/user_upload/forschung /forschungsdialog/ZUKUNFTSbotschaften_des_FORSCHUNGSministers_0808bmwf.pdf

Bundesministerium für Wissenschaft und Forschung (2009a). *Universitätsgesetz 2002. Österreichisches Hochschulrecht Heft 14* [University act 2002].Wien: bmw_f².

Bundesministerium für Wissenschaft und Forschung (2009b). *Bericht über den Stand der Umsetzung der Bologna Ziele in Österreich. Berichtszeitraum 2000-2008.* [Bologna Progress Report Austria, 2000-2008].Wien: bmw_fa.

Bundesministerium für Wissenschaft und Forschung (2010). *Dialog Hochschulpartnerschaft. Empfehlungen zur Zukunft des tertiären Sektors* [Dialogue 'Higher Education Partnership', recommendations for the future of the tertiary sector]. Retrieved August 13, 2010, from http://www.bmwf.gv.at/ fileadmin/user_upload/Endbericht_Dialog_Hochschulpartnerschaft.pdf

Campbell, D.F.J. & Brechelmacher, A. (2007). *Bachelor Neu und der Arbeitsmarkt. Analyse der Sichtweisen von wirtschaftlichen Unternehmen und von Universitäten und Fachhochschulen. Formulierung von Empfehlungen.* Forschungsprojekt im Auftrag der WKÖ (Wirtschaftskammer Österreich) [The New Bachelor degree on the labour market]. Wien: IFF. Retrieved August 13, 2010, from http://www.uni-klu.ac.at/wiho/downloads/studie_bachelor_FINAL.pdf

derstandard.at (2010). *Arbeitslosigkeit bei Akademikern steigt trotz positiver Tendenz* [Unemployment among graduates increases]. Retrieved August 13, 2010, from http://derstandard.at/127733 9011003/Arbeitslosigkeit-bei-Akademikern-steigt-trotz-positiverTendenz

Eurydice (2009). *Higher education in Europe 2009: Developments in the Bologna Process.* Brussels: Education, Audiovisual and Culture Executive Agency.

Fachhochschul-Studiengesetz (FHStG) [Fachhochschule Studies Act] (2010). Retrieved August 13, 2010, from http://www.jusline.at/FachhochschulStudiengesetz_%28FHStG%29.html

Guggenberger, H., Kellermann, P. & Sagmeister, G. (2001). *Wissenschaftliches Studium und akademische Beschäftigung. Vier Jahre nach Studienabschluss. – Ein Überblick* [Study and graduate employment four years after graduation]. Institut für Soziologie der Universität Klagenfurt. Klagenfurt.

Guggenberger, H., Kellermann, P., Sagmeister, G. & Steingruber, A. (2007). *Wandel der Erwerbsarbeit in einer wissensbasierten Gesellschaft. Neue Herausforderungen an die Hochschulbildung in Europa. Österreich-Bericht* [The flexible professional in the knowledge society. New demands on higher education in Europe. Austrian report]. Klagenfurt: IfS. Retrieved August 13, 2010, from http://www.uni-klu.ac.at/sozio/bilder/Bericht_Langfassung.pdf

Heissenberger, S., Mark, V., Schramm, S., Sniesko, P. & Süss, R.S. (Eds.) (2010). *Uni brennt. Grundsätzliches – Kritisches – Atmosphärisches* [University burning].Wien, Berlin: Turia + Kant.

Kellermann, P., Boni, M. & Meyer-Renschhausen, E. (Eds.) (2009). *Zur Kritik europäischer Hochschulpolitik. Forschung und Lehre unter Kuratel betriebswirtschaftlicher Denkmuster* [Critique on European Higher Education policy]. Wiesbaden: VS.

Liessmann, K.P. (2006). *Theorie der Unbildung. Die Irrtümer der Wissensgesellschaft* [Theory of miseducation]. Wien: Zsolnay.

Prisching, M. (2008). *Bildungsideologien. Ein zeitdiagnostischer Essay an der Schwelle zur Wissensgesellschaft* [Ideologies of education]. Wiesbaden: VS.

Schneeberger, A. & Petanowitsch, A. (2010b). *Zwischen Akademikermangel und prekärer Beschäftigung. Zur Bewährung der Hochschulexpansion am Arbeitsmarkt.* ibw Forschungsbericht Nr. 153

[Between shortage of graduates and precarious occopation: Probation of the expansion of higher education on the labour market]. Wien: ibw. Retrieved August 13, 2010, from http://www.ibw.at/de/pruefungsunterlagen/lap?page=shop.getfile&file_id=392&product_id=348

Schneeberger, A., Petanovitsch, A. & Nowak, S. (2010). *Akzeptanz des Bachelors in der Wirtschaft. Befragungsergebnisse mittlerer und großer Unternehmen.* ibw-Forschungsbericht Nr. 155 [Acceptance oft the Bachelor on the labour market. A survey among medium and large enterprises]. Wien: ibw. Retrieved August 13, 2010, from http://www.ibw.at/de/pruefungsunterlagen/lap?page=shop.getfile&file_id=403&product_id=364

Unger, M., Zaussinger, S., Angel, S., Dünser, L., Grabher, A., Hartl, J., Paulinger, G., Brandl, J., Wejwar, P. & Gottwald, R. (2010). *Studierenden-Sozialerhebung 2009* [Survey on the social and economic conditions of students]. Retrieved August, 13, 2010, from http://www.bmwf.gv.at/uploads/tx_contentbox/Studierenden_Sozialerhebung_2009.pdf

Wirtschaftskammer Österreich & Bundesministerium für Wissenschaft und Forschung (2010). *Bachelor welcome!* Retrieved August 13, 2010, from http://portal.wko.at/wk/format_detail.wk?AngID=1&StID=547824&DstID=0&titel=Brosch%C3%BCre,%22Bachelor,Welcome%22

RADIM RYŠKA AND MARTIN ZELENKA

PROFESSIONAL SUCCESS DUE TO SCARCITY? BACHELOR GRADUATES IN THE CZECH REPUBLIC

STUDY STRUCTURE IN THE CZECH REPUBLIC

Before 1989, the Czech higher education system was highly centralised, very small and elitist in nature. The development of tertiary education had stagnated and did not respond to the rising educational aspirations or to the demand for tertiary education. It can be defined as a unitary system of traditional university education that offered only Master degrees. Because of the low income returns to higher education and the orientation of the economy towards heavy industry there was little motivation to study at university on the part of less educated lower classes (for educated higher classes a degree was a way of maintaining their social status) and little demand on the labour market. After 1989, a need for shorter and vocationally oriented types of tertiary education emerged. However, in the first half of the 1990s, tertiary education still consisted only of traditional universities focusing on academically-oriented studies. It was necessarily selective, and its limited capacity could not satisfy demand.

In the mid-1990s, a new type of tertiary institution, the *higher professional schools* (ISCED 5B) gradually came into existence in the Czech Republic. While it was originally presumed that they would become the main way of diversifying higher education (which was deemed necessary as a corollary to its expansion) as its lower tier, these institutions were not granted higher education status, and the only way they could come into existence was to create them as an extension of (upper) secondary vocational education, i.e. without any systemic links to existing universities (enabling, for instance, transfers of credits or recognition of studies).

A few years later – more or less at the same time as the Bologna Process – *universities started to offer vocationally-oriented Bachelor programmes* (ISCED 5A). Hence, further development and even the very existence of higher professional schools became thwarted. Although the duration of studies was the same, links to enterprises were closer and vocational orientation was more pronounced in higher professional schools, their diploma enjoyed less prestige than a first university degree and did not open the way to Master programmes.

During the second half of the 1990s and particularly after the turn of the century, when substantial changes (strengthening vocational education at the tertiary level, massive expansion of Bachelor studies and setting-up of private non-university higher education institutions) were introduced, the number of study places greatly increased – gradually at the beginning and quite steeply in the last few years. As a result, the tertiary education sector in the Czech Republic is now predominantly composed of public higher education institutions (with slightly less than 80 per cent of all students), followed by a constantly increasing number of

---

H. Schomburg and U. Teichler (eds.), Employability and Mobility of Bachelor Graduates in Europe, 69–88.
© 2011 *Sense Publishers. All rights reserved.*

private higher education institutions (with over 10 per cent of all students) and constantly diminishing higher professional schools (with less than 10 per cent of all students).

Bachelor studies underwent massive expansion – while in the year 2002 there were not even 16,000 Bachelor graduates (accounting for about a quarter of all higher education graduates), in the year 2009 there were more than 79,000 (accounting for almost 55 per cent of all HE graduates). However, most continue study in Master programmes and do not enter the labour market directly. Their share is gradually increasing, and as of 2009 three quarters of all Bachelors continued to study.

To sum up, tertiary education in the Czech Republic is composed of higher professional schools (introduced in 1992/93, with a two- to three-year study programmes) and higher education institutions (of a university and a non-university type). Conform to the Bologna process, there are three types of programmes: three- to four-year Bachelor programmes, Master programmes – five- to six-year single-cycle Master programmes or two- to three-year second-cycle Master programmes – and doctoral programmes leading to a PhD degree.

THE GRADUATE SURVEYS USED FOR THE ANALYSIS

Three main graduate surveys were used for this analysis. They were supplemented by data from the Czech Labour Force Survey, the European Social Survey, the Ministry of Labour and Social Affairs, and the Combined Register of Students.

The first graduate survey was *undertaken in the framework of the REFLEX project* involving partners from 16 countries (Austria, Belgium/Flanders, the Czech Republic, Estonia, Finland, France, Germany, Italy, Japan, the Netherlands, Norway, Portugal, Spain, Sweden, Switzerland and the United Kingdom) and was coordinated by the Research Centre for Education and the Labour Market (ROA) of Maastricht University. It focused on higher education graduates who had more or less than five years of experience since leaving higher education. The sample was restricted to ISCED 5A level (Bachelors and Masters or equivalent) graduates. The target cohort of graduates for the Czech Republic was defined in terms of the calendar years 2001 and 2002. A two-stage sampling was used: First a sample of higher education institutions, at the second stage a random sample within these institutions. Data were collected between March and June 2006. Overall 6,794 completed questionnaires were returned with a response rate of 27 per cent. The non-weighted sample consisted of 17 per cent of Bachelor graduates and of 82 per cent of Master graduates. Weighting was applied so that the sample represented the population of HE graduates in relevant years (with regard to the type of programme, field of study, sex, region, etc.). The disadvantage of this data source is that it is quite outdated as it relates to years 2001 and 2002. The advantage is, of course, a large sample of tertiary education graduates and international comparability.

The second graduate survey was the *REFLEX 2010 survey* – "Employability and situation of higher education graduates in the labor market", which is part of a national project in the Czech Republic and builds significantly on the previous

REFLEX project. Data were collected between May and September 2010. The target cohort of graduates was defined in terms of the calendar years 2005 and 2006. Overall 20 public, one state and three private higher education schools took part in the project. The questioning was done via Internet. Overall 8,629 students completed questionnaires with response rate at 20 per cent. The non-weighted sample consists of those who graduated in the years 2005 or 2006 as Bachelor graduates in nearly 32 per cent of the cases, as Masters in almost 68 per cent of the cases and as doctors in about 1 per cent of the cases. There are more than 800 respondents (almost 9 per cent of the sample) whose highest education level at the time of the survey is the Bachelor degree. Weighting was applied so that the sample represented the population of HE graduates in relevant years.

The third graduate survey was the Czech School Leaver Survey *School to Work Transition of Graduates and Skill Requirements*. It was conducted as part of the Quality II project (under the ESF Operational Programme Human Resource Development), and the data were collected between October 2007 and January 2008. The sample was chosen by the quota sample technique. Quotas were gender, age, level of education, region and economic activity and they were calculated on the basis of data from the Czech Labour Force Survey. Data was collected by means of face-to-face interviews using the CAPI (Computer Assisted Personal Interviewing) technique. Overall 5,853 respondents between the ages of 19 and 59 were questioned. For the purposes of the original project the sample emphasised young people and several other specific groups (people studying in tertiary education). Weighting was used. Hence, the sample was fully representative for the relevant population. Weights were based on data about gender, education, economic activity, age and region gathered in the Czech Labour Force Survey 2008. The response rate was 60 per cent. This survey made it possible to compare the number of Bachelor graduates with primary, secondary and post-secondary non tertiary education graduates, which is much lower than in the REFLEX projects.

The survey had two main focuses. The first contained several questions: What is the process of transition of school leavers from school to work, how far has the school leavers' position in the labour market changed, and how do graduates value their education and their school? What are the ensuing recommendations for education policy (for example for the structure of the Czech school system and for educational content) and for employment policy? The second contained questions such as: What is the relation between job qualification requirements and workers' educational level? How does their education match with skill requirements and how can it be used in the labour market? What are the cases of over-qualification or of under-qualification? What will it mean for further development of education and work and what does it mean for lifelong learning?

As for the *additional data sources*, the Czech Labour Force Survey is a standardised ILO Labour Force Survey. It is carried out four times a year as a random sample of households (about 60,000 respondents per quarter), and focuses on identifying the economic status of the population in the country. The European Social Survey, which so far has been conducted in four rounds in the years 2002-2009, focuses on examining social structure and value orientation, and on moni-

SOCIO-BIOGRAPHIC BACKGROUND AND COURSE OF STUDY

toring attitudes, beliefs and behaviour patterns in current European societies. A sample size for all participating countries is about 40,000 (for the Czech Republic it is about 2000) in each round.

Bachelor studies in the Czech Republic are dominated by *women*, and a Master degree is more often obtained by men. According to the latest Czech Labour Force Survey, of all Bachelor graduates, more than 56 per cent are women, while in the group of Master graduates they represented about 45 per cent.

Much empirical evidence shows that *social origin* is an important factor that affects young people's chances of continuing education or dropping out early with different labour market outcomes. The relationship between parents' and children's education in the Czech Republic is very strong. According to data from research undertaken in 2007/08, young people who have attained higher levels of education more often have parents with tertiary education than parents with primary or secondary education. For example, graduates with a Master degree have fathers with tertiary education in more than 30 per cent of the cases, and mothers with tertiary education in almost 20 per cent of the cases. At least one parent obtained a higher education degree in nearly two fifths of the cases. Compared to that, graduates with a Bachelor degree had at least one parent with tertiary education in one of four cases (a father in 19 per cent and a mother in 14 per cent of the cases). The proportion of graduates of higher professional schools and of all types of upper secondary schools with parents where at least one has attained tertiary education, ranges from 13 per cent to 19 per cent. At lower levels of education, the share is less than 6 per cent.

Similar results can be found in REFLEX 2010: Nearly 35 per cent of Master graduates of the years 2005 and 2006 have a father with tertiary education and 26 per cent (23 per cent in REFLEX 2006 of the graduation years 2001 and 2002) of them have a mother with tertiary education. Bachelor graduates on the other hand have a father with tertiary education in 26 per cent of the cases and a mother with tertiary education in more than 16 per cent of the cases. While these figures are generally higher than those taken from the 2007 survey, it clearly shows the same quite substantial difference between Master and Bachelor graduates. It seems that while Bachelor studies often serve as a way to upgrade on the level of parents education, Master studies are more often a way of reproducing parents education. Of course, the number of tertiary graduates is substantially higher than in the past so quite large share of Master graduates' parents did not achieve tertiary level.

In looking at the relationship between parents' occupation and children's educational attainment, we find the most substantial difference between Bachelor and Master graduates in the share of fathers who are working in a professional/managerial occupation. According to data of the REFLEX 2010 survey, more than 37 per cent of fathers of Master graduates of the years 2005 and 2006 were working (when the respondent was 15 years old) in this occupation – a share comparatively higher than the 29 per cent in case of Bachelor graduates. The difference in case of mothers is about the same – 36 per cent and 27 per cent. In the case of the share of parents working in associate professional occupation there is also quite small discrepancy between Bachelor and Master graduates. Fathers of Master graduates were working in this occupation in nearly 17 per cent of the cases and mothers in 22 per cent of the cases. Comparable numbers for Bachelor graduates are 14 per cent in the case of fathers and 22 per cent in the case of mothers.

According to the data of the 2007/08 survey, more than 33 per cent of fathers of Master graduates were working in the same occupation when the respondent was 15 years old – a share comparatively higher than the 15 per cent in the case of Bachelor graduates. The difference in the case of mothers is much lower – 22 per cent and 18 per cent. Even if the proportion of parents working in associate professional occupation is considered, a small difference between Bachelor and Master graduates remains. Fathers of Master graduates were working in this occupation in about 23 per cent of the cases and mothers in less than 22 per cent of the cases. Comparable numbers for Bachelor graduates are 20 per cent in the case of fathers and 17 per cent in the case of mothers.

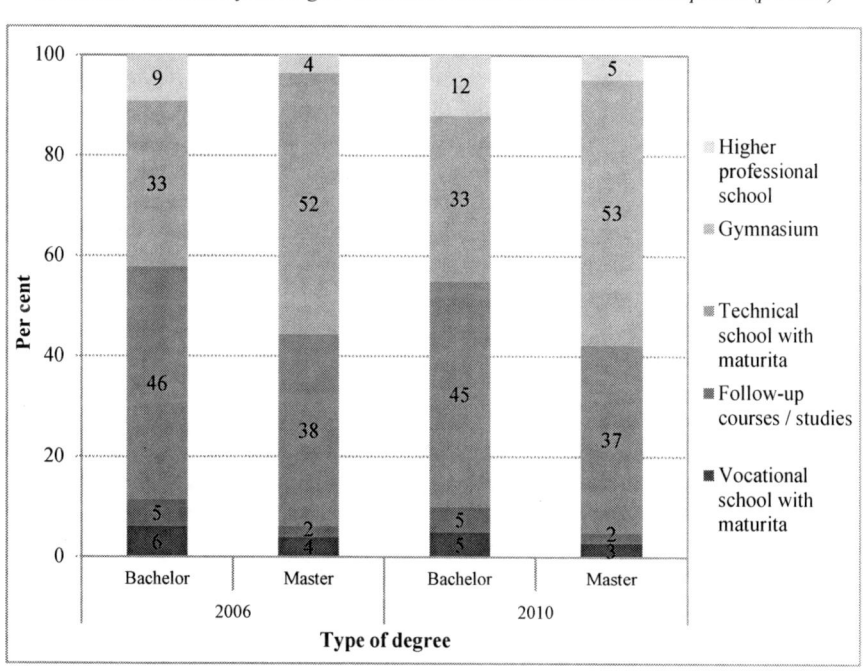

Figure 1. Prior Education to Higher Education Studies of 2001-2002 and 2005-2006 Bachelor and Master Graduates from Higher Education Institutions in the Czech Republic (per cent)

Source: REFLEX 2006 and REFLEX 2010

Bachelor and Master graduates also differ substantially in their course of study at secondary level. While both generally quite often follow general secondary education, in the case of Master graduates this happen considerably more often. On the other hand, Bachelor graduates graduate from technical schools, secondary vocational schools and higher professional schools before their higher education studies much more often than Master graduates.

According to the REFLEX 2010 data which relate to the years 2005 and 2006, Bachelor graduates most often took the route of secondary technical schools (more than 45 per cent), quite a substantial number graduated from general secondary schools (one third), and more than one tenth completed higher professional education. The route via secondary vocational schools was also an important one (more than 10 per cent including the follow-up courses).

As Bachelor programmes last for three to four years and some Bachelor graduates spend time in Master programmes without successfully completing them, the average *length of time spent on higher education study* for Bachelor graduates is about 3.7 years. On average, their age on graduation is about one and a half years more than Master graduates. According to the REFLEX 2010 project, Bachelors in 2005 and 2006 graduated at the age of 28.0 years, whereas Masters graduated at the age of 26.3 years. This is mainly because Bachelor programmes often serve as a supplementary way of obtaining a degree for those who, for various reasons, were not able to do so in their early 20s. Graduates are also getting older as, according to the data from REFLEX 2006, the average age of graduation of the 2001 and 2002 graduates was 25.8 years for Bachelors and 25.2 years for Masters.

One must ask whether Bachelor graduates are *satisfied with their choice of course of study*. The results of the 2007/08 survey show that most have responded positively, however also a significant number would have liked to continue their studies and obtain a higher degree. 78 per cent are satisfied with their educational path, but more than 15 per cent would have chosen a higher level, and less than 2 per cent a lower level. In comparison, 91 per cent of Master graduates are satisfied with their educational path, less than 6 per cent would have chosen a higher level, and about 3 per cent a lower level.

INTERNATIONAL MOBILITY

There is not much information about graduates' international mobility. Fortunately, in the REFLEX 2010, there were questions about the time Czech 2005 and 2006 graduates had spent abroad during their course of study or after graduation for study, study-related activities or work. As can be seen in figure 2, only a small share of Bachelor graduates (6 per cent) had *studied abroad* for at least 3 months during their course study. In contrast, many Master graduates had spent a period abroad during their studies. This cannot be explained merely by the length of the overall study period. Rather, Bachelor students do not have as much flexible time as Master graduates who often go abroad in the later stages of their course of study.

There is much smaller yet still considerable difference between Bachelors and Masters who *go abroad for work-related reasons*. Some 16 per cent of Bachelors and 26 per cent of Masters were working outside the Czech Republic for at least three months during or after their studies.

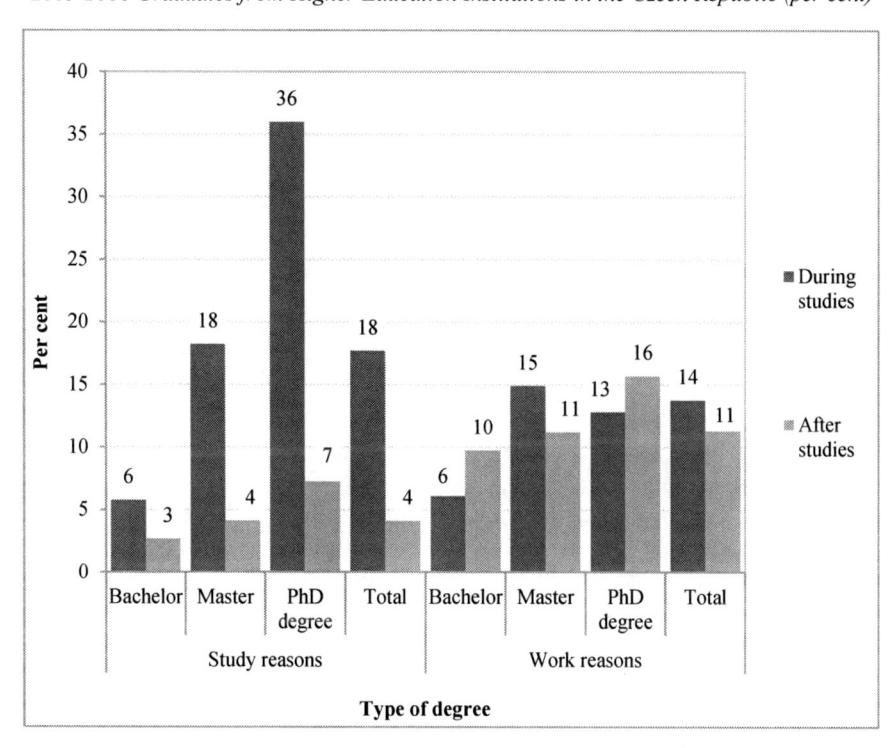

Figure 2. Mobility for at Least Three Months during and after the Course of Study of 2005-2006 Graduates from Higher Education Institutions in the Czech Republic (per cent)

[Bar chart showing mobility percentages by degree type (Bachelor, Master, PhD degree, Total) for Study reasons and Work reasons, split between During studies and After studies:

Study reasons — Bachelor: 6, 3; Master: 18, 4; PhD degree: 36, 7; Total: 18, 4
Work reasons — Bachelor: 6, 10; Master: 15, 11; PhD degree: 13, 16; Total: 14, 11]

Source: REFLEX 2010

Even though the REFLEX 2006 data on 2001-2002 graduates do not offer full comparability with the results above, it can be assumed that the experience of studying abroad is becoming available to a growing number of higher education students. Unfortunately, this only applies to Master graduates. Their share who had studied abroad during studies was about 10 per cent (compared to 18 per cent in the data from 2010 on 2005-2006 graduates), while for Bachelors it was 6 per cent (the same as in the 2010 survey).

EMPLOYMENT AND FURTHER STUDY OF BACHELOR GRADUATES

The employment situation of Bachelor graduates is greatly influenced by the expansion of their numbers and the economic situation of the country.

First information about what Bachelor graduates are *doing several years after graduation* is provided by the REFLEX data. Five years after graduation, most of those who graduated from higher education institutions in the Czech Republic in 2001 and 2002 did not continue their studies. More than 81 per cent were only employed, almost 13 per cent were neither studying nor employed, and only 6 per cent were still studying (about three quarters of those were studying and employed and about one quarter were only studying). These figures resemble those of Master graduates. The biggest difference is that there was a share of those who were neither studying nor employed (less than 9 per cent). Slightly more Master graduates were employed (almost 83 per cent) and, surprisingly, more Master students were still studying (9 per cent) five years after graduation.

However, these data are somewhat outdated and do not present the situation just after graduation. We therefore used data about *unemployed graduates* gathered by labour offices and processed at the Czech Ministry of Labour and Social Affairs twice a year. An unemployed graduate is defined as a person registered as a jobseeker at a labour office within the first two years after graduation. This registered unemployment differs from the ILO definition. Data on the number of higher education graduates and on the number of those who continue their studies after graduation are provided by a Combined Register of Students (SIMS in Czech). They enable us to analyse the situation of Bachelor graduates up to seven years after graduation.

In 2002 only about 16,000 Bachelors graduated. Within six months after graduation, 58 per cent were continuing their studies, 18 per cent were unemployed, and almost one quarter was in employment or economically inactive for other reasons than higher education (unfortunately we are unable to distinguish between both groups but we assume that most are employed and only a small share is inactive). Within the subsequent six months, i.e. to one year after graduation, the share of unemployed is always radically reduced, and also in 2002 the share of unemployed dropped to 9 per cent. Correspondingly, the share of those who continued their studies and those in employment increased. In the second year after graduation, the share of the unemployed had decreased and the share of the other two groups had increased.

The dynamics within the first two years after graduation do not change much over time. What changed dramatically was a significant rise in the number of graduates, an increase in the share of those who continued to study, and significant changes in the economic situation of the country. While in 2003 there were only slightly more than 16,000 Bachelor graduates, this figure greatly increased to almost 80,000 in 2009, and while in 2003 not even two-thirds of Bachelors continued their (mostly Master) studies, there were about three-quarters of them in 2009. The overall unemployment rate rapidly decreased, as did the share of unemployed Bachelor graduates. It was lowest in the years 2007 and 2008 when the share of unemployed Bachelors within six month after the graduation was 8 per cent; it was 4 per cent in the second half-year after graduation and 3 per cent in the second year after the graduation. Those figures have increased since then and are expected to be substantially higher in 2010. This is, of course, due to the effect of the economic crisis which has caused a significant increase in the overall unemployment rate, and the decreasing proportion of the employed in recent years. In spite of this, due to a large increase in the number of Bachelor graduates, the absolute number of Bachelors entering the labour market continues to grow substantially. As of 2009, almost 20,000 graduates entered the labour market, which is about four times more than in 2002.

These data can only partly be compared to those of Master graduates. Logically, the share of Master graduates who continue their studies is much lower, and thus the share of those who enter the labour market within the first two years after graduation much higher. Therefore, it only makes sense to compare the share of unemployment. The most recent figures show that right after graduation (within the first six months) the share of unemployed is slightly higher for Masters (10 per cent) than for Bachelors (10 per cent). But thereafter, Masters become much less often unemployed than Bachelors. In the second six months after graduation, there were 3 per cent unemployed Masters compared to 4 per cent Bachelors. In the second year after graduation, this proportion changed to 2 per cent and 3 per cent respectively.

Table 1. Employment and Study within Two Years after Graduation of the 2002-2009 Graduates from Higher Education Institutions in the Czech Republic (per cent)

Year	2002	2003	2004	2005	2006	2007	2008	2009
Numbers of graduates from Bachelor's programmes	15,861	16,036	20,125	28,947	40,996	54,062	67,873	79,418
Proportion of Bachelor's graduates pursuing further study at the same or other institution in period								
Within 6 months of graduation	58	52	53	59	66	69	68	68
From 6 to 12 months after graduation	64	59	56	60	63	69	72	72
From 12 to 24 months after graduation	65	61	61	65	69	74	74	n/a
Proportion of Bachelor's graduates who are unemployed in period								
Within 6 months of graduation	18	18	16	13	13	10	8	9
From 6 to 12 months after graduation	9	10	9	6	6	4	3	4
From 12 to 24 months after graduation	8	6	4	3	3	2	3	n/a
Proportion of Bachelor's graduates who are not unemployed and not opting to pursue further study in period								
Within 6 months of graduation	24	30	30	28	21	21	24	23
From 6 to 12 months after graduation	27	31	35	34	32	27	25	24
From 12 to 24 months after graduation	27	34	35	31	28	24	23	n/a

Source: Ministry of Labour and Social Affairs, SIMS

PROFESSIONAL SUCCESS OF BACHELOR GRADUATES

Areas of professional success

The concept of professional success is very complex. It concerns societal and personal outcomes which are interconnected. We can see how new knowledge is acquired and how it is used. We can also focus on how people with specific personal characteristics act in their professional and personal life. Different approaches as to how to measure professional success and different data are available, and different indicators can be used.

On the one hand, data can be used to indicate how certain groups of persons with specific characteristics affect measurable economic gains. On the other different data describe certain characteristics of the transition from study to work (or to another job with better use of the knowledge acquired), including the quality of the job (the type of contract, income, etc.) or the quality of the knowledge transfer from higher education to work (whether employment corresponds to the level and field of education and how the knowledge is used in the job). Other questions concern job satisfaction.

Data used to measure professional success can come from different sources and be of different quality. Most come from surveys such as the labour force survey conducted on a large sample or from special surveys like those on graduate transition to the labour market that can include personal characteristics, views and attitudes. In what follows, we use data from two projects on the transition of graduates to the labour market – the Labour Force Survey and the European Social Survey.

From the societal and economic point of view, the key points of professional success concern the way the knowledge acquired is transformed into economic outcomes. We will analyse the distribution of Bachelor graduates and compare it to that of graduates of upper secondary and Master levels. First, we will examine the jobs of Bachelor graduates.

Positive situation for a small share of graduates in the labour force

Compared to similarly developed economies, the number of tertiary graduates in the Czech economy is still low, which creates a positive environment for tertiary graduates as a whole. Moreover, many Bachelor graduates continue their study. In the economy, there are 18 per cent of tertiary graduates, of whom 84 per cent are Master graduates, 7 per cent Bachelor graduates, 6 per cent higher professional school graduates and 4 per cent PhD graduates (2009 data). Changes were noted mainly among Master and Bachelor graduates. Compared to 2005, the share of Masters graduates has dropped from over 86 per cent to the above 84 per cent, while the share of Bachelors has increased from 4 per cent to 7 per cent. An increase, although lower, was observed in the case of graduates of higher professional schools; however their future is uncertain due to the demographic decline and to their ambiguous position in the tertiary system.

Occupational category

Compared to developed economies with a higher proportion of tertiary graduates, most of the relatively small proportion of tertiary graduates in the Czech Republic are still working in managerial and professional (or associate professional) occupations. However, in recent years, a change can be seen, as a growing number of tertiary graduates in the labour market has caused more of them to occupy professions in ISCO 4-9 groups. This is the case not only for new but also for older tertiary graduates.

Table 2. *Proportion of Tertiary Education-Trained Persons in the Czech Republic in Various Occupational Categories (per cent)*

	Age 20-29		Age above 30	
	2005	2009	2005	2009
ISCO 1+2	60	52	71	67
ISCO 3	32	38	24	26
ISCO 4-9	8	10	5	7

Source: Labour Force Survey

The situation of Bachelor degree holders is similar to that of the whole group of tertiary education-trained persons. However, their proportion occupying a profession in the lower-level ISCO 4-9 groups is even more pronounced. A stronger movement between the groups ISCO 1+2 and ISCO 3 is visible in the case of Bachelor graduates: Recent graduates of Bachelor studies are entering professions at the ISCO 3 level more often than the ISCO 1+2 than was the case a few years ago. In the case of Master graduates, this effect is weaker. An obvious difference can be seen between groups of Bachelor and Master graduates occupying jobs at ISCO 4-9 level: Bachelor graduates more often work in these jobs. The change between 2005 and 2009 in the group of older Bachelor graduates is not as high in other groups; this may be an effect of older workers taking Bachelor courses to improve their job positions and further career prospects.

Table 3. Proportion of Bachelor and Master Degree Holders in the Czech Republic in Various Occupational Categories (per cent)

	Bachelor graduates				Master graduates			
	Age 20-29		Age above 30		Age 20-29		Age above 30	
	2005	2009	2005	2009	2005	2009	2005	2009
ISCO 1+2	45	31	46	38	66	60	71	68
ISCO 3	39	52	41	49	28	34	24	25
ISCO 4-9	16	18	14	14	6	6	5	7

Source: Labour Force Survey

Bachelor graduates do not occupy jobs equally across the board, but they can be found more often in certain professional groups. In the managerial occupations (ISCO 1), the percentage in categories such as *Heads of offices, secretaries and executives of district and municipal authorities, Executives of smaller units,* or among *Senior public officials* is small. In the professional occupations (ISCO 2), there are many Bachelor graduates in jobs such as *Teachers at special schools, Archivists, librarians and professionals in related fields* and *Other administrative professionals*. Among associate professional occupations (ISCO 3), the greatest share of Bachelor graduates can be found in the following jobs: *Health care assistants, opticians and rehabilitation staff, Professional caregivers, nurses, Police inspectors and detectives, Social workers*; and notable numbers are working as *Teachers for preschool education of children and youth, Teachers in special schools, Professionals – brokers commercial and financial transactions, Representatives – agents, Administrative associate professionals* and *Customs and Excise staff and workers in related fields*.

Income

Income differences are one element of professional success. They are connected to the structure of graduates' jobs and to their position in the economy. Concerning Bachelor graduates, their qualification is relatively recent and their experience is limited in the Czech Republic. Differences by tertiary level according to the average hourly wage (as indicated by the information on average earning) fall into two groups. One comprises Bachelor graduates and graduates of higher professional schools, the other includes Master and PhD graduates. The hourly wage of Bachelor and higher professional school graduates is 51 per cent lower than that of Master and PhD graduates; but it is 15 per cent higher than that of higher secondary graduates with maturita, 54 per cent higher than that of higher secondary graduates without maturita, and 85 per cent higher than that of those with only basic or no education.

Table 4. Employees in the Czech Republic in the Various Rankings of Gross Monthly Earnings according to Data of the Czech Statistical Office, by Level of Educational Attainment (per cent)

Education / earnings (CZK)	All	Basic education	Secondary without maturita	Secondary with maturita	Higher professional and Bachelor	Master's and PhD
Till 15,000	18	47	27	10	5	1
15,001 till 20,000	22	29	30	20	15	4
20,001 till 24,000	18	12	19	21	18	9
24,001 till 28,000	14	6	12	17	17	15
28,001 till 32,000	9	3	6	11	12	13
32,001 till 40,000	9	2	4	12	16	18
40,001 and more	11	1	2	10	16	39

Source: Czech Statistical Office, 2010, 1st quarter

Table 5. Employees in the Czech Republic in the Various Rankings of Gross Monthly Earnings according to Data of the REFLEX 2010 Survey, by Level of Educational Attainment (per cent)

	Bachelor	Master's	PhD	Total
Till 20,000				
First job	69	64	62	65
Current	29	22	24	24
20,000 – 29,999				
First job	24	27	21	26
Current	39	33	31	34
30,000-39,999				
First job	5	6	10	6
Current	16	20	20	19
40,000 and more				
First job	2	3	7	3
Current	11	21	18	18
Gross monthly earnings				
First job	18,278	19,549	21,402	19,253
Current	28,217	32,996	31,200	31,641

Source: REFLEX 2010

Distribution of employees by earnings provides us with another perspective of how Bachelor graduates convert their education into monetary value (see tables 4 and 5). Though there is a visible advantage as compared to graduates of a lower level of education, the difference as compared to graduates of Master and doctoral programmes is greater than would be expected when taking into account three-year education of Bachelors and only another two-year education of Masters. From the Reflex 2010 survey difference between first and current job is also obvious.

Transition to employment and employment conditions

We will explore different aspects of how Bachelor graduates obtained their first jobs and how stable these were compared to graduates of other levels of education. As in the case of many other indicators, the position of Bachelor graduates here is also between Master graduates and higher secondary school graduates. We must keep in mind that this implies many other characteristics of a personal nature, and that it does not necessarily draw a correct picture of the effectiveness of Bachelor study programmes. From the 2007/08 survey, we saw that Bachelors need half the time to find a job compared to graduates from higher secondary school and Masters half of the time that Bachelors need. Reflex 2010 shows that it took the 2005-2006 Bachelor graduates 2.7 months on average to find a job as compared to 2.0 months for Master graduates. The situation of PhD graduates (only 0.4 months on average) is different, as they mostly already hold a job.

Although the duration of job contract can be considered as another indicator of a successful transition from school to work, there is no significant difference between Bachelors and Masters. 85 per cent of the Bachelor graduates and 86 per cent of the Master graduates obtain a long term or unlimited term contract. Similarly, 84 per cent of the Bachelor graduates and 87 per cent of the Master graduates are employed full-time.

Link between level of educational attainment and job requirements

An appropriate use of the highest level of education attained is important to assess the effectiveness of both public and private expenditure on education. More important is that people have jobs that correspond more to their level of education than to their field of study. We find significant differences between graduates of Bachelor and Master programmes. Graduates of Master's programmes have jobs that correspond to their level of education much more often than Bachelors, and Bachelors are more likely to have jobs that would require Masters. This reflects an unclear position of Bachelor education in the labour market, and also a still insufficient number of tertiary graduates in the Czech economy, as can be seen in table 6.

Table 6. Educational Level Perceived as Most Appropriate for the First and Current Job Four to Five Years Later for the 2005-2006 Graduates from Tertiary Education in the Czech Republic (per cent)

Most appropriate education	Bachelor	Master	PhD	Total
PhD and other postgraduat qualification				
First Job	2	4	43	5
Current Job	4	8	64	9
Master				
First Job	34	71	50	60
Current Job	46	79	32	69
Bachelor				
First Job	36	9	2	16
Current Job	34	6	2	13
Higher professional school				
First Job	7	3	1	4
Current Job	5	2	0	2
Lower than higher education				
First Job	22	12	3	14
Current Job	11	5	2	7

Source: REFLEX 2010

Graduates of Master programmes hold jobs that correspond to their level of education (71 per cent as regards the first job and 79 per cent as regards the job some years later) much more often than Bachelors (36 per cent and 34 per cent respectively); Bachelors are more frequently convinced a few years after graduation that their job would be better held by a Master graduate (46 per cent). Altogether, fewer graduates, Bachelors and Masters alike, think that their job a few years later would require a lower level of education than concerning their first job. This reflects the still unclear position of Bachelor education in the labour market in the Czech Republic, where the number of tertiary graduates is still insufficient and where the proportion of Bachelor graduates among all graduates is still low. The number of Master graduates is still too low for the needs of the current structure of the economy, thus opening up the door to higher-level jobs for Bachelor graduates.

Use of knowledge

In the REFLEX project, tertiary graduates assessed how their knowledge acquired in the course of study is used in their current job. The ratings of Master graduates (67 per cent) hardly differ from those of Bachelor graduates (65 per cent). On the basis of the assessment of the links between actual and most suitable educational attainment reported above, one could have expected that Bachelors would use their knowledge to a much greater extent, as many are working in positions that would need a Master degree. It could be that the graduates had more specific areas of knowledge in mind than the overall level of competences needed.

Job satisfaction

73 per cent of Bachelor graduates expressed great satisfaction with their work situation a few years after graduation, i.e. slightly more than Master graduates (71 per cent).

Personal characteristic for professional success

Even if we do not have an exact measure of professional success, these results indicate that about three quarters of tertiary education graduates consider their professional life as successful. This is because many perceive key elements of professional success as corresponding to their competences and their personal characteristics. The following personal characteristics are considered to be very important for professional success: (a) a *positive attitude* (not to lose energy on negative thinking, not to complain); (b) *openness to change* (flexibility and adaptability are qualities many employers seek as well as searching for new pathways, responses need to be quick); (c) *resilience* (the ability to overcome barriers, not to get frustrated, not to give up); (d) the *power of choice* (successful people understand that it is their choice that determines their success, they do not blame others for their failure). These characteristics – or at least some of them -have been included in a new data collection in June and July 2010 carried out as part of a new round of the REFLEX project. Further analyses may shed more light on these matters.

Taking into account all the dimensions of professional success mentioned above, we will focus on how satisfied graduates are with their education, as it would help us to describe the interaction between the world of education and the labour market. A factor analysis of data gathered over the last ten years has found two essential dimensions: the overall readiness and the use in practice. Overall readiness expresses how the level of education attained has prepared graduates for their working life, in particular whether the school has provided a broad base of knowledge and good opportunities for specialisation. The second dimension is concerned with whether the things taught have been well used in practice, assessing their possible obsolescence and proportion of theoretical knowledge that is not very applicable in practice. Taken together, both factors cover 65 per cent of the variance (the first factor 34 per cent, the second 31 per cent).

Using these factors, factor scores were calculated for each respondent from the surveys of the years 1997, 2002 and 2007. The resulting graph shows both dimensions and the position of different types of schools in the period examined. As far as Bachelor studies (marked as Bach) are concerned, overall readiness has improved during the period but the use in practice has been reduced. This reflects the development in the 1990s, when new practically-oriented Bachelor programmes were introduced, but the other Bachelor programmes only more or less replaced the first part of Master studies. Therefore, graduates of Master programmes (Master) as and those of higher professional schools (HPS) give a more positive assessment of their education from the point of view of its use than Bachelor graduates.

Figure 3. Usability of Education in Practice and General Readiness of School Leavers in the Years 1997 – 2007

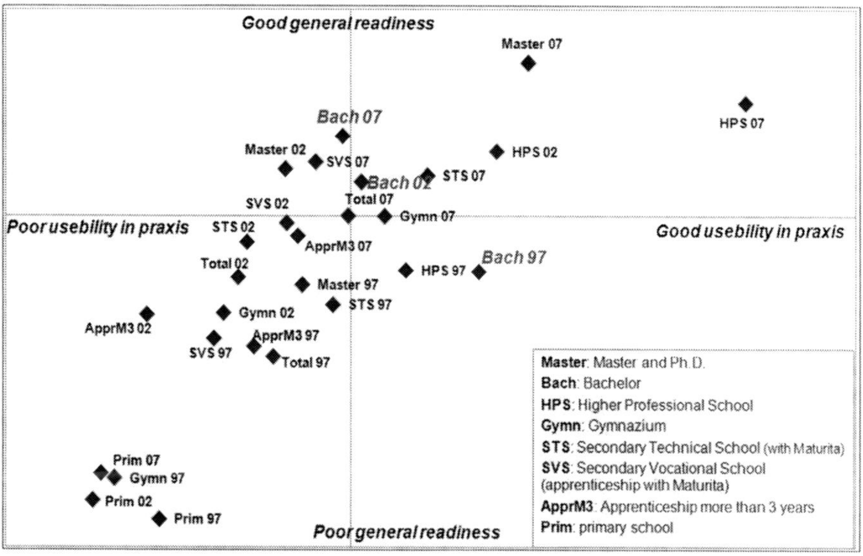

Source: School leavers' survey 1997, 2002 and 2007/08

CONCLUSIONS

Available data gathered by the REFLEX 2006 and 2010 projects and by the 2007/08 Czech School Leaver Survey allow us to formulate some tentative conclusions concerning the difference between Bachelor and Master graduates. We observed differences in socio-biographic background, educational paths, as well as employment and professional success.

There is empirical evidence that social origin is an important factor that affects young people's chances of continuing education or dropping out early, and of achieving different labour market outcomes. The relationship between parents' and children's education in the Czech Republic is very strong. For Master graduates, at least one parent obtained a higher education degree in nearly two fifths of cases. Graduates with a Bachelor degree had at least one parent with tertiary education in one of four cases. It seems that while Bachelor studies often serve as a way to upgrade the level of parents' education, Master studies are more often a way of reproducing parents' education (of course, the number of tertiary graduates is much higher than in the past so that many Master graduates have parents who did not achieve tertiary level). As for the relationship between parents' occupation and children's educational attainment, the biggest difference between Bachelor and Master graduates is in the share of fathers who are working in a professional/managerial occupation.

Bachelor and Master graduates also differ substantially in other aspects. One is the course of study they take at secondary level. While both generally quite often follow general secondary education, in the case of Master graduates this happens considerably more often. As for the average age of graduation, it is surprisingly about a year and half higher in the case of Bachelors. This is mainly because Bachelor programmes often serve as a supplementary way of obtaining a degree for those who were unable to do so in their early 20s. The graduates' satisfaction with their choice of course of study also differs. Almost all Master graduates are positive, while almost one fifth of Bachelor graduates would have liked to continue their studies and obtain a higher degree.

Experience of studying abroad for substantial period of time is not something students of Bachelor programmes go through very often. In fact only about 6 per cent had studied abroad for at least 3 months during their course study – a considerably lower share than in case of Master graduates who have much more flexible time available to do that mainly in the later stages of their course of study. In case of going abroad for work-related reasons there is smaller difference between Bachelors and Masters. About every sixth Bachelor have experience of working outside of Czech Republic for extended period of time during or after the course of study.

The employment situation of Bachelor graduates is mainly influenced by the rise in their numbers and the economic situation of the country. Particularly in recent years, the number of graduates has risen significantly, from 16,000 to 80,000, as has the proportion of those who continue to study, from less than two thirds to about three quarters. As the overall unemployment rate was rapidly decreasing before the economic crisis, so did the share of unemployed Bachelor graduates. Although today the economic crisis has caused significant increase in the overall unemployment rate, due to a large increase in the number of Bachelor graduates, the number of Bachelors entering the labour market continues to grow substantially, being in 2009 four times more than in 2002. Just after graduation (within the first six months), the unemployment rate of Bachelor and Master graduates is roughly the same, but later the proportion of unemployed Master graduates is lower, representing only about two thirds of the proportion of unemployed Bachelor graduates.

Different data can be used to measure professional success. Some relate to specific personal characteristics, others to characteristics concerning the transition from school to work, the quality of the job, the relationship between the education attained and job requirements, and job satisfaction. The number of tertiary graduates in the Czech economy is still relatively low, which creates a positive environment for them in the labour market. Moreover, a large proportion of Bachelor graduates continue their studies. Most tertiary graduates are still working in managerial and professional (or associate professional) occupations. However, in the last few years a growing number of tertiary graduates in the labour market has led to the fact that more of them, and particularly Bachelor graduates, occupy professions in ISCO 4-9 groups. Furthermore, new Bachelor graduates are entering more often professions at the ISCO 3 level compared to ISCO 1+2 than a few years ago. In the case of Master graduates this effect is weaker.

Income differences are another element of professional success. Concerning Bachelor graduates, their qualification is relatively new and experience with it limited in the Czech Republic. In the labour market they are still in quite low numbers performing only a limited number of jobs. An hourly wage of Bachelor graduates is half that an hourly wage of Master graduates, 15 per cent higher than that of upper secondary graduates with maturita and 54 per cent higher than that of upper secondary graduates without maturita.

In considering the time span between graduation and the first job and the stability of the first job, we observe a position of Bachelor graduates between Master graduates and upper secondary school graduates. As regards job contracts, there is no significant difference between Bachelor and Master graduates. Regarding the appropriate use of education attained, more important is that people do jobs corresponding to their level of education than jobs corresponding to their field of study. Graduates of Master programmes do jobs corresponding to their level of education much more often than Bachelors, and Bachelors do much more likely jobs that would require Masters. This fact reflects still an unclear position of Bachelor education on the labour market, and also a still insufficient number of tertiary graduates in the Czech economy.

Some key elements of professional success are closely connected to personal characteristics (positive attitude, openness to change, resilience, and the power of choice), which may thus play a great role in assessing both how much graduates use the knowledge and skills they gained and their job satisfaction. There is almost no difference between Bachelor and Master graduates in this respect, about three quarters of all tertiary graduates would see their professional life as successful.

Finally, an essential criterion of professional success is how satisfied graduates are with their education. A factor analysis of data gathered during the past ten years has found two essential dimensions: the overall readiness and the usability in practice. The first dimension expresses how education attained has prepared graduates for their working life, the second dimension is rather concerned with the fact whether the things taught have been well usable in practice.

In the period examined, as far as Bachelor studies are concerned, their overall readiness has improved during the period but the usability in practice has been reduced. This reflects the development in the 1990s, when some new practically oriented Bachelor programmes were introduced, but other Bachelor programmes only more or less replaced the first part of Master studies but did not change much in order to become more focused on usability in practice. Therefore Master graduates assess their education from the point of view of its usability in practice better than Bachelor graduates.

REFERENCES

Allen, J. & van der Velden, R. (Eds.) (2007). *The flexible professional in the Knowledge Society: General results of the Reflex project.* Maastricht: Research Centre for Education and the Labour market.

Centrum pro studium vysokého školství (2006). *OECD thematic review of tertiary education: Country background report for Czech Republic.* Prague: Centre for Higher Education Studies.

Koucký, J., Voříšek, P. & Zelenka, M. (2008). *Absolventi vysokých škol na pracovním trhu* (Higher education graduates in the labour market). *Aula, 16*(2), 1-10.

Koucký, J., Bartůšek, A. & Kovařovic, J. (2009). *Who is more equal? Access to tertiary education in Europe.* Prague: Charles University, Faculty of Education.

Koucký, J., Kovařovic J. & Zelenka, M. (2011). Czech Republic. In I. Kogan, M. Gebel & C. Noelke (Eds.), *Making the transition: Education and labor market entry in Central and Eastern Europe.* Stanford: Stanford University Press (in press).

Ryška, R. (2009). *Evaluace a přidaná hodnota ve vzdělání* [Evaluation and value added in education]. Prague: Pedagogická fakulta, Universita Karlova.

Straková, J. (2008). Czech Republic. In I. Kogan, M. Gebel & C. Noelke (Eds.), *Europe enlarged: A handbook of education, labour and welfare regimes in Central and Eastern Europe* (pp. 123-49). Bristol: Policy Press.

Zelenka, M. (2008). *Přechod absolventů škol ze vzdělávání na pracovní trh* [The transition of school graduates from education to employment]. Prague: Pedagogická fakulta, Universita Karlova.

HARALD SCHOMBURG

BACHELOR GRADUATES IN GERMANY: INTERNATIONALLY MOBILE, SMOOTH TRANSITION AND PROFESSIONAL SUCCESS

THE STUDY STRUCTURE IN GERMANY

From the 1970s to the 1990s, the higher education system in the Federal Republic of Germany was characterised by a two-type structure. Most study programmes at universities required 4-5 years of study and led to "Magister", "Diplom" or "Staatsexamen" degrees, all considered as equivalent to a Master. The study programmes at *Fachhochschulen* (translated into English as universities of applied sciences) were called three-year programmes with additional internships and possible examination periods until the 1980s and four-years programmes including internships and possible examination periods in the 1990s leading to a "Diplom" degree; this tended to be considered internationally as "Bachelor+" and also was counted in UNESCO statistics as ISCED 5A. About one tenth of graduates from universities of applied sciences (*Fachhochschulen*) continued their studies at universities. In 1998, 11 per cent of the corresponding age group was awarded a university degree and 6 per cent a Fachhochschule degree. Graduates from both types were about 28 years old on average at the time of graduation.

There was no concept of "tertiary education" in Germany, but an institution with less than one per cent of the age group existed in that domain: The *Berufsakademien* offering three-year programmes with somewhat more than half of the time spent for study and almost half in an enterprise. The 10 per cent of the age group who successfully completed ISCED 5B education were technicians, associate professionals in the medical area, kindergarten teachers, etc. who were trained in advanced vocational training schemes.

The introduction of a Bachelor-Master system started in Germany as early as in 1998, but progressed slowly (see figure 1).

In 2008, Bachelor and Master graduates comprised 20 per cent of the total number of graduates in Germany. In 2009, almost 80 per cent of new students started studying in the new system, while in 2005 this was the case for less than 20 per cent (see Hochschulrektorenkonferenz [HRK], 2010).

H. Schomburg and U. Teichler (eds.), Employability and Mobility of Bachelor Graduates in Europe, 89–110.
© 2011 Sense Publishers. All rights reserved.

Figure 1. New Students and Graduates in the Bachelor-Master System in Germany 2000-2009 (per cent)

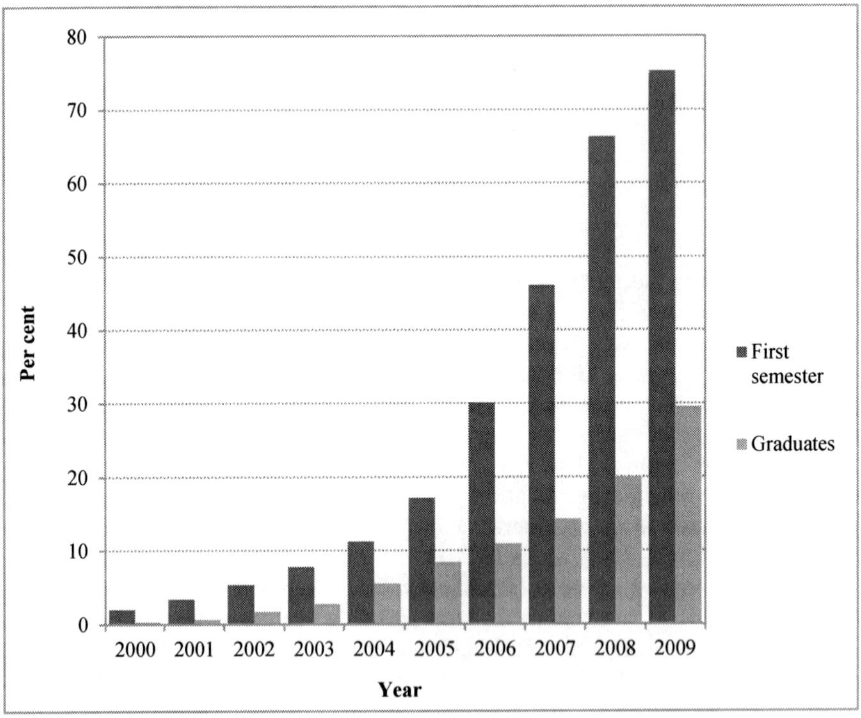

Source: Hochschulrektorenkonferenz (2010)

Both universities and universities of applied sciences (*Fachhochschulen*) in Germany are entitled to offer Bachelor and Master programmes. No formal distinction is made between Bachelor programmes; most comprise three years (180 ECTS credits), but some three-and-a-half or four years. Master programmes comprise two years in most cases but in some cases one-and-a-half years or one year, and Bachelor and Master programmes altogether should last for "not more than five years". Masters are labelled differently:
(a) "theory-oriented" (more often but not exclusively at universities) vs. "application-oriented" (more often but not exclusively at universities of applied sciences (*Fachhochschulen*)),
(b) "consecutive" (in the same field as the Bachelor) vs. "not consecutive", and
(c) "continuing" (students are not admitted immediately upon the award of a Bachelor degree) vs. "not continuing".

It remained controversial, and different regulations were implemented as regards the transition from a Bachelor degree to a Master programme: In some cases, all

Bachelor graduates are accepted while often additional selection criteria are put in place; in some cases, all Bachelors from the same field at the same institution are accepted, while others are selected. More than 70 per cent of the Bachelor graduates transfer to Master programmes according to information available for 2007. Moves to upgrade ISCED 5B vocational training to "Bachelor (professional)" programmes led to controversial debates and have not been implemented so far.

The new Bachelor-Master structure has not consistently been implemented in all fields of study in Germany. The traditional single-cycle long programmes have been preserved in medical fields, law, theology, education and as well as in a relatively high number of study programmes in fine arts.

THE DATA BASE: THE KOAB GRADUATE SURVEY

In the following, the results of graduate surveys which were conducted in the years 2009 and 2010 by 52 higher education institutions in Germany (see table 1) are reported[1]. The institutions undertook these studies with common core questionnaires in the framework of a network coordinated by the International Centre for Higher Education Research of the University of Kassel (INCHER-Kassel). In this survey network, a total of some 70,000 graduates responded (response rate: 50 per cent) who had graduated in the years 2007 and 2008, or more precisely in most cases from October 2006 to September 2008. The surveys took place during the winter semesters of the respective years, i.e. about 1½ years after graduation. In most cases, all graduates of the respective graduation cohort were surveyed, i.e. those from Bachelor and Master programmes, those from the traditional university and *Fachhochschule* programmes as well as all persons awarded a doctoral degree.

This graduate survey (referred to as KOAB graduate survey in the following text) constitutes the most comprehensive data set on the further study and career paths of graduates of a Bachelor's or Master's course of studies in Germany (main results were published in Schomburg & Teichler; 2009; Alesi, Schomburg & Teichler, 2010; Schomburg, 2010). In the survey conducted decentrally (by the individual higher education institution) and coordinated by INCHER-Kassel, a standard core questionnaire was used in all cases. Every individual higher education institution used an adapted questionnaire with supplementary individual questions. The higher education institutions funded their studies themselves, while the coordination on the part of INCHER-Kassel was supported financially by the Federal Ministry of Education and Research.

---

[1] Some of the 52 higher education institutions participated only in one of the two surveys.

Table 1. The KOAB Graduate Surveys in Germany 2009 and 2010

	Survey 2009	Survey 2010
Cohort of graduates (year of graduation)	2007	2008
Field phase	Oct. 2008 – Jan. 2009	Oct. 2009 – Feb. 2010
Number of participating institutions of higher education	48	46
Number of addresses	86,800	78,000
Number of valid addresses	75,000	69,000
Number of responses	37,500	33,000
Response rate (higher education institutions average)	50 %	49 %

Source: INCHER-Kassel, KOAB graduate surveys 2009 and 2010

Figure 2. Number of 2007 and 2008 Graduates from Higher Education Institutions in Germany Surveyed about One and a Half Years After Graduation, by Type of Degree

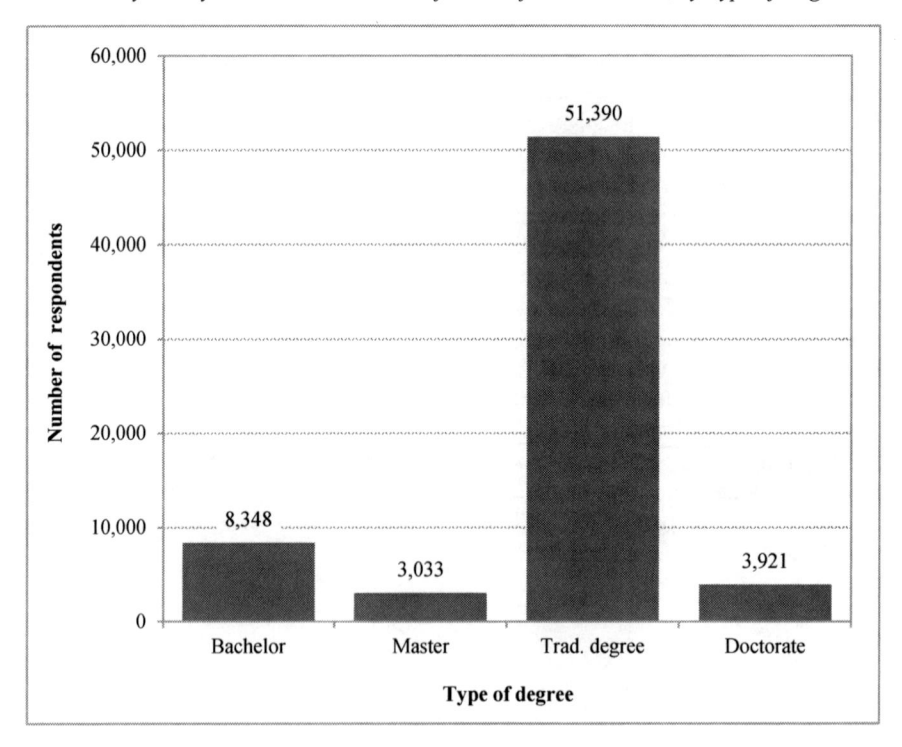

Source: INCHER-Kassel, KOAB graduate surveys 2009 and 2010

The subsequent analysis is based on the responses of about 62,000 graduates (see figure 2). Comparisons are made between Bachelor graduates from universities and universities of applied sciences (*Fachhochschulen*) with Master graduates from these two types of institutions as well as graduates from the traditional programmes of these two types of institutions. PhD holders are not included here, since there is no clear distinction between a traditional and a Bologna-based system.

SOCIO-BIOGRAPHICAL BACKGROUND AND COURSE OF STUDY

The graduate study examined several aspects of the socio-biographic background and the course of study which could help to explain subsequent employment. Several of them will be addressed here (see table 2).

Most respondents are *women* (52 per cent). They are most frequent among Bachelor graduates from universities (63 per cent), and also their proportion among Bachelor graduates from universities applied sciences is about half (51 per cent). The respective shares are lower among graduate of the traditional programmes and even lower among Master graduates (50 per cent from universities and 34 per cent from universities of applied sciences).

Table 2. Socio-biographical Background and Course of Study of 2007 and 2008 Graduates from Higher Education Institutions in Germany

	University of applied sciences BA	Trad. degree	MA	University BA	Trad. degree	MA	Total
Female graduates	51	44	34	63	57	50	52
A-typical entry qualification for HE (not "Abitur")	37	42	37	4	4	19	20
Vocational training before HE	51	54	52	16	19	24	32
Father or mother with higher education degree	53	43	52	58	60	60	55
Foreign graduates	4	4	21	4	4	23	5
Entry qualification from abroad	3	2	19	3	4	22	4
Father or mother born abroad (%)	17	20	33	17	17	32	19
Study duration for that degree							
Arithmetic mean (years)	3.3	4.7	2.9	3.3	5.6	3.2	5.0
Median (years)	3.0	4.5	2.5	3.0	5.5	2.5	5.0
Total study duration							
Arithmetic mean (years)	3.9	5.2	5.5	3.8	6.2	5.1	5.6
Median (years)	3.5	4.5	5.5	3.5	6.0	5.0	5.5
Age at time of graduation							
Arithmetic mean (years)	26.7	28.4	31.8	24.8	28.0	28.4	28.0
Median (years)	25.0	27.0	30.0	24.0	27.0	27.0	27.0
Total	1,280	8,613	530	7,068	42,409	2,503	62,403

Source: INCHER-Kassel KOAB graduate surveys 2009 and 2010

On average (arithmetic mean), the surveyed graduates are 28 *years old at the time of graduation*. The median age of 27 is somewhat lower. University Bachelor graduates are on average 25, i.e. about three years younger than university Master graduates and university graduates with traditional degrees. The relative high age of graduates from universities of applied sciences reflects their higher age of entry as a consequence of the fact that many participated in vocational training and were employed before enrolling in higher education.

The typical *entry qualifications* for first-cycle study did not change substantially in the wake of the introduction of the two-cycle structure of study programmes. Both 96 per cent of university graduates from traditional programmes and from Bachelor programmes possessed the general entry qualification for universities. At universities of applied sciences, however, the proportion of those entering higher education on the basis of other, as a rule more vocationally- oriented schooling declined from 42 per cent in traditional study programmes to 37 per cent in Bachelor programmes. More than half of the graduates from universities of applied sciences had been involved in *vocational training prior to study*, as compared to less than one fifth of the university graduates.

In contrast to university Bachelor graduates, the proportion of university Master graduates who had not acquired the general entry qualification, was as high as 19 per cent. This indicates that a substantial number of university Master graduates had been awarded the Bachelor degree by a university of applied sciences.

Overall, 4 per cent of respondents of Bachelor graduates from both types of higher education institutions are *foreigners* – of whom three per cent who had *not acquired their entry qualification in Germany*. In contrast, more than 20 per cent of Master graduates are foreigners and almost as many had acquired their entry qualification abroad. This indicates that the Master programmes in Germany are very attractive for students from other countries. Finally, less than 20 per cent of graduates from Bachelor levels and from traditional study programmes of both types of higher education institutions have a migrant background (at least father or mother born abroad) as compared to more than 30 per cent among Master graduates from both types of institutions.

The *actual duration of study* exceeds the required length of study to a lesser extent in the new Bachelor-Master system than in the traditional study system. The following proportion of graduates report that they have completed their study programme within the required length:
- 73 per cent of the Bachelor graduates from universities of applied sciences and
- 57 per cent of the Master graduates from universities of applied sciences as compared to
- 41 per cent of the graduates with traditional degrees from universities of applied sciences;
- 66 per cent of the Bachelor graduates from universities and
- 59 per cent of the Master's graduates from universities as compared to
- 37 per cent of the graduates with traditional degrees from universities.

INTERNATIONAL MOBILITY

The promotion of international student mobility is a central concern of the Bologna Process. In the Leuven Communiqué in 2009, the European ministers responsible for higher education stated: "*We believe that mobility of students, early stage researchers and staff enhances the quality of programmes and excellence in research; it strengthens the academic and cultural internationalization of European higher education. Mobility is important for personal development and employability, it fosters respect for diversity and a capacity to deal with other cultures. It encourages linguistic pluralism, thus underpinning the multilingual tradition of the European Higher Education Area and it increases cooperation and competition between higher education institutions. Therefore, mobility shall be the hallmark of the European Higher Education Area. We call upon each country to increase mobility, to ensure its high quality and to diversify its types and scope. In 2020, at least 20 per cent of those graduating in the European Higher Education Area should have had a study or training period abroad.*" (Leuven-communiqué, 2009) Thus a specific target for the increase in mobility was set which refers to mobility during the course of study which can best be measured with the help of graduate surveys; however, this statement does not define clearly the type of experience abroad: would this be, for example, at least three months of study or internship abroad, or would summer schools and language courses also count?

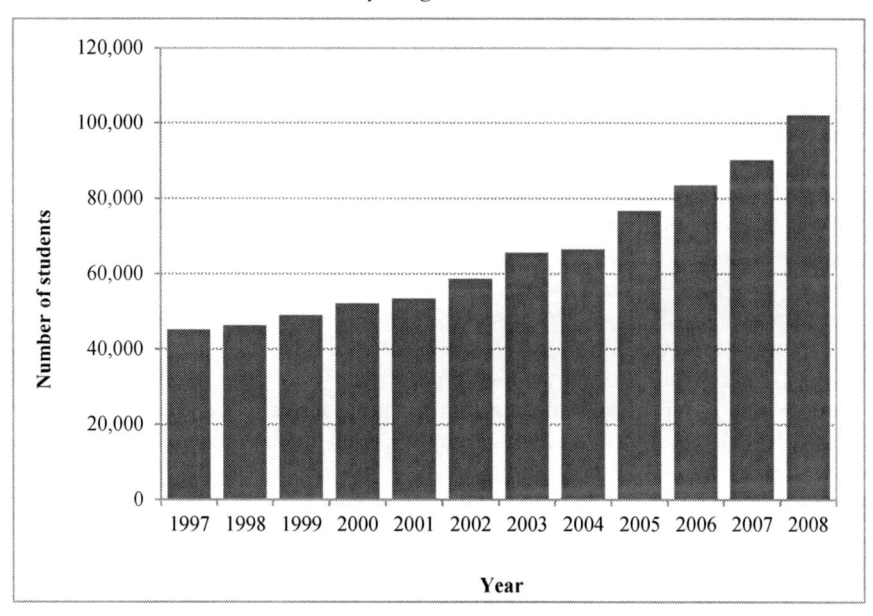

Figure 3. German Students Studying Abroad for Extended Periods or the Whole Study Programme* 1997-2007

* The data are derived by asking agencies of other countries to provide the number of German students, whereby in most cases only students who spend an extended or whole study period abroad are counted.

Source: Statistisches Bundesamt (2010)

The proportion of German students can be estimated with the help of two sources. First, the number of German students who spend the total study period abroad or major parts of it can be estimated at about 4 per cent. Because about 90,300 German students (more than 4 per cent) studied abroad in 2007 (see figure 3) according to international statistics which, according to recommendations by the international data collection agency, should only include students studying for a longer period abroad or for the complete study period abroad (= "degree mobility").

Second, graduate surveys can provide information about the proportion of students who have spent a period abroad during the course of study (temporary mobility). Table 3 shows that 28 per cent of university Bachelor graduates and almost the same proportion (27 per cent) of Bachelor graduates from universities of applied sciences spent a period abroad for study or for other study-related activities, of whom about half for the purpose of regular study. In the case of university Bachelor graduates this proportion is lower than among graduates from the traditional university programmes, but in taking into account the high transition quota of Bachelor graduates to Master programmes and the data on study after graduation as well as on study abroad of Master graduates we can conclude that the temporary mobility of German university students has increased in the wake of the Bologna Process. The proportion of Bachelor graduates from universities of applied sciences is higher than the respective proportion of graduates from the traditional study programmes at universities of applied sciences.

In adding up both the estimates of German students studying abroad for extended periods or for the whole study programme and of graduates from German higher education institutions who spent a period abroad for the purpose of study, we conclude that the proportion of German students studying abroad during the course of their study had already exceeded 20 per cent before 2010. If we add internships – also quoted in the Leuven Communiqué – the proportion is even higher, and if we add other study-related activities abroad, more than one third of German students experiences at least some study-related time abroad during their course of study.

Table 3 also provides information on employment abroad after graduation. 6 per cent of the university Bachelor graduates and 13 per cent of the Bachelor graduates from universities of applied sciences worked abroad at some time during the first 1½ years after graduation. The respective figures for graduates from traditional study programmes are 12 per cent each according to type of higher education institutions. In taking into account the high proportion of university Bachelor graduated who continue to study we conclude that mobility abroad after graduation hardly differs according to type of study programmes. Also, the high rates of Master graduates working abroad in the early period after graduation can be disregarded, because the data comprise a high proportion of foreign students who go abroad after graduation.

Table 3. *International Mobility before and during Study and after Graduation of 2007 and 2008 Graduates from Higher Education Institutions in Germany (per cent)*

	University of applied sciences			University			Total
	BA	Trad. degree	MA	BA	Trad. degree	MA	
A. Prior to study							
Foreign graduates	4	4	21	4	4	23	5
Entry qualification abroad	3	2	19	3	4	22	4
Foreign graduates who got their entry qualification abroad	2	2	18	3	3	20	3
B. During the course of study							
Study abroad and/or short study-related activities abroad	27	20	22	28	37	35	31
... Temporary study abroad	14	9	9	16	19	17	15
... Short study related activities abroad	21	16	17	19	27	27	23
... Internship	15	10	8	12	15	15	13
C. After study							
Study and/or practical training abroad after graduation	12	5	8	24	8	11	9
... Study abroad after graduation	7	2	5	15	4	6	4
... Practical training abroad after graduation	7	4	5	13	6	7	6
Employment abroad after graduation	13	12	23	6	12	20	12
... Temporary employed abroad	13	12	21	6	11	16	11
... At present employed abroad	8	4	8	7	5	11	5
N	1,279	8,605	529	7,060	42,355	2,493	62,321

Source: INCHER-Kassel KOAB graduate surveys 2009 and 2010

WHEREABOUTS OF THE BACHELORS

The newly introduced Bachelor programmes in German higher education in the Bologna Process, in principle, have both the function of being "professionally qualifying" for embarking in employment after the award of the Bachelor degree and preparing for subsequent study at Master level. In Germany, it was taken for granted that only moderate changes in the traditional study programmes at universities of applied sciences would be needed to transform them into Bachelor programmes and that most Bachelor graduates from these institutions would transfer to employment; however, the opportunity to continue to study was viewed as an important element to raise the status of study programmes at universities of applied sciences vis-à-vis those at universities. On the other hand, a substantial change in the study programmes at universities was viewed as needed to create Bachelor programmes that serve transition to employment and prepare for further study – similarly to the concern expressed by the ministers who signed the Bologna Declaration and called for the professional relevance of university programmes: "The degree awarded after the first cycle shall also be relevant to the European labour market". Therefore, some advocates of the new cycle system of study programmes and degrees in Germany called for fixed quota of transition to Master programmes in order to avoid too high a quota; and some critics of the new cycle system suggested that university Bachelor graduates should as a rule transfer to Master programmes. Therefore, it is interesting to note how the whereabouts of Bachelor programmes develop.

As table 4 shows, of the 2007 and 2008 Bachelor graduates from universities of applied sciences in Germany,
- 24 per cent solely study one-and-a-half years after graduation (i.e. are not employed concurrently),
- 17 per cent work and study,
- 2 per cent are in publicly coordinated professional training, and
- 52 per cent only work.

Table 4. Further Study and Employment about One and Half Year after Graduation of 2007 and 2008 Graduates from Higher Education Institutions in Germany (per cent)

	University of applied sciences			University			Total
	BA	Trad. degree	MA	BA	Trad. degree	MA	
Regular work (no study)	52	82	81	18	43	53	55
Professional training	2	3	2	3	25	9	15
Study and work	17	7	11	24	23	25	18
Only study (not employed)	24	4	2	51	5	8	8
Search for job (without employment)	4	3	3	2	2	3	2
Other (family, etc.)	2	2	2	2	2	2	2
Total	100	100	100	100	100	100	100
N	1,200	8,025	454	6,377	38,280	2,221	56,557

Source: INCHER-Kassel KOAB graduate surveys 2009 and 2010

Thus, the ratio of work after graduation (including possible concurrent study and training) is 71 per cent among Bachelor graduates from universities of applied sciences but the ratio of further study and training (including possible concurrent work) is 43 per cent.

Of the 2007 and 2008 university Bachelor graduates
- 51 per cent only study,
- 24 per cent work and study,
- 3 per cent are in publicly coordinated professional training (notably in training for legal professions and in teacher training), and
- 18 per cent only work.

Thus, the ratio of further study and training (including possible concurrent work) is 78 per cent among university Bachelor graduates and the ratio of further work (including possibly concurrent study and training) is 45 per cent.

Most but not all the Bachelor graduates who continue to study after graduation enrol in Master programmes. As figure 4 shows, 65 per cent of university Bachelor graduates and 30 per cent of graduates from universities of applied sciences transfer to Master programmes within one-and-a-half years after the award of the Bachelor degree.

Figure 4. Transition to Master Study on the Part of 2007 and 2008 Graduates from Higher Education Institutions in Germany (graduates from various study programmes and institutions; per cent)

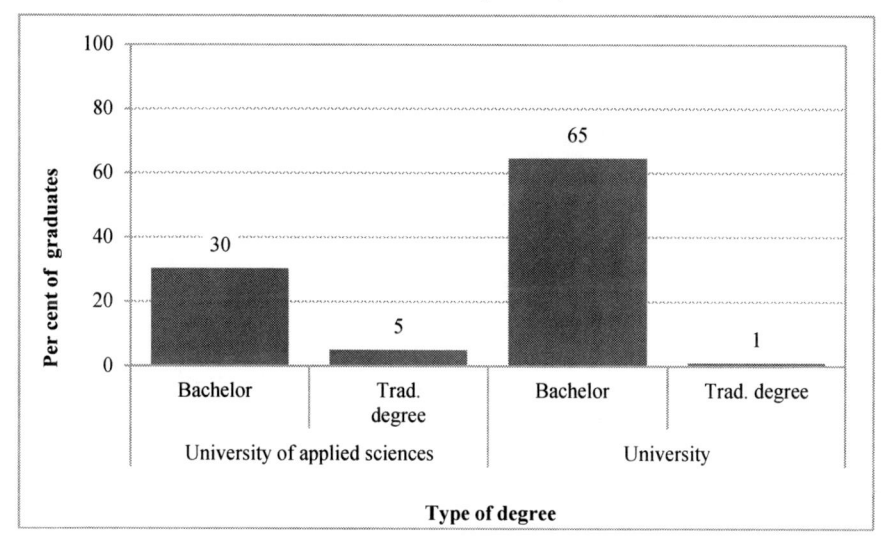

Type of degree	Per cent of graduates
Bachelor (University of applied sciences)	30
Trad. degree (University of applied sciences)	5
Bachelor (University)	65
Trad. degree (University)	1

Source: INCHER-Kassel KOAB graduate surveys 2009 and 2010

The further study was predominantly a Master's programme. For the Bachelor graduates from universities of applied sciences this is almost exclusively a Master's degree at a university of applied sciences. For the Bachelor graduates from universities the transition to a Master's programme at a university dominates, but other degrees are also pursued.

Previous graduate surveys of the Hochschul-Informations-System (HIS) (Minks & Briedis, 2005; Briedis, 2007) noted similar rates of continuing study among university Bachelor graduates (78 per cent). On the other hand, a higher rate of continuous study was identified for graduates from universities of applied sciences (59 per cent) in the 2002/2003 cohort, i.e. at a very early stage of the implementation of Bachelor programmes in Germany (Minks & Briedis, 2005). A later graduate survey reported slightly lower proportions for Bachelor graduates from universities of applied sciences, but about the same proportion for university Bachelor graduates, without further specification (Briedis, 2007). The graduate survey undertaken at the University of Konstanz (Auspurg, Bargel, Hinz & Pajarinen, 2009) states similar results as the KOAB graduate survey (72 per cent).

According to the KOAB survey, the rate of those who only continue to study varies substantially by field of study. In the case of university Bachelor graduates, the highest study rates are observed in mathematics and natural sciences (89 per cent), agricultural, food and forestry sciences (86 per cent), computer science (75 per cent), cultural and social sciences (74 per cent) and engineering (71 per cent), while the respective rate is only 65 per cent in economic fields. In the case of universities of applied sciences, the rates of further study are high in engineering (60 per cent), about average in agricultural, food and forestry sciences, as well as in computer science (48 per cent each), but only 32 per cent in economic fields and 31 per cent in cultural and social sciences.

The data presented cannot provide a full picture of the ratios of Bachelor and Master degrees. On the one hand, some Bachelors may opt for further study at a later stage than one-and-a-half years after graduation. On the other, some Bachelor graduates who continue to study after graduation may not complete their subsequent study; for example, they may take part-time or full-time study as having a well-accepted status in an extended search for a suitable job.

The data presented above make clear that there can be different rates of transition to employment after the award of the Bachelor degree:
– the rate of sole employment after the award of the Bachelor degree: 18 per cent of university Bachelor graduates and 52 per cent of Bachelor graduates from universities of applied sciences;
– the rate of employment and vocational training: 21 per cent of university Bachelor graduates and 54 per cent of Bachelor graduates from universities of applied sciences;
– the rate of employment including training and concurrent study: 44 per cent of university Bachelor graduates and 71 per cent of Bachelor graduates from universities of applied sciences.
– The unemployment rate (search for job without being employed) for 2007 and 2008 graduates was only 2 per cent in the case of university Bachelor graduates one-and-a-half years after graduation and 4 per cent in the case of Bachelor graduates from university of applied sciences. These rates are similar to those of Master graduates from both types of higher education institutions (3 per cent each) as well as of graduates from the traditional programmes at universities (2 per cent) and universities of applied sciences (3 per cent).

Information provided on the *duration of job search* suggest that university Bachelor graduates did not face any particular difficulties in the process of transition to employment. They reported on average a search period of 3.0 months as compared to 2.9 months reported by graduates from traditional university degrees and 3.4 months by university Master graduates. Bachelor graduates from universities of applied sciences as well as graduates from the traditional programmes of these institutions spent on average 2.8 months on job search as compared to 3.4 months on the part of Master graduates from universities of applied sciences.

The period between graduation and first employment was about two months longer for university Bachelor graduates than the search period, i.e. 5.3 months on average. This is one to two months more than for the other groups of graduates, not necessarily an indication of enormous difficulties. Actually, this transition period lasted for 4.0 months on average for graduates from traditional university programmes and 3.7 months for Master graduates. The respective time span was slightly shorter for graduates from universities of applied sciences: 3.9 months for Bachelors, 2.9 months for Masters and 3.2 months for those from traditional programmes.

THE PROFESSIONAL SUCCESS OF BACHELOR GRADUATES

Views vary about what can be taken as the most salient measures of the professional success of graduates. Hence, a variety of measures are addressed here: as regards employment conditions, whether graduates are employed full-time or part-time, whether they have an unlimited or a fixed-term employment contract, and how much they earn; as regards the links between higher education and professional assignment, the extent to which the level of educational attainment corresponds to the professional position and the extent to which the knowledge acquired during the course of study is used on the job. Finally, the graduates were asked to rate their level of overall satisfaction with their job. An overview of their responses is provided in table 5.

Table 5. Aspects of the Professional Success of 2007 and 2008 Graduates from Higher Education Institutions in Germany Being Employed Solely One and a Half Years after Graduation (per cent)

	University of applied sciences BA	Trad. degree	MA	University BA	Trad. degree	MA	Total
Full-time employed	90	92	91	85	85	91	89
Unlimited term contract	66	75	85	55	65	68	70
Gross annual income (arith. mean; thousand Euro)	33.8	36.5	45.0	29.4	36.9	36.2	36.6
Adequate level of employment	81	86	85	75	82	78	83
High use of competences	48	51	64	35	50	56	51
High job satisfaction	69	67	65	63	66	66	66
N	614	6,443	359	1,094	17,309	1,148	26,967

Source: INCHER-Kassel KOAB graduate surveys 2009 and 2010

It should be noted that the following analysis addresses only those employed graduates who are only employed. Excluded are those who study along employment or are formally participating in initial professional training programmes. This decision was taken because many Bachelor graduates who are studying part-time do not try to find a job that is commensurate to their competences and career aspirations.

Part-time and full-time employment

Nine out of ten graduates from higher education institutions in Germany who are solely employed are employed full-time two years after graduation. The respective proportion does not differ between university Bachelor graduates and graduates from traditional university programmes (85 per cent each), and are similar for Bachelor graduates and graduates from traditional programmes of universities of applied sciences (90 per cent and 92 per cent respectively).

Fixed-term and unlimited employment

As table 5 shows, the rates of Bachelor graduates from higher education institutions in Germany employed on an unlimited contract are 10 per cent lower each in the case of graduates from universities (55 per cent as compared to 65 per cent) and from universities of applied sciences (66 per cent as compared to 75 per cent) than the respective rates among graduates from traditional programmes. Table 5 also shows that the rates of unlimited employment are highest for Master graduates. One must bear in mind that graduates from universities embark more often on careers in the public sectors where a high proportion of employees has a fixed-term contract in the initial years than those from universities of applied sciences.

Table 6. Unlimited-term Contracts of 2007 and 2008 Graduates from Higher Education Institutions in Germany Being Employed Solely One and a Half Years after Graduation, by Group of Fields of Study (per cent)

	University of applied sciences			University			Total
	BA	Trad. degree	MA	BA	Trad. degree	MA	
Humanities and social sciences	40	45	74	45	49	50	47
Economics	83	81	94	71	80	80	82
Mathematics and natural sciences	61	53	67	45	68	69	65
Computer science	81	87	90	88	88	87	87
Engineering	77	84	82	79	83	73	83
Agriculture, food science, forestry	60	67	56	55	59	62	65

Source: INCHER-Kassel KOAB graduate surveys 2009 and 2010

Table 6 shows the differences in permanent employment by group of fields of study. Obviously, there is no regular pattern of differences between graduates from universities and universities of applied sciences across disciplines. On the one hand, university Bachelor graduates in mathematics and natural sciences are far less often employed on a permanent contract than those in traditional programmes;

on the other hand, graduates from universities of applied sciences in mathematics and natural sciences are even more often employed permanently than those in traditional programmes.

Table 6 indicates that unlimited term contracts are obtained by at most half of the solely employed graduates one-and-a-half years after graduation in select groups: university graduates from all types of programmes in humanities and social sciences, graduates from Bachelor and traditional programmes in humanities and social sciences of the universities of applied sciences, and university Bachelor graduates in mathematics and natural sciences.

Income

As can be seen in table 5, the annual gross income of university Bachelor graduates (29,400 Euro) is on average 20 per cent less than that of graduates from traditional university programmes (36,900 Euro). A comparison of the information provided in table 5 and table 7, however, suggests that this large difference is a compositional effect of fields of study. Within the individual groups of field of study, the difference is only that large in mathematics and natural sciences (21 per cent), whereas it is somewhat less in engineering (15 per cent) and clearly less in economic fields (12 per cent), cultural and social sciences (11 per cent), agricultural, food and forestry sciences (8 per cent) and computer science (4 per cent). We must bear in mind that Bachelor programmes are viewed in the German public sector as leading to second-rank careers ("gehobener Dienst"), whilst Master programmes are supposed to lead to first-rank careers ("höherer Dienst"), whereby the income according to career varies by more than 15 per cent.

Table 7. *Gross Annual Income of 2007 Graduates from Higher Education Institutions in Germany Being Employed Solely One and a Half Years after Graduation, by Group of Fields of Study (arithmetic mean in thousand Euro)*

	University of applied sciences			University			Total
	BA	Trad. degree	MA	BA	Trad. degree	MA	
Humanities and social sciences	28.1	30.5	41.3	26.0	29.1	32.7	29.7
Economics	37.8	39.2	54.1	35.7	40.5	39.8	40.2
Mathematics and natural sciences	35.9	34.7	33.8	28.4	36.0	38.3	35.7
Computer sciences	42.5	40.5	40.5	40.6	42.5	40.4	41.3
Engineering	37.1	39.3	43.1	34.7	41.1	37.9	39.9
Agriculture, food science, forestry	27.9	28.0	29.7	25.0	27.3	31.6	28.3
Total	33.8	36.5	45.0	29.4	36.9	36.2	36.6

Source: INCHER-Kassel; KOAB Graduate Survey 2009

The average income of graduates from traditional university programmes in Germany and that of graduates from university Master programme are about the same. This suggests that the new university degree is accepted by German employers more or less equally well as the traditional university degree. Table 7, however, shows that there are enormous variations by group of field of study. In some groups, the graduates from traditional university programmes earn clearly more than Master graduates, but the reverse is true for other groups of fields of study.

The income of Bachelor graduates from universities of applied sciences is on average 7 per cent less than that of Bachelor graduates from traditional programmes at these institutions. The differences vary by field: The former earn 8 per cent less in cultural and social sciences, 6 per cent less in engineering, 4 per cent less in economic fields, but 3 per cent more in mathematics and natural science and 5 per cent more in computer science. As the new Bachelor programme at university of applied sciences is usually one year shorter than the traditional programmes at these institutions and often comprises less practical experiences, this income difference could be viewed as normal by employers.

Table 7 shows that the annual income of graduates from traditional programmes at universities of applied sciences across all fields is as high as that of graduates from traditional programmes from universities. This finding – surprising at first glance – is due to the fact that fields of study which are not closely linked the respective occupational areas are not represented in the universities of applied science. In large fields represented both at universities and universities of applied sciences, notably engineering and economic fields, the income of university graduates is somewhat word missing than that of graduates from universities of applied sciences.

The most surprising information in table 7 as regards remuneration is the high income of the Master graduates from universities of applied sciences which is clearly higher than that of university Master graduates. This is due to the fact that many Master programmes of the former institutions have set a longer period of professional work as entry requirements. As a consequence, graduates from these programmes are not viewed by the employers as being in the phase of initial adjustment to the world of work about one-and-a-half years after graduation, but already as somewhat experienced professionals.

Link between level of educational attainment and employment

An "adequate level of employment" is stated in tables 5 and 8 if graduate in response to the question "In your opinion, which academic degree is best suited for your current job?" responded either "A higher academic degree" or "My academic degree". According to this mode of analysing the vertical link between study and employment, the proportion of university Bachelor graduates who consider themselves as not adequately employed is 25 per cent; this is somewhat higher than among their colleagues from traditional university programmes (18 per cent) and Master programmes (21 per cent). Graduates from universities of applied sciences consider themselves more seldom as inappropriately employed, whereby the quota among Bachelor graduates (18 per cent) is also slightly higher than among graduates from traditional programmes (15 per cent each).

Table 8. Link between Level of Education and Present Job Perceived by 2007 and 2008 Graduates from Higher Education Institutions in Germany Being Employed Solely One and a Half Years after Graduation (per cent)

	University of applied sciences			University			Total
	BA	Trad. degree	MA	BA	Trad. degree	MA	
A higher academic degree	12	7	10	14	5	6	6
My academic degree	70	79	75	61	77	72	77
A lower academic degree	5	7	13	6	11	16	9
No academic degree necessary	13	8	2	19	7	5	8
Total	100	100	100	100	100	100	100
N	407	4,780	250	941	16,001	1,042	23,421

Source: INCHER-Kassel; KOAB Graduate Survey 2009 and 2010

Altogether, many graduates in Germany perceive a close link between their level of educational attainment and their early-career job. Only 9 per cent believe that a lower-level degree would be appropriate, and 8 per cent deem a higher education degree as not necessary. There are differences, though, by groups of field of study, as is seen in table 8. University Bachelor graduates in mathematics and natural sciences (62 per cent) as well as in agriculture (67 per cent) consider their job least often as corresponding to their level of education. University graduates of all categories in agriculture as well as in humanities and social sciences note such a match between level of education and job less often than the graduates on average.

Table 8. Adequate Level of Education for Present Job Perceived by 2007 and 2008 Graduates from Higher Education Institutions in Germany Being Employed Solely One and a Half Years after Graduation, by Group of Fields of Study (per cent)

	University of applied sciences			University			Total
	BA	Trad. degree	MA	BA	Trad. degree	MA	
Humanities and social sciences	85	86	83	73	75	72	78
Economics	85	83	82	85	83	80	83
Mathematics and natural sciences	78	83	100	62	85	83	84
Computer sciences	88	88	92	91	84	84	86
Engineering	91	91	91	86	87	84	89
Agriculture, food science, forestry	86	78	80	67	72	75	78

Source: INCHER-Kassel; KOAB Graduate Survey 2009 and 2010

Use of competences and links between field of study and work tasks

The horizontal link between study and work was addressed in the German study with the question: "To what extent are the knowledge and skills you acquired during study used in your current job?". Hardly any links (the lowest two points on a five-point scale from 1 "to a very high extent" to 5 "not at all") were noted by 25 per cent of the university Bachelor graduates as compared to 16 per cent each of the university graduates from traditional programmes and from Master programmes (table 5). The corresponding rates for graduates from universities of applied sciences were 17 per cent, 15 per cent and 11 per cent. Hardly any links were observed by university Bachelor graduates in humanities and social sciences (29 per cent as compared to 21 per cent among graduates from traditional programmes) and university Bachelor graduates in mathematics and natural sciences (29 per cent as compared to 20 per cent). In contrast, there are hardly any differences in this respect between the various types of degrees and types of higher education institutions in the field of computer science.

Table 9. Link between Field of Study and Work Tasks Perceived by 2007 and 2008 Graduates from Higher Education Institutions in Germany Being Employed Solely One and a Half Years after Graduation (per cent)

	University of applied sciences BA	Trad. degree	MA	University BA	Trad. degree	MA	Total
My field of study is the only possible/by far the best field for my present work tasks	38	43	32	21	38	31	40
Some other fields could prepare for the area of work as well	46	44	55	48	45	52	46
Another field would have been more useful for my present work tasks	12	8	7	17	10	10	9
In my present work the field of study does not matter	4	4	6	14	7	7	6
Total	100	100	100	100	100	100	100
N	482	5,400	276	893	15,270	939	23,260

Source: INCHER-Kassel; KOAB Graduate Survey 2009 and 2010

In addition, the affinity of study and work was addressed with respect to the relationship between field of study and work tasks. Again, the university Bachelors most often missed a link between study and work tasks: 31 per cent stated either that another field of study would have been more useful or that the field of study would not matter. As table 9 shows, less than 20 per cent each of the other categories of graduates noted such a discrepancy between field of study and work tasks. The highest rates of such a limited or non-existing link between field of study and occupational tasks were reported by university Bachelor graduates in the humanities and social sciences (39 per cent) and in mathematics and natural sciences (35 per cent).

Job satisfaction

The graduates from German higher education institutions less often expressed a high extent of job satisfaction (66 per cent) than the graduates from most countries addressed in this publication. Thereby, the rates hardly differ between the different categories of graduates that were analysed:
- 69 per cent of Bachelor graduates from universities of applied sciences,
- 65 per cent of Master graduates from universities of applied sciences, and
- 67 per cent of graduates from traditional programmes at universities of applied sciences;
- 63 per cent of university Bachelor graduates,
- 66 per cent of university Master graduates, and
- 66 per cent of the traditional programmes at universities.

There are variations by field of study. It is worth noting that Bachelor graduates in computer sciences are most highly satisfied: 85 per cent at universities as compared to 77 per cent among their peers in traditional programmes and 79 per cent as compared 72 per cent at universities of applied sciences.

CONCLUSION

In the summary of the main findings it is important to note that the proportion of graduates with a Bachelor's and Master's degree only makes up a small part of all graduates. Second, the graduate survey one-and-a-half years after graduation cannot illustrate long-term professional development.

16 per cent of the Bachelor graduates of German universities report that they completed one semester abroad during the course of their studies. At Master's level 17 per cent study temporarily abroad (Bachelor graduates from universities). Considering that three-quarters of university Bachelor graduates continue their studies, one can estimate that about 27 per cent of students in the Bachelor-Master system have studied abroad before the degree with which they start employment. Among the graduates from university programmes of the old system, the corresponding percentage is much lower at 19 per cent.

The relatively high international mobility of graduates of the new programmes, however, can partly be explained by the high proportion of humanities and social sciences graduates among them. This field of study group already had an above average international mobility in the past.

Of the graduates from the universities of applied sciences, 14 per cent studied abroad during the course of the Bachelor study. Among the graduates of the old traditional degree programmes from universities of applied sciences, this figure is only 9 per cent. Here too, the new study system clearly proves beneficial for studies abroad.

In addition, almost as many graduates have been abroad during their studies for other study-related purposes (foreign language courses, summer schools, internships, etc.). Summing up these shorter stays abroad during their studies with semesters abroad, it turns out that in total 28 per cent of Bachelor graduates from universities and 27 per cent of the Bachelor graduates from universities of applied sciences acquired experience abroad during their studies.

The European ministers called for a target of the Bologna process whereby 20 per cent of graduates should have spent some time abroad from studying or internships in 2020.

Considering the estimated value of other statistics that about 3 per cent of German graduates spend their entire study up to the degree abroad, the result is: German higher education institution students have already reached the Bologna target for mobility for 2020 a decade earlier.

The KOAB surveys can help to answer the question of which percentage of Bachelor graduates goes into employment after they graduate, and which percentage continues their studies. It was shown that there are several variants in calculating the rate of continuing studies, depending on whether you consider people who are exclusively studying or people who are working while studying. The rate of continuing studies among Bachelor graduates determined in this report as 78 per cent at universities and 43 per cent at universities of applied sciences includes both groups, people who are exclusively studying and those who are working while studying.

In an international comparison between countries with a longer experience with the Bachelor-Master system (USA, UK and Australia), these rates seem high. However, it should be considered that these countries have a much higher entrance rate. On the other hand, if you make a comparison between the rate of graduates from long study programmes in Germany (about 10 to 11 per cent of a cohort) and the rate of Master graduates in these countries (about 12 per cent of a cohort), these differences appear small. Since it is not foreseeable that in the near future the entrance rates in Germany will dramatically increase, a high rate of continuing studies as determined in the KOAB graduate survey seems adequate to keep to the qualification level in its current state. Countries whose higher education system also consists of two types of higher education institutions (universities and universities of applied sciences) report similarly high rates of continuing studies.

Only 4 per cent of Bachelor graduates from German universities and 6 per cent of graduates from German universities of applied sciences remain unemployed. The average job search duration of Bachelor graduates from German higher education institutions does not differ from that of graduates of the old system.

57 per cent of Bachelor graduates of German universities are employed full-time compared to 67 per cent of graduates from the old long study programmes. This can be explained by the fact that Bachelor graduates more often study while working. Considering only the regular employees (exclusively working) then almost 90 per cent of graduates are working full-time and there are no relevant differences in the contract situation between the new and the old degrees.

The rate of employees with unlimited term contracts 1½ years after graduation among university Bachelor graduates (36 per cent) and other university graduates (38 per cent) is almost equal. In both cases, the initially fixed-term employment in public service has a heavy impact. Considering only regular employees, somewhat larger differences between old and new study programmes become apparent, the latter having fewer unlimited term contracts .

The income of graduates from new study programmes in most of the fields of study groups is slightly lower than among the traditional study programmes. The differences are less obvious (less than 10 per cent) at universities of applied sciences. The differences are highest among graduates in mathematics / natural science (-21 per cent to the disadvantage of the Bachelor's), engineering (-15 per cent), of economics (-12 per cent) and humanities and social sciences (-15 per cent).

The graduates from university Bachelor programmes in Germany do not rate the relationship between study and work as positively as the graduates from the old long university study programmes. This is reflected in the assessment of whether employment matches the level of qualification (77 per cent compared to 87 per cent; 69 per cent compared to 84 per cent for regular employees), and in the statement that knowledge acquired during the studies can mostly be used in the job (45 per cent compared to 55 per cent, 35 per cent compared to 50 per cent for regular employees). With regard to high job satisfaction the picture is similar: 53 per cent compared to 63 per cent (63 per cent compared to 66 per cent for regular employees).

The results of the KOAB graduate survey of 2009 cannot support the fears of an acceptance issue of university Bachelor graduates in general.

Looking at the individual fields of study it shows two extremes (both STEM[2] subjects): Bachelor graduates in mathematics and natural science seem to have a much more problematic entry into professional life than traditional graduates. For most of the above mentioned indicators they fare far less well than traditional graduates. The margin increases (for some indicators even significantly) when compared to Master graduates. However, for Bachelor graduates in computer science there are next to no differences, both in comparison to traditional university graduates and Bachelor graduates from universities of applied sciences.

A comparison of the results from the years 2009 and 2010 shows no significant changes. Only a higher rate of continuing studies among graduates of the cohort of 2008 can be seen. Whether this was influenced by economic development (financial and economic crisis in 2008/2009) cannot be clarified with our data.

---

[2] STEM: Science, Technology, Engineering, and Mathematics

REFERENCES

Alesi, B., Schomburg, H. & Teichler, U. (2010). Humankapitalpotenziale der gestuften Hochschulabschlüsse: Weiteres Studium, Übergang in das Beschäftigungssystem und beruflicher Erfolg von Bachelor- und Master-Absolventen in Deutschland [Human ressources potential of tiered degrees: further study, transition to employment and vocational success of bachelor and master graduates in Germany]. In Bettina Alesi & Nadine Merkator (Eds.), *Aktuelle hochschulpolitische Trends im Spiegel von Expertisen. Internationalisierung, Strukturwandel, Berufseinstieg für Absolventen* (129-195). Werkstattberichte 72. Kassel: Internationales Zentrum für Hochschulforschung Kassel.

Auspurg, K., Bargel, H., Hinz, T. & Pajarinen, A. (2009). *Studium und Verbleib der Bachelorabsolventen 2007/08 der Universität Konstanz* [Study and whereabouts of bachelor graduates 2007/08 of the University of Konstanz]. Konstanz. Retrieved October 20, 2010 from http://kops.ub. uni-konstanz.de/volltexte/2009/8278/pdf/BA_Absolventenstudie_2009_final.pdf

Briedis, K. (2007). Übergänge und Erfahrungen nach dem Hochschulabschluss. Ergebnisse der HIS-Absolventenbefragung des Jahrgangs 2005 [Transitions and experiences after graduation. Results of the HIS graduate survey of the year 2005]. HIS: Forum Hochschule, 13. Hannover: HIS

Hochschulrektorenkonferenz (2010). *Statistische Daten zur Einführung von Bachelor- und Masterstudiengängen Wintersemester 2010/2011* [Statistical data about implementation of bachelor and master programmes winter term 2010/2011]. Statistiken zur Hochschulpolitik 2/2010. HRK: Bonn.

Leuven-communiqué (2009). *The Bologna Process 2020 - The European Higher Education Area in the new decade.* Communiqué of the Conference of European Ministers Responsible for Higher Education, Leuven and Louvain-la-Neuve, 28-29 April 2009. Retrieved February 7, 2011 from http://www.bmbf.de/pub/leuvener_communique.pdf

Minks, K.-H. & Briedis, K. (2005). *Der Bachelor als Sprungbrett? Ergebnisse der ersten bundesweiten Befragung von Bachelorabsolventinnen und Bachelorabsolventen. Teil II. Der Verbleib nach dem Bachelorstudium* [Bachelor as stepping stone? Results of the first nationwide survey about bachelor graduates]. HIS-Kurzinformation A4/2005. Hannover: HIS.

Schomburg, H. & Teichler, U. (2009). Der Bachelor – besser als sein Ruf [Bachelor – better than its reputation]? *duzMAGAZIN, 65(*10), 22-23.

Schomburg, H. (Ed.) (2010). *Generation Vielfalt. Bildungs- und Berufswege der Absolventen von Hochschulen in Deutschland 2007-2008* [Generation diversity. Educational and vocational careers of graduates of higher educational institutions]. Werkstattberichte 71. Kassel: Internationales Zentrum für Hochschulforschung Kassel (in press).

Statistisches Bundesamt (2010). *Deutsche Studierende im Ausland. Ausgabe 2010* [German students abroad]. Wiesbaden: Statistisches Bundesamt.

JEAN-FRANÇOIS GIRET, CHRISTINE GUEGNARD
AND CLAIRE MICHOT

THE VOCATIONALISATION OF UNIVERSITY PROGRAMMES IN FRANCE: ITS CONSEQUENCES FOR EMPLOYABILITY AND MOBILITY

OVERVIEW OF THE FRENCH HIGHER EDUCATION SYSTEM

France has a multi-track higher education system which includes four key components: *Grandes Écoles*, short vocational training tracks, specialised higher education institutions (in social work, healthcare and the arts), and universities. Access to higher education is traditionally defined by the contrast between universities (which enrol all holders of the *baccalauréat* without any selection process) and the extremely selective *Grandes Écoles*. The other tertiary courses are not directly accessible to all *baccalauréat* holders who wish to enrol because the number of study places is limited; applications to these tracks involve a selection process (based on educational records or a competitive entrance exam, test, interview, etc.).

Until 1960, the French higher education was characterised by a contrast between the *Grandes Écoles* and the universities. In the 1960s, two technological degrees were created to provide a more vocationally oriented programme in tertiary education (short vocational tracks): the *Diplôme Universitaire de Technologie* (DUT), conferred by autonomous university institutes (IUT), and the *Brevet de Technicien Supérieur* (BTS), a higher education vocational course offered by secondary schools (*lycée*). While recent studies conducted in a range of countries have emphasised the "academic drift" of tertiary education (Teichler, 2007), French higher education seems to be driven by an opposite trend. In the last three decades, universities have offered new vocational programmes (*DESS, Miage, IUP, Magisters*) and more recently vocational Bachelor degrees. Their purpose was to offer vocational training in universities, comprising work placements and the involvement of professionals. This was partly an attempt to improve a university system which was widely criticised for being too theoretical and academic and for producing a growing number of unemployed graduates (Agulhon, 2007).

In France the *baccalauréat* is the final certificate of upper secondary education and the entry qualification to higher education. *Baccalauréat* holders can enrol in first-year undergraduate courses at universities where the *licence* degree is awarded after three years of study. Students can choose a general (*licence générale*) or a vocational Bachelor degree (*licence professionnelle*). A clear distinction is maintained between these according to student access, their programmes, and their opportunities.

The introduction of vocational Bachelors in 1999 was designed to develop the "vocationalisation" of French university education. Before 1999, universities only offered a purely academic, general Bachelor degrees based on subject-specific teaching and training. The award of the Bachelor degree was conditional on fol-

H. Schomburg and U. Teichler (eds.), Employability and Mobility of Bachelor Graduates in Europe, 111–128.
© 2011 *Sense Publishers. All rights reserved.*

lowing three years of university study (in humanities, science and technology, engineering, law and economics). The Bachelor level was not considered an appropriate professional entry qualification, except for careers in teacher education and public administration. By establishing a close partnership with potential employers in the design of curricula, the vocational Bachelor degree was designed to provide a specific response to the local demands for high-level vocational training, particularly in the private sector. It is a one-year training course offered to holders of a diploma awarded after two years of tertiary education. It includes a 12- to 16- week work placement in a company. Some 77 per cent of vocational Bachelor graduates had completed a placement lasting for at least three months, as compared to 30 per cent of general Bachelor graduates (Calmand, Epiphane & Hallier, 2009).

One of the major objectives of the vocational Bachelor programme was to promote the transition from higher education to work after three years of post-*baccalauréat* study (Giret, 2011). It is expected to correspond to the first level of the European structure of higher education diplomas defined in the Sorbonne and Bologna Declarations. The *licence* is now commonly considered as equivalent to a Bachelor's degree in international terms and represents the first stage of the three-cycle *licence/Master/doctorat* (LMD equivalent to Bachelor/Master/doctorate, 3-5-8) of European harmonised degrees (associated with 180 European Credit Transfer Systems). Unlike general Bachelor degrees, access to vocational Bachelor programmes in France is selective. Selection is based on students' educational record and on evidence of a professional project.

Moreover, vocational Bachelor degrees were intended to attract second-year students studying for a general Bachelor degree who wished (following a period of general study) to enrol in a vocational course that would enable them to enter the labour market directly after graduation. Yet it quickly became apparent that most of these graduates opted for the third-year vocational Bachelor programmes: More than half hold a BTS and more than one third a DUT, while only 12 per cent had completed two years of general university studies. Thus, these new Bachelor programmes have become a way of extending training for those students who have already completed a post-*baccalauréat* vocational track. While students from general programmes are reluctant to pursue such training, graduates from BTS and DUT tracks generally view it as further vocational development and as a precondition for securing a more highly qualified job. Some vocational Bachelor programmes had already existed in DUTs and also, although less frequently, in BTS tracks, whereby the degree was awarded officially by a university.

In principle, vocational Bachelor degrees, like other Bachelor degrees, are also entry qualifications to Master-level studies. Yet, the recommendations of the French Ministry of Higher Education, which have been largely adopted by the course providers, discourage these graduates from pursuing Master-level studies. The proportion of students continuing their studies after a vocational Bachelor degree is approximately 17 per cent, i.e. well below that of those pursuing postgraduate studies after a general Bachelor degree.

The – professional or research – *Master degree* is awarded to students who have successfully completed five years of study after the *baccalauréat*. It was introduced in the academic year 2002/2003 and replaced the *Diplôme d'Études Supérieures Spécialisées* (*DESS*, vocational) and the *Diplôme d'Études Approfondies* (*DEA*, research). The implementation of the new LMD system also encouraged the *Grandes Écoles* to reflect the general trend. The degrees they currently award are usually regarded as Master-level qualifications. Some *Grandes Écoles* encourage students to obtain a university degree as well. The creation of the LMD system led to an increase in professional Master degrees at the expense of research Masters. Common Master programmes (i.e. research and professional) were created to compensate for the declining numbers of students wishing to pursue a career in research. Moreover, access to doctoral studies became progressively more open to holders of a professional Masters degree. This may lead to a gradual disappearance of the research Masters programmes.

The shift to the LMD system occurred while the number of higher education students declined. There were 2,232,000 students in the academic year 2008/2009 (Ministry of Education, 2009).

Both the gradual increase in the number of degrees awarded in the (third-year) vocational Bachelor programmes and the transition from the former maîtrise programmes to the new Master programmes are documented in table 1.

Table 1. The Number of Diplomas and Degree awarded at Higher Education Institutions in France 2000, 2004 and 2008

	2000	2004	2008
BTS	95,530	108,839	106,025
DUT	47,478	47,018	46,714
General Bachelor (Licence)	135,017	137,307	124,289
Vocational Bachelor (Licence professionnelle)	•	17,159	37,665
Maîtrise	93,304	94,146	1,915
DEA	23,428	26,339	7
DESS	32,612	47,351	110
Master (professional)	•	2,415	65,111
Master (research)	•	2,544	23,218
Master	•	581	7,069
Grandes Écoles (Engineering, Business studies)	42,966	51,996	50,865
Doctorate	9,991	8,931	10,678

Source: Ministry of Education, Repères et statistiques

About 56 per cent were female. The number of students in public universities (roughly 1,400,000) decreased to a slightly lesser extent than in private study programmes (private BTS and business schools). Private tertiary education only represented about 17 per cent of the total enrolment. At universities, 56 per cent of students were enrolled in Bachelor programmes and 39 per cent in Masters programmes, while 5 per cent undertook a doctorate. There is an increase in the number of university students in vocational programmes, while the number of students in general university programmes (particularly in the first years of the Bachelor degree) is declining.

Vocational programmes at French universities have recently been established or extended to bring the professional world closer to the educational system, promote the professional transition of students and respond to the skills required for the world of work (Dupeyrat, 2002). Continuously increasing numbers of vocational Bachelor graduates enter the labour market, sometimes at levels which they had never entered before. This is particularly the case of the L level (i.e. three years of post-*baccalauréat* university study), which was not previously considered to be an appropriate level for leaving the educational system. The inflow of these graduates in the labour market raises the issue of their professional prospects amid changing economic and social circumstances. Are they well prepared for forthcoming social changes? The aim of this paper is to provide some indications concerning vocationalisation and employability based on an analysis of the current links between training courses and the jobs of young people and recent Bachelor graduates.

THE CEREQ "GENERATION 2004" GRADUATE SURVEY

This article focuses on the specific studies and subsequent employment of students in vocational programmes at French universities. It analyses how they progress from study to professional life. Data from Cereq's surveys is used. In spring 2007, Cereq surveyed by phone 65,000 persons who had graduated from their initial education in 2004 at all educational levels – a sample representative of 737,000 leavers of the educational system. This survey, called "Generation 2004', analysed the first three years of active life after initial education. It includes information on young people's characteristics (family's socio-economic status, age, highest grade obtained, highest grade attended, university area, job during their study, study time abroad, internship, etc.) and their work history from 2004 to 2007. The employment situation of 2004 graduates will be compared with the findings of a previous Cereq survey conducted in 2004 of the 2001 graduates, i.e. the first cohort of vocational Bachelor graduates.

In the sample of 2004 graduates, 2,226 respondents left higher education with a Bachelor degree: 671 a vocational Bachelor, 1,207 an academic Bachelor in humanities and social sciences, and 407 an academic Bachelor in mathematics, physics or engineering sciences. They are representative of the 50,748 Bachelors graduating in 2004 in France. However, the survey does not interview graduates who continue their studies after 2004.

*Table 2. Socio-biographic Background and Course of Study of 2004
Higher Education Graduates in France (per cent)*

	BA (Uni)	BA (Voc.)	BA other	BAC+4	MA (Uni) Bac+5	MA (Other) *Grandes Écoles*	Trad. long cycle	Total
	1	2	3	4	5	6	7	8
Female graduates	70	37	58	61	55	33	49	56
Entry qualification other than *baccalauréat*	0	0	2	1	0	0	0	1
Father in professsional/ managerial position	33	26	24	37	43	53	56	33
Mother in professsional/ managerial position	20	17	13	24	26	32	36	20
Father in associate professional occupations	10	14	12	13	12	14	9	12
Mother in associate professional occupations	7	8	6	8	9	9	10	7
Prior HE diploma of Bachelor graduates	12	88	•	•	•	•	•	•
Total years of study in higher education (arithmetic mean)	5.5	3.8	3.4	5.8	6.5	5.9	10.6	5.9
Age at time of graduation in 2004 (arithmetic mean)	24.0	22.5	22.2	24.3	24.8	24.1	28.7	24.4
N	38,441	12,307	135,241	37,207	38,981	30,611	14,214	307,003

(1) BA (Uni): General Bachelor (Licence Générale, Bac +3)
(2) BA (Voc): Vocational Bachelor (Licence Professionnelle)'
(3) BA other: BA or other diploma (ISCED5b) (BTS, DUT, DEUG, DEUST, Bac +2 healthcare & social work, other Bac +2)
(4) BAC +4: Maîtrise, Bac +4, MST + MSG, Bac +4 Écoles de commerce
(5) MA (Uni): Bac +5, DEA, Master Recherche, DESS, DRT, Master Pro, Magistère
(6) MA (Other): Grandes Écoles de commerce, d'ingénieur
(7) Trad. long cycle/university: Doctorate

Source: Cereq "Generation 2004" survey

It should be noted that the data are not representative, as far as international mobility after graduation is concerned. This is because graduates living abroad were not included.

JEAN-FRANÇOIS GIRET, CHRISTINE GUEGNARD AND CLAIRE MICHOT

THE SHARE OF BACHELOR GRADUATES

The cohort of students in this survey carried out their studies in a context of significant change. The LMD system was implemented in the framework of the Bologna Process in order to create a convergent system of higher education programmes and degrees throughout Europe which, in France, led to an increasing vocationalisation of higher education. In recent years, the provision of training at L-level has developed significantly (Calmand et al., 2009): In 2004, students could choose from some 1,600 vocational Bachelor degrees (as compared to 178 in 2000). The introduction of vocational Bachelor degrees enabled holders of a vocational diploma (BTS or DUT) to continue their higher education studies.

However, of the almost 307,000 graduates leaving the educational system in 2004 (out of 737,000 young people leaving education), only a small number left tertiary education at L-level (i.e. as a rule after three years of study). This indicates that Bachelor-level degrees continue to be viewed primarily as the entry qualification to a Masters programme. Bachelor graduates represented only 17 per cent of all tertiary education graduates leaving the education system in 2004 (*see* table 2). Almost 44 per cent had obtained a short post-*baccalauréat* vocational degree (ISCED 5 B), 23 per cent held a five-year degree (Masters and *Grandes Écoles*), and 5 per cent entered the labour market with a doctorate (including a corresponding degree in medicine).

GRADUATES' SOCIO-BIOGRAPHIC BACKGROUND

For many years, women have accounted for the majority of higher education students in France. Ten years ago, they represented 55 per cent and this trend has continued to this day. However, differences according to type of institution and field of study persist. While women represented only one third of *Grandes Écoles* graduates, they accounted for 90 per cent in health care (nursing, etc.) and social work. Their proportion varied between 37 per cent of vocational Bachelor degree holders and 70 per cent of general Bachelor degree holders (*see* table 1). 34 per cent obtained a Bachelor degree in management and 26 per cent in language and literature, while 44 per cent of men graduated with a vocational Bachelor degree in science and technology.

Compared to other European countries, students in France rarely interrupt their studies to take a sabbatical year or to work in a full-time job. Delays in educational careers are more commonly related to failure and drop-out in the first years of study. This is most frequent in university Bachelor programmes, where less than half the students spend the first two years without having repeated at least a year. The mean age at the time of graduation (for the total number of tertiary graduates) is 24. The mean length of tertiary studies ranges from three to four years for graduates from vocational courses to 11 years for those awarded a doctoral degree; as is seen in table 2, it is six years. Vocational Bachelor graduates were among the youngest, with a mean age of 22 on entering the labour market.

As has already been pointed out, the *baccalauréat* is the usual entry qualification for higher education. Less than one per cent of the 2004 graduates had another equivalent entry qualification (2 per cent of those graduating from social and paramedical higher schools, as is shown in table 2).

Various reports and studies have challenged the idea of an increasing democratisation of higher education in France in terms of the students' socio-economic background (e.g. Prost, 1986; Merle, 2000). In their book *La Reproduction*, Bourdieu and Passeron (1970) had already pointed out that the increase in enrolments in higher education did not necessarily lead to democratisation. Access to the *baccalauréat* and thereby to higher education remains a privilege. According to 1995 longitudinal data provided by the French Ministry of Education, the children of managers and professionals, while making up 16 per cent of pupils entering *sixième* (i.e. first year of secondary school), made up 23 per cent of *baccalauréat* holders seven years later. Children of working-class parents made up 38 per cent of those entering *sixième*, but only 29 per cent of *baccalauréat* holders (Lemaire, 2008). The process of selection and orientation at every stage of a pupil's educational career, influenced by various educational, social, economic and geographical factors, continues beyond access to higher education: Students with parents in professional and managerial occupations make up almost a third of the number of higher education students (see table 2). We note substantial differences by sector: Students with parents in professional and managerial professions are substantially over-represented in the *Grandes Écoles* as well as in many university science programmes (particularly medical studies). In contrast, many students in vocational two-year programmes and vocational Bachelor programmes come from a more modest socio-economic background. Of the graduates from vocational Bachelor programmes who leave the education system, only 26 per cent had fathers and 17 per cent had mothers in managerial and professional positions, while 14 per cent of fathers and 8 per cent of mothers worked in associate professional occupations.

WORK EXPERIENCE DURING THE COURSE OF STUDY

Work experience during the course of study tends to be seen as a means of enhancing students' professional competences. Therefore, an overview is provided here of various types of work experiences during the course of study.

In France, few students are employed while studying. However, apprenticeships have spread significantly in recent years. In the academic year 2006/2007, almost 80,470 students were concurrently apprentices; this figure has increased by almost 12 per cent every year over a decade; this phenomenon is most frequent among students heading for a BTS (about half) (Ministry of Education, 2008). Altogether, about 20 per cent of the vocational Bachelor graduates surveyed and less than 1 per cent of the general Bachelor graduates had studied as apprentices, notably those graduating from management and business studies.

However, many students in France work during their course of study, either to fund their studies or to be more independent. According to the Génération 2004 survey, about 80 per cent of tertiary education graduates (85 per cent of the Bachelor graduates among them) had worked during their course of study, mostly in summer or part-time jobs (see Calmand et al., 2009).

Just 11 per cent of vocational Bachelor graduates stated that they had regular work during the course of study in compared to 37 per cent of the general Bachelor graduates. The low rate among the formers reflects the character of the vocational programmes: regular attendance is often compulsory while attendance tends to be optional (except for a small number of lessons) in general courses. The number of weekly hours also is inclined to be higher in vocational courses. In addition vocational programmes require students to complete a formal period of work placement during the academic year, which means that students are rarely able to have a professional activity alongside their studies.

It might be added here that almost 50 per cent of the graduates in France continued to work in the same regular job after graduating – thus having a period of gainful employment in the process of transition between higher education and full-time employment. Almost ten per cent of all graduates were still working on a job they had held during the course of study, when they were surveyed in the Cereq study about three years after graduation.

Almost 77 per cent of the vocational Bachelor graduates had participated in internships lasting more than three months during their course of study. This only slightly higher than among students in Master programmes and in *Grandes Ecoles* study programmes but substantially higher than the figure reported by general Bachelor graduates, i.e. 30 per cent (Calmand et al., 2009).

INTERNATIONAL MOBILITY DURING THE COURSE OF STUDY

The number of foreigners moving to France to pursue their higher education studies increased to 266,400 (Ministry of Education, 2010) in 2009. In ten years, their share grew from 7 per cent to 12 per cent of the total number of students. In 2008, almost half were Africans (25 per cent from the Maghreb and 19 per cent from other Africa countries). Less than a quarter was from Europe, of whom 18 per cent were from the European Union (about two thirds of the latter were women). A quarter was from Asia and 8 per cent were from the American continent.

Of the higher education graduates who responded to the Cereq survey in 2004, only 4 per cent were foreigners. As is seen in table 3, their share is relatively high among those with a Masters degree. One must bear in mind, though, that the Cereq survey did not address graduates living abroad and therefore only covered a relatively small proportion of foreign graduates.

A considerable number of graduates studies abroad for some period. In the academic year 2008/2009, about 28,300 French students studied in another European country in the framework of the ERASMUS programme and France has regained its position as "champion of student mobility" (a position it had conceded to Germany since 2003/2004). The top foreign destinations were Spain (22 per cent) and the United Kingdom (19 per cent), followed by Germany (12 per cent), Sweden and Italy (7 per cent each).

Table 3. Inwards and Outwards Mobility during the Course of Study on the Part of 2004 Graduates in France

	BA (Uni)	BA (Voc.)	BA other	BAC+4	MA (Uni) Bac+5	MA (Other) Grandes Écoles	Trad. long cycle	Total
	1	2	3	4	5	6	7	8
Total mobility short and long	20	22	19	32	29	54	33	26
Foreign graduates	3	3	2	5	6	4	5	4
Temporary degree mobile (at least 6 months)	6	2	1	13	12	22	11	7
Study-related stay abroad in training institutions (at least 6 months)	3	1	•	6	6	8	6	3
Study-related stay abroad in firms (at least 6 months)	3	2	1	7	7	13	6	4
Short study-related stay abroad (less than 6 months)	13	19	17	19	17	32	21	19

(1) BA (Uni): General Bachelor (Licence Générale, Bac +3)
(2) BA (Voc): Vocational Bachelor (Licence Professionnelle)'
(3) BA other: BA or other diploma (ISCED5b) (BTS, DUT, DEUG, DEUST, Bac +2 healthcare & social work, other Bac +2)
(4) BAC +4: Maîtrise, Bac +4, MST + MSG, Bac +4 Écoles de commerce
(5) MA (Uni): Bac +5, DEA, Master Recherche, DESS, DRT, Master Pro, Magistère
(6) MA (Other): Grandes Écoles de commerce, d'ingénieur
(7) Trad. long cycle/university: Doctorate

Source: Cereq "Generation 2004" survey

Periods of study abroad remain relatively undeveloped in university programmes, including those with a strong vocational purpose. Over half of *Grandes Écoles* graduates and a third of doctoral and Master graduates had completed at least one period of study in a foreign country as part of their higher education studies, as opposed to just 20 per cent of Bachelor graduates (see table 3 on the mobility). Most of these periods lasted for less than six months, and over half of them were carried out in English-speaking countries (Calmand et al., 2009). Two thirds of *Grandes Écoles* graduates, research Master graduates and doctoral graduates completed a period of study lasting less than six months. A greater number of general Bachelor graduates engaged in a period of study abroad lasting at least six months than vocational Bachelor graduates (6 per cent as opposed to 2 per cent). These periods of study were equally likely to be conducted in companies and training institutions.

PROFESSIONAL SUCCESS OF VOCATIONAL BACHELOR GRADUATES

The whereabouts of graduates

The 2004 graduates entered the French labour market in a difficult economic situation, although it was less serious than during the economic crisis that hit France in 2008 (Joseph, Lopez & Ryk, 2008). Three years after entering the labour market, 7 per cent of Bachelor graduates were unemployed (see table 4). The proportion of graduates beginning a fixed-term contract remained constant at around 20 per cent.

Table 4. Whereabout of 2004 Graduates Three Years Later in France

	Count	Per cent
Bachelor graduates*		
Study	3,682	7
Employment	42,302	83
Neither study nor employment nor unemployment	1,486	3
Unemployment	3,278	7
Total	50,748	100
Master + Grandes Écoles Graduates		
Study	1,362	2
Employment	63,545	91
Neither study nor employment nor unemployment	1,127	2
Unemployment	3,560	5
Total	69,594	100

* Excluding those continuing study in the first year after graduation

Source: Cereq "Generation 2004" survey

Overall, the analysis of the first three years after graduation indicates that vocational Bachelor graduates have coped with the adverse economic conditions successfully by securing qualified and permanent jobs. In 2007, almost 90 per cent were employed, and the vast majority had secured a permanent contract (see table 4). The number of graduates working part-time was low. Vocational Bachelor graduates also tended to be better paid than general Bachelor graduates, even if access to manager and professional positions remained relatively rare. Three years after entering the labour market, 15 per cent of the vocational Bachelor graduates had been recruited as managers or professionals as compared to 17 per cent of the general Bachelor graduates, 63 per cent of the Master graduates and 81 per cent of the *Grandes Écoles* graduates (see table 5). A closer examination of the positions according to different fields of study confirms that the jobs obtained by graduates were mostly qualified and related to their training. Overall, graduates in industrial fields seemed to be in a better position in the labour market than other graduates.

Table 5. Professional Situation of 2004 Employed Graduates Three Years Later in France

	BA (Uni)	BA (Voc.)	BA other	BAC+4	MA (Uni) Bac+5	MA (Other) *Grandes Écoles*	Trad. long cycle	Total
	1	2	3	4	5	6	7	8
Period from graduation to first employment (in months)								
Arith. mean	3.4	2.1	2.7	3.9	3.5	3.2	2.4	3.0
Median	2.0	0.0	1.0	2.0	1.0	2.0	0.0	1.0
Duration of job search from 2004 to 2007 (in months)								
Arith. mean	3.3	3.2	3.4	4.3	4.6	3.7	3.6	3.7
Median	0.0	0.0	0.0	0.0	2.0	1.0	0.0	0.0
Full-time employment (per cent)	79	96	88	86	90	98	85	88
Long-term employment (per cent)	70	80	73	71	77	91	71	75
Net income (in €)								
Arith. mean	1,368	1,575	1,483	1,618	1,904	2,313	2,383	1,806
Median	1,411	1,514	1,408	1,510	1,800	2,167	2,150	1,514
Graduates in managerial/professional occupation (per cent)	17	15	6	33	63	81	91	30
Graduates in associate professional occupation (per cent)	64	67	62	50	29	15	7	49
Employment three years after appropriate to level of competences (per cent)	61	60	61	54	63	69	76	62
Employment three years after appropriate to level of education (per cent)	55	40	70	59	82	88	97	70
Job satisfaction three years after (per cent)	76	82	82	78	82	85	89	82

(1) BA (Uni): General Bachelor (Licence Générale, Bac +3)
(2) BA (Voc): Vocational Bachelor (Licence Professionnelle)'
(3) BA other: BA or other diploma (ISCED5b) (BTS, DUT, DEUG, DEUST, Bac +2 healthcare & social work, other Bac +2)
(4) BAC +4: Maîtrise, Bac +4, MST + MSG, Bac +4 Écoles de commerce
(5) MA (Uni): Bac +5, DEA, Master Recherche, DESS, DRT, Master Pro, Magistère
(6) MA (Other): Grandes Écoles de commerce, d'ingénieur
(7) Trad. long cycle/university: Doctorate

Source: Cereq "Generation 2004" survey

The Cereq surveys only address those who have left the education system for at least one year. Hence, they do not provide a full account of the number of graduates who continue their studies after having been awarded a degree. However, many graduates returned to education after having been employed for a while. As can be seen in table 4, seven per cent of the 2004 Bachelor graduates (primarily graduates from the general programmes) having been employed for some time returned to higher education or were engaged in other further training (most often teacher training programmes).

Data provided by the French Ministry of Higher Education provides a more complete picture of further study and training subsequent to the Bachelor award. There is a clear dichotomy between the two types of graduates. Most General Bachelors graduating in 2004/2005 continued their education (82 per cent), notably in Master programmes (approximately two thirds), in teacher training (10 per cent) and in other training programmes (5 per cent). Two years after graduation from a general Bachelor, about 30 per cent obtained a Master degree. In contrast, only 20 per cent of the vocational Bachelor graduates continued their education and training in the subsequent academic year, of whom 17 per cent at universities (mostly in Master programmes) and 3 per cent in teacher training institutes (Ministry of Education, 2007).

Enviable professional prospects?

As most vocational Bachelor graduates held a vocational two-year diploma (BTS or DUT), the professional value of the vocational Bachelor can be established by the advantage of their employment situation in relation to that of graduates of two-year programmes. The available data suggest that the additional third year of study is very profitable: unemployment rates were lower and the number of permanent contracts and executive and intermediate positions was significantly higher. The average salary was also higher (by approximately 150 Euros). Most vocational Bachelor graduates (87 per cent) were employed in private companies.

The 2004 general Bachelor graduates transferring to employment – a small minority, as pointed out above – were in a less favourable position. Even though a slightly higher number obtained executive positions (see above), they earned on average 80 Euros less than vocational Bachelor graduates. The rate of unemployment was also marginally higher (7 per cent as compared to 5 per cent of vocational Bachelor graduates), particularly for those with a degree in language, literature, law and economics. The job stability three years after graduation was clearly lower for general Bachelor graduates: 70 per cent had a permanent contract as compared to 80 per cent of vocational Bachelor graduates, 77 per cent of Master graduates and 91 per cent of *Grandes Écoles* graduates. Part-time work was also more common: 21 per cent as compared to only 4 per cent of vocational Bachelor graduates. 30 per cent of the women among the general Bachelor graduates were in part-time employment as compared to 13 per cent of men.

In assessing the professional situation of general Bachelor graduates, we must take into consideration that almost 60 per cent of those in literature and the humanities were employed three years later as primary school teachers, supply teachers, teaching assistants or student monitors. A smaller number of graduates – notably in law and economics – were employed as professionals in intermediate positions, either in public administration or in private business companies. General Bachelor graduates in the public sector tend be in unfavourable positions (Dauty & Lemistre, 2006).

Overall, vocational Bachelor graduates experienced fewer problems in the transition process than those with a vocational two-year diploma. They find more stable and better paid jobs and are employed in higher positions. Compared to general Bachelor graduates transferring to employment, the vocational Bachelor graduates did not obtain higher positions, but they had a higher income and more satisfying work.

Altogether, more than half the Bachelor graduates were still working with their first employer. Most had never experienced unemployment and the average period of job search was very short (3 months for Bachelor graduates, 5 months for Master graduates).

Among both general and vocational Bachelor graduates, women had a less favourable position in the labour market than men. Gender-related differences remain significant as regards income: Female students graduating in 2004 with a university qualification earned 15 per cent less than their male counterparts. There are also other socio-economic disparities. The children of immigrants, who were less likely to pursue higher education studies, were more at risk of unemployment, particularly those from North African countries (Frickey, Murdoch & Primon, 2004; Brinbaum & Guégnard, 2010). To understand these disparities beyond the strictly discriminatory phenomena highlighted in studies of the French labour market (Duguet & Petit, 2005), differences in inherited educational, social and economic capital (which generally tend to combine in making youth vulnerable upon entering the labour market) need to be taken into account.

Work linked to training

The relationship between study and work has been an issue of concern on the part of many experts and scholars who warned that the gap between the level of qualification and the level of employment and work would widen with higher education expansion (see for example Duru-Bellat, 2006). Yet tertiary graduates tended not to perceive such a gap when surveyed in 2007 three years after graduation. Almost 70 per cent stated that their level of qualification was necessary to carry out their job to a satisfactory level (see table 5).

As pointed out above, vocational Bachelor graduates seem to have a relatively favourable employment situation. The picture is less favourable with respect to their views about appropriate employment and work. Only 40 per cent felt that their jobs matched their level of education; this is low compared to the respective statements of general Bachelor graduates (55 per cent) and the average of all graduates (70 per cent). 45 per cent of the vocational Bachelor graduates stated that a lower qualification (two years of post-*baccalauréat* study) would be sufficient to carry out their job satisfactorily. This relatively negative assessment can be explained by their difficulties in having access to executive positions and thereby demarcating themselves from tertiary technicians recruited after two years of post-*baccalauréat* study (BTS or DUT).

However, these results need to be put into perspective, because the ratings of the vocational Bachelor graduates are positive. 60 per cent consider that their employment matches their level of competences (as compared to 61 per cent of the general Bachelor graduates and 62 per cent on average of all graduates). 82 per cent wished to remain in their current job and were satisfied in it. Finally, 27 per cent of vocational Bachelor graduates believed that they were well or very well paid; this is higher than the average of all tertiary graduates (20 per cent).

For the most part, graduates enjoyed enviable professional prospects and had found employment quickly and permanently. One positive indication of professsional integration is that nearly 60 per cent of Bachelor graduates stated that their skills were valued in their current job, reflecting the feelings of most higher education graduates. Two thirds wished to remain for as long as possible in their current job.

As is seen in table 5, however, the lowest rate of job satisfaction is stated by general Bachelor graduates. Yet, their job satisfaction is relatively high: almost three quarters are satisfied with their job.

Geographical mobility

Three Bachelor graduates out of ten have worked outside the region since graduation. This ratio is low as compared to about half of the Master graduates and doctoral award holders.

Half the Bachelor graduates stated that they would be prepared to leave the region where they work to advance their career. This is higher than the actual mobility, but they are less prepared to leave the region than Master graduates (66 per cent) and doctorate holders (57 per cent). Other studies show that young people generally view geographical mobility as a requirement for career advancement (Centre d'études et de recherches sur les qualifications [Cereq], 2008).

Change over time

As Cereq has undertaken a similar survey in 2004 of the 2001 generation of graduates in France (see Giret, Molinari-Perrier & Moullet, 2006), a change over time can be observed. As table 6 shows, the 2001 vocational Bachelor graduates have differed in their employment situation three years later from the general Bachelor graduates of their generation: also the 2001 vocational Bachelor graduates reached more often a stable employment and a higher education income and were less frequently unemployed, while fewer were employed as professionals and managers than general Bachelor graduates.

Table 6. Employment of Bachelor Graduates 2001 and 2004 in France Three Years Later (per cent)

	Unemployment rate	Employed as professionals & managers	Permanent employment contract	Median net monthly income (Euro)
Graduates 2004:				
Vocational Bachelor graduates	5	15	80	1,514
General Bachelor graduates	7	17	70	1,411
Graduates 2001:				
Vocational Bachelor graduates	9	17	78	1,380
General Bachelor graduates	12	22	67	1,300

Source: Cereq "Generation 2004" and "Generation 2001" surveys

There are similar differences between the 2001 cohort and the 2004 cohort both for general Bachelor graduates and for vocational Bachelor graduates. We note a slight improvement of the employment situation in two respects: the unemployment rate decreased by 5 per cent and 2 per cent respectively; similarly, the proportion of graduates with a permanent employment contract increased by 3 per cent and per cent respectively. The increase of the net income by about 8-9 per cent must be seen as being linked to inflation. But the employment in professional or managerial positions decreased slightly by 5 per cent and 2 per cent respectively.

SOME CONCLUDING REMARKS

At the end of this analysis, the findings of the survey need to be viewed in a more general theoretical framework. One of the objectives of any transition survey is to establish the extent to which the qualification obtained at the end of training is used by graduates in employment. The human capital theory suggests that training is one of the best ways of securing a good job and satisfactory work conditions. Our results confirm these findings in the French labour market. A higher education degree constitutes a relative protection against unemployment and nearly two thirds of young people claimed that their skills were recognised in their current professional activity. At the other end of the scale, young people with no diplomas were highly exposed to unemployment: 32 per cent were still unemployed after three years in the labour market (Cereq, 2008). In France, a Bachelor-level degree is currently deemed to represent a first threshold. This is confirmed among vocational Bachelor graduates. While the employability of Bachelor graduates is undeniable, the level of international mobility does not appear to be a determining factor for French graduates. Only students in engineering courses are strongly encouraged to undertake a period of study abroad to achieve the level of proficiency in English required as part of their degree.

Overall in 2004, vocational higher education graduates entered the labour market in better conditions than their predecessors. After three years, a greater number had a permanent job and were better paid. A diploma has never been a more valuable asset than today. Despite unfavourable economic circumstances and significant changes in the provision of training, the hierarchy of diplomas remains unchanged. It is worth recalling that the careers and income of higher education graduates are significantly more favourable than those of school leavers, with the likelihood of a rapid and permanent access to employment being very high. Tertiary graduates also tend to be less exposed to the effects of changing economic circumstances, despite continuing disparities between *Grandes Écoles* and university graduates.

These observations highlight the continuing influence of forms of higher education inherited from the past (Brennan & Tang, 2008) – an influence that is likely to change as a result of the increasing vocationalisation of university education, not unlike the changes affecting other European countries. As noted by Teichler (2007), the debate surrounding the conflict between general and vocational courses is seldom addressed in British universities, while vocationalisation is becoming increasingly important in France and to a lesser extent in Germany. This reflects the levels of job satisfaction felt by students and recorded in Cereq and REFLEX (*Research into Employment and professional Flexibility*) surveys (Allen & van der Velden, 2007; Guégnard, Calmand, Giret & Paul, 2008). In the British context, job satisfaction is primarily related to income, while in Germany it is more closely related to the type of job or professional occupation.

Human capital and employability constitute a crucial challenge for all the countries. At the moment when Europe and the rest of the world are moving towards a knowledge society, an effective higher education and an efficient vocational system appear more important for the economy and society. Recent and current developments in the French educational system have raised a number of issues concerning the competition between vocational and general programmes in a context of significantly expanding training provision. Attempts to build bridges between training courses to enable students to continue their studies more easily have also raised a debate concerning the gap between vocational and general courses. Some training programmes initially designed to be vocational and to result in entry in professional life have lost their unique appeal and distinctiveness. The current difficulties encountered by providers of vocational courses who are keen to integrate the LMD system reflect the ambiguous status of such programmes in French higher education, while their graduates are highly valued by industry employers.

REFERENCES

Agulhon, C. (2007). *La professionnalisation à l'université, une réponse à la demande sociale* [The vocationalisation at University: An answer to the social request]. *Recherche et Formation, 54*, 11-27.

Allen, J. & van der Velden, R. (Eds.) (2007). *The flexible professional in the Knowledge Society: General results of the Reflex project.* Maastricht: Research Centre for Education and the Labour market.

Brennan, J. & Tang, W. (2008). *The employment of UK graduates: Comparisons with Europe.* Report to HEFCE by the Centre for Higher Education Research and Information, the Open University. Retrieved june 30, 2010, from http://www.open.ac.uk/cheri/documents/reflex_report_1.pdf

Birnbaum, Y. & Guégnard, C. (2010). Orientation, parcours de formation et insertion: Quelles relations pour les jeunes issus de l'immigration [Orientation, training and transition careers: Which relations for the young people from immigration]? In T. Couppié et al. (Eds.), *Évaluation et données longitudinales: Quelles relations?* (323-338). Marseille : Céreq.

Bourdieu, P. & Passeron, J.C. (1970). *La reproduction: Éléments pour une théorie d'enseignement* [The reproduction: Elements for a teaching theory]. Paris: Minuit.

Calmand, J., Epiphane, E. & Hallier, P. (2009). De l'enseignement supérieur à l'emploi: Voies rapides et chemins de traverse. Enquête « Génération 2004 ». Interrogation 2007 [From higher education to employment: Expressways and short roads. Cereq "Generation 2004" survey]. *Note Emploi Formation*, 43.

Centre d'études et de recherches sur les qualifications (2008). *Quand l'école est finie... Premiers pas dans la vie active de la Génération 2004* [When school is finished... First steps in active life for the Generation 2004]. Marseille: Céreq.

Conseil d'Orientation pour l'Emploi (2009). *L'orientation scolaire et professionnelle des jeunes* [School and vocational guidance for the youth]. Propositions du Conseil d'orientation pour l'emploi.

Dauty, F. & Lemistre, P. (2006). Jeunes dans la fonction publique territoriale: Entre gestion publique et marchande [Young people in territorial: Between public and commercial management]. *Formation Emploi*, 95, 41-59.

Duguet, E. & Petit, P. (2005). Hiring discrimination in the French financial sector: An econometric analysis on field experiment data. *Annales d'Économie et de Statistique*, 78, 79-102.

Dupeyrat, G. (2002). *Les formations professionnelles supérieurs* [The higher vocational trainings]. Rapport à Monsieur le Ministre délégué à l'enseignement professionnel. Paris: Ministère de l'Enseignement supérieur et de la Recherche.

Duru-Bellat, M. (2006). *L'inflation scolaire: Les désillusions de la méritocratie* [School inflation: Disillusions of the meritocraty]. Paris: Le Seuil.

Frickey, A., Murdoch, J. & Primon, J.L. (2004). *Les débuts dans la vie active des jeunes issus de l'immigration après des études supérieures* [The first steps in the in active life of youth from immigration after higher studies]. Marseille: Céreq

Giret, J.-F. (2011). Does vocational training facilitate transition from university to work? The example of the new vocational Bachelor degree in France. *European Journal of Education* (in press).

Giret, J.-F., Molinari-Perrier, M. & Moullet, S. (2006). *2001 – 2004: Les sortants de l'enseignement supérieur face au marché du travail* [2001 – 2004 : The higher education to work transition]. Marseille: Céreq

Guégnard, C., Calmand, J., Giret, J.-F. & Paul, J.-J. (2008). Recognition of higher education graduates' competences on european labour markets. *Training and Employment*, 83.

Haut Comité Education Economie Emploi (2006). *Objectif 50% d'une génération diplômée de l'enseignement supérieur* [Objective 50% of a graduate generation of the higher education]. Paris: La Coumentation Francaise.

Joseph, O., Lopez, A. & Ryk, F. (2008). *Génération 2004, des jeunes pénalisés par la conjoncture* [Generation 2004, Young people penalized by the economic situation]. Bref, 248.

Lemaire, S. (2008). Disparités d'accès et parcours en classes préparatoires [Disparities of access and course in preparatory classes]. *Note d'information*, 08.16. Retrieved March 30, 2010, from http://media.education.gouv.fr/file/2008/83/1/ni0816_25831.pdf

Merle, P. (2000). Le concept de démocratisation de l'institution scolaire: Une typologie et sa mise à l'épreuve [The concept of democratization of the school institution: A typology and its test]. *Population*, 1, 15-50.

Ministère de l'Éducation (2007). La réussite en licence professionnelle [Success in vocational Bachelor]. *Note d'information*, 07.13. Retrieved March 30, 2010, from http://media.education.gouv.fr/file/03/6/5036.pdf

Ministère de l'Éducation (2008). L'apprentissage: Une voie de formation attractive, entre tradition et mutation [Apprenticeship: An attractive course, between tradition and change]. *Note d'information*, 08.33. Retrieved March 30, 2010, from http://media.education.gouv.fr/file/2008/19/2/NI0833_40192.pdf

Ministère de l'Éducation (2009). Les effectifs d'étudiants dans le supérieur en 2008: Stabilisation après deux années de recul [Students in higher education: Stabilization after two years of retreat]. *Note d'Information*, 09.25. Retrieved March 30, 2010, from http://media.enseignementsup-recherche.gouv.fr/file/2009/53/9/NI0925_128539.pdf

Ministère de l'Éducation, Ministère de l'Enseignement Supérieur & Recherche (2010). Les étudiants étrangers dans l'enseignement supérieur français: Augmentation à la rentrée 2008-2009 après deux années de baisse [Foreign students in the French higher education: Increase in 2008-2009 after two years of decrease]. *Note d'information Enseignement supérieur et Recherche*, 10.02. Retrieved March 30, 2010, from http://media.enseignementsup-recherche.gouv.fr/file/2010/61/1/NIMESR10_02_138611.pdf

Powell, J.W., Coutrot, L., Graf, L., Bernhard, N., Kieffer, A. & Solga, H. (2009). *Comparing the relationship between vocational and higher education in Germany and France* (Discussion Paper SP I 2009-506). Berlin: Wissenschaftszentrum für Sozialwissenschaften (WZB). Retrieved June 30, 2010, from http://bibliothek.wz-berlin.de/pdf/2009/i09-506.pdf

Prost, A. (1986). *L'enseignement s'est-il démocratisé. Les élèves des lycées et collèges de l'agglomération d'Orléans de 1945 à 1980* [The democratization of the education? The pupils in secondary schools in Orleans region from 1945 to 1980]. Paris: Presses Universitaires de France.

Teichler, U. (Ed.) (2007*). Careers of university graduates, views and experiences in comparative perspectives*. Dordrecht: Springer.

LÁSZLÓ KISS AND ZSUZSANNA VEROSZTA[1]

BACHELOR GRADUATES IN HUNGARY IN THE TRANSITIONAL PERIOD OF HIGHER EDUCATION SYSTEM

STRUCTURE OF HUNGARIAN HIGHER EDUCATION

The institutional system of Hungarian higher education has been traditionally formed by universities and colleges as state, private or religious institutions. Altogether 71 higher education institutions operated in Hungary in 2010 of which 19 offered only religious programmes.

Prior to the introduction of Bologna-type study programmes, universities focused on more theoretical, university-level education, while colleges provided more practice-oriented, college-level training. The typical duration of studies was five years universities and four years at colleges. In the Bologna Process, a gradual transition started in 2004 from the traditional university or college degrees a higher education system based on three phases built one on the other: BA/BSc, Master and PhD programmes. Beside the new BA/BSc and the Master programmes, single-cycle 10-12 semester programmes were preserved, where the degree level corresponds the Master degree: in veterinary medicine, architecture, forestry engineering, dentistry, pharmacy, law and medicine as well as in some arts majors and theological studies. On single-cycle education 5-6 per cents of all students are studying.

In addition to undergraduate and Master programmes, the higher education institutions in Hungary also provide postgraduate programmes: first, postgraduate specialist training programmes, which provide a new technical qualification based on a higher education degree (their duration ranges from one to three years); second, the PhD and DLA programmes leading to science degrees. The entry qualification for toth programmes is a university degree or equivalent qualification obtained abroad; universities select on the basis of an entrance examination and made set other entry requirements (e.g. professional experience).

The first Bologna-type undergraduate study programmes begin in 2004 and 2005 – initially only on an experimental basis. The real transition was realized in 2006, when over 76 thousand students started their Bachelor studies. Some Bachelors require three years of study and others three-and-a-half years. Five years of study are required for a Master degree. Master programmes constituting the second level of the Bologna system followed the commencement of BA/BSc majors with some delay. In 2007, only about five hundred students, but in 2008 already more than four thousand students commenced studies in Master programmes. Master programmes became significant in 2009 when over twelve thousand new Master students were admitted to the institutions; this was facilitated

---

[1] Matild Sági and Péter Róbert (TÁRKI Social Research Institute) provided professional help in preparing the present study.

H. Schomburg and U. Teichler (eds.), Employability and Mobility of Bachelor Graduates in Europe, 129–141.
© 2011 *Sense Publishers. All rights reserved.*

by an increasing number of start up programmes resulting from progress in the accreditation process and the widening choice of majors as well as triggered by a substantial increase the numbers of persons graduating from the new BA/BSc programmes in that year. Although traditional university and college programmes/ majors were no longer started after 2006, relatively high numbers of such students remain in Hungarian higher education.

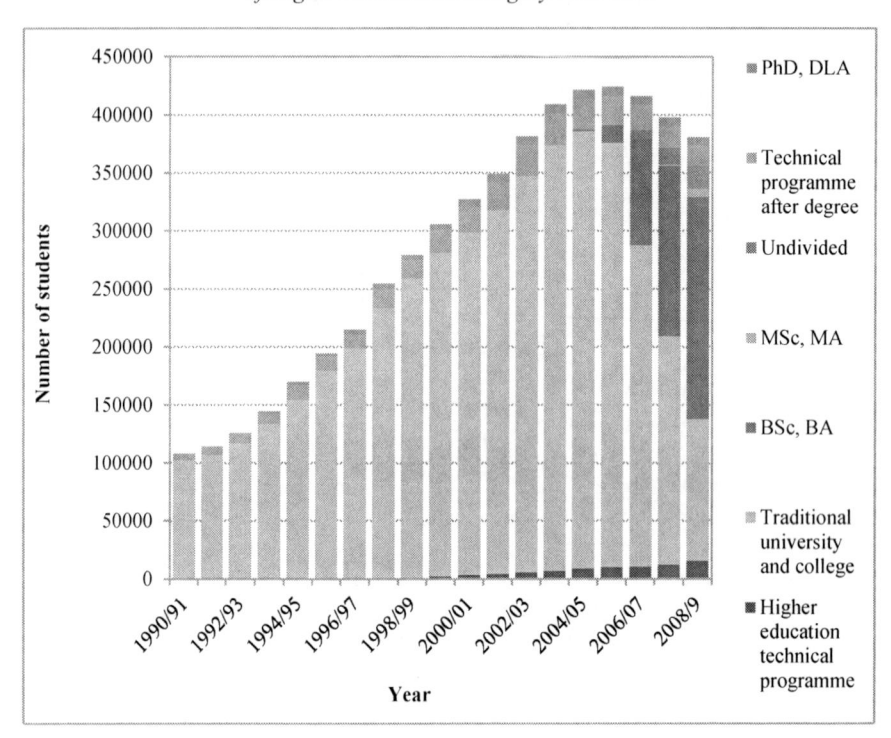

Figure 1. Number of Students in Various Types of Study Programmes at Institutions of Higher Education in Hungary 1990-2009

Source: Nemzeti Erőforrások Minisztériuma Statisztika (2008)

The introduction of the Bachelor-Master structure occured at a time of rapid expansion of higher education. Around 1990, enrolment rates in higher education in Hungary were relatively low. A sudden growth in the number of students and institutions began in the mid-1990s. The increase in the number of applicants continued after 2000, reaching a peak in 2004 when a total of 167,371 people applied to higher education, 109,581 of whom were admitted to an institution. The number of applicants started to decrease from 2005 and by 2008 it had declined to 96,991 persons, i.e. 57 per cent of the number seen in 2004. Many researchers have studied the reason for the decrease, many theories and ideas have arisen about the background to the processes – the most remarkable phenomena is the rapid decrease in the application rates of older age groups, which was also catalysed by the transformation of the training structure (temporary lack of Master programmes) after 2006 (Veroszta, 2010).

The tendency turned around in 2009, the number of applicants increased again, to a great extent due to the Bologna structure. As mentioned above, the relatively complete range of Master programmes was established by that year and the first BA/BSc students graduated in every educational field in that year, too.

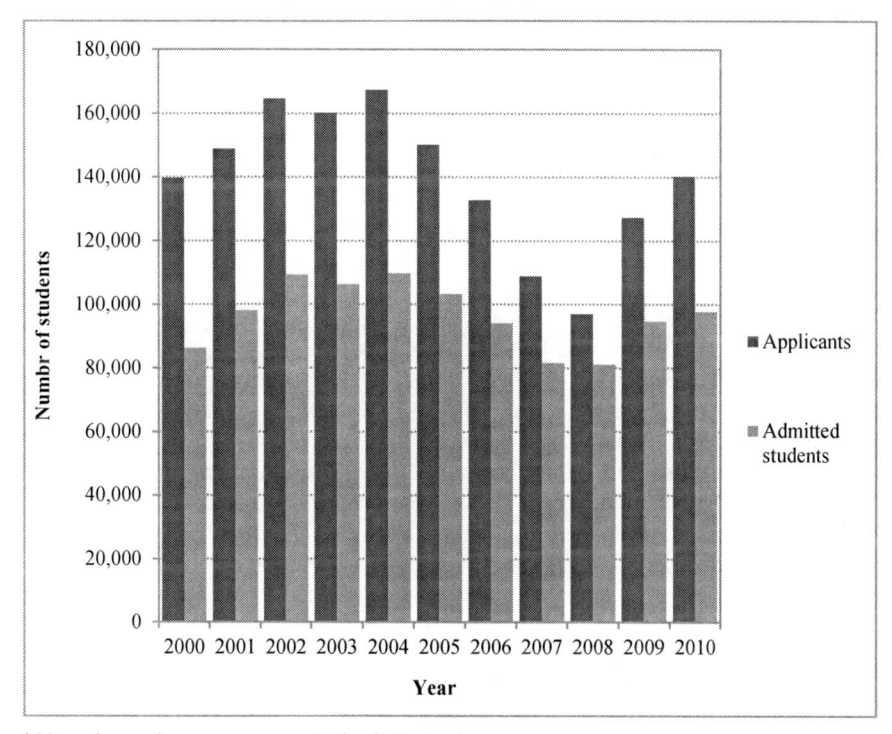

Figure 2. Number of Applicants and Admitted Students* at Institutions of Higher Education in Hungary 2000-2010

* Normal procedure, programmes starting in September

Source: Educatio Public Service Non-profit Llc.

The increase in the number of students in higher education has become one of the central issues of labour market and higher education research (see Hrubos, 2001, 2007; Róbert, 2009). Some researchers focus on the problems of "graduate overeducation" and the expected employment and work difficulties arising from "graduate oversupply" (see for example Polónyi, 2000), others investigate the sociological causes of the increase in the number of graduates, drawing parallels with entering the middle class and the spread of a middle-class mentality (see Gábor & Dudik, 2000). Research projects on the graduate labour market have not confirmed the theory of difficulties directly arising from the increase of the number of graduates: the targeted research of the Central Statistics Office found that the employment prospects of young graduates are better than those of non-graduates (Szilágyi, 2005); moreover, their wage advantage significantly increased in the first half of the past decade compared to young people with the final school examination (see Galasi, 2004; Kertesi & Köllö, 2005).

The forecast and examination of how the labour market receives young people who have graduated in the Bologna system has become a new and important issue in research on the labour market. The interview studies conducted in recent years show that participants on the labour market, the representatives of employers, were quite uncertain about the (future) employment opportunities of Bachelor graduates (see Horváth, 2007). Considering that the first graduating BA/BSc year with higher number of students only left universities and colleges last year, the question is still open-clear perception is not easy due to the still "mixed" nature of education, the parallel of traditional and Bologna type programmes and traditional and new BA/BSc graduates freshly appearing together on the labour market. Question marks are even larger with regard to Master programmes since the first Master year with a significant number of graduates could only complete studies in 2010, this year.

THE GRADUATE CAREER TRACKING SYSTEM IN HUNGARY AND THE DATABASE OF THIS REPORT

The Act on Higher Education of 2005 requires all higher education institutions to conduct compulsory career-tracking studies in Hungary. Several such developments were started in recent years; however, these created systems of studies, that are typically separated and do not communicate with each other, work under different methodologies and appear with different processing demands (see Horváth, 2008). The special development programme known as "System level development of higher education services" was started in 2008 from European Union resources, and the application programme also announced intended to supplement these organisational and operational deficiencies. The nationwide programme conducted by Educatio Public Service Non-profit Llc. aims to operate a career-tracking system based on unified methodology although on basic conditions at institutions. In order to do so, it provides the services and professional support – in addition to unifying data collection – through which the institutions can implement and later maintain and incorporate into their operation the development of career tracking with the help of resources through tendering.[2] but a professional development sup-

---

[2] Representative career tracking research based on nationwide sampling was conducted in May-June 2010. The survey had a dual aim. On the one hand, as a survey conducted with a yet unique methodology in Hungary and larger sample element number than any previous studies, it will provide data about the labour market situation of new graduates; on the other hand, the nationwide survey not examining institutions but educational fields provides an opportunity to interpret the results in a wider contextual system. – More about the Hungarian graduate career tracking system: Tamás Horváth: Central system for tracking graduates' careers. http://www.felvi.hu/diploman_tul/szakmai_tamogatas/kiadvanyok/dpr1_angol

porting institutional level career tracking establishing the long term operation of that.

Hungarian career-tracking data collections were based on institutional-level, overall on-line surveys. Two compulsory, unified questionnaires were developed in the central career-tracking programme, one of which is for the entire actual sphere of students, while the other is for all members of two given years of graduates (one and three years after graduation).[3] Universities and colleges naturally have the opportunity of expanding the questionnaire with their own questions.

2010 was the first full year of operation of this programme, resulting in the completion of the first institutional data collections and the first national career-tracking database. The survey was conducted by using the student address lists of the institutions with an on-line questionnaire method. Institutions addressed students who graduated in 2007 and 2009 with the questionnaire.

Table 1. Types of Degrees of the 2009 Graduates Surveyed from Institutions of Higher Education in Hungary in Comparison to National Graduate Statistics

Degree	National data (HEIS) Number of	per cent	Sample data Number of	per cent	Response rate per cent
Bachelor	17,061	34	2,898	30	17
University	11,769	23	3,176	33	27
College	20,541	41	3,075	32	15
Single-cycle	712	2	215	2	30
Master	509	1	241	3	47
Total	50,592	100	9,605	100	19

Source: Hungarian Graduate Survey 2010

The following analysis concentrates on 2009 graduates, where information was obtained with the help of 28 institutions of higher education institutions from 9,605 graduates (response rate of 19 per cent). Of the respondents, actually 6,251 had graduated from traditional higher education programmes (3,176 of them from university programmes and 3,075 from college programmes), 2,898 from Bachelor programmes, and only 241 from Master programmes. A further 215 graduated from new single-cycle programmes (see table 1). A weighting process ensuring representativeness was performed on the available sample.

The Hungarian Graduate Survey 2010 does not address international mobility. According to another survey of 2007 graduates from traditional study programmes, altogether have studied abroad during their course of study or within three years after graduation.

---

[3] The English version of the questionnaire blocks can be read at the following web page: http://www.felvi.hu/diploman_tul/szakmai_tamogatas/online_kerdoivek/online_kerdoivek_angolul

SOCIO-DEMOGRAPHIC BACKGROUND OF GRADUATES

68 per cent of the 2009 Bachelor graduates in Hungary are women. This high rate is close to that among all graduates surveyed (66 per cent) as well as that among graduates from the new single-cycle programmes (69 per cent). It is higher among graduates from traditional college programmes (72 per cent) than among graduates from traditional university programmes (58 per cent).

The average age of Bachelor graduates is 27.8 years at the time of obtaining the pre-degree certificate. This is close to the average of all graduates surveyed (28.0 years). Bachelor graduates are somewhat older on average than university graduates (27.2 years) while they are younger than the college graduates (29.1 years). It might be added that the small numbers of new single-cycle graduates was about 27 years and that of Master graduates about 29 years on average upon graduates

Obviously, the relatively high average age of Bachelor graduates cannot be viewed as being primarily deermined by the duration of the study programme itself, since the traditional university programmes have the longest educational cycle. The average age is related to the composition of students according to educational background: a higher rate of students at colleges study in non full-time programmes, potentially alongside work or not directly after the final examination. Among the new Bachelor, we note the backgrounds of both the traditonal university students and college students. In considering, however, that the Bachelor programmes are shorter in principle, we have to identify further causes for the relatively high average age of Bachelor graduates. It is most probably caused by specific conditions related to the period of transition to the two-cycle system. In the great wave of the establishment of new BA/BSc programmes in the Hungarian higher education around 2006, also many students from the age groups could enrol who took their final school examinations earlier and jointed the new study programmes after having waited for several years; this is also supported by the figure that the average age of students admitted to BA/BSc programmes is between 22 and 23 years.[4] Moreover, the average age of graduates may also be quite high that planning of study was complicated in the period of the inauguration of the new programmes. Finally, some programmes could not really be completed within six semesters, for example due to the fact that a compulsory professional practice semester was not integrated into the six-semester schedule.

---

[4] The average age of students admitted is "pulled up" by correspondent students – the average age of student admitted to correspondent programmes was 27.5 years, while the average age of students admitted to regular programmes was only 19.6 years. Source: *Jelentkezési és felvételi adatok 2005; Jelentkezési és felvételi adatok 2006* (Application and admittance data 2005; Application and admittance data 2006). Budapest: Educatio Public Service Non-profit Llc.

TRANSITION TO EMPLOYMENT AND FURTHER STUDY

The transition of Bachelor graduates from study to employment deserves special attention, since the first degree obtained in the two-cycle system offers an option for continuing studies or stepping out onto the labour market. We should bear in mind that the Bachelor graduates surveyed here graduated in the year 2009, when Master programmes started in large numbers in the Hungarian higher education system. On the one hand, we observe the first year of Bachelor graduates who have a realistic option of embarking into Master programmes. on the other hand, the establishment of new Master programmes was not yet complete in 2009; therefore, we might expect a further increase of the proportion of Bachelor students continuing study from 2010 onwards.

Therefore, surveys are of interest here which examine the intentions of Bachelor students with regard to further study and training (see for example Verosta 2009) motivations of BA/BSc students. According to the data of the Student Motivation Survey conducted by Educatio Non-profit Llc in 2009 within the GCT programme (Educatio Public Service Non-profit Llc., 2010b), 66 per cent of BA/BSc graduates obtaining Bachelor degrees plan to study on a Master programme. A survey conducted in 2005 of the students of new Bachelor programmes had shown that 50 per cent certainly wanted to continue study and an additional 27 per cent consider further study.

Table 2 shows that actually only 44 per cent of the 2009 Bachelor graduates from higher education institutions in Hungary continued study. More precisely,
- 28 per cent of Bachelors graduates continued study solely,
- 16 per cent combined further study and work,
- 39 per cent worked solely, and
- about one sixth did neither work nor study at the time the survey was undertaken.

Actually, Master study comprised less than half of the further study options of the 2009 Bachelor graduates. Only 18 per cent embarked on Master programmes (14 per cent as study only and 4 per cent with concurrent work).

Bachelor graduates from colleges officially have the same rights to continue to study as Bachelor graduates from universities. Table 2, however, shows, as one might expect, that more Bachelor graduates from universities continue to study without concurrent employment (32 per cent as compared to 18 per cent). In contrast, graduates from colleges more often opt for employment only or study along employment.

Table 2. Employment and Further Study One Year after Graduation of 2009 Bachelor Graduates from Higher Education Institutions in Hungary

	Total		University		College	
	Per cent	Number	Per cent	Number	Per cent	Number
Master study (only)	14	434	17	400	6	36
Master study and (full-time) employment	4	123	4	103	3	21
Other further study (only)	14	433	15	356	12	75
Other further study and (full-time) employment	12	377	11	257	19	119
(Full-time) Employment (only)	39	1,184	38	917	43	267
Neither study nor (full-time) Employment	15	467	15	363	17	104
Total	100	3,018	100	2,396	100	622

Source: Hungarian Graduate Survey 2010

It might be added here that about 70 per cert of the graduates each of the traditional university and traditional college programmes transfer to employment after graduation. Among graduates from new single-cycle programmes, this rate is even higher (80 per cent). But higher transition rates from these programmes are to be expected.

This notwithstanding, the rate of less than half of the Bachelor graduation transferring toe employment is clearly lower than expected. Several factors might explain that. As already pointed out, the situation in 2009 was exceptional because the establishment of new Master programmes was not yet fully completed. It is also interesting to note that more than half of the new Master students were graduates from traditional study programmes (Educatio Public Service Non-profit Llc., 2009), because many students of the first large Bachelor generation, starting to study in 2006, had not yet completed their study.

Moreover, the transition from graduation to further study might be long, because there is a specific characteristic in Hungary of a period between the award of a provisional degree certificate and the actual award of the degree. There might be requirements for the award of the degree which are fullfilled after the study period, i.e. primarily language certificates. The provisional award does not prevent the graduation to transfer to employment, but does not allow them to continue study immediately. According to the previously mentioned nationwide central survey of graduates (of traditional programmes) conducted in 2007, 16 per cent of graduates did not receive their degrees immediately after their final examination due to the lack of language certificates; however, 76 per cent of them stated that this has not affected their opportunity of transferring to employment (Educatio Public Service Non-profit Llc, 2010a). Accepting the above named facts, we expect that the rate of BA/BSc graduates participating in Master programmes will grow in the near future, which will most probably not reach the rates explored in the motivation surveys.

PROFESSIONAL SUCCESS OF BACHELOR GRADUATES

The professional success of Bachelor graduates can be measured worked with objective and subjective success criteria. As regards objective criteria, information on the length or the transition I worth to be taken into consideration. According to the data from the national career-tracking survey conducted in 2007, the average time of seeking employment at the end of higher education studies (of the traditional programmes is 3-4 months (Educatio Public Service Non-profit Llc., 2010b).

In calculating annual gross income as another objective success indicator, we only take full-time employed graduates into consideration and adress the gross monthly income (calculated from information provided on net income with the help of available information on progressive tax rates), thereby including the monthly average amount of benefits, extras and salary bonuses. The amount of Euro reported was calculated with a 0.00348 multiplier for the Hungarian currency according to the data of 31st August 2010.

Actually, the 2009 Bachelors from higher education institutions in Hungary earn one year after graduation, as table 3 shows, on average 26 per cent less than graduates from traditional university programmes. This is less than the average income of graduate from traditional college programmes, who earn 22 per cent less than graduates from traditional university programmes.

Table 3. Annual Gross Income One Year after Graduation of 2009 Full-time Employed Graduates from Institutions of Higher Education in Hungary (in Euro)

	Bachelor	Traditional university	Traditional college	Single-cycle	Total
Arithmetic mean	8,884	11,958	9,327	10,166	10,254
Median	7,099	10,231	7,099	8,143	7,726
N	1,294	2,022	1,789	145	5,250

Source: Hungarian Graduate Survey 2010

The differences shown in table 3 are affected by the composition of fields: Graduates from medical fields are included in the graduates from traditional university programmes, but not in the Bachelor graduates (who are among the single-cycle graduates of the new system). Moreover, no distinction is provided here between Bachelor graduates from universities und colleges. This notwithstanding, the income of Bachelor graduates is on average remarkably low.

The new Bachelor graduates in Hungary are professionally very successful, as far as the their occupational category is concerned about a year after graduation. 62 per cent are in manegerial and professional occupations, i.e. as many as graduates from the traditional university programmes and slightly more than graduates from traditional college programmes (58 per cent). As table 4 shows, a further 29 per cent of Bachelor graduates are active as associate professionals, and only 9 per cent in other occupations.

Table 4. Occupational Category One Year after Graduation of 2009 Full-time Employed Graduates from Institutions of Higher Education in Hungary (per cent)

	Bachelor	Traditional university	Traditional college	Single-cycle	Total
Managerial and professional occupations(ISCO 1-2)	62	62	58	76	61
Associate professional Occupations (ISCO 3)	29	31	34	22	31
Other occupations	9	7	9	2	8
Total	100	100	100	100	100
N	692	751	816	41	2,300

Source: Hungarian Graduate Survey 2010

As a first subjective category, a respective question addressed the relationship between work and level of educational attainment. Graduates were asked: "To what extent does your present/last main activity match your qualification?"; the responses are shown in table 5. Actually, 61 per cent of the Bachelor graduates from Hungarian institutions of higher education stated that they note a match either completely or to a great extent. In comparison to other countries, this can be viewed as a high proportion. It is slightly higher than the respective proportion among graduates from traditional programmes at colleges (59 per cent), but it is considerably lower than among graduates from traditional programmes at universities (76 per cent) and even more so than among graduates from the new single-cycle programmes (94 per cent). The graduates from single-cycle programmes stand out in various respects, as one might expect, because they are mostly the privileged group of those from medical fields.

Table 5. Extent of Match between Qualification and Current or Last Main Work Activity of 2009 Graduates from Higher Education Institutions in Hungary (per cent)

	Bachelor graduates	Traditional university graduates	Traditional college graduates	Single-cycle graduates	Total (N=6,421)
Not at all	19	8	17	1	14
To a small extent	20	17	24	5	20
To a great extent	29	31	27	23	29
Completely	32	45	32	71	38
Total	100	100	100	100	100

Source: Hungarian Graduate Survey 2010

Finally, graduates were asked to rate their job satisfaction. Table 6 shows the extent of satisfaction (5 means "very satisfied") with various aspects of employment and work conditions. Accordingly, differences between graduates from the various types of study programmes and institutions are small in most cases. However, graduates from traditional university programmes are somewhat satisfied as regards the opportunities for professional progress and the professional prestige. Surprisingly, graduates from single-cycle programmes are least satisfied with income and benefits: As they income, as shown above, is close to the average, the findings shows that these graduates (mostly in medical fields) have higher expectations as regards income, as it is realized at this stage of their career.

Table 6. Satisfaction with Various Aspects of Employment and Work on the Part of 2009 Graduates from Higher Education Institutions in Hungary (mean)*

	Bachelor programmes	Graduates from Traditional university programmes	Traditional college programmes	Single-cycle	Total
Professional, contextual part of work	3.7	3.8	3.7	3.7	3.7
Professional progress, career building	3.1	3.3	3.1	3.3	3.2
Professional prestige	3.2	3.4	3.2	3.4	3.3
Income, benefits	3.0	3.1	3.0	2.7	3.0
Personal working conditions	3.7	3.8	3.6	3.5	3.7
Objective working conditions	3.6	3.7	3.5	3.4	3.6
N	1,696	2,455	2,320	177	6,649

* Mean on a scale from 1 = "not satisfied at all" to 5 = "completely satisfied"

Source: Hungarian Graduate Survey 2010

In response to a questions about the overall satisfaction, a high extent of satisfaction (scale point 4 and 5 of a five-point scale) was expressed by 82 per cent of the graduates surveyed, among them
- 81 per cent of Bachelors graduates,
- 84 per cent of graduates from traditional university programmes,
- 79 per cent of graduates from traditional college programmes and
- 77 per cent of graduates from single-cycle programmes.

Bachelor graduates are obviously highly satisfied. This holds true both in comparison to graduates from other types of study programmes and institutions in Hungary, where the differences are small, as well as in comparison to Bachelor graduates from other countries addressed in this publication. As shown above, Bachelor graduates in Hungary report a professional success that could be viewed as very similar to that of graduates from traditional university progammes similar in some respects, but as lower in other respects. As the overall extent is more or less identical, we can infer that Bachelor graduates consider some differences in their career from that of universities as normal given the shorter overall study period and thus the level of educational attainment, but concurrently believe that their employment and work situation is relatively good.

SUMMARY

The introduction of the Bologna system has been practically completed in Hungary in a very short time mostly between 2006 and 2010. Almost all initial study programmes were transferred into BA/BSc study programmes. However, since most Master programmes have been established since 2009, there are not yet any reliable data available about the differences of employment and work between the Bachelor graduates and the new Master graduates.

The proportion of 2009 Bachelor graduates opting for continued study – either solely or along employment – is relatively small in comparison to the other European countries addressed in this publication: less than half of the graduates. The 2009 figures are certainly influenced by the fact that the new Master system was incompletely established at that time; therefore, an increase of this proportion is to be expected, but it might be possible that a smaller transition quota than in other countries will become customary in Hungary. This can be seen in accordance with the basic idea of the Bologna reform that Bachelor programmes should serve both the transition to the world of work and the continuation of study towards advanced levels.

As far as the the employment and work success is concerned, the situation for the Bachelor graduates is is somewhat more subtle. It is a great success for them in Hungary in comparison to other European countries that the majority are employed in managerial and professional occupations, and this quota is even as high as among graduates from traditional university programmes. Bachelor graduates, again report a relatively frequent link between qualification and level of job, though less often than gradutes from traditional university programmes. In those respects, the new Bachelor graduates are closer to the graduates of the traditional college programmes. In one respect – the income – Bachelor graduates fare substantially worse than graduates from from traditional university programmes and even somewhat worse than from traditional college programmes.

In terms of satisfaction with their work, however, Bachelor graduates assess their situation almost as positive as graduates from traditional university programmes. This seems to reflect the successes named above as well as the insight that graduates from the first cycle of studies cannot end up as a rule on the same level of positions and income as the graduates from the second level.

In sum, if we wish to position Hungarian BSc graduates, we can say that the labour market and the new study programmes are still in the process of accmmodation, whereby the position of the new Bachelors seems to become closer to that of the graduates from traditional college programmes form than to that of graduates from traditional university programmes of education are still feeling their way towards each other, but the first signs of matching show a similar pattern to that of the college qualification. The Bachelor degree is comparable to the traditional college degree on the labour market in several respects. However, the Bachelor degree might more clearly differ from that of the traditional college degree in one respect, i.e. in the larger rates transferring to further study.

REFERENCES

Educatio Public Service Non-profit Llc.(2009). *Jelentkezési és felvételi adatok 2009* [Application and admittance data 2009]. Budapest: Educatio Public Service Non-profit Llc.
Educatio Public Service Non-profit Llc. (2010a). *Diplomás pályakövetés – Diplomás kutatás 2010* [Graduate career tracking – Graduate survey 2010]. Budapest: Educatio Public Service Non-profit Llc.
Educatio Public Service Non-profit Llc. (2010b). *Diplomás pályakövetés – Hallgatói motivációs kutatás 2009-2010* [Graduate career tracking – Student motivation survey 2009-2010]. Budapest: Educatio Public Service Non-profit Llc. Retrieved August 30, 2010, from http://www.felvi.hu/diploman_tul/ szakmai_tamogatas/eredmenyek/diplomas_kutatas
Gábor, K. & Dudik, E. (2000). Középosztályosodás és a felsőoktatás tömegesedése [Entering the middle class and masses in higher education]. *Educatio, 1*, 95-114.
Galasi, P. (2004). *Túlképzés, alulképzés és bérhozam a magyar munkaerőpiacon – 1994-2002* [Overeducation, undereducation and wage yield on the Hungarian labour market – 1994-2002]. Budapesti Munkagazdaságtani Füzetek, 4.
Horváth, D. (2008). Hazai gyakorlatok a diplomás pályakövetésben [Hungarian practices in tracking graduates' careers]. In I. Fábri, T. Horváth. & A. Nyerges (Eds.), *Diplomás pályakövetés 1* (pp. 9-51). Budapest: Educatio Public Service Non-Profit Llc.
Horváth, T. (2007). Az átalakuló hazai felsőoktatás munkaerő-piaci szemmel [Transforming Hungarian higher education from the aspect of the labour market]. *Felsőoktatási Műhely, 1*, 43-49.
Hrubos, I. (2001). Transition to a modern mass education system: Career chances for women graduates in Hungary. In L.-M. Lurén & A.H. Ronning (Eds.), *Gendering Empowerment* (pp. 127-134). Geneva: International Federation of University Women.
Hrubos, I. (2007). Une exigence de transformation rapides: L'université hongroise entre massification et ouverture européenne [A demand for quick changes. The Hungarian university: Between massification and the opening to Europe]. *Revue Internationale d'Éducation, 45*, 63-74.
Kertesi, G. & Köllő, J. (2005). Felsőoktatási expanzió, "diplomás munkanélküliség" és a diplomák piaci értéke [Expansion in higher education, "graduate unemployment" and the market value of degrees]. *Budapesti Munkagazdaságtani Füzetek, 3*.
Nemzeti Erőforrások Minisztériuma Statisztika (2008). *Felsőoktatási Statisztikai Adatok 2008* [Higher education statistics 2008]. Retrieved August 30, 2010, from http://db.okm.gov.hu/statisztika/fs08_fm/
Polónyi, I. (2000). Egyre többet, egyre kevesebbért [More and more for less and less]? *Educatio, 1*, 43-61.
Róbert, P. (2009). The consequences of educational expansion for returns to education in Hungary. In A. Hadjar & R. Becker (Eds*.), Expected and unexpected consequences of the educational expansion in Europe and the US. Theoretical approaches and empirical findings in comparative perspective* (pp. 201-212). Bern: Haupt.
Szilágyi, E.L. (Ed.) (2005). *A fiatalok munkaerő-piaci helyzete* [Youth in the labour market]. Budapest: Hungarian Central Statistics Office.
Veroszta, Z. (2010). Az idősebb korosztály jelentkezési tendenciái [Application tendencies of older age groups]. *Felsőoktatási Műhely, 1*,49-57.

ANDREA CAMMELLI, GILBERTO ANTONELLI, ANGELO DI
FRANCIA, GIANCARLO GASPERONI AND MATTEO SGARZI

MIXED OUTCOMES OF THE BOLOGNA PROCESS IN ITALY

INTRODUCTION

A country study in the framework of a comparative analysis – in this case on issues of mobility and employability of Bachelor graduates in Italy in comparison to other European countries – runs the risk of misunderstandings if the characteristics of the individual countries are not sufficiently taken into account. Therefore, we must stress two stylized facts on the Italian setting.

First, despite the strong inflow of immigrants in the last 25 years, the absolute number of nineteen-year-olds in Italy dropped by 38 per cent (for a more comprehensive analysis see Cammelli, di Francia & Guerriero, 1997). This brings about strong direct and indirect effects, both on the demand for higher education and the potential supply of graduates.

Second, even if in the last decade the catching-up process has been remarkable, in 2007 the ratio of graduates in the population in the 25-34 age group was only 19 per cent, as compared with an OECD average of 34 per cent (Organisation for Economic Co-operation and Development [OECD], 2010, chapter 9; for further evidence see also Cammelli, 2009a). This is the effect of a delay with deep historical and structural roots, where firm size and local system of production must be taken into consideration to explain the demand for graduates (see Antonelli, 1987, p. 161; Antonelli, di Francia & Guidetti, 2006; Antonelli & Guidetti, 2008): In the 55-64 age group, the ratio reaches only 9 per cent, i.e. less than half the corresponding OECD average. This also involves occupational groups such as entrepreneurs and managers, both in the private and public sectors. This is why the setting of a minimum threshold of 40 per cent in the framework of the European Higher Education Area (EHEA) can be highly relevant for Italy.

STUDY STRUCTURE IN ITALY

Before the Bologna Process, Italy was one of the few countries with neither a two-cycle structure of study programmes and degrees nor a two-type or multi-type system of higher education institutions. Before the introduction of the "3+2" reform, which took place in the academic year 2001/02 (in some universities already in 2000/01), university study programmes mostly lasted for four-years and led to a degree called *laurea*. Moreover, since the end of the 1960s, access to study programmes has been granted to virtually all upper secondary school leavers. Some required five (e.g. engineering) or six (medicine) years of study. Universities also offered three-year programmes conferring a *diploma universitario*, but students who enrolled in these programmes represented a minority of only about 10 per cent, as shown in table 1.

H. Schomburg and U. Teichler (eds.), *Employability and Mobility of Bachelor Graduates in Europe*, 143–170.
© 2011 Sense Publishers. All rights reserved.

Table 1. Development of Diplomas and Degrees Awarded by Italian Institutions of Higher Education 2000-2009

	2000	2001	2002	2003	2004	2005	2006	2007	2008	2009
Absolute figures										
Pre-reform degrees	143,892	153,976	164,531	164,375	161,050	142,993	100,078	63,864	40,864	27,797
Diplomas of higher education for specific purposes	17,592	16,556	13,367	8,021	3,921	1,689	810	446	226	162
First-cycle (Bachelor) degrees		1,267	20,626	50,705	91,653	137,545	160,861	173,270	172,591	171,115
Single-cycle Master degrees		6	817	5,825	7,299	7,855	9,423	11,616	15,422	19,525
Second-cycle Master degrees		1	99	1,132	2,983	10,280	29,109	50,139	64,975	73,588
Total	161,484	171,806	199,440	230,058	266,906	300,362	300,281	299,335	294,078	292,187
Percentages										
Pre-reform degrees	89	90	83	71	60	48	33	21	14	10
Diplomas of higher education for specific purposes	11	10	7	4	2	1	0	0	0	0
First-cycle (Bachelor) degrees		1	10	22	34	46	54	58	59	59
Single-cycle Master degrees		0	0	3	3	3	3	4	5	7
Second-cycle Master degrees		0	0	1	1	3	10	17	22	25
Total	100	100	100	100	100	100	100	100	100	100

Source: Miur-Ufficio di Statistica, *Indagine sull'istruzione universitaria* and, for 2009, *Rilevazione degli iscritti al 31 gennaio* (provisional data); excluding the qualifications within the "Defence and security" field of study.

The Italian higher education system was strongly influenced by the Bologna Process, aimed at introducing a more transparent and comparable structure of university degrees, fostering student and scholar mobility, promoting employability of graduates, ensuring educational quality and placing emphasis on the European dimension of higher education. The first of these objectives has been pursued by organising university programmes in two main cycles:
- a first cycle leading to a Bachelor degree (laurea"), geared to professional outcomes and lasting (at least) three years; and
- a second cycle, leading to a Master degree ("laurea magistrale", formerly "laurea specialistica"), conditional upon the completion of the first cycle.[1]

In some fields of study – medicine, veterinary medicine, dentistry, pharmacology, architecture[2] – there is only a long "single-cycle" lasting for 5 years (6 for Medicine) to which admission is limited. Also, law moved as from the academic year 2007/08 to a single-cycle, five-year programme (see Antonelli et al., 2010; Cammelli, 2006a). Moreover, university study programmes in educational science have maintained their prior 4-year duration.

Two sets of legislative measures were adopted in Italy to implement the Bologna Process: (1) The first reform (Ministerial Decree No. 509 of 1999, "Regulation establishing rules on didactical autonomy of universities", implemented since the academic year 2001/02), introduced the "3+2" system on a general basis with a two-cycle degree structure consisting of a first degree obtained after at least 180 ETCS credits and a second degree requiring at least 300 ETCS credits (including those previously obtained for a first cycle degree); (2) the second reform (Ministerial Decree No. 270 of 2004, "Amendments to the regulation establishing rules on didactical autonomy of universities" and the following decrees issued on 16 March 2007) aimed at reducing the number of the new study programmes and exams in each study programme, as well as introducing a budget constraint on resources, in addition to establishing the *laurea magistrale*, with a total workload of 120 ECTS credits and increasing the number of corresponding study programmes, and finally introducing single-cycle study programmes in the field of law. The "3+2" reform was also aimed at addressing traditional endemic weaknesses of the Italian university system: a low rate of graduates, a high rate of drop-outs from university, and a strong discrepancy between the officially required and the actual duration of studies.[3]

Italy has 61 state universities (including four polytechnics and two universities for foreigners), 17 non-state, but legally acknowledged universities (4 are promoted by public institutions, 13 are privately run), 11 on-line (private) universities and

---

[1] The Italian reform also created degree courses called "Masters" (*"Master di primo livello"* – typically following a first-cycle degree – and *"Master di secondo livello"* – following a second-cycle degree); in the subsequent text, only the second-cycle or single cycle will be called Master programmes and degrees in order to avoid misunderstandings.
[2] These study programmes are also regulated by specific European directives which define the scientific basis and the practical training needed to practise the corresponding professions.
[3] A third reform process has been triggered by the approval at the very end of the last year of the Law N° 240 of 2010, beginning from the transformation in the governance system of Italian universities.

6 special schools or higher institutes (specialising in research and usually catering only to doctorate-level students). Italy's higher education system is unique in that almost all participation in higher (post-secondary) education is university-based. Non-university higher education is offered through a variety of institutions, including arts academies, music conservatories (which are also included in the Bologna reform), higher schools for linguistic mediators, psychotherapy training institutes, military and police academies, higher integrated training schools and institutes, and regional vocational training centres.

The net entry rate of Italians to tertiary education institutions according to OECD statistics was 53 per cent (as compared to 56 per cent in OECD countries), up from 39 per cent in 2000. The graduation rate from tertiary education was estimated to be 35 per cent as compared to 39 per cent in OECD countries (see Cammelli, 2009b; AlmaLaurea-Consorzio Interuniversitario, 2010a).

The "3+2" reform, starting earlier than in most other European countries (see Cammelli, 2009c; Roversi Monaco, 2008), triggered a very rapid and partly uncontrolled increase in the number of degree programmes: While in the academic year 2000/01, 2,262 university study programmes (and less than 1,000 university diploma programmes) were available in the framework of the old system, there were more than 3,000 first-cycle programmes, over 1,200 second-level programmes and some 180 single-cycle Master programmes in 2003/04. The respective figures increased to over 3,100, around 2,400 and around 270 in 2007/08. Thereafter universities and their controlling ministry attempted, with some success, to reduce the number of degree programmes.

The reform led a higher number of young people – as well as older adults "returning" to formal education (cf. Cristofori, 2008) – to undertake university studies: The number of newly enrolled students increased from 284,000 in 2000/01 to a peak of 338,000 in 2003/04; the total number of university students grew from 1.69 million in 2000/01 to 1.82 million in 2005/06. Thereafter, a reduction in the number of enrolments and students was recorded, partly due to demographic changes (a decline in upper secondary school leavers). Furthermore, families faced growing difficulties to cover the direct and indirect costs of higher education.

As table 1 shows, the reform process and the dynamics of the university system have proven to be slow and sticky; therefore, the composition of degrees has changed slowly. This is also due to the fact that the establishment of new programmes is the result of different legislative waves. The number of graduates of the new "3+2" programmes increased gradually over the decade, surpassing half the total of university graduates in 2007. Only in 2008 did the number of new-type Master graduates exceed that of old system graduates.

The "3+2" reform has led an increasing number of students to complete their university studies.[4] Altogether, the number of university degrees awarded (including university diplomas) increased from 161,484 to more than 300,000 in 2005. However, this was partly due to the fact that many students were awarded both a

---

[4] Or, at least, it has implied the awarding of a greater number of university qualifications.

Bachelor and a Master degree. The number of years of study completed increased by 23 per cent between 2001 and 2009 (AlmaLaurea-Consorzio Interuniversitario, 2010b). And the number of graduates earning a second-level degree (pre-reform or new Master-*specialistica* or single-cycle) grew from 143,892 in 2004 to 171,332 in 2004 and thereafter dropped to 120,910 in 2009 (table 1). The most recent decline could be interpreted both negatively as a decrease in the number of highly qualified graduates and positively as a success in routing students towards shorter and employment-oriented university programmes.

The university reform has had a different impact according to field of study. Among Bachelors, for the vast majority of fields, such as science[5], engineering, architecture, economics-statistics, socio-political science, psychological science, the number of graduates initially increased and then reached a plateau. Graduates in art and humanities stand out because of their steadily increasing number. Law graduates have seen an increase in their number up to the year 2006 and subsequently a drop as a result of the introduction of single-cycle programmes. Single-cycle and two-year Master graduates both show positive trends and no quantitative stabilisation has been reached yet. In terms of *university degrees as a whole* (excluding PhDs), the number of graduates in medicine is constant; the number of law graduates corresponds to an inverted U-curve, where the decline might have been caused by the introduction of single-cycle degree programmes; other fields, e.g. health care and physical education, arts and humanities as well as socio-political and psychological sciences, display a more regular and growing trend (cf. Gasperoni, 2010; Camillo, 2010).

According to the Alma Laurea survey for the year 2009, 57 per cent of the 2008 Bachelor graduates continued their academic studies in a Master programme at one year from graduation.[6]

---

[5] The degrees in chemistry, physics, mathematics need further clarification. In observing the increase in the number of degrees in this area between 2001 and 2009, we note an increase that is far below the average. This is particularly critical, because Italy suffers a substantial shortage in this area. In the meantime, the duration of study also decreased. The Ministry, the universities and the business associations started an action around 2005 to attract more students to this area, but no impact is visible yet (AlmaLaurea, 2010b).

[6] This result is coherent with the expectations expressed just before graduation. In order to compare pre-reform and post-reform prospects of further studies, we could refer to the overall expectations of the 2009 graduates' cohort as compared with the 2001 ones: accordingly, 77 per cent and 63 per cent expected to continue study and training (including internships, postgraduate specialization schools and doctoral study).

THE ALMALAUREA GRADUATE SURVEYS

The following analysis is based on the surveys undertaken by the AlmaLaurea-Interuniversity Consortium (AL) which covers now 62 Italian universities and 76 per cent of the total number of graduates.[7] University students belonging to the Consortium get in contact with AL when they are about to complete their study programme and obtain their user name and password to access the available functions. They fill in an online questionnaire addressing study conditions and provisions as well as subsequent study and work prospect. The results are used both for statistical analyses, and, if the students so wish, for the purpose of job search and recruitment.[8] More than 90 per cent of the graduates respond every year (92 per cent in 2009 graduates' profile survey).

After graduation, universities send their respective records – e.g. type of final degree, marks as well as entry qualification, duration of study and age – to AL, thus providing the opportunity to detect any inconsistency or incompleteness between the administrative data and the information formerly provided by the students.

Both sets of information contribute to create the curriculum vitae of each graduate, which accrue the AL CV database of all AL surveys and, thus, a *fully integrated information system* – being periodic, well-timed and updatable – serving both research activities and services supply. By the end July 2010, it included the curricula of almost 1.5 million graduates.[9]

Two main reports are produced every year. The first is the *Survey on graduates' employment condition* as surveyed one, three and five years after graduation.[10] The most recent is the XIIth report on graduate employment conditions in the year 2009 (AlmaLaurea-Consorzio Interuniversitario, 2010a). It investigated 210,000 gradu-

---

[7] This result has been achieved gradually, in the frame of a bottom up approach based on the subsidiarity principle.

[8] An independent assessment of the impact of the AL model on the functioning of Italian labour markets can be found in Bagues and Sylos Labini (2009).

[9] Companies have direct access to published CVs in the data-base through a wide set of services. Companies may consult CVs through a self-service facility, with payment when the names and addresses of the graduates are obtained. From the start, around three million CVs have been provided to firms and Italian and foreign organisations (www.almalaurea.it/en/aziende/). AL has a non-profit statute and private companies co-finance the provision of AL services. Associated universities also co-finance the initiative.

[10] Graduates are interviewed on their occupational status: attendance/not attendance of a second cycle post-degree course and reasons for further enrolment/not enrolment in second cycle post-degree course (both only for first cycle graduates); graduate training activities; occupational situation immediately after graduation as well as at the time of interview; match between the current job and the job held at the time of graduation; improvement in the employment position; number of months elapsed between obtaining the degree and seeking/finding the first job; job-seeking channel used for job held at the time of interview; frequency of the actions taken to find a job; type of job (employee/self-employed); professional position; legal and contractual job characteristics; full-time or part-time employment; economic sector and field; firm size; region and province where the job is located; extent to which knowledge/skills acquired at the university are used; requirements for performing the job; satisfaction felt regardings various characteristics of the job; net monthly income; reasons for inactivity in the labour market; frequency of the actions implemented to find a job.

ates of the year 2008 from 49 Italian universities. The survey response rates reached 90 per cent for first cycle graduates, 89 per cent for second-cycle graduates and 87 per cent for single-cycle graduates. The study also included pre-reform graduates from the summer sessions in the years 2006 and 2004 interviewed after three and five years after graduation. Their response rates were 82 per cent and 76 per cent. The data thus gathered were subjected to a statistical procedure known as "re-weighting" (AlmaLaurea-Consorzio Interuniversitario, 2010a).

The second annual report is the *Graduates' profile survey*, published annually on the web free of charge. Information is provided on graduates' performance and characteristics and, thus, on the quantitative and qualitative characteristics of the human capital produced by the universities. Comparisons of different generations of graduates can be also undertaken (AlmaLaurea-Consorzio Interuniversitario & Osservatorio Statistico dell'Università di Bologna, 2008).

The most recent XIIth report on the graduate profile refers to the year 2009 (AlmaLaurea-Consorzio Interuniversitario, 2010b). It includes responses by 190,000 persons from 51 universities graduating in 2009 (110,000 Bachelors; 47,000 Masters and 13,000 single-cycle degree holders). The response rate for the first cycle graduates was almost 92 per cent. The survey released in May 2010, reports extensive and detailed information up to each degree course, making it possible to notice the extreme variability across the different aspects it covered, notwithstanding the common reform framework.[11] Three fields of study were most frequent among the Bachelor graduates: social-political sciences (15 per cent), economics and statistics (14 per cent) and medicine and health care (12 per cent); engineering and humanities each comprise about ten per cent, while other fields range from 7 per cent (foreign languages) to 2 per cent (chemistry and pharmacology).

SOCIO-BIOGRAPHIC BACKGROUND AND COURSE OF STUDY

In comparing pre-reform and post-reform findings we must take into consideration that the transition is still under way. Among the critical methodological issues, in comparing structural characteristics, study performances and employment outcomes, we must consider that the pre-reform and reform study programmes had been designed with entirely different objectives, features and study careers prospects. Second, the entire period examined (2001-2009) is characterised by the coexistence of groups with different structural characters over time. Third, the performances of pre-reform graduates have become more and more uneven over time (e.g. age at graduation, marks, study abroad). Fourth, we must distinguish between "pure" graduates, who complete their curriculum in the post-reform setting, and "hybrid" graduates, who within the pre-reform setting completed their study within the reform setting. In the framework of this analysis, we focus on the 2008 and 2009 Bachelor cohorts where the incidence of the "hybrid" graduates became marginal (only 9 per cent; see also Cammelli, 2005, 2006b).

---

[11] The other subset of data presented in this paper is drawn from this second survey.

Data on the *socio-economic background* of graduates show an over-representation of youngsters from socio-economically advantaged families, with no discrepancy between geographical areas. While the percentage of graduates among the male population in Italy aged 45 to 69 is under 9 per cent, it represents 20 per cent among graduates' fathers; the pattern is similar for graduates' mothers. Yet 72 per cent were the first in their families to obtain a university qualification; this proportion was 73 per cent for graduates from pre-reform study programmes (among them 87 per cent in educational science and 84 per cent in health care), 75 per cent for Bachelor graduates and 69 per cent for Master graduates, but only 51 per cent for graduates from the new single-cycle programmes.

The most frequent *upper secondary school background* is the scientific lyceum (34 per cent, often among graduates in geo-biology and engineering fields). Second most frequent is the technical secondary school leaving certificate, which increased from 27 per cent in 2001 to 30 per cent in 2009; it is most frequent among graduates in economics-statistics and agriculture. The classical lyceum leaving certificate represents 12 per cent; it is most common among graduates in humanities and law.

The Bologna reform process has led to a substantial increase in *class attendance*: About 67 per cent of the Bachelors attended more than three quarters of the classes – a much higher rate than that recorded for the pre-reform graduates. Rates of more than three quarters vary substantially according to the field of study of Bachelor graduates: They range from 92 per cent in medicine and health care, to 86 per cent in engineering and 85 per cent in chemistry-pharmacology on the one hand and to 43 per cent in educational sciences and 35 in law on the other.

Work practice during the course of study is very frequent in Italy, since it is an important determinant of choices and performances. Studying workers (those having held a full-time job for at least six months during their course of study) represent 10 per cent all Bachelors. Their share is only 4 per cent or less among students in engineering and geo-biology, but almost 20 per cent in education science and social-political sciences.

Internships and training periods acknowledged by the universities (undertaken by more than 80 per cent outside the university) are very widespread. As figure 1 shows, 60 per cent of the 2009 Bachelor graduates report this kind of practical experience during their course of study. This varies from 91 per cent in agriculture, 86 per cent in educational sciences and 85 per cent in psychology to 49 per cent in economics and statistics and 24 per cent in law. It is worth mentioning that internships and training periods are associated with a higher employment rate: The latest survey on graduates' employment condition confirms a differential of 6 per cent between those who underwent a training period and those who did not (see Alma-Laurea-Consorzio Interuniversitario, 2010a, p. 168).

The *age at the time of first enrolment* has increased in recent years, due in part to the growing diversity of the study provisions. The share of persons starting study two years later than usual increased from 11 per cent in 2001, i.e. before the reform, to 23 per cent in 2009. There is an even higher increase among those enrolling for the first time 10 years after the conventional age: from 3 per cent to 7 per cent (8 per cent among the Bachelors). It is not certain, whether this is a transitory effect due to a shortage of study places prior to the reform.

The average *age of graduation* among the graduates of pre-reform study programmes is 28 years. It is 26.2 years for Bachelor graduates, 27.3 years for Master graduates and 26.5 years for graduates from the new single-cycle programmes. We must bear in mind, though, that more than two years' delay on average of the Bachelor and Master graduates is due to the increase in late enrolment since the reform of the study programmes.

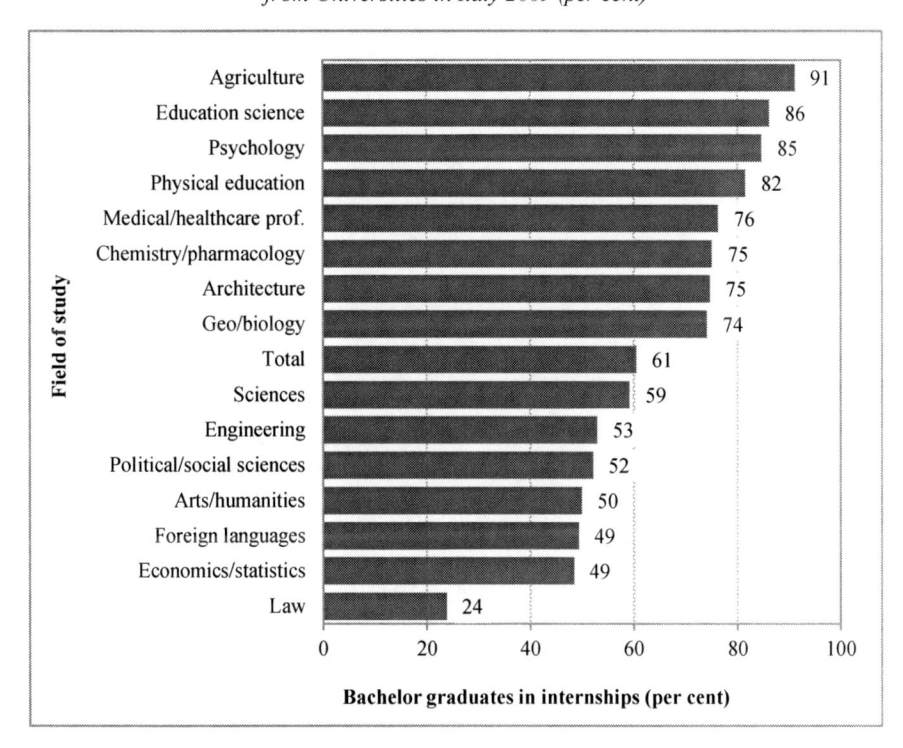

Figure 1. Internships during the Course of Study among of Bachelors Graduates from Universities in Italy 2009 (per cent)

Field of study	Bachelor graduates in internships (per cent)
Agriculture	91
Education science	86
Psychology	85
Physical education	82
Medical/healthcare prof.	76
Chemistry/pharmacology	75
Architecture	75
Geo/biology	74
Total	61
Sciences	59
Engineering	53
Political/social sciences	52
Arts/humanities	50
Foreign languages	49
Economics/statistics	49
Law	24

Source: AlmaLaurea-Consorzio Interuniversitario, Indagine 2010: Profilo dei Laureati 2009[12]

The *time to graduate* seems to have become more regular and thus shorter in the reform process. 39 per cent of graduates of the new programmes graduated within the required period, as compared to 10 per cent of those from pre-reform programmes. Up to one year of extension holds true for 25 per cent and 18 per cent respectively. Thus, the extension beyond one year is less than half in the former

---

[12] Retrieved February 03, 2011, from http://www.almalaurea.it/universita/profilo/profilo/2009/index.shtml

than in the latter category. As table 2 shows, however, completion within the required period of study varied substantially by field among the Bachelor graduates: from 18 per cent in law to 73 per cent and medicine and health care.

Table 2. Bachelor Graduates from Universities in Italy 2009 Having Completing Studies within at Most One Year above the Required Period (per cent)

	Completing their studies within the prescribed time limit	Completing their studies with one year of delay
Medical/healthcare professions	73	17
Foreign languages	37	31
Chemistry/pharmacology	41	25
Psychology	38	28
Economic/statistics	38	26
Political/social sciences	39	25
Physical education	39	24
Geo/biology	33	26
Architecture	28	31
Arts/humanities	30	28
Agriculture	31	27
Sciences	37	21
Education science	31	26
Engineering	34	23
Law	18	23
Total	39	25

Source: AlmaLaurea-Consorzio Interuniversitario, Indagine 2010: Profilo dei Laureati 2009[13]

INTERNATIONAL MOBILITY

In 2009, 5,059 graduates in Italy surveyed in the AlmaLaurea study were *foreign* (excluding those from San Marino). As figure 2 shows, their percentage grew steadily from 1 per cent in 2001 to 3 per cent in 2009. Almost 70 per cent come from European countries – with a rising share from non-EU and a decrease in those from EU countries: 11 per cent from Asia, 11 per cent from North and South America and 9 per cent from Africa. Those from Greece were most frequent and from Albania second most frequent in 2001; this reversed to 21 per cent Albanians and 7 per cent Greeks among the 2009 graduates.

The highest proportion of foreign graduates can be found in medicine, health care and dentistry (6 per cent), followed by foreign languages (5 per cent). They make up 4 per cent of the graduates of the new single-cycle study programmes

---

[13] Retrieved February 03, 2011, from http://www.almalaurea.it/universita/profilo/profilo2009/index.shtml

(among them the medical fields), 3 per cent of the Bachelor programmes and 3 per cent of the Master programmes, as compared to only 2 per cent of the pre-reform graduates. Foreign students more often come from a higher social background: 43 per cent of them had at least one parent with a higher education qualification, as compared to 26 per cent among Italian graduates.

Where do foreign graduates want to make use of their university qualifications? In response to a corresponding question, 23 per cent stated that they were willing to find a job outside Italy and 48 per cent were open for a job both in Italy and abroad, while 25 per cent declared that they wanted to find a job in Italy.

Figure 2. Persons with Foreign Citizenship among Bachelor Graduates from Universities in Italy 2001-2009 (per cent)

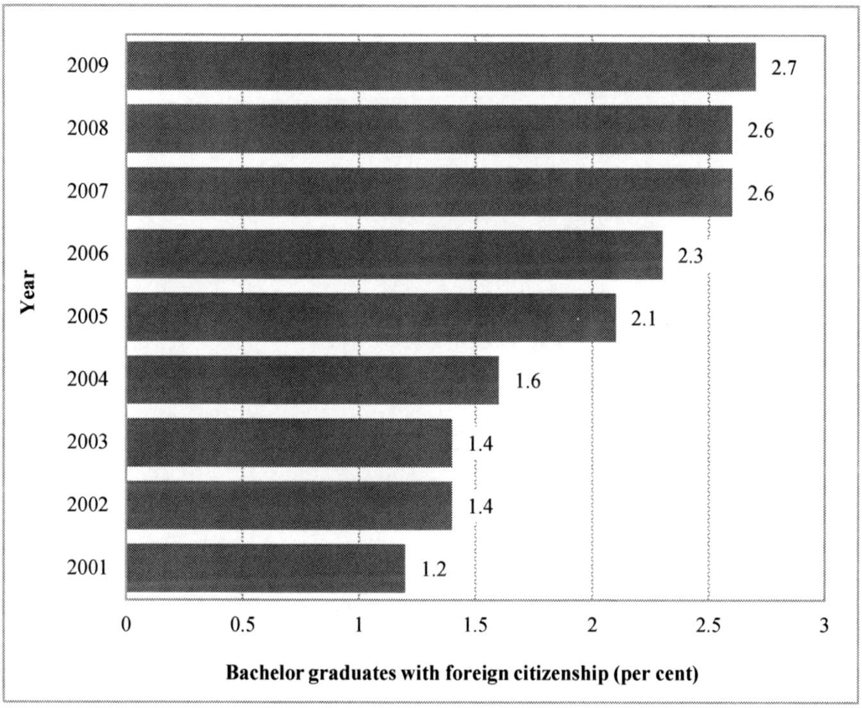

Year	Bachelor graduates with foreign citizenship (per cent)
2009	2.7
2008	2.6
2007	2.6
2006	2.3
2005	2.1
2004	1.6
2003	1.4
2002	1.4
2001	1.2

Source: AlmaLaurea-Consorzio Interuniversitario (2010b, p. 176)

Study periods abroad for Italian students have grown during the first years of the Bologna reform. Of the 2001 graduates, 8 per cent had studied abroad in the framework of ERASMUS or other EU programmes. Of the 2009 Bachelor graduates, only 5 per cent studied abroad in the framework of ERASMUS or other EU programmes – due to the shorter study period. The respective quotas were 15 per cent for 2009 Master graduates and 10 per cent for single-cycle programme graduates.

By taking into account other study abroad arrangements acknowledged by the university programme and study abroad on individual initiative, we note an overall rate of 14 per cent of the 2009 graduates, of which an overall rate of 18 per cent of Master graduates. Moreover, 6 per cent of Italians graduated abroad and then validated their exams on their return. It can be added that 5 per cent of doctoral degree recipients did a significant part of their doctoral work abroad. In both respects, we also note an increase over time.

Study abroad varies substantially by field of study. The respective rate for 2009 Bachelor graduates having studied abroad in European countries ranged from less than 2 per cent in medicine and health care, psychology and chemistry-pharmacology to 7 per cent in political-social sciences and 23 per cent in foreign languages.

Work abroad after graduation becomes increasingly an option for Italian graduates. According to the most recent data, 4 per cent work abroad one year after graduation.

A detailed analysis was undertaken of the 3 per cent of 2002 graduates with Italian citizenship surveyed in the AL system who worked abroad in 2007 (see Cammelli, 2008; Brandi & Segnana, 2008). Their employment conditions were better on average than those of graduates working in Italy and they were more highly satisfied than those working in Italy. Many had international work assignments. 45 per cent stated that they would probably not return to Italy, whilst about a third wished to do so.

TRANSITION TO EMPLOYMENT AND FURTHER STUDY OF BACHELOR GRADUATES

One year after graduation, 46 per cent of the Bachelors having graduated in 2008 (including the "hybrid" ones who started their study in the pre-Bologna system) were employed: 31 per cent worked without concurrent study and 15 per cent combined work and study. Among the others, 42 per cent were entirely dedicated to their Master degree studies, 9 per cent were neither enrolled nor employed, but were seeking a job and, finally, about 3 per cent were not employed and not seeking a job. The employment rate of 2008 Bachelor graduates was lower than in the preceding years – partly due to worse economic conditions and partly to a greater inclination to continue their studies.

Employment of Bachelor graduates one year after varied substantially by *field of study*. On the upper end, 83 per cent of the graduates from medicine and healthcare were employed and an additional 2 per cent both employed and enrolled in a Master course. As table 3 shows, the fields of physical education and education science also showed very high employment rates (68 per cent and 61 per cent respectively) and high rate of employment and concurrent study as somewhat higher (27 per cent and 18 per cent respectively). As will be seen below, in these two fields, the number of graduates pursuing the job held prior to graduation was significantly higher than in other fields. On the lower end, only about 10 per cent were in psychology and geo-biology, with rates of concurrent employment and study of 27 per cent and 13 per cent respectively.

The transition to employment within the first year after graduation did not differ substantially by *gender*. 46 per cent of both men and women were employed, among them about one third concurrent with study. Almost 44 per cent of men as compared to almost 42 per cent of women were enrolled in advanced study. However, the rates of the unemployed (10 per cent and 8 per cent respectively) and of those not seeking a job (both 3 per cent respectively) were higher among women.

Table 3. Employment and Study One Year after Graduation among 2008 Bachelors Graduates from Universities in Italy (per cent)

	Work only	MA study + work	MA study only	Other	Job search
Geo/biology	10	13	69	3	6
Engineering	15	13	67	1	4
Architecture	21	15	51	4	10
Law	18	19	55	2	6
Psychology	10	27	58	1	3
Chemistry/pharmacology	29	9	45	4	13
Economics/statistics	23	16	51	3	8
Arts/humanities	20	19	47	4	10
Sciences	28	13	51	2	6
Foreign languages	27	15	41	5	13
Agriculture	30	15	40	4	11
Social/political sciences	33	17	34	5	12
Education science	43	18	23	4	12
Physical education	41	27	17	5	10
Medical/healthcare professions	83	2	1	2	11
Total	31	15	42	3	9

Source: AlmaLaurea-Consorzio Interuniversitario (2010a, p. 42)

The geographical location plays an important role for the employment opportunities of graduates in Italy. Prior to the Bologna reform, the transition rate to employment during the first year after graduation was more than 20 per cent lower in the Southern regions than in the Northern regions. This gap became smaller, as table 4 shows. The employment rate of Bachelor graduates residing in Northern Italy was 53 per cent (16 per cent thereby combining study and work) and 38 per cent (13 per cent) in the South. But more Bachelor graduates from the South enrol in Master programmes (62 per cent as compared to 53 per cent). A more detailed regional classification shows that the graduates from Central Italy figure between those from the North and the South in those respects.

It is interesting to note in this framework that work practice during the course of study is more common among students in Northern Italy than in the South (42 per cent and 29 per cent respectively). The difference in economic situation is also reflected in the cause stated for embarking on Master studies. 33 per cent of the

Bachelor graduates from the South stated that they transferred to Master studies for reasons of employment opportunities, as opposed to 20 per cent of graduates living in the North.

Table 4. Employment and Study One Year after Graduation among 2008 Bachelors Graduates from Universities in the North and in the South of Italy* (per cent)

	North	South	Total*
Work only	37	25	31
Work and Master study	16	13	15
Master study only	37	49	42
Not searching for employment	3	3	3
Searching for employment	7	11	9

* Graduates residing in Central Italy and abroad also included.

Source: AlmaLaurea-Consorzio Interuniversitario (2010a, p. 49)

Further study was by no means uncommon among university graduates prior to the Bologna reform. Of the 2001 graduation cohort, 64 per cent undertook some study or training a year later, but the structural reform puts further study on a more structured route and also provides more choices. 57 per cent of the 2008 Bachelor graduates in Italy reported one year later that they were enrolled in a Master programme (among them 15 per cent concurrent to work). Transition to Master study, thereby, was most frequent among graduates from 85 per cent of all psychology (82 per cent), geo-biology fields (82 per cent) and engineering (80 per cent). Not surprisingly, transition to further study was low in fields with a single-cycle structure.

Many Bachelor graduates consider the transition to a Master programme as natural. This is true of about two thirds if they transfer to a Master programme in the same field. Others see the Master as an opportunity to enhance knowledge in another field. Actually:
- 65 per cent of those having transferred to a Master programme continued their studies at the same faculty of the same university,
- 7 per cent remained in the field, but changed university,
- 20 per cent had changed faculty at the same university, and
- 7 per cent had changed both faculty and university.

Interestingly enough, Bachelor graduates who had spent time abroad in the framework of the ERASMUS programme, showed greater readiness to change university for their Master study. 31 per cent of former ERASMUS students changed university when embarking on Master study as compared to 13 per cent of new Master students who had not.

PROFESSIONAL SUCCESS OF BACHELOR GRADUATES

Job security

A substantial proportion of Bachelor graduates from universities in Italy was already employed at the time of graduation. Of those graduating in 2008 and being employed one year later, 45 per cent *kept the job they held prior to graduation*. A further 16 per cent who were employed changed job. Keeping the job held prior to graduation is a frequent feature among graduates in law (68 per cent), physical education (66 per cent), psychology (63 per cent), political-social sciences (55 per cent) and education sciences (54 per cent).

Figure 3. Employment Characteristics One Year after Graduation among 2008 Employed Bachelor Graduates from Universities in Italy, by Gender, Employment Status and Job Held Prior to Graduation (per cent)

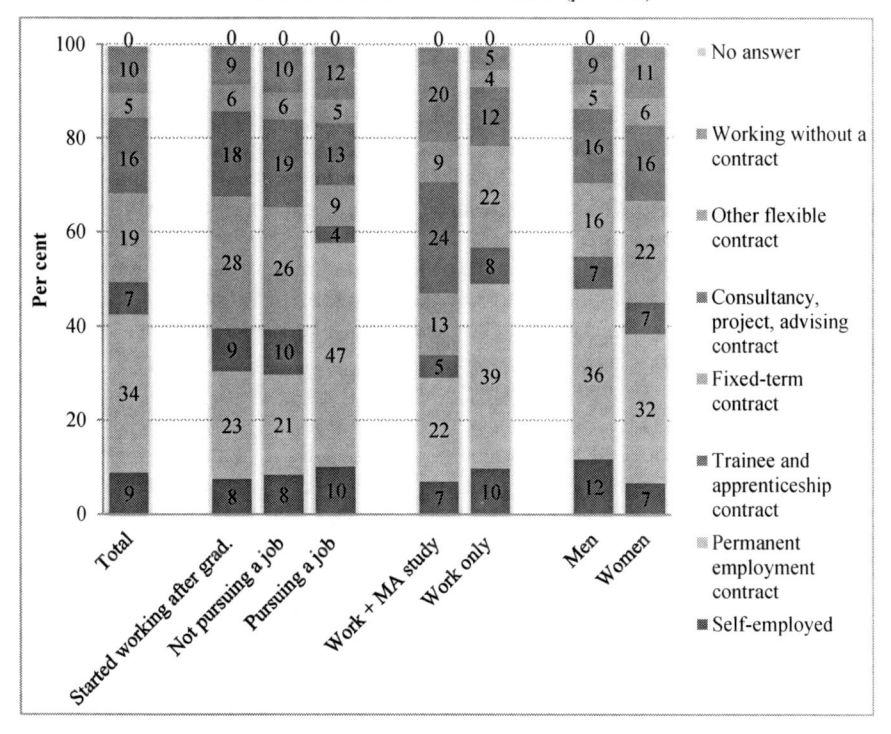

Source: AlmaLaurea-Consorzio Interuniversitario (2010a, p. 60)

In 2008, one year after graduation, 43 per cent of all employed Bachelor graduates (including those keeping the job which they held prior to graduation) had a *secure job* – defined here as either having a permanent employment contract or being self-employed. 40 per cent had a *flexible or "atypical" contract*, defined as a fixed-term contract, ad hoc or project employment, "occasionally accessory work",

157

working without contract, etc. A secure job was most frequent among graduates in medicine and health care (57 per cent) and law (56 per cent). It was also slightly above average among graduates in political-social sciences, educational sciences and economics-statistics, but only below 30 per cent in humanities, geo-biology, physical education and foreign languages.

Job security is almost twice as high among employed Bachelor graduates who already had work prior to graduation (58 per cent) as among those who start their job after graduation (30 per cent). Contract work applies to 28 per cent of the latter as compared to 9 per cent of the former and the respective figures for "collaboration contracts" are 18 per cent and 13 per cent.

Not surprisingly, a secure job is less common among employed Bachelor graduates studying concurrently (33 per cent) than among those who do not study alongside (67 per cent). For example, a quarter of the former as compared to 12 per cent of the latter is employed in the framework of a "collaboration contract".

Job security varies by *gender*, as figure 3 shows. Among women with a Bachelor degree awarded in 2008 who work in 2009, 32 per cent hold a permanent contract as compared to 36 per cent of men. 7 per cent of the women are self-employed as compared to 12 per cent of the men. In contrast, 22 per cent of women have a fixed-term compared to 16 per cent of men. Women work more often without any contract (11 per cent) than men (9 per cent). These differences can be explained to a large extent by the different composition of the fields of study and the related employment conditions.

Finally, job stability as defined above can be found more frequently in the South (50 per cent) than in the North (42 per cent). In contrast, Bachelor graduates from the North report more often "atypical" contracts and fixed-term contracts.

Graduates' earnings

The net monthly income of 2008 Bachelor graduates from Italian universities one year later was 1,020 Euros. As figure 4 shows, those who do not concurrently study earned about 60 per cent more than those studying along employment. It also shows that those who keep the job which they held prior to graduation have an above average income.

As one might expect, the income one year after graduation varies substantially by field of study. It is clearly above average for graduates in medicine and health care (1,325 Euros), law (1,111 Euros) economics-statistics (1,086 Euros) and is below 800 Euros per month) for graduates in geo-biology, humanities, physical education, psychology, foreign languages and architecture. In some but not all the latter fields we note a high percentage of graduates who were both studying and working.

Men with a Bachelor degree earn 23 per cent more than their women colleagues (1,144 Euros as compared to 927 Euros). Such differences hold true both for graduates exclusively working (1,294 Euros as compared to 1,070 Euros) and for those who are both working and studying (839 Euros as compared to 615 Euros). We also note respective gender differences by field of study. An in-depth study (AlmaLaurea-

Consorzio Interuniversitario, 2010a) taking into account the range of variables that influences gender earnings differences (especially field of study, enrolment in a Master course, pursuing the job held prior to graduation, full or part-time job) showed that, *ceteris paribus*, all men were earning more than women.

Figure 4. Net Monthly Earnings One Year after Graduation among 2008 Employed Bachelor Graduates from Universities in Italy, by Gender, Employment Status and Job Held Prior to Graduation (average Euro)

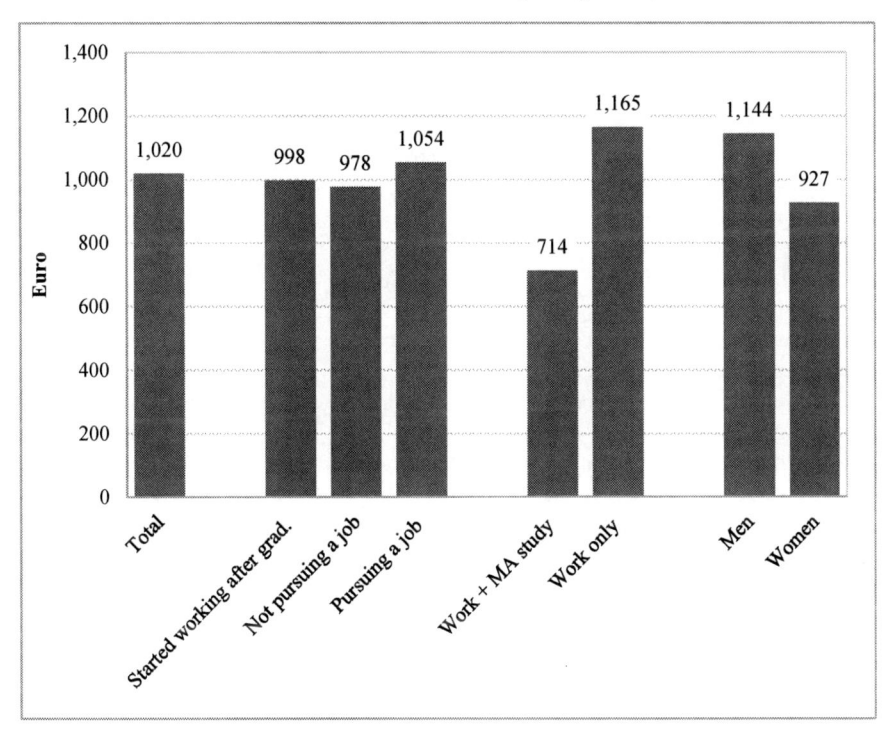

Source: AlmaLaurea-Consorzio Interuniversitario (2010a, p. 64)

The average nominal earnings for Bachelor graduates employed in Northern Italy (1,048 Euros) are only marginally higher than those of their Southern colleagues (1,006 Euros). In taking into account the respective employment situation, we note larger differences. For example, among those starting to work after graduation, those in the North earn about 10 per cent more than those in the South. By field of study, the North-South differences represent from 2 per cent in agriculture to 30 per cent in law, psychology and educational sciences.

Horizontal and vertical match between study and work

In order to measure how closely the graduates' knowledge and skills are linked to the requirements of their jobs, we devised a matching index.[14] Accordingly, the link between abilities of Bachelor graduates from universities in Italy and their work one year after graduation seems to be quite close. For 73 per cent, the "match" was at least "fairly effective". As figure 5 shows, this proportion is substantially higher for those employed and not studying (80 per cent) than for those studying alongside work (59 per cent). It is interesting to note that there is a closer link between study and work among graduates who started working after graduation (81 per cent) than among those who were employed prior to graduation and kept this job after graduation (66 per cent) – even though the former have less job security and a lower income.

In looking separately at the two major variables included in the matching index we note that 40 per cent of the employed Bachelor graduates, according to their self-ratings, make substantial use one year after graduation of the knowledge and skills acquired in the course of study. In contrast, 37 per cent noted relatively little use and about one out of five absolutely no use of the skills learned during the first-cycle course of study. Substantial use was most frequently reported by the graduates in medicine and health care (76 per cent), physical education (53 per cent) and educational science (46 per cent) and least by those in geo-biology and humanities.

The second variable refers to the formal link between credentials and access to employment. 28 per cent of the employed Bachelor graduates stated that their degree was mandatory for their job. 13 per cent considered the Bachelor degree not as formally required, but necessary. A further 37 per cent considered the degree as useful, while 22 per cent viewed it as neither necessary nor useful. As expected, the degree was seen as required most frequently in medicine and health care (82 per

---

[14] The match index combines two dimensions involved in measuring the capability of the graduate endowment of knowledge and skills to cope with job needs: the formal requirement of a specific degree in order to hold the job; the actual knowledge and skills learned while studying in a university course. Therefore, this index includes features related to both horizontal and vertical match/mismatch. We have defined five levels of matching:
- *very effective*: there is a formal or de facto requirement for graduates to hold the specific degree and they use to a large extent the knowledge and skills learned in the course of study;
- *effective*: Despite the fact that there is no formal requirement to hold a specific degree, this is nonetheless necessary or useful and graduates make use of the knowledge and skills learned in the course of study;
- *fairly effective*: Although not required, a degree is de facto necessary or useful, but graduates do not make much use of the knowledge and skills learned in the course of study;
- *not very effective*: A degree is neither required formally, nor, in any way useful, and graduates hardly ever use the knowledge and skills learned in the course of study; or a degree, although not formally required, is useful, but graduates do not make any use of the knowledge and skills learned;
- *in no way effective*: A degree is neither required formally, nor, in any way, useful and graduates make no use whatsoever of the knowledge and skills learned.

These levels are mutually exclusive, although not exhaustive, since they do not include the non-respondents or the answers that do not fit any of the levels.

MIXED OUTCOMES OF THE BOLOGNA PROCESS IN ITALY

cent). In contrast, almost half of the graduates in geo-biology and humanities considered their degree as neither required nor useful.

The degree obtained proves at least "fairly effective" slightly more frequently for men (75 per cent) than for women (72 per cent). A small difference holds true almost across all fields and also, if controlled by work along or not along study as well as new employment vs. continuation of job held prior to employment.

Figure 5. Link between Study and Work One Year after Graduation among 2008 Employed Bachelors Graduates from Universities in Italy, by Gender, Employment Status and Job Held Prior to Graduation (per cent*)

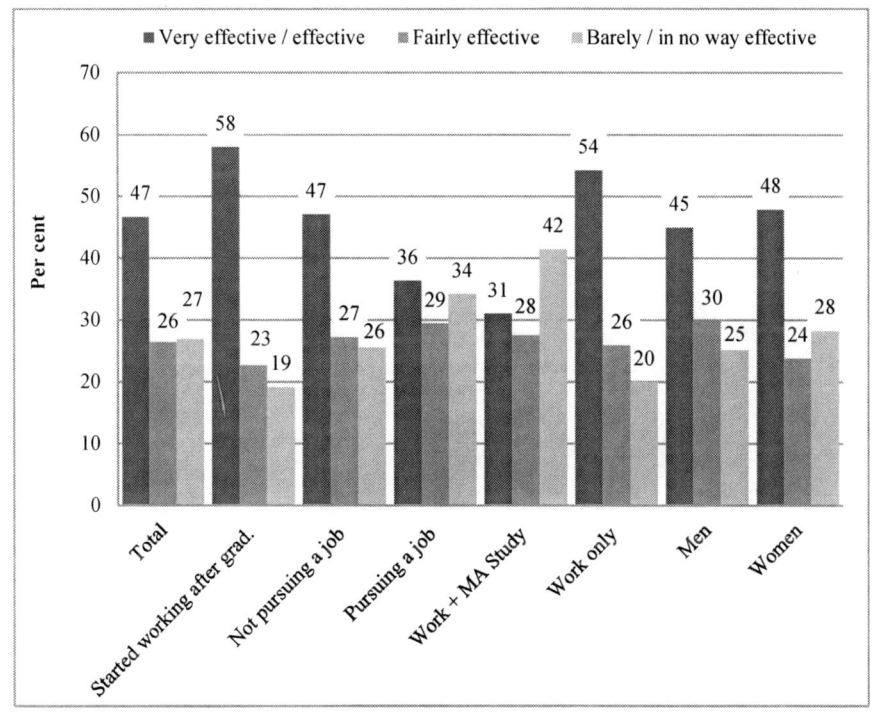

* Per cent very effective/effective and fairly effective

Source: AlmaLaurea-Consorzio Interuniversitario, Efficacia della laurea ad un anno per genere [Link between study and work one year after graduation][15]

---

[15] Retrieved February 03, 2011 from http://www.almalaurea.it/universita/occupazione/occupazione08/slides.shtml?slide=45

The professional success of newly and genuinely employed Bachelor graduates

In analysing employment and work of all Bachelor graduates employed some time after graduation, we do not indicate the full potentials of the reform of study programmes and degrees. There is a bias, because many Bachelor students were already employed prior to education and often continued their job after graduation; This is not a minor concern, since in Italy about one third of the first and second cycle graduates of the 2008 cohort was employed at the time of graduation, as compared to only 16 per cent of the single-cycle graduates. Nor should it be forgotten that the share of graduates continuing their studies after a Bachelor degree is higher than that of the second cycle graduates. Therefore, a direct comparison of the employment conditions would penalise Bachelor graduates. Hence, figures 9-11 refer only to graduates who were not employed at the time of graduation and, in the case of Bachelor graduates, only to those who were not enrolled in further study.

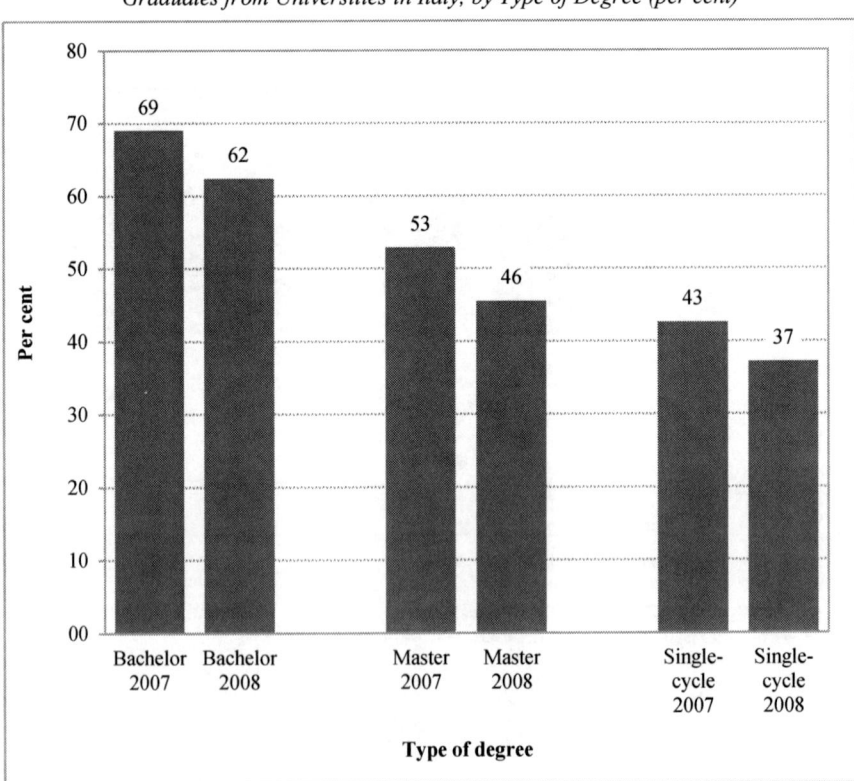

Figure 6. Rate of New Employment* One Year after Graduation among 2007 and 2008 Graduates from Universities in Italy, by Type of Degree (per cent)

Type of degree	Per cent
Bachelor 2007	69
Bachelor 2008	62
Master 2007	53
Master 2008	46
Single-cycle 2007	43
Single-cycle 2008	37

*Only graduates not employed at graduation and, in the case of Bachelor graduates, only those not enrolled in further studies

Source: AlmaLaurea-Consorzio Interuniversitario (2010a, p. 17)

The rate of employment one year after graduation of the newly and genuinely employed 2008 Bachelor graduates is 62 per cent. This is clearly higher than in the case of Master graduates (46 per cent) and single-cycle graduates (37 per cent), as figure 6 shows. The lower rate of employment for Master graduates is partly due to the fact that the survey was carried out on the first cohorts of graduates of the new system, who are by definition the best and therefore more inclined to pursue postgraduate studies.

Also the proportion of those with secure positions, defined as those permanently employed or self-employed, among the newly and genuinely employed 2008 Bachelor graduates, is relatively high. As figure 7 shows, the rate of 36 per cent is more or less as high as that for single-cycle graduates (36 per cent) and substantially higher than for Master graduates (26 per cent).

Finally, the monthly average net income of the newly and genuinely employed 2008 Bachelor graduates exceeds on average 1,050 Euros for all types of graduates and varies only to a very small extent, as figure 8 shows: 1,109 Euros for Bachelor graduates, almost the same, i.e. 1,110 Euros, for single-cycle graduates and even slightly less, i.e. 1,057 Euros, for Master graduates.

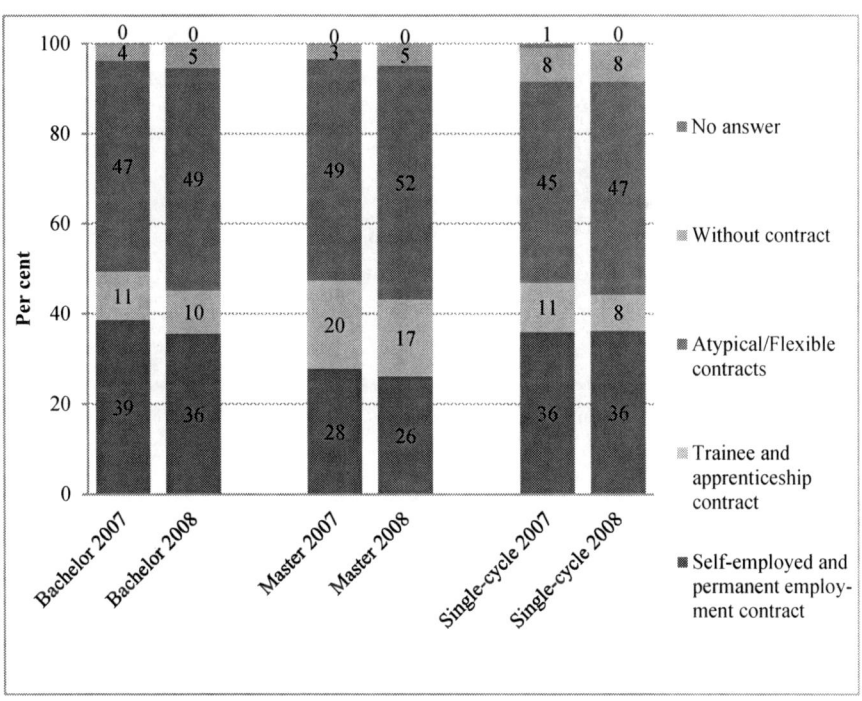

Figure 7. Employment Characteristics One Year after Graduation among 2007 and 2008 Bachelor Graduates from Universities in Italy, by Type of Degree (per cent*)

*Only graduates not employed at graduation and, in the case of Bachelor graduates, only those not enrolled in further studies.

Source: AlmaLaurea-Consorzio Interuniversitario (2010a, p. 20)

Differences in professional success between 2007 and 2008 graduates

A comparison of the data obtained for the 2007 and 2008 cohort of graduates, all interviewed one year after graduation, clearly shows an impact of the specific labour market conditions at a certain moment of observation. From this comparison the impact of the global crisis on the employment situation of the 2008 graduates clearly emerges.

Comparing the 2008 cohort with the 2007 one, all types of graduates show a slowdown in their capacity to be absorbed by the demand for labour (see figure 6). Among the Bachelor graduates, the rate of employment dropped by almost seven per cent (62 per cent as compared to 69 per cent) and similarly among the Master graduates (46 per cent as compared to 53 per cent), while among the single-cycle graduates it was 5 per cent (37 per cent as compared to 43 per cent).

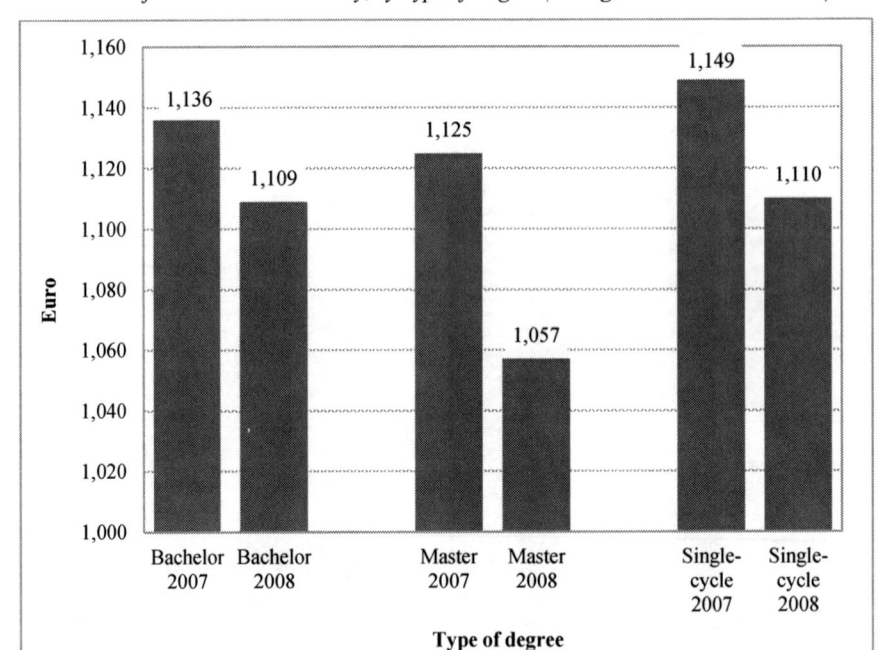

Figure 8. Net Monthly Earnings One Year after Graduation among 2007 and 2008 Bachelors Graduates from Universities in Italy, by Type of Degree (average at 2009 Prices in Euro)*

Type of degree	Euro
Bachelor 2007	1,136
Bachelor 2008	1,109
Master 2007	1,125
Master 2008	1,057
Single-cycle 2007	1,149
Single-cycle 2008	1,110

*Only graduates not employed at graduation and, in the case of Bachelor graduates, only those not enrolled in further studies.

Source: AlmaLaurea – Consorzio Interuniversitario, Guadagno mensile netto ad un anno [Net monthly earnings after one year][16]

---

[16] Retrieved February 03, 2011 from www.almalaurea.it/universita/occupazione/occupazione08/slides.shtml?slide=9

Job security dropped slightly as well, as figure 7 shows. However, the differences are small for Bachelor graduates and Master graduates, while job security remained on the same level for single-cycle graduates. Finally, the net monthly earnings decreased slightly, when calculated on the basis of 2009 figures. As figure 8 shows, the decrease was two per cent on average for Bachelor graduates, three per cent for single-cycle graduates, six per cent for Master graduates and 3 per cent for single-cycle graduates.

CONCLUSION

According to many commentators, within and outside the academic world, the "3+2" reform in Italy has been a failure or even a disaster. Furthermore, the attitude towards the Bologna Process is not always positive in Europe, especially in some fields of study. The surveys carried out by the AL Consortium do not confirm such a negative conclusion for Italy. Rather, there is a mixed outcome of positive and negative features in which variety is overriding.

First, we should observe that the empirical evidence and the database used in this public debate have been usually rather poor. The habit has prevailed to project personal experiences and opinions at a very general level. As a consequence, there is great scope for improvement and the AL data-base is ready for this.

The aim of the AlmaLaurea surveys is not to support the opposing views in such a debate. Instead its task is to favour a convincing assessment of the empirical outcomes of the reform. After all, AL cornerstones are the idea that, as Luigi Einaudi maintained, in order to govern you need to know, and that, as Galileo Galilei put it, in order to know, you need "to measure what is measurable, and to make measurable what it is not yet measured". In this spirit, AL gathers the appropriate information, disseminates statistics, offers services and issues reports and papers that are useful in national and international debates.

Using the available documentation we can say for certain that, at about ten years from the take-off of the Bologna reform, the Italian system of higher education has achieved the following positive results:
(i) the number of graduates has increased;
(ii) the age at graduation has decreased considerably and a higher share of students graduate in the required period or in a somewhat longer period;
(iii) class attendance has improved;
(iv) the interactions with the business world have improved, enhancing internship experiences;
(v) the European targets as regards study abroad are almost met, at least for Master programmes;
(vi) the number of graduates (especially Bachelors) coming from households in which there was no graduate has increased, and there is no proof that their performances are weakening;
(vii) the impact of social class is still relevant, but evidence points to the progressive inclusion of graduates from less privileged backgrounds;
(viii) Bachelors' earnings do not seem to have declined despite the increase in their supply.

This means that the outcomes of the reform have been more positive than most commentators think. At the same time, there is room for further improvement of the overall performance of the higher education system which continues to be unsatisfactory, due to poor budgets. This means that the human resources engaged in higher education provision are valuable and that their efforts should be better assessed and provided with the appropriate incentives.

However, among the several persisting flaws that characterise the Italian system of higher education, despite the improvements obtained with the reform, we must stress the following:
(a) a high dropout rate, especially in the first twelve months after enrolment;
(b) a poor performance in reducing the age of graduation and the time to graduate;
(c) a rigidity of the overall syllabus organisation and coursework recognition;
(d) the lack of a comprehensive "open" university system, offering education both to adults and working students;
(e) little geographical mobility for study reasons;
(f) a still low international openness of the system;
(g) ambivalent motives to engage in further studies.

An additional flaw that is not strictly speaking attributable to the higher education system is the low level of earnings, in general and specifically for highly qualified human resources. This is linked to the production structure of the country and its sectoral and territorial organisation. To give evidence of this, while the demand for highly qualified labour in Italy is predicted at 12 per cent for graduate manpower in Italian firms (see Unioncamere-Ministero del Lavoro, 2009), the corresponding figure in the United States is estimated to be 31 per cent (see US Department of Labor, 2009).

More controversial is the issue concerning the relevance of mismatch and over-education. In this respect, AL is carrying out studies which combine supply-side and demand-side analyses in conjunction with other databases available for Italy. The results are referred to above. A study has been carried out estimating a regression model in which the dependent variable is the opinion of the graduates about the on-the-job use of the skills learned while studying in a university course (see Camillo, 2010): a dichotomic variable whose modalities correspond to a higher or lower use in comparison with pre-reform graduates. The independent variables are: gender; pre or post-reform degree; age at graduation; graduation mark; delay in graduating; social class. This analysis seems to show a lower probability of Bachelor graduates being satisfied with their on-the-job use of the skills acquired at university, as compared with the pre-reform graduates.

However, we must emphasise once again that this study refers only to the graduates' situation one year after graduation, and this limits the understanding of an intrinsically long-term phenomenon. Moreover, we should take into consideration the scale effect when we speak about mismatch and over-education. The very low share of graduates in the employed labour force in Italy makes this case not easily comparable with more developed countries.

Further investigation must be undertaken to improve the methodology of the study. However there are two likely interpretations. In a *wage-competition* framework (see Antonelli & Guidetti, 2008), the mismatch increases in the transition from the pre to the post-reform setting. Even a privileged social class origin does not seem to close the gap and work experience seems to foster criticism. The natural interpretation, therefore, is: In the post-reform courses, a redefinition of contents has taken place which tends to reduce the perceived usefulness of the learned skills and excessively raise the Bachelors' expectations. In a *job-competition* framework, in which part of the mismatch is physiological and firms actively contribute to lowering it, an increase of the mismatch (measured as lower satisfaction in the use of own skills) in the transition from the pre to the post-reform setting, is to some extent natural, due to the mandatory reduction of the duration of study determined by the reform. Moreover, it can be at least partly explained as the result of the transfer to firms of higher educational requirements. Incidentally, the job-competition framework can better explain the absence of a price adjustment for the Bachelors while their supply is increasing. The more appropriate assessment of the reform process and which of the two interpretations is more convincing need to be further explored. However, all the authorities involved in the management of the higher education system should take into consideration the risk that a whole generation of young graduates, including the best equipped, can be trapped, especially in the midst of a global economic crisis, between a production system which is not able to recruit them and a research system that lacks resources.

Taking into consideration the entire decade, we have observed a first phase characterised by an increase in first-year enrolments, followed by a second phase of decline. In both phases expenditure did not match the needs of a quality-driven system. In the same period, the employment conditions of all pre-reform and post-reform graduates have worsened, and the economic cycle seems to have brought about serious shocks for all types of graduates in Italy.

These are the graduate cohorts which form the fundamental resource for any country. But this is especially true for Italy, due to the rapid ageing of the population and the scarcity of youths, both in absolute terms and in terms of highly qualified manpower. This is why we consider as highly beneficial the adoption by the Council of European Union of the new decennial strategy "Europe 2020", and the goal to improve education levels, in particular by aiming to reduce school drop-out rates to less than 10 per cent and by increasing to at least 40 per cent the share of 30-34-year-olds having completed tertiary or equivalent education.

Finally, we would like to stress the need for comparative studies that help in developing both methods and empirical evidence on the production processes in higher education and on the functioning of graduates' labour markets. And, in our view, the Euro-Mediterranean area is particularly significant in this respect.

REFERENCES

AlmaLaurea-Consorzio Interuniversitario (Ed.) (2005). *La qualità del capitale umano dell'università in Europa e in Italia* [The Universities' human capital quality in Europe and Italy]. Bologna: Il Mulino. Retrieved September 17, 2010, from www.almalaurea.it/universita/profilo/profilo2003/

AlmaLaurea-Consorzio Interuniversitario (Ed.) (2006a). *VIII Rapporto sulla condizione occupazionale dei laureati. I laureati di primo livello alla prova del lavoro* [8th AlmaLaurea survey on Italian graduates' employment conditions. The Bachelors graduates at the at proof of labor]. Bologna: Il Mulino.

AlmaLaurea-Consorzio Interuniversitario (Ed.) (2006b). *VIII Profilo dei laureati italiani. I primi figli della riforma* [8th AlmaLaurea survey on Graduate's profile. The first sons of the reform]. Bologna: Il Mulino.

AlmaLaurea-Consorzio Interuniversitario (Ed.) (2008a). *X Rapporto sulla condizione occupazionale dei laureati. Formazione universitaria ed esigenze del mercato del lavoro* [10th AlmaLaurea survey on Italian graduates' employment conditions. University and training and labour market requirements]. Bologna: Il Mulino.

AlmaLaurea-Consorzio Interuniversitario (Ed.) (2008b). *IX Profilo dei laureati italiani. La riforma allo specchio* [9th AlmaLaurea survey on graduates' profile. The reform at the mirror]. Bologna: Il Mulino.

AlmaLaurea-Consorzio Interuniversitario (Ed.) (2009a). *XI Rapporto sulla condizione occupazionale dei laureati italiani. Occupazione e occupabilità dei laureati. A dieci anni dalla Dichiarazione di Bologna* [11th AlmaLaurea survey on Italian graduates' employment conditions. Ten years after the Bologna Declaration]. Bologna: Il Mulino.

AlmaLaurea-Consorzio Interuniversitario (Ed.) (2009b). *XI Profilo dei laureati italiani. Valutazione dei percorsi formativi nell'università a dieci anni dalla Dichiarazione di Bologna* [11th AlmaLaurea survey on graduate's profile. Assessment of academic training pathways a decade after the Declaration of Bologna]. Bologna: Il Mulino.

AlmaLaurea-Consorzio Interuniversitario (Ed.) (2010a). *XII Rapporto sulla condizione occupazionale dei laureati. Investimenti in capitale umano nel futuro di Italia ed Europa* [12th AlmaLaurea survey on Italian graduates' employment conditions. Investing in human capital: The Italian and European future]. Bologna: AlmaLaurea.

AlmaLaurea-Consorzio Interuniversitario (Ed.) (2010b). *XII Profilo dei laureati. L'istruzione universitaria nell'ultimo decennio. All'esordio della European Higher Education Area* [12th AlmaLaurea survey on graduate's profile. Academic education over the last decade. The opening of the European higher education area]. Bologna: AlmaLaurea.

AlmaLaurea-Consorzio Interuniversitario & Osservatorio Statistico dell'Università di Bologna (2008). *L'Università, la sua capacità formativa e le sue infrastrutture nella valutazione di 12 generazioni di laureati dell'Alma Mater* [The university, its education capacities and its structures assessed by 12 generations of Alma Mater graduates]. Bologna: AlmaLaurea. Retrieved September 17, 2010, from http://www.almalaurea.it/universita/altro/12generazioni2008/giudizi_bologna_1996-2007.pdf

Antonelli, G. (1987). Human resources and labour incomes. Demand for education, labour supply and comparisons between private and public sector. *Labour, 1*, 153-190.

Antonelli, G., di Francia, A. & Guidetti, G. (2006). Domanda ed offerta di laureati: Una interazione complessa [Graduates demand and supply: a complex interaction]. In AlmaLaurea-Consorzio Interuniversitario (Ed.), *VIII Rapporto sulla condizione occupazionale dei laureati. I laureati di primo livello alla prova del lavoro* (183-206). Bologna: Il Mulino.

Antonelli, G., Ferioli, E., Gerussi, E. & Kozovska, K. (2010). *The Bologna Process and internationalization: General and specific trends* (Background Paper). Bologna: University of Bologna, Faculty of Law.

Antonelli, G. & Guidetti, G. (2008). *Economia del lavoro e delle risorse umane* [Labour and human resources economics]. Novara: UTET Università.

Bagues, M.F. & Sylos Labini, M. (2009). Do online labor market intermediaries matter? The impact of AlmaLaurea on the university-to-work transition. In D.H. Autor (Ed.), *Studies of Labor Market Intermediation* (127-154). Chicago: University of Chicago Press.

Brandi, M.C. & Segnana, M.L. (2008). Lavorare all'estero: Fuga o investimento [Working abroad: escape or investment]? In AlmaLaurea-Consorzio Interuniversitario (Ed), *X Rapporto sulla condizione occupazionale dei laureati. Formazione universitaria ed esigenze del mercato del lavoro* (205-224). Bologna: Il Mulino.

Camillo, F. (2010). Measurement and models for the evaluation of some outcomes of Italian universities in the reform period: Delay at graduation, income, employment (Report prepared for the Giovanni Agnelli Foundation). Bologna: AlmaLaurea.

Cammelli, A. (2005). La qualità del capitale umano dell'università. Caratteristiche e performances dei laureati 2003 [The universities' human capital quality. Features and performances]. In AlmaLaurea-Consorzio Interuniversitario (Ed.), *La qualità del capitale umano dell'università in Europa e in Italia* (9-32). Bologna: Il Mulino.

Cammelli, A. (2006a). *Laureati in Giurisprudenza: L'organizzazione degli studi e gli sbocchi professionali in Italia* [Graduates in law: Study organization and professional outcomes in Italy]. Retrieved September 17, 2010, from http://www.almalaurea.it/universita/altro/giurisprudenza2006/giurisprudenza2006.pdf

Cammelli, A. (2006b). La riforma alla prova dei fatti [The reform at the proof of the facts]. In AlmaLaurea-Consorzio Interuniversitario (Ed.), *VIII Profilo dei laureati italiani. I primi figli della riforma* (17-33). Bologna: Il Mulino.

Cammelli, A. (2008). Il X Rapporto sulla condizione occupazionale dei laureati [The 10th AlmaLaurea survey on Italian graduates' employment conditions]. In AlmaLaurea-Consorzio Interuniversitario (Ed.), *X Rapporto sulla condizione occupazionale dei laureati. Formazione universitaria ed esigenze del mercato del lavoro* (19-89). Bologna: Il Mulino.

Cammelli, A. (2009a). *Università e ricerca: Numeri e spunti di riflessione* [University and research: Figures and food for thought]. Paper prepared for the Conference "Università e ricerca", Società italiana per il progresso delle scienze, Accademia nazionale dei Lincei, Roma, 6 May.

Cammelli, A. (2009b). XI Rapporto sulla condizione occupazionale dei laureati [The 11th AlmaLaurea survey on Italian graduates' employment conditions]. In AlmaLaurea-Consorzio Interuniversitario (Ed.), *XI Rapporto sulla condizione occupazionale dei laureati italiani. Occupazione e occupabilità dei laureati. A dieci anni dalla Dichiarazione di Bologna* (22-54). Bologna: Il Mulino.

Cammelli, A. (2009c). Le caratteristiche del capitale umano dell'università: Prima e dopo la riforma [The university's human capital: Before and after the reform]. In AlmaLaurea-Consorzio Interuniversitario (Ed.), *XI Profilo dei laureati italiani. Valutazione dei percorsi formativi nell'università a dieci anni dalla Dichiarazione di Bologna* (15-37). Bologna: Il Mulino.

Cammelli, A., di Francia, A. & Guerriero, G. (1997). Le déclin des entrées à l'université italienne d'ici 2008 [The decline of the Italian university admissions from now to 2008]. *Population, 52*, 365-380.

Cristofori, D. (2008). *L'esperienza universitaria: Giovani e adulti a confronto* [The higher education experience: Comparing youngsters and adults]. Retrieved September 17, 2010, from http://www.almalaurea.it/universita/altro/adulti/adulti2008.pdf

Gasperoni, G. (2010). *Reform of the university educational systems and evolution of some characteristics of Italian graduates (2000-2009)*. Report prepared for the Giovanni Agnelli Foundation.

Istituto nazionale di statistica (2003). *Classificazione dei titoli di studio italiani* [Classification of Italian qualifications]. Roma: Istat. Retrieved September 20, 2010, from http://www.istat.it/strumenti/definizioni/titoli_di_studio/

Istituto nazionale di statistica (2009). *Università e lavoro. Orientarsi con la statistica* [University and labour. Orientation at the statistic]. Roma: Istat. Retrieved September 20 2010, from http://www.istat.it/lavoro/unilav/unilav_2009.pdf

Organisation for Economic Co-operation and Development (2010). *Factbook 2010: Economic, environmental and social statistics*. Paris: OECD.

Roversi Monaco, F. (2008). Premessa [Foreword]. In AlmaLaurea-Consorzio Interuniversitario (Ed.), *IX Profilo dei laureati italiani. La riforma allo specchio* (19-20). Bologna: Il Mulino.

Unioncamere-Ministero del Lavoro (2009). *Progetto Excelsior. I fabbisogni occupazionali delle imprese italiane nell'industria e nei servizi per il 2009* [Excelsior Project: The employees needs of Italian industry and services for the year 2009]. Roma: Ufficio Studi Unioncamere.

US Department of Labor (2009). *Employment projections: 2008-2018.* Washington, DC: US Department of Labor.

JIM ALLEN AND JOHAN COENEN

EMPLOYABILITY AND MOBILITY OF BACHELOR GRADUATES IN THE NETHERLANDS

INTRODUCTION

In this paper, we provide a brief sketch of some relevant features of new study programmes introduced in the Netherlands in accordance with the Bologna Process, as reported by graduates of those programmes in the annual surveys that have been held since the early 1990s in the *HBO-Monitor* and WO-Monitor. We focus on the situation of graduates of Bachelor and Master programmes. There are several comparisons that are of interest when looking at these programmes, the explanation of which requires a brief digression in order to describe some salient features of the Dutch higher education system before and after the implementation of the Bologna Process.

The key feature of Dutch higher education is its differentiation between HBO (higher professional education, taught at universities of applied sciences *(hogescholen)*) and WO *(wetenschappelijk onderwijs*, academic or scientific education, taught at research universities *(universiteiten)*. Before the implementation of the Bologna model of a system of study programmes and degrees, most programmes in both HBO and WO required four years of study, with a degree at an HBO institution *(HBO-diploma)* usually equated with a Bacherlor level and a degree at a WO institution *(doctoraal* – not to be confused with the *doctoraat,* which is equivalent to a PhD*)* usually equated with a Master level. The reason for the difference in level between HBO and WO is due to the difference in entry requirements, with WO programmes requiring pre-university secondary education *(VWO)* or its equivalent (12 years of schooling), and HBO programmes requiring senior general secondary education (HAVO) (11 years of schooling). Moreover, most HBO programmes comprise up to one year of practical work experience.

With the implementation of the Bologna two-stage model, HBO programmes have more or less been directly converted into Bachelor programmes. The main consequence for students is that after completing a HBO Bachelor degree, they are entitled to apply for a Master programme at a university. In order to do so, they may sometimes have to follow one year of pre-Master education if the gap between the HBO Bachelor qualification and the requirements of the WO Master programme is seen as too great for a direct transition.

The Bologna Process has more far-reaching consequences for WO institutions. Prior to its implementation, most studies consisted in a *"propedeuse"* in the first year followed by the three-year *"doctoraal"* phase. Although separate degrees were awarded for both the *"propedeuse"* and the *"doctoraal",* in practice, they formed two parts of a single four-year programme for almost all students. With the implementation of the new model, this has been replaced by a three-year Bachelor programme followed by a Master programme that may take one, two or even three

H. Schomburg and U. Teichler (eds.), Employability and Mobility of Bachelor Graduates in Europe, 171–183.
© 2011 *Sense Publishers. All rights reserved.*

years. In the new regime, many students still regard the Bachelor as the first phase towards their Master degree in the same field and at the same institution, but the distinction is real and has real consequences. The main consequence is that entry to the Master programmes is, in principle, open to Bachelors from other programmes and from other higher education institutions (including HBO institutions). Of course, there are strong restrictions as to which Bachelors are allowed entry into which Masters programmes and in which conditions (see for example the remark above concerning pre-Master programmes), but there is scope for mobility between the Bachelor and Master, and even from a WO-Bachelor programme to the labour market, although this is still relatively unusual. A Master degree is an entry requirement for a PhD.

Taking these changes into account, the comparisons of interest in this paper are between the traditional programmes before the implementation of the Bologna Process – the *HBO-diploma* and the *doctoraal* degree awarded by WO-institutions – and the three Bologna-model degrees – the HBO-Bachelor, the WO-Bachelor and the WO-Master. As far as possible, we will provide comparisons between these five degree types.

Two final points need to be made which will influence the comparison. The first is that, because higher education institutions have been gradually replacing pre-Bologna by post-Bologna programmes over the last ten years or so, with post-Bologna graduates only appearing since the graduate surveys conducted in 2004 (reflecting graduates of the academic year 2002-2003), any information on pre-Bologna graduates will necessarily reflect an earlier point in time than comparable information on post-Bologna graduates. This may bias some information, particularly on the position of graduates in the labour market, because the economy improved considerably in the years 2003-2007 (although there has been a slight downturn again since then). As a result, the labour market position of the post-Bologna programmes may show a slight upward bias.

The second point, which is related to the first, is that the introduction of Bologna-style programmes has taken place earlier in some fields of study than in others. Figures 1 to 3 illustrates this. Figure 1 shows the percentage of HBO graduates surveyed in 2003 to 2008 (reflecting academic years 2002/03 to 2006/07) who obtained a Bachelor degree by area of study. It is clear that programmes in agriculture were relatively early in implementing the Bologna Process and that the same applies to around half the arts programmes.[1] The implementation was slowest in the broad field of education, where around one in six graduates approached in 2008 still obtained pre-Bologna qualifications. This means that the former two fields are somewhat over-represented in Bologna-model programmes and under-represented in pre-Bologna programmes, while the opposite will be true of the latter programmes. Because agriculture and arts generally show the worst results in terms of labour market outcomes, this may give a downward bias to the results for pre-

---

[1] The drop in the percentage of Arts-Bachelors between 2004 and 2005 is due to a temporary surge in the number of graduates of "old-style" arts programmes.

Bologna programmes (perhaps somewhat counterbalancing the upward bias described above).

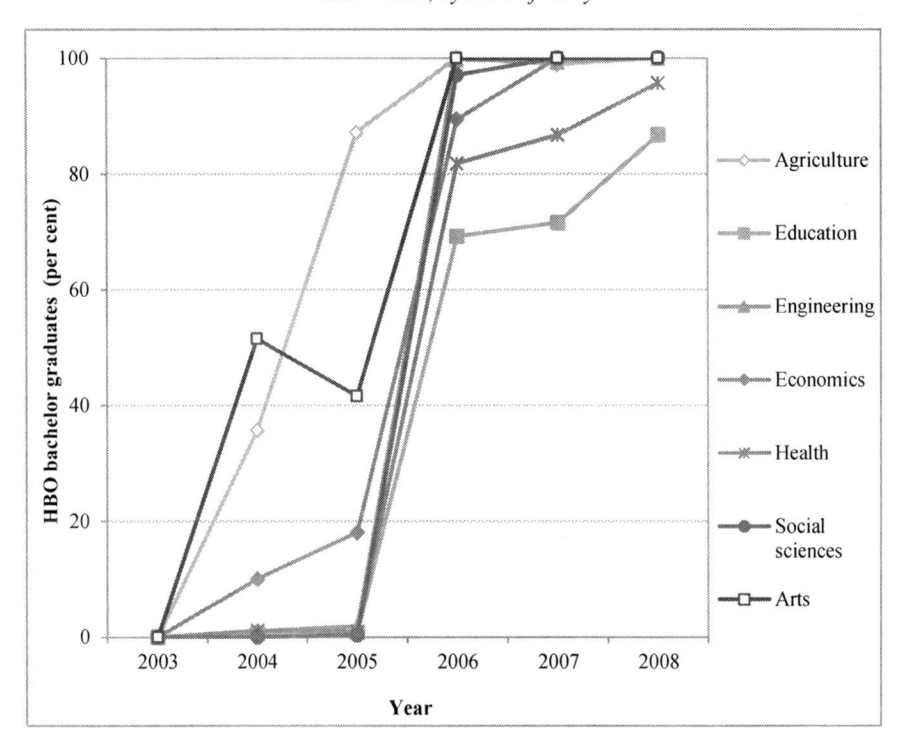

Figure 1. Graduates from HBO Bachelor Programmes in the Netherlands 2003 – 2008, by Area of Study

Source: Dutch graduate surveys 2003-2008

The situation is again a little more complicated for WO-programmes than for HBO programmes. The introduction of Bologna-model programmes resulted in a change in the population definition for the WO-Monitor. The population now not only includes WO-Masters (who are more or less equivalent to old-style WO *doctoraal* degree holders), but also some WO-Bachelors. It was decided to approach only those WO-Bachelors who left higher education (at least for the time being) after completing their Bachelor degree. WO-Bachelors who remained in higher education (either at the same or in a different institution) were not asked to participate in what is essentially a labour market monitor for graduates. Figure 2 shows the share of university Masters programmes each year among all university graduates per broad field of study.

It is obvious that Bachelor programmes form a small part of the study programmes at university level. Further interpretation of figure 2 is complicated by the fact that not only does the timing of the introduction of university Bachelor programmes differ by field of study, but also their number will also differ once the Bologna-model has been fully implemented. We can see that there are very few Bachelor programmes in the field of health studies, whereas they are quite common in economics, arts, natural sciences and especially engineering. In engineering, the implementation was relatively late but very rapid, rising from 1 per cent in 2006 to 16 per cent in 2007. It remains to be seen whether the percentage will stabilise at this level. In most other fields, the introduction was spread over a longer period. Since the fields that introduced Bachelors programmes early and/or have a high number of university Bachelors are somewhat of a mix that have a rather good labour market position, it is not clear whether this will result in any systematic bias in the results.

Figure 2. Graduates from University Bachelor Programmes in the Netherlands 2003 – 2007, by Area of Study

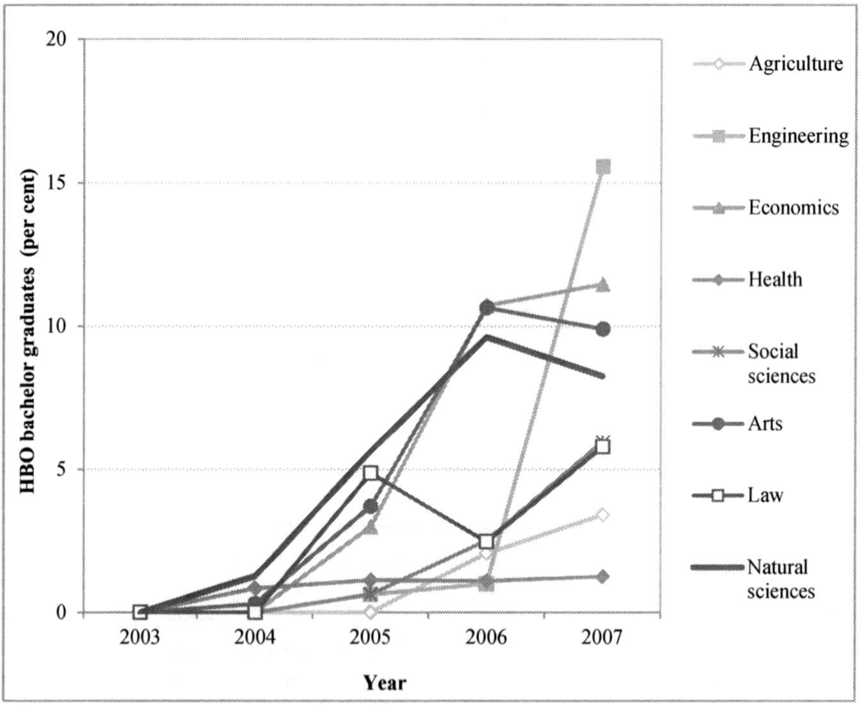

Source: Dutch graduate surveys 2003-2007

Figure 3 shows the timing of the introduction of Master programmes at university level. Again, those in engineering were introduced quite abruptly, rising from almost none in 2004 to around 50 per cent in 2005. Despite this, the implementation of Bologna-model programmes is not yet complete in this field, as is evidenced by the fact that, in 2007, the total share accounted for by Bachelors (16 per cent) and

EMPLOYABILITY AND MOBILITY OF BACHELOR GRADUATES IN THE NETHERLANDS

Masters (55 per cent) is just over 70 per cent, leaving almost 30 per cent of pre-Bologna programmes that will be phased out in the next few years. As was the case with Bachelor programmes, the introduction of Master programmes in most other fields has been much more gradual and the timing differs quite substantially per field of study. Again, the fields in which the highest number of Bologna-model programmes has been introduced to date are something of a mix, with rather good labour market outcomes (engineering) and programmes that have a less favourable outlook (agriculture). Hence, it is not clear whether this will lead to any systematic bias.

Figure 3. Graduates from University Master Programmes in the Netherlands 2003 – 2007, by Area of Study

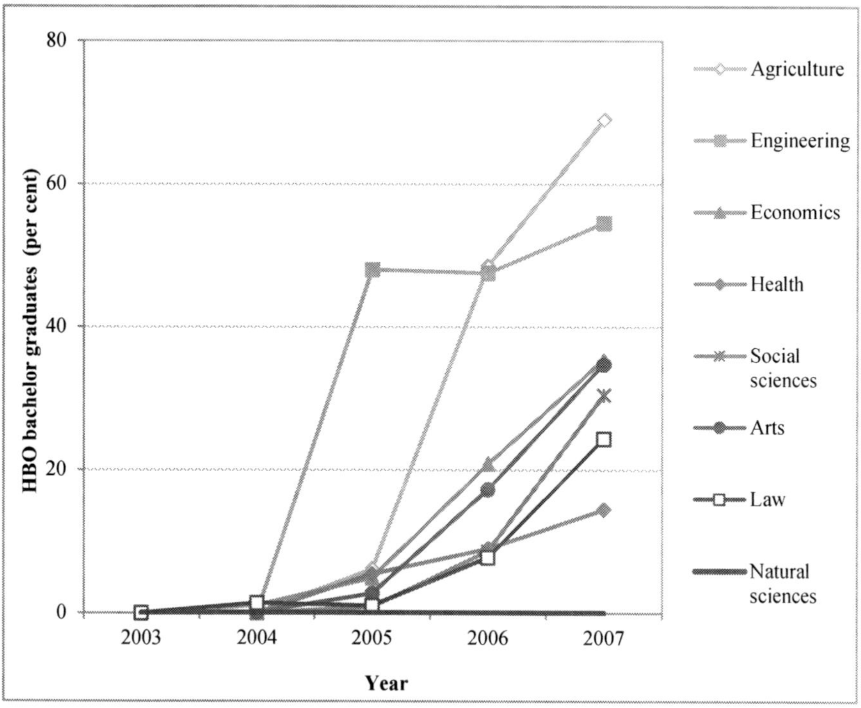

Source: Dutch graduate surveys 2003-2008

JIM ALLEN AND JOHAN COENEN

SOCIO-BIOGRAPHIC BACKGROUND AND COURSE OF STUDY

Table 1 presents some key socio-biographic information on graduates from Dutch higher education institutions. It should be noted that all information in table 1 and subsequent tables is derived from the annual surveys of higher education graduates in the Netherlands conducted by the Research Centre for Education and the Labour Market (ROA) of the University of Maastricht. In these surveys, graduates of a given academic year (extending from the start of September to the end of August the following year) were approached in the autumn of the following year. For example, graduates who completed their degree in academic year 2006/07 were approached in the autumn of 2008, i.e. one to two years after graduation, depending on the exact time of graduation and of completion of the questionnaire. The information contained in the tables is based on the five combined cohorts from 2002/03 to 2006/07 (surveyed from 2004 to 2008).

Although women are now somewhat overrepresented in higher education, there are differences between the types of programmes. The highest share is found in former HBO (pre-Bologna) programmes and the lowest in university Bachelor programmes. These results are probably influenced by the differences by field of study, as described in Section 1, with strongly "female" fields such as HBO education, health and social sciences being slow to implement HBO Bachelor programmes, while the strongly "male" fields of engineering and economics have introduced the most university Bachelor programmes.

Table 1. Socio-biographic Background of 2002/03-2006/07 Graduates from Higher Education Institutions in the Netherlands (per cent)

	HBO Trad. model	HBO Bachelor	University Trad. model	University Bachelor	Master	Total
Gender (per cent female graduates)	60	55	56	47	54	56
A-typical entry qualification	49	49	24	22	*	42
Prior degree or HE certification	12	8	26	26	*	16
Total years of study in HE (mean)	44	46	66	60	*	50
Age at time of graduation (mean)	28	27	28	28	27	28

* No reliable data available for university Masters

Source: Dutch graduate surveys 2003-2008

Table 1 also shows the share of atypical entry qualifications, i.e. the number of graduates entering higher education with a qualification that is different from that normally required for the type of higher education concerned. It must be pointed out that "typical" qualifications, and thus also "atypical" qualifications, are defined differently according to types of higher education institutions/programmes. For HBO programmes (both the old and the new model), the "typical" entry qualification is a diploma in senior general secondary education *(HAVO)*, and "atypical" qualifications are either pre-university secondary education *(VWO)* or senior vocational secondary education *(MBO)*. For university programmes (both old style and Bachelor programmes), the "typical" entry qualification is pre-university secondary education *(VWO)*, and "atypical" entry can be either senior via general *or* vocational secondary education *(HAVO or MBO)*, or a prior HBO degree.[2] "Typical" entry to a university Master programme is based on a Bachelor, either at HBO or university level. No reliable information is available.. Although atypical entry qualifications are more common for HBO graduates than for university graduates, there is little difference between old model and Bachelor programmes at either level.

Not surprisingly, university graduates are more likely than HBO graduates to have obtained a prior degree in higher education. As was pointed out above, a HBO qualification is one of the "atypical" – but far from unusual – routes into a university programme. There is hardly any difference between the old and the Bachelor programmes at university level. Among HBO graduates, "those who completed old-model programmes are somewhat more likely to have had prior higher education experience than those who completed a HBO Bachelor degree programme".

Although the nominal duration of HBO programmes and old university programmes is usually four years, the actual study duration is substantially shorter for HBO graduates than for university graduates. Whereas HBO graduates complete their studies in less than the nominal duration on average, old-model university graduates take around five-and-a-half years on average to complete their degree. This is partly due to the fact that some university programmes have a nominal duration of five or even six years – notably medical degrees and many engineering programmes -, but university graduates of four year programmes are also more likely to exceed their nominal duration than HBO graduates. As we might expect, university Bachelor programmes, which usually have a nominal duration of three years, show a shorter mean duration. However, the difference between university Bachelor graduates and university graduates of the old model is smaller than we might expect on the basis of nominal duration. We also see that HBO Bachelor graduates have taken slightly longer on average to complete their degrees than HBO graduates of the old system. It could be that some of these differences are due to differences in composition by field of study.

Somewhat surprisingly, there is little or no difference in mean age between HBO and university graduates. We would expect HBO graduates to be younger, since they start at a younger age and normally take less time to complete their programme. On closer inspection, it appears that they are more likely to have completed their programme in part-time study than university graduates. Graduates of full-time university programmes are around two years older on average than those of full-time HBO programmes (27 versus 25). Similarly, the difference between pre-Bologna and Bologna-model programmes at both HBOs and universities is due to the higher share of part-timers among pre-Bologna model graduates.

---

[2] Entry to HBO based on a prior HBO or university degree and entry to university programmes based on a prior university degree are not included here, since this is clearly not initial entry to higher education. This is covered by the percentage of graduates with prior HE qualifications indicator in table 1.

INTERNATIONAL MOBILITY

Table 2 provides information on international mobility prior, during and after the higher education course of study. The number of foreign graduates (defined as graduates born outside the Netherlands) and of graduates who lived abroad at the age of 16 is clearly higher for Bologna-model programmes than for old-model programmes – with the exception of university Bachelor graduates, who were only slightly more likely to have been born abroad than those of the old-model university programmes, and slightly less likely to have lived abroad at the age of 16. The latter finding gives the best indication of study mobility into Dutch higher education, since many of the graduates who were born abroad arrived in the Netherlands at a young age where they attended much or all of their education prior to entering higher education. Most of those who lived abroad at age 16 are likely to have come to the Netherlands to attend higher education.

Temporary mobility during the course of study – mostly periods abroad for study or work as part of the study programmes – is considerably more common among university graduates than among HBO graduates. University graduates of the old model are likely to have spent time abroad as part of their programme. In contrast, HBO Bachelor graduates are more likely than HBO graduates of the old model to have spent time abroad during their studies. It is not immediately clear whether these differences reflect a real shift or are a product of compositional differences.

Table 2. International Mobility of Persons Having Graduated in 2002/03-2006/07 from Higher Education Institutions in the Netherlands (per cent)

	HBO Trad. model	HBO Bachelor	University Trad. model	University Bachelor	University Master	Total
Foreign graduates	5	9	7	8	12	7
Lived abroad at age 16	2	4	4	4	10	5
Temporarily mobile during the course of study	16	21	35	28	28	23
Employed abroad	2	3	4	5	7	3

Source: Dutch graduate surveys 2003-2008

University graduates are also more likely to work abroad for one to two years after graduation than HBO graduates. Both HBO Bachelor graduates and university Bachelor and Master graduates are more likely to work abroad than those of the old models. Again, it is unclear how far these differences are due to compositional effects.

WHEREABOUTS OF GRADUATES ONE TO TWO YEARS AFTER GRADUATION

Tables 3 and 4 provide basic information about the study or employment situation of graduates one to two years after graduation. According to table 3, there are only minor differences between graduates of HBO traditional-model programmes and those of HBO Bachelor programmes. Almost three quarters of both groups are employed full-time and about one sixth combines employment with study, resulting in slightly less than nine out of every ten graduates being in some form of employment at the time of the survey. Some 7-8 per cent are studying full-time – usually in a Master programme; altogether, i.e. including those working and studying, 23 per cent each embarked in some form of further education. Only 4 per cent are neither studying nor working.

Table 3. Study or Employment Situation of 2002/03-2006/07 Graduates from HBO Institutions in the Netherlands One to Two Years after Graduation (per cent)

	HBO	
	Traditional model	Bachelor
Master study (only)	7	6
Master study and employment	8	8
Other further study (only)	1	1
Other further study and employment	7	8
Employment (only)	74	73
Neither study nor employment	4	4
Total	100	100
N	36,942	54,663

Source: Dutch graduate surveys 2003-2008

As already pointed out, the graduate surveys address only university Bachelors who transfer to employment; hence, no data can be presented on the basis of these surveys on the whereabouts of university Bachelor graduates; hence, table 4 provides only information about the whereabouts of university Masters of the new Bologna-model. Table 4 shows that there are only moderate differences between graduates of pre-Bologna university programmes and those of university Master programmes, although the differences are slightly greater than in the case of HBO.

Table 4. *Study and Employment Situation of 2002/03-2006/07 Pre-Bologna Model and Master Graduates from Universities in the Netherlands One to Two Years after Graduation (per cent)*

	University	
	Traditional model	Master
Doctoral study (only)	0	0
Doctoral study and employment	8	10
Other further study (only)	3	3
Other further study and employment	13	9
Employment (only)	71	75
Neither study nor employment	5	4
Total	100	100
N	33,258	9,317

Source: Dutch graduate surveys 2003-2008

Again, almost three quarters of university graduates are employed full-time, with a slightly higher share in the case of Master programmes. This is almost entirely compensated by the slight difference in the number of those combining study and work, so that more than nine out of ten graduates in both groups are involved in some form of employment at the time of the survey. It is relatively rare for university graduates to be studying full-time, but taken together with those who combined study and work, somewhere between a fifth and a quarter of all graduates are involved in some form of further education. Only 4-5 per cent are neither studying nor working.

PROFESSIONAL SUCCESS OF GRADUATES

Table 5 provides information on the labour market success of graduates one to two years after graduation. In general, graduates find work rather quickly. The mean search period after graduation is only one month. Graduates of Bologna-model programmes have a slightly shorter average search period than those of the pre-Bologna model, but the difference is very small and can probably be attributed to the better situation of the Dutch labour market between 2004 and 2008 (before the current economic crisis).

As regards employment conditions, we note slightly more full-time employment one to two years after graduation among graduates of the new model than among the corresponding group in the pre-Bologna model. This can be explained in a similar way as the slightly shorter search period of the former. As regards unlimited-term contracts, however, the situation is mixed. HBO Bachelor graduates are slightly less likely to have an unlimited term contract than graduates of old-style HBO programmes, despite the fact that they entered the labour market under more favourable circumstances. This may be due to the overrepresentation of agriculture and arts programmes among the HBO Bachelor graduates. The higher proportion of university Bachelor graduates with an unlimited term contract compared to traditional university programmes and university Master graduates probably reflects the fact that Bachelor graduates only entered the labour market after the Dutch economy had recovered from its mid-decade dip.

As regards occupational position, we note that more or less the same share of pre-Bologna HBO graduates, HBO Bachelor graduates and university Bachelor graduates work in "Managerial or professional occupations" (slightly over 50 per cent); it is only slightly higher for university Bachelor graduates than for the other two groups. It is too early to establish whether this reflects employers' preference for university Bachelor graduates over their HBO peers or just compositional and/or timing effects. University Bachelor graduates do not reach such positions as often as pre-Bologna university graduates and university Master graduates (71 per cent each). In contrast, HBO graduates (both traditional model and Bologna model) work more often (more than 20 per cent) than university graduates of any kind (about 10 per cent) in "Associate professional occupations". Since many HBO programmes are specifically designed to train people for such occupations, this is only to be expected. On average, the income of HBO Bachelor graduates is slightly higher that that of the pre-Bologna HBO graduates.

Table 5. Professional Success of 2002/03-2006/07 Graduates from Higher Education Institutions in the Netherlands One to Two Years after Graduation

	HBO Trad. model	HBO Bachelor	University Trad. model	University Bachelor	Master	Total
Foreign graduates (per cent)	5	9	7	8	12	7
Duration of job search (mean months)	1.0	0.9	1.5	1.3	1.3	1.1
Full-time employment (per cent)	59	65	76	78	81	67
Unlimited-term contract (per cent)	66	63	50	63	52	60
Monthly gross income						
Mean (Euro)	1,938	2,040	2,476	2,589	2,439	2,159
Median (Euro)	1,958	2,050	2,409	2,460	2,400	2,153
Managerial or professional occupation (per cent ISCO 1 or 2)	52	52	71	57	71	58
Associate professional occupation (per cent ISCO 3)	23	22	9	11	10	18
At least own level of education required (per cent)	78	81	64	47	64	74
High utilization of knowledge and skills (per cent)	64	62	66	54	66	64
High job satisfaction (per cent)	64	65	69	63	70	66

Source: Dutch graduate surveys 2003-2008

The average income of HBO Bachelor graduates is somewhat higher than that of HBO graduates of the pre-Bologna model. It hardly differs between pre-Bologna university graduates and university Master graduates. Surprisingly, though, university Bachelor graduates on average have a higher income than university Master graduates. Again, we have to be cautious in considering this as a success of the new model of study programmes and degrees because it could reflect the fact that Bachelor graduates only entered the labour market after the Dutch economy had recovered from its mid-decade dip.

In terms of working in a job requiring at least one's level of education, most HBO graduates old and now consider their education as appropriate. The same number of university Master graduates and graduates of the old-model university programmes expresses such views slightly less often. The most striking finding in this respect is the difference between university Bachelor graduates and the other university graduates: Less than half the university Bachelor graduates consider their job as requiring their degree. However, this could be an artefact, because no distinction was made in the questionnaire between university Bachelor level jobs and university Master level jobs (the questionnaire only addressed jobs at "university level", which could have misled the Bachelor graduates to compare the job requirements with the university Master and old-model level. Yet, fewer university Bachelor graduates might consider their job as not requiring a higher education degree, as a comparison with the responses to a further question suggests. Only slightly more than half the university Bachelor graduates stated that they used their knowledge and skills to a high extent, as compared to more than 60 per cent of the other graduates.

Finally, we note that overall job satisfaction does not differ substantially by type of degree. University graduates from the pre-Bologna mode programmes (69 per cent) as well as university Master graduates (70 per cent) express a high or very high degree of satisfaction slightly more often than pre-Bologna mode HBO graduates, HBO Bachelor graduates and university Bachelor graduates (63-65 per cent).

CONCLUSION

Perhaps the major conclusion that can be drawn at this stage is that it is very difficult to draw firm conclusions about the effects of introducing Bologna-model programmes in higher education institutions in the Netherlands. In general, the differences between old-model and Bologna-model programmes are not substantial and the actual differences shown by the data may well be due to compositional effects in terms of fields of study and the timing of introduction in relation to the economic cycle. A definitive analysis of the effects will only be possible after more time has passed: Then it will be possible to distinguish between the artefacts of the transition period and real changes. But even then, we will have to distinguish structurally-caused shifts from fluctuations due to the economic cycle. In that respect we can say that the current economic situation makes things even more difficult, since the first cohorts of Dutch graduates who have been trained almost exclusively under the new regime are faced with one of the most severe economic crises in recent decades.

There is another reason to conclude that a proper analysis of the effects of the new system of study programmes and degrees in the wake of the Bologna reforms will take more time. Employers will need time to become accustomed to the changes that have been made in the study programmes and to fully realise the potential of the new types of graduates presenting themselves in the labour market. This applies particularly to university Bacherlors. There have been frequent discussions about the extent to which a university Bacherlor degree represents a final qualification in its own right or if it should be regarded as simply a preparation for a university Masters degree. It will certainly take time for employers to decide whether they consider this entirely new degree as a qualification that is useful as a preparation for work. At this historical stage, we can tentatively conclude that there is little justification for the extreme pessimism that some people express in this respect. For example, the rates of full-time employment and average income of new university Bacherlors look promising, even if we do not know yet how far this can be explained by labour market cycles. Although there seems to be room for improvement in some areas such as the use of knowledge and skills, there is certainly nothing in the current results that suggests that university Bacherlor graduates opting for a transition to the world of work will face extreme difficulties. The available data suggest that they are well paid, even if their skills are not used as much as those of other graduates. The latter findings, however, could be viewed as an indication that graduates themselves – and possibly employers – are still in the process of becoming accustomed to the changes in the study programmes. Only time will provide the answer to this question.

REFERENCES

Allen, J., Coenen, J., Kaiser, F. & de Weert, E. (2007). *WO-Monitor 2004 en 2005 VSNU-kengetallen, Analyse en Interpretatie* [Academic Education-Monitor 2004 and 2005 VSNU (Association of Universities in the Netherlands) – Facts and Figures, Analysis and Interpretation]. Den Haag: VSNU. Retrieved January 31, 2011, from http://arno.unimaas.nl/show.cgi?fid=14068

Allen, J., van Breugel, G., Coenen, J., Fouarge, D., Meng, C., Ramaekers, G., et al . (2009). *Afgestudeerden van het hbo tijdens een crisis: geen verloren generatie* [Polytechnical graduates during a crisis: no lost generation]. Den Haag: HBO-raad. Retrieved January 31, 2011, from http://www.han.nl/start/bachelor-opleidingen/studeren-bij-de-han/_attachments/hbomonitor2008_1_.pdf

Researchcentrum voor Onderwijs en Arbeidsmarkt (2010). Schoolverlaters tussen onderwijs en arbeidsmarkt 2009 (ROA-R-2010/7) [School leavers between education and labour market 2009]. Maastricht: Research Centre for Education and the Labour Market. Retrieved January 31, 2011, from http://www.roa.unimaas.nl/pdf_publications/2009/ROA_R_2009_4.pdf

LIV ANNE STØREN, JANNECKE WIERS-JENSSEN AND
CLARA ÅSE ARNESEN

EMPLOYABILITY AND MOBILITY OF NORWEGIAN GRADUATES POST BOLOGNA

THE STUDY STRUCTURE OF NORWAY

A new degree structure in Norwegian higher education was implemented in 2003 following the "Quality Reform" (Ministry of Education and Research, 2001). It follows up the objectives of the Bologna Process in the European higher education and aims at the implementation of a 3 + 2 + 3 degree system with a Bachelor's, Master's and PhD structure in accordance with European standards. The reform also introduced a new grading and quality assurance system in line with the Bologna Process.

Norway has a binary higher education system, with universities situated in the larger towns and university colleges spread all over the country. There are (in 2011) eight universities (Ministry of Education and Research, 2010a, 2010b), all state-run, of which three are former university colleges and ten are specialised institutions at university level – eight of them state-run. There are 21 state-run university colleges and more than 20 (mostly small, publicly supported) private colleges (some of them also officially university colleges). The university colleges play an important role for decentralised access to higher education and generally attract students with a more diverse social origin than the universities.

The university colleges predominantly offer 3-year professional Bachelor programmes (engineering, nursing, social work, etc.). There are also professional programmes of varying length, from one to five years, for example in teacher training and business administration. Several university colleges offer Master's programmes and three have the right to award doctorates in one or more subjects.

Prior to the reform, a lower university degree (cand. mag.) existed which took 4 years to obtain. With the implementation of the Quality Reform in 2003, the "cand.mag." degree was replaced by the Bachelor degree, with three years of full-time study (180 ECTS). Concurrently, the *Master* degree replaced the previous higher degree ("hovedfag"). The Master degrees mainly take two year of study subsequent to a Bachelor degree to obtain.

The three-year study programmes at the *university colleges* (among them *engineers, nurses* etc.) were hardly affected by the new structure, but they obtained a new label: "Bachelors". These programmes may be considered as "traditional Bachelors", although the former degrees had other titles.

The 3+2+2 model was implemented in most fields of study. Exceptions are professionally-oriented five-year Master degree programmes in some fields. Moreover, a few programmes kept their previous degree structure and the duration of six years (medical doctors and psychologists). Finally, teacher training lasts for four

H. Schomburg and U. Teichler (eds.), Employability and Mobility of Bachelor Graduates in Europe, 185–208.
© 2011 *Sense Publishers. All rights reserved.*

years instead of three. Students commencing on a Master programme in 2003 or a few years later and who completed it up to spring term 2007 had started their initial studies in the old structure. Thus, many of them had completed a cand.mag. degree (see above) before entering Master studies. Others had completed a three-year full-time study programme, i.e.180 ECTS (Bachelor degree equivalent), at a university college before commencing a Master programme. In addition, up until 2007 it was possible, as a transitional arrangement, to choose the "hovedfag" programme instead of a Master programme.

The introduction of the Quality reform was based on the report "Do your duty – Demand your rights (Report No. 27 to the Storting, 2000-2001)" submitted by the Government on 9 March 2001 whereby the new lower degree – the Bachelor degree – will *provide professional qualifications and/or qualify for admission to higher degree studies*. The Master degree confers professional qualifications and/or qualifies for admission to doctoral studies.

The Report stresses the relationship between higher education and working life without distinguishing between Bachelor and Master degrees. It states, for instance, that it is the responsibility of the higher education institutions (HEI) to make sure that the content of the study programmes is relevant and attractive for the working life into which the students are likely to enter (p.8); the content of study programmes and degrees should provide an education that students will need in future professional life (p. 29). Further, the Report states that the universities should arrange the study programmes in such a way that they are well organised and improved as far as vocational orientation is concerned (p. 37). The Report finally states that all higher education institutions should offer their students a period of study abroad as a component of the Norwegian study programmes. Overall, the Report emphasizes the importance of student mobility (cf. Ministry of Education and Research, 2001).

THE EMPLOYMENT SITUATION IN NORWAY

According to the Norwegian Labour Force Survey (LFS), only 2 per cent of the labour force were unemployed in the fourth quarter of 2007.[1] The labour market situation was very good in terms of demand for labour in 2007. Also, in Norway, the unemployment rate increased as a consequence of the financial crisis of autumn of 2008 and 4 per cent of the labour force were unemployed the first quarter of 2010. This is still much lower than in other European countries.

The percentage of *employed* people in Norway is high compared to most other OECD countries. In 2009, the employemnt rate was 77 per cent, whereas the OECD average was 65 per cent. In particular, the employment rate of *women* is

---

[1] Employed persons worked for a salary or profit for at least one hour in the survey week or were temporarily absent from work because of illness, holiday, etc. Unemployed persons were not employed in the survey week and had been seeking work during the preceding four weeks, and were available for work in the survey week or within the following two weeks. Persons in the labour force are either employed or unemployed.

higher in Norway than in most other countries. It is 74 per cent, as compared to the OECD average of 57 per cent (Organisation for Economic Co-operation and Development [OECD], 2010).

With regard to different age goups, the Norwegian LFS shows that the employment rate of 15-24 year-olds was 51 per cent in the first quarter of 2010, and somewhat higher among females than males (52 versus 50 per cent respectively) (Statistics Norway, 2010a) despite the fact that the female participation rate in higher education is higher than males. In the 25-66 age group, the percentage of employed people is 82 per cent for men and 77 per cent for women.

Newcomers on the labour market are more deeply affected by the increase in unemployment than others in the labour force. The LFS shows that in the last quarter of 2007 5 per cent of *15-24-year*-olds in the labour force were unemployed. In this age group, the unemployment rate increased to 9 per cent in the first quarter of 2010 (Statistics Norway, 2008; 2010b).

The fact that unemployment is higher among newcomers also applies to newcomers with HE, even though their situation is better than that of school-leavers with a lower education level.

THE NORWEGIAN GRADUATE SURVEY 2007

In Norway, NIFU has conducted national graduate surveys on a regular basis since 1972[2]. The "regular" survey is conducted every second year six months after graduation.[3] The most recent was conducted in November 2009. However, it did *not* include new university Bachelors. Hence, this chapter presents data from the 2007 Graduate Survey.

The 2007 NIFU STEP Graduate survey is the only national Norwegian graduate survey that includes Bachelor study programmes that were introduced in universities with the "Quality Reform" in 2003. It was conducted closer to graduation than the surveys of most other countries.[4] One should bear in mind that the unemployment rate among graduates is higher six months after graduation than one or more years after graduation.

The survey includes the following groups of graduates from the spring 2007 cohort:

---

[2] The research institute NIFU (Nordic Institute for Studies in Innovation, Research and Education) was named NIFU STEP from 2005 to 2010, but changed back to NIFU in December 2010.

[3] Every other year "special" graduate surveys are conducted, targeting different groups and/or conducted several years after graduation.

[4] The reason why the Norwegian graduate survey is conducted six months after graduation is to avoid breaking the time series which go back to 1972. The regular Norwegian graduate surveys (six months after graduation) are held every second year, and, in the years in between, different types of special follow-up or retrospective surveys are held, for instance 2 ½ years after graduation or four to six years after.

- Bachelors graduating from the Universities of Oslo, Bergen, Trondheim and Tromsø (traditional universities). These are "new Bachelors", labelled "University Bachelors" in the tables;
- Bachelors in engineering graduating from university colleges, labelled "Engineering Bachelors";
- Graduates with higher degrees/Master degrees (except for medicine) from all universities (six at the time), as well as from university colleges providing such programmes, labelled "Masters".

Only one group of Bachelors from the university colleges, i.e. engineers, was included in the 2007 graduate survey. They serve here as a comparison group with new university Bachelors. It is not possible to compare the results for the new university Bachelors with the old system's previous lower degree cand.mag. graduates (see above), as they were never included in the Norwegian graduate surveys. It is also important to note that only university colleges graduate engineers. University Bachelor programmes in science and technology do not include engineering.

As mentioned above, 2007 was the final year when it was possible to graduate with a degree based on the old structure. This implies that some graduates with the highest degree did not graduate as Masters, but with the "hovedfag" (higher degree) which required one year more than the new Master degree. Yet, about two-thirds of the Master degree/higher degree graduates studied in the new structure, at least for the last part of their studies, thus graduating as Masters. For the sake of simplicity we will refer to the total group as "Masters" in the text.

Information was collected from the higher education institutions, and the graduates received a questionnaire. The respondents could choose between answering a paper questionnaire and a web survey. Three reminders were sent. The gross sample included 7,425 persons, whereas the net sample included 4,298 persons, of whom 2,515 are Masters/higher degree graduates, 722 are engineers, and 1,061 are university Bachelors. The overall response rate was 58 per cent; 61 per cent for graduates with a higher/Master degree; 52 per cent for the Bachelors in engineering and 53 per cent for the university Bachelors.

For most target groups, *all graduates* were included in the survey, but a sample was drawn with regard to some large groups among the *Masters*. All the results presented below are weighted: Groups from which a sample was drawn are weighted according to their original share of the graduates included in the survey. The weighted samples consist of 5,497 observations, of which 3,714 were made by Masters/higher degree graduates.

SOCIO-BIOGRAPHIC BACKGROUND AND COURSE OF STUDY

Like in other Western countries, there is a majority of *females* among the higher education students in Norway. However, as is shown in table 1, they are a minority among graduates in engineering. Among university Bachelors, the proportion of females in science and technology is 47 per cent.

Table 1. Gender of 2007 Graduates from Higher Education Institutions in Norway

	University Bachelors (new Bachelors)			Engineering Bachelors, university colleges	Master/ higher degree	Total
	Science and technology	Other fields	Total university Bachelors			
Per cent female	47	66	63	17	59	54
N (total number of observations)	134	927	1,061	722	3,714	5,497

Source: Norwegian Graduate Survey 2007

The most sex-segregated study programmes in higher education in Norway are – in addition to engineering – nursing, teacher training and pre-school teacher training, the former with a majority of male students and the latter three with a vast majority of female students. Except for these programmes, the gender gap in most studies has been narrowing in recent decades, mainly because female participation has increased in all fields (Statistics Norway, 2010b). In many study programmes where females used to be a minority or where their gender distribution was more or less balanced, females have become a majority. Examples of the latter are medicine and law. In Master degrees, the share of females is lower in science and technology at about 40 per cent, but this still represents a large increase in the last 20 years.

The educational level of the graduates' parents is shown in table 2. Here, the data regarding Master graduates are sub-divided by type of higher education institution, because the parental background of the Masters differs by type of higher education institutions, as it does among the Bachelors.

Table 2. Father and/or Mother with Higher Education among 2007 Graduates from Higher Education Institutions in Norway (per cent)

	Mother	Father	One of parents	Both parents
University Bachelors				
Science and technology	59	63	72	46
Other fields	58	59	71	44
Total	58	59	71	44
Engineering Bachelors, university colleges	42	47	56	32
Masters				
From university colleges	42	51	60	32
From universities	53	59	68	44
N (total, all graduates included in the survey)	51	57	66	41

Source: Norwegian Graduate Survey 2007

The figures presented in table 2 are not representative of *all* graduates in Norway. First, the graduate survey did not comprise *all* Bachelors from university colleges, but only the engineers. Second, some respondents may have overestimated their parents' educational level. Third, one of the categories regarding parental education in the questionnaire referred to *1-4 years* of higher education and this could lead to the inclusion of parents who would not have been registered in the official statistics.

Therefore, the proportion of parents with higher education is presented in table 3 for both new entrants in upper secondary education and new entrants in higher education.[5] These figures based on register data show that parents of students in higher education in Norway have a higher level of educational attainment than those of the average young persons. According to table 3, the share of students in Norway with higher education-trained parents is lower than that of the respondents shown in table 2.

Yet, the differences between the groups presented in table 2 are valid in principle. University college students represent a group with a somewhat lower parental educational attainment level than that of university students. The large geographical diffusion of these colleges is probably the reason why the share of students who have parents with higher education is lower at these institutions than among the university students.

---

[5] The figures in table 3 refer to persons who mainly belong to the 1983 – 1984 birth cohorts. The Bachelors in table 2 represent, on average, persons who are two years older, and thus also refer to parents who are somewhat older.

Table 3. *New Entrant Students in Upper Secondary Education and Higher Education with Higher Education-Trained Parents in Norway (per cent, register data)*

	Mother	Father	One of parents
Persons who started in upper secondary education in 1999 or 2000 (N=98,452)	27	27	38
Persons who started in upper secondary education in 1999 or 2000, and who started in HE in 2002 or 2003 (N=24,035)	40	41	55

Source: Støren, Helland and Grøgaard (2007); Støren (2009)

The educational attainment of the parents of engineers is lower than among university Bachelors and Masters. The finding that the university *Bachelors* have somewhat more highly educated mothers than the university *Masters* may be coincidental: it may be because Bachelors are younger than Masters and thus have younger parents who are more likely to be highly educated.

Regarding prior study and degree, the question was formulated as follows in the Norwegian graduate survey: *"Did you complete any other university or college education with a full-time duration of at least one year, before the one you completed in the spring of 2007, and which is not part of the degree you were awarded in the spring of 2007?"* The graduates were also asked what kind of education this referred to. These answers were coded in accordance with the Norwegian 6-digit Standard Classification of Education. Some graduates mentioned education at a lower level than ISCED 5. They are excluded here. 22 per cent of university Bachelor graduates, 12 per cent of engineering Bachelor graduates, 29 per cent of Master graduates, and 26 per cent of all graduates surveyed had completed higher education (between at least one year of study at ISCED 5 level and a degree) prior to the current degree.

In the case of Masters one should bear in mind that they could have included "cand.mag.", Bachelor or another equivalent degree, although the questionnaire specified that the respondents should not include education that is part of the degree they were awarded in the spring of 2007. We can infer such errors because the respective quota is quite high among Master graduates.

The 2007 graduate survey does not provide a complete picture of the total *years of study up to the degree* awarded in 2007. Yet, some useful information can be presented here as regards *prolongation of study*. The following questions were asked: *Did you take more time than prescribed (standard) time to be awarded this degree?* (The graduates were given the instruction not to include studies that were not necessary to obtain the degree.) (If yes:) *Estimate the number of semesters that exceed prescribed study time.* The share of those spending more time was 28 per cent among university Bachelor graduates, 14 per cent among engineering Bachelor graduates, 54 per cent among Master graduates, and 44 per cent of all

graduates surveyed. Of those who answered "yes", 23 per cent gave no answer to the follow-up question to estimate the number of semesters. With regard to the duration *among those who gave an answer*, the arithmetic means were:
- 2 semesters for university Bachelor graduates,
- 2.6 semesters for engineering Bachelor graduates,
- 4.0 semesters for Master graduates and
- 3.7 semesters for all graduates surveyed.

Obviously, the Master graduates frequently reported that they had studied longer than the prescribed time because work on the Master thesis may be quite demanding and require more time than estimated; some students spent much time on paid employment while studying; some had children while being a student; moreover, the student support system allows for some delays.

The average *age at the time of graduation*, according to the 2007 survey, was:
- 25.9 years for university Bachelor graduates,
- 26.6 years for engineering Bachelor graduates,
- 32.3 years for Master graduates and
- 30.3 years for all graduates surveyed.

The average age among Masters was increased by the fact that graduates were included in 2007 who had their last chance that year of obtaining this degree in the old system. The respective mean among 2009 graduates was 30.3 years. Yet, the average age of Norwegian graduates is quite high for the reasons quoted above. Although incentives are provided for rapid study progress, the Norwegian system is relatively flexible with regard to studying at an older age.

The relatively late age of engineers and new Bachelors does not seem to be caused by slow study progression. As shown above, only 14 per cent of the engineers had used more than the prescribed time on their degree, with an average of 2.6 semesters. The main reason is postponement of higher education enrolment and the fact that a relative high share had completed a higher education degree prior to the current degree. Another point worth mentioning is the fact that, in Norway, the normal age for leaving upper secondary education is 19, whereas it is 18 in many other countries.

INTERNATIONAL MOBILITY

Immigrants

The Norwegian Graduate Survey does not include information on citizenship, but information on the graduates' country of birth and that of their parents. We may thus identify first-generation immigrants, who are persons born abroad with both parents being also born abroad. They make up:
- 6 per cent of university Bachelor graduates,
- 5 per cent of engineering Bachelor graduates,
- 6 per cent of Master graduates from university colleges,
- 5 per cent of Master graduates from universities, and
- 5 per cent of all graduates surveyed.

The differences in the rate of first-generation migrants by type of study are small. However, additional analyses showed the share of immigrants from *non-Western* countries is relatively high among engineering graduates. Those from the Nordic countries are highly represented among Master graduates from the university colleges, and European (and North-American) immigrants are relatively numerous among the new university Bachelors.

Recent immigrants or inward mobile students

The Norwegian Graduate Survey does not distinguish between foreign inward mobile students and recent immigrants. However, it includes information on place and country of residence at the age of 17.

Table 4. First-generation Immigrants from Various Regions Arriving in Norway at the Age of 18 or Older among the 2007 Graduates from Higher Education Institutions in Norway (per cent)

	Bachelors from universities	Engineering Bachelors university colleges	Masters from university colleges	Masters from universities	Total
Nordic countries	1	0	2	1	1
Europe, except the Nordic countries	2	1	2	1	2
Africa, Asia, Latin-America	1	1	1	1	1
North-America, Oceania and unknown	0	0	0	0	0
Total	3	3	5	3	4

Source: Norwegian Graduate Survey 2007

Graduates who were not born in Norway (and whose parents were not born in Norway), and who lived outside Norway at the age of 17 are most often immigrants who subsequently came to Norway. Some may be what is ordinarily understood as foreign inward mobile graduates. However, many graduates in the latter group have probably left Norway and are thus not included in the survey. We assume that most of the foreign inward mobile students are from the Nordic or other European countries. In table 4 we present the proportion of graduates who are first generation immigrants not having resided in Norway at the age of 17, by region of origin.

These recent immigrants make up 4 per cent of all the 2007 graduates surveyed, as is shown in table 4. As the total share of immigrants is only 5 per cent, as shown above, we note that most foreign (immigrant) graduates did not live in Norway at the age of 17. This holds true for all regions of origin.

It does not come as surprise, however, that many respondents among Nordic graduates – 3 per cent – arrived in Norway at the age of 18 or later. Many are certainly inward mobile persons, but this group also comprises "regular" immigrants or refugees, for instance from Bosnia, as well as persons who have moved to Norway because they have a Norwegian spouse/partner.

Temporary outward mobility

The proportion of outwards temporarily mobile students, i.e. persons that has spent at least one semester abroad as a part of their Norwegian study programme, before they eventually graduated from a Norwegian higher education institution in Norway in 2007, is
– 20 per cent among university Bachelor graduates,
– 5 per cent among engineering Bachelor graduates,
– 23 per cent among Master graduates from university colleges,
– 25 per cent among Master graduates from universities, and
– 21 per cent of all graduates surveyed.
Accordingly, this outward temporary mobility is highest among Master students; this is not surprising, given that they have been students for more years. Bachelors in engineering are less likely to have studied abroad; this could be because these study programmes are less flexible, making it difficult to find time to go abroad. Mobility statistics from the Norwegian Centre for International Cooperation in Higher Education (SIU) show that the proportion of Bachelor students undertaking a sojourn abroad is generally lower among university college students than among university students (Senter for internasjonalisering av høgre utdanning [SIU], 2010). Also, fewer students in natural sciences study temporarily abroad than students in most other fields.

Internationalisation of higher education is high on the political agenda in Norway, and student mobility is an important part of this. Temporary mobility, such as participation in student exchange programmes like ERASMUS and NORDPLUS, is strongly encouraged. The number of exchange students increased by almost 70 per cent between 1999 and 2009 (Lånekassa, 2009). This means that more than three per cent of the total student body goes abroad on exchange sojourns every year.

Graduating abroad

A high share of the total student body goes abroad, compared to many other Western countries (see OECD, 2005; UNESCO, 2006). Full degree students abroad have in recent years constituted approximately 6-7 per cent of the total Norwegian student body (Senter for internasjonalisering av høgre utdanning [SIU], 2008) thanks to a generous student support scheme for mobile students (Saarlikallio-Torp & Wiers-Jenssen, 2010).

Norwegian students graduating abroad are not included in the regular NIFU surveys six months after graduation. However, those graduating from foreign universities are included in two "special" graduate surveys conducted 3-4 years after graduation in the years 2002 and 2007. They show that those who have taken a full degree abroad are more likely to face difficulties in entering the labour market than graduates who obtained their diploma from a Norwegian HEI (Wiers-Jenssen & Try, 2005; Wiers-Jenssen, 2010). On the positive side, Norwegians who obtain their diplomas abroad have higher wages.

Mobility after graduation

The regular Norwegian graduate surveys undertaken six months after graduation do not contain information about mobility after graduation. The special graduate surveys 3-4 years after graduation conducted in 2002 and in 2007 include graduates working abroad, but they did not address the new Bachelor graduates. According to the 2007 surveys, five per cent of those Norwegian graduates who studied for the whole study period in Norway worked abroad at some stage during the first 3-4 years after graduation. Mobility after graduation was much higher among those who had been mobile during their course of study: 16 per cent of graduates from Norwegian higher education institutions who spend a study period abroad, and 22 per cent of persons from Norway who spent their whole study programme and graduated abroad (Wiers-Jenssen, 2008). As the rate of students who study abroad is increasing, one could also expect an increasing international mobility of Norwegian graduates.

TRANSITION TO EMPLOYMENT AND FURTHER STUDY

Altogether, 72 per cent of the 2007 Bachelor graduates from Norwegian universities continue their studies – more than half to Master level and more than one fifth to other further study. More than half each work and study concurrently. This is in accordance with the graduates' response to a question regarding the envisaged qualifications. 68 per cent of the university Bachelor graduates intend to study up to a Master degree and 13 per cent to a doctoral degree (Arnesen & Waagene, 2009). The proportion of those planning to obtain a Master degree was almost the same among females and males (69 versus 66 per cent), while more men planned to obtain a doctoral degree (17 versus 10 per cent) (Arnesen & Waagene, 2009).

62 per cent of the 2007 university Bachelor graduates are employed six months after graduation; however, as table 5 shows, only 23 per cent are employed but do not study. Finally, about 5 per cent neither study nor are employed.

The situation is different for engineering Bachelor graduates from university colleges. 29 per cent, i.e. less than half as many as university Bachelor graduates, continue their studies, of whom 11 per cent work at the same time. Altogether, 25 per cent of the engineering Bachelors transfer to Master study. In reverse, 78 per cent of engineering Bachelor graduates take up employment during the first six months after graduation, of whom 67 per cent without concurrent study.

Table 5. Employment and Study Six Months after Graduation of 2007 Bachelor Graduates from Higher Education Institutions in Norway (per cent)

	Bachelors universities	Engineering Bachelors university colleges	Total Bachelors
Per cent			
Master study (only)	25	17	22
Master study and employment	27	8	19
Other further study (only)	9	2	6
Other further study and employment	12	3	8
Employment (only)	23	67	41
Neither study nor employment	5	4	4
Total	100	100	100
Count			
Master study (only)	262	122	384
Master study and employment	284	59	343
Other further study (only)	93	12	105
Other further study and employment	128	19	147
Employment (only)	244	483	727
Neither study nor employment	49	27	76
Total	1,060	722	1,782

Source: Norwegian Graduate Survey 2007

While university Bachelor graduates predominantly conceived the Bachelor as a stage in their studies and continue to study, Master graduates as a rule transfer to employment: 95 per cent, as table 6 shows, of whom 11 per cent with concurrent study. Five per cent neither study nor are employed.

Table 6. Employment and Study Six Months after Graduation of 2007 Master Graduates from Higher Education Institutions in Norway (per cent)

	Per cent	Count
PhD study and employment*	2	90
Other further study (only)	2	78
Other further study and employment	7	249
Employment (only)	83	3,094
Neither study nor employment	5	199
Total	100	3,712

* PhD study (only): too few to be reported

Source: Norwegian Graduate Survey 2007

PROFESSIONAL SUCCESS OF GRADUATES

Period from graduation to employment

The Norwegian graduate survey does not provide any information on the duration of the period from graduation to first employment. However, it indicates the timing of the *start of current employment*. For most graduates this is the first significant employment after graduation.

The responses indicate that about 28 per cent started their current job prior to the year of graduation; obviously, they were employed during study and continued their job after graduation, possibly thereby increasing their working hours. This proportion might be even higher because some graduates providing information on the start of their current employment after graduation report that they already had been in this job prior to graduation.

Table 7 comprises only graduates having started the current employment upon or after graduation in the upper part, while the lower part of the table informs about all employed graduates.

Table 7. Number of Months from Graduation to Current Employment on Average of all 2007 Graduates from Higher Education in Norway Employed Six Months after Graduation

	Engineering Bachelors	University Bachelors	Master / higher degree	Total
Started in current employment after graduation or in the month of graduation				
Mean	1.5	2.7	2.3	2.2
Median	1	2	2	2
N	440	294	2,191	2,925
*All employed graduates**				
Mean	1.2	1.2	1.5	1.4
Median	1	0	1	1
N	561	656	3,433	4,650

* Number of months is set to zero for those who started current employment before graduation.

Source: Norwegian Graduate Survey 2007

University Bachelor graduates started employment on average 2.7 months after graduation. This period from graduation to employment is even shorter for Master graduates (2.3 months) and engineering Bachelor graduates from university colleges. Also, other data provided below suggest that the labour market situation for university Bachelor graduates in Norway is more difficult than for other graduates.

However, as already pointed out, many university Bachelor graduates continue to work on the job they held prior to graduation. If we count their transition period to employment as zero, the overall average transition period from graduation to the current job is 1.2 months on average. We must bear in mind, though, that the jobs held prior to graduation are mostly not very demanding; 79 per cent reported that their work did not require higher education or that it was irrelevant.

Employment situation

Six months after graduation, the rate of *full-time employment* is:
- 30 per cent among university Bachelor graduates,
- 87 per cent among engineering Bachelor graduates from university colleges,
- 85 per cent among Master graduates, and
- 77 per cent of all graduates surveyed.

The share of university graduates employed full-time is higher than that of Bachelor graduates who are employed without concurrent study (23 per cent, as shown above). Also, very few university Bachelor graduates reported that their part-time work was involuntary (see figure 3 below). Thus, part-time study seems to be chosen voluntarily in order to be able to pursue work and further study concurrently.

About half the employed university Bachelor graduates had *long term or unlimited contracts* six months after graduation. As figure 1 shows, the proportion is lower than that of other groups, but the difference is less than in the case of full-time employment.

Again, the relatively low percentage of permanent employment of university Bachelors can be explained by the fact they often understand their concurrent study and work as a first step to employment, but not as a real integration in the employment system. In contrast, the transition of engineering Bachelor graduates from university colleges is in most cases a transition to full-time regular and relevant work.

It is interesting to note that the number of Master graduates who have a long-term or unlimited contract, though higher than among university graduates, is clearly lower than among engineering Bachelor graduates. This could be due to the fact that a higher percentage of engineers than Master graduates are employed in the private sector (83 per cent for engineering Bachelor graduates and 47 per cent for Master graduates). The private sector is more strictly regulated than the public sectors when it comes to temporary labour contracts, while many careers in the public sector start with a limited time contract.

The wages of university Bachelor graduates is 15 per cent lower than those of engineering graduates, and 17 per cent lower than those of Master graduates. This can be explained by the difference in educational level. However, the wage difference between engineering Bachelor graduates and university Bachelor graduates is interesting because their education level is equivalent. There are three main reasons for this difference. The first is that engineers have a vocationally-oriented education that is well adapted to the demands of the labour market, whereas university Bachelor graduates have a (new) generic education that is not very well adapted to the demands of the labour market. The second is that engineers were highly demanded in the labour market as a result of the economic boom in the period 2005-2007. The third is that engineers, to a great extent, find their jobs in the private sector where wages are generally higher and more flexible than in the public sector. This means that the favourable labour market will have a more positive effect on their wages than for graduates who mainly find work in the public sector.

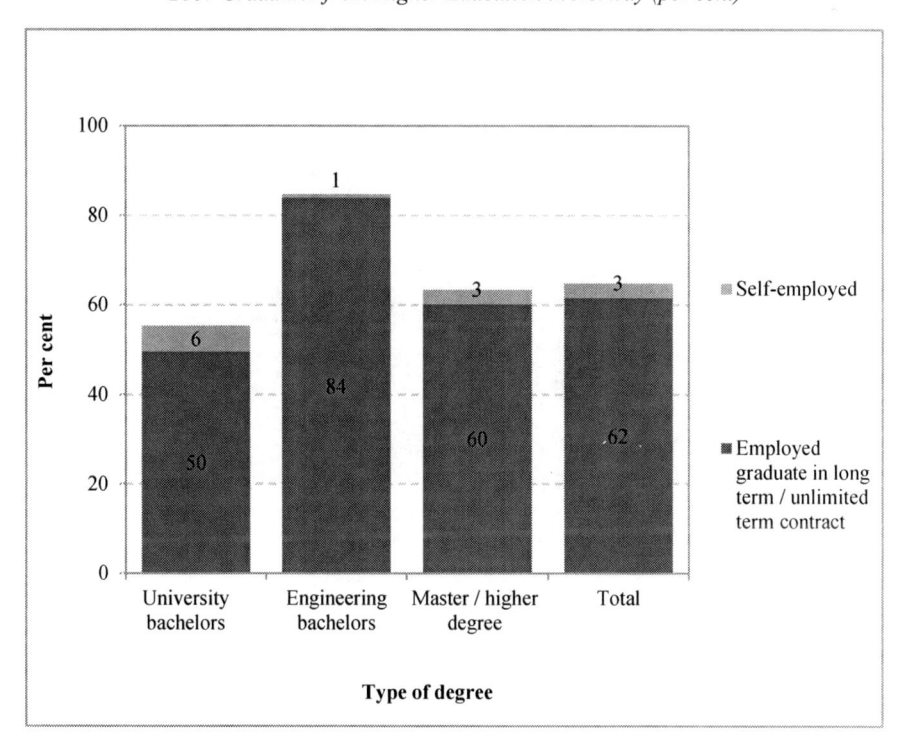

Figure 1. Long-term/Unlimited Term Contract Six Months after Graduation among 2007 Graduates from Higher Education in Norway (per cent)

Source: Norwegian Graduate Survey 2007

Figure 2 shows the average *annual gross income* of those in full-time employment. University Bachelor graduates earn 17 per cent less than Master graduates. This difference can be viewed as normal, i.e. as reflecting the difference in the level of educational attainment.

Although engineers had a very favourable labour market in 2007, it is surprising that Master graduates only earned 2 per cent more. The wage difference was exceptionally small in 2007 and must be seen in light of the positive labour market situation in 2007 and the high percentage of engineers who found jobs in the higher paying private sector. As already mentioned, 83 per cent of the engineers worked in the higher paying private sector, while this was the case for only 47 per cent of Master graduates.

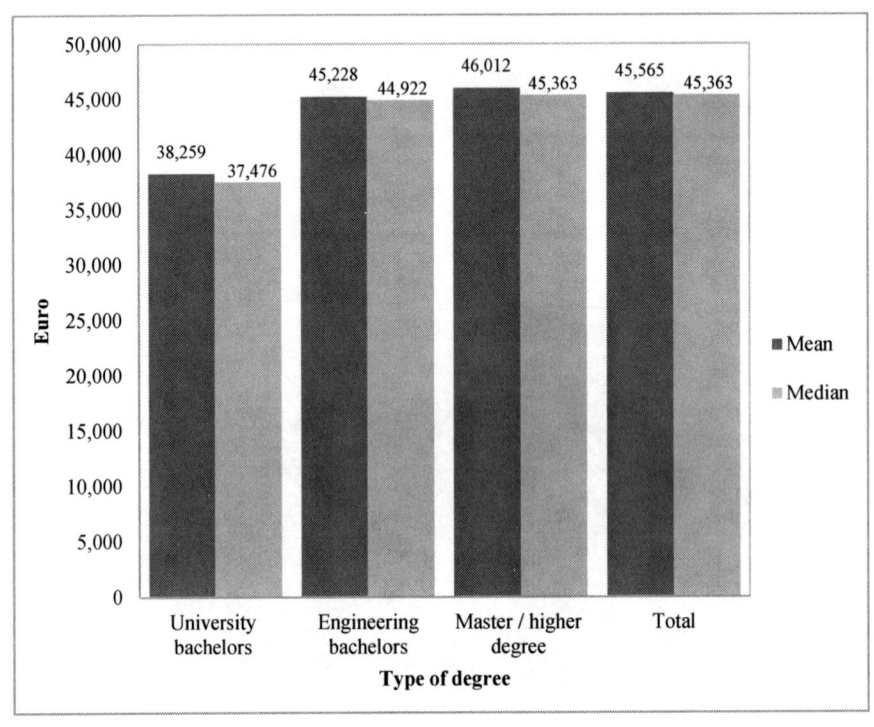

Figure 2. Estimated Annual Gross Income* Six Months after Graduation of Full-time Employed 2007 Graduates from Higher Education Institutions in Norway (mean and median, Euro)

Type of degree	Mean	Median
University bachelors	38,259	37,476
Engineering bachelors	45,228	44,922
Master / higher degree	46,012	45,363
Total	45,565	45,363

* Calculation of the annual gross income: monthly regular gross income in NOK * 12, whereby 7.9360 is NOK: Euro rate in November 2007.

Source: Norwegian Graduate Survey 2007

Another point worth mentioning with regard to the results in figure 2 is the small difference between the median and the arithmetic mean. This indicates that the wage distribution is not very skewed.

Type of positions

Only some 27 per cent of university Bachelor graduates in Norway hold professional positions shortly after graduation, as table 8 shows, while 11 per cent are in associate professional and 62 per cent in other positions. As already pointed out, many university Bachelor graduates studying along employment do not really opt for a professional career. But also among those who were employed only (i.e. not combining work and study) all a minority (39 per cent) held professional positions, while 15 per cent held associate positions and 46 per cent were employed in other occupations. In contrast, almost three quarters of engineering Bachelors – almost as many as among the Master graduates – held professional positions.

Table 8. Occupational Category of 2007 Graduates from Higher Education Institutions in Norway Employed Six Months after Graduation (per cent)

	University Bachelors	Engineering Bachelors	Master / higher degree	Total
Professional	27	74	75	68
Associate	11	4	13	11
Other occupations	62	22	12	20
Total	100	100	100	100

* Only graduates providing information on occupational category

Source: Norwegian Graduate Survey 2007

Link between study and work

While table 8 addresses the link or mismatch between study and work according to occupational category, the graduates' *assessments of the vertical match or mismatch* are shown in table 9. The correspondence between the two is fairly good. As the data provided above have shown, only Bachelor graduates considering employment as their "main activity" are really comparable to other graduates. The upper part of table 9 presents data for those employed as their main activity, while data for all (i.e. including those working concurrent to study) is provided in the lower part of the table.

Accordingly, we note that 57 per cent of graduates who are mainly employed consider their job as requiring their level of higher education or even a higher level. This holds true for 47 per cent of the university Bachelor graduates in science and technology, but only for 36 per cent of the other university Bachelor graduates. The respective quota is higher for Master graduates (58 per cent) and even slightly higher for engineering Bachelor graduates from university colleges (63 per cent).

Table 9. Assessment of the Link between Work and Level of Educational Attainment by 2007 Graduates from Higher Education Institution in Norway Employed Six Months after Graduation (per cent)

	University Bachelors, science and technology	University Bachelors, other fields	Total university Bachelors	Engineering Bachelors, university colleges	Master/ higher degree	Total
Employed graduates considering employment as their main activity						
The work requires higher education at the same level	41	29	30	57	55	54
The work requires higher education, but at a higher level	6	7	7	6	3	3
The work requires higher education, but at a lower level	6	7	7	7	23	20
The work does not require higher education, but it is an advantage to have it	24	32	31	25	14	16
Higher education is irrelevant	24	25	25	5	5	7
Total	100	100	100	100	100	100
All employed graduates						
The work requires higher education at the same level	23	16	17	53	52	47
The work requires higher education, but at a higher level	4	4	4	6	3	3
The work requires higher education, but at a lower level	14	5	7	7	22	19
The work does not require higher education, but it is an advantage	18	27	26	23	15	17
Higher education is irrelevant	41	48	47	12	8	14
Total	100	100	100	100	100	100

Source: Norwegian Graduate Survey 2007

Moreover, graduates were asked whether the content of their study was related to their current work. The responses, indicating the extent of *horizontal link or mismatch* between higher education and work, are presented in table 10.

Table 10. Assessment of the Link between the Content of Study and Work by 2007 Graduates from Higher Education Institution in Norway (per cent)

Content of study corresponds to work ...	University Bachelors, science and technology	University Bachelors, other fields	Total university Bachelors	Engineering Bachelors, university colleges	Master/ higher degree	Total
Employed graduates considering employment as their main activity						
To a high extent	41	26	28	39	49	47
To some extent	24	40	39	49	38	40
Not at all	35	34	34	12	12	14
Total	100	100	100	100	100	100
All employed graduates						
To a high extent	30	18	20	36	47	42
To some extent	23	29	28	45	37	37
Not at all	47	53	52	18	15	21
Total	100	100	100	100	100	100

Source: Norwegian Graduate Survey 2007

A clear horizontal mismatch six months after graduation is reported by about one third of university Bachelor graduates for whom employment is the main activity. In contrast to the previous question about a vertical link or mismatch, a horizontal mismatch is not more frequently reported by university graduates in other fields of study than by those in science and technology. The corresponding share among engineers and Masters is only 12 per cent.

In figure 3, information on vertical and horizontal links versus mismatch is combined. The category *irrelevant work* is used here in a strict sense for those who consider *higher education as for their positions and* the *contents* of their education as not at all corresponding to their work. The data refer to all graduates in the labour market, i.e. including those combining study and work and those who are unemployed. Finally, those who are involuntarily employed part-time are presented in a separate category.

Figure 3 shows that the category "irrelevant work" applies to a little more than one third of university Bachelor graduates. In contrast, the respective proportion is 8 per cent for engineering Bachelor graduates from university colleges and 7 per cent for Master graduates.

Figure 3. Different Forms of "Match/Mismatch" Six Months after Graduation among 2007 Graduates from Institutions of Higher Education in Norway (percentage of graduates in the labour force)

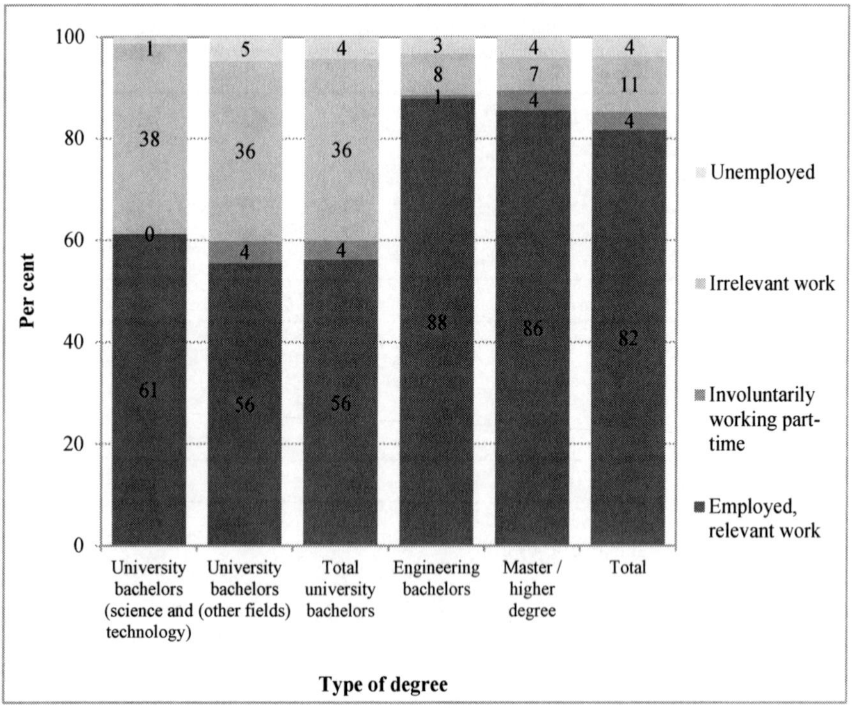

[Bar chart showing percentages by type of degree:
- University bachelors (science and technology): Employed relevant work 61, Involuntarily working part-time 0, Irrelevant work 38, Unemployed 1
- University bachelors (other fields): 56, 4, 36, 5
- Total university bachelors: 56, 4, 36, 4
- Engineering bachelors: 88, 1, 8, 3
- Master / higher degree: 86, 4, 7, 4
- Total: 82, 4, 11, 4]

Source: Norwegian Graduate Survey 2007

In 2007, the demand for labour was very high in Norway, and thus the unemployment rate among graduates six months after graduation was low, i.e. 4 per cent. This rate was both 4 per cent among university Bachelor graduates and Master graduates.

The survey undertaken in 2009 showed that the unemployment rate of recent Master graduates increased as a consequence of the economic crisis from 3.9 per cent in 2007 to 6 per cent in 2009. As pointed out above, the analysis of graduate employment is based here on the 2007 survey, because Bachelor graduates were not included in the 2009 Graduate Survey.

Satisfaction with relevance of study for work

Among the questions included in the Norwegian graduate survey about *job satisfaction* the question on satisfaction with the relevance of study for work is most salient. In combining the categories "very satisfied" and "a little satisfied" presented in table 11, we note the highest level of satisfaction among Master graduates (74 per cent). It is clearly lower among university Bachelor graduates (48 per cent) – 60 per cent among those in science and technology and 46 per cent among those in other fields.

Table 11. Extent of Satisfaction with the Relevance of Study to Work Six Months after Graduation on the Part of 2007 Graduates from Institutions of Higher Education Institutions in Norway (percentage of employed graduates)

	University Bachelors, science and technology	University Bachelors, other fields	Total university Bachelors	Engineering Bachelors, university colleges	Master/ higher degree	Total
Very dissatisfied	6	8	8	4	2	3
A little dissatisfied	8	21	19	14	10	12
Neither nor	26	25	25	21	15	17
A little satisfied	33	31	32	42	38	37
Very satisfied	27	15	16	20	36	31
Total	100	100	100	100	100	100

Source: Norwegian Graduate Survey 2007

The engineering Bachelor graduates from university colleges (61 per cent) are more satisfied than the university Bachelor graduates. The degree of satisfaction, however, is clearly lower than on the part of Master graduates, although the responses to the other questions regarding the link and the mismatch between study and work were otherwise similar between these two groups.

CONCLUDING REMARKS

The labour market situation was very good in Norway in 2007 – the year in which the survey analysed here was undertaken. Hence, all groups of higher education graduates in Norway fare relatively well in the labour market compared to those in many other European countries.

The Norwegian case study, however, shows that the labour market situation for the new university Bachelor graduates was far from good. Their situation was not bad in terms of risk of becoming unemployed, but in terms of difficulties in finding a relevant job. University Bachelor graduates more frequently than the other groups:
– have limited-term contracts and part-time jobs,
– have occupations that do not necessarily or do not require higher education,
– hold jobs that do not correspond to the content of their study,
– are dissatisfied, as far as relevance of their study to the labour market is concerned.

More than 60 per cent of the university Bachelor graduates are employed six months after graduation; most combine study and employment. Almost 40 per cent study and work, and in addition one third are studying without having an employment. Even more stated that they intended to go on studying; in total about 80 per cent plan to take a Master degree or a PhD degree.

Employed university Bachelor graduates who consider that employment is their main activity more often have work that corresponds to their education level than those who do not. Still, when comparing groups who consider employment as their main activity, there remains a gap between university Bachelor graduates on the one side and Master graduates and engineering Bachelors on the other.

Continuing to study directly after the award of a Bachelor degree, for instance by combining work and study, may not have been a free choice for all university Bachelor graduates. We do not know how many preferred this and how many chose this option after having faced difficulties in finding a suitable job. The work situation of university Bachelor graduates suggests, overall, that the universities have not prepared them well for employment and that employers welcomed the new generic Bachelor educations.

The main objective of the introduction of Bachelor programmes at universities in Norway was to prepare students for Master study. However, it was also a central goal that a Bachelor degree should give students an opportunity to enter the labour market and obtain jobs based on their first degree. It was said in the Report to the Storting (Ministry of Education and Research, 2001) that universities should go through their study programmes in order to organise good study courses with a better vocational orientation.

The study has shown that the opportunities for mobility during the course of study are relatively high in Norway in a comparative perspective. For example, one out of five university Bachelor students and one out of four Master students from Norway has taken the opportunity to study abroad for some period. Taking into account the period of study, we note that university Bachelor students in Norway are most likely to study abroad. In contrast, only about five per cent of the engineering Bachelor students from university colleges study abroad for some period; this could be because these study programmes are less flexible, making it difficult to find time for an exchange.

But even though the temporary outward mobility of students from Norway is quite high, current mobility figures are far from the goal that all students should have the opportunity to study abroad. Whether many students are not interested in the opportunities provided or whether action would be needed to increase opportunities cannot be judged on the basis of the survey analysed. However, data from another survey show that there are both personal and practical barriers for studying abroad, but that personal reasons, such as family/partner, are the most important ones (SIU, 2010).

REFERENCES

Ministry of Education and Research (2001). *Gjør din plikt – Krev dinrett. St. meld. nr. 27(2000-2001)* [Do your duty – Demand your rights. Report No. 27 to the Storting (2000-2001)]. Oslo: Ministry of Education and Research

Ministry of Education and Research (2010a). *Homepage Ministry of Education of Research.* Retrieved January 25, 2011, from http://www.regjeringen.no/nb/dep/kd.html?id=586

Ministry of Education and Research (2010b). *Bodø University College turns into University of Nordland*". Retrieved January 25, 2011, from http://www.regjeringen.no/en/dep/kd/press-contacts/Press-releases/2010/Bodo-University-College-turns-into-University-ofNordland.html?id=625269

Organisation for Economic Co-operation and Development (2005). *Education at a glance 2005. OECD Indicators 2005*. Paris: OECD.

Organisation for Economic Co-operation and Development (2010). *How does your country compare – Norway.* Retrieved January 25, 2011 from http://www.oecd.org/document/46/0,3746,en_2649_37457_43219182_1_1_1_37457,00.html

Saarlikallio-Torp, M. & Wiers-Jenssen, J. (Eds) (2010). *Nordic students abroad. Student mobility patterns, student support systems and labour market outcomes.* Helsinki: Kela.

Senter for internasjonalisering av høgre utdanning (2008). *Mobilitetsrapport 2008* [Mobility report 2008]. Bergen: Senter for internasjonalisering av høgre utdanning [The Norwegian Centre for International Cooperation in Higher Education (SIU)].

Senter for internasjonalisering av høgre utdanning (2010). *Hvorfor studere i utlandet* [Why study abroad]? Bergen: Senter for internasjonalisering av høgre utdanning [The Norwegian Centre for International Cooperation in Higher Education (SIU)]. Retrieved January 25, 2011 from http://www.siu.no/eng/content/download/4563/48614/file/Mobilitetsanalyse%202010_endelig.pdf

Statistics Norway (2008). *Arbeidsledige 15-74 år, etter kjønn og alder (AKU). 1 000 og present* [Unemployed 15 – 74 years, by sex and age (LFS). In 1000 and as per cent]. Retrieved January 25, 2011 from http://www.ssb.no/aku/arkiv/tab-2008-10-29-13.html

Statistics Norway (2010a). *Arbeidsstyrken og sysselsatte 15-74 år, etter alder og kjønn (AKU). I prosent av befolkningen* [The labour force, and employed persons, 15-74 years, by age and sex (LFS). Percentage of the population]. Retrieved January 25, 2011 from http://www.ssb.no/emner/06/01/aku/tab-2010-05-05-03b.html

Statistics Norway (2010b). *Arbeidsledige 15-74 år, etter kjønn og alder (AKU). 1 000 og present* [Unemployed 15 – 74 years, by sex and age (LFS)].In 1000 and as per cent]. Retrieved January 25, 2011 from http://www.ssb.no/emner/06/01/aku/arkiv/tab-2010-05-05-13.html

Statistics Norway (2010c). *Kvinneandel for studenter i høyere utdanning, etter fagfelt. Tall per 1.oktober 1980-2008. Prosent* [Per cent females of students in higher education, by field of study. Per 1. October 1980-2008]. Retrieved January 25, 2011 from http://www.ssb.no/samfunnsspeilet/utg/201001/03/tab-2010-03-01-02.html

Støren, L. A. (2009). *Choice of study and persistence in higher education by immigrant background, gender and social background. Rapport 43/2009.* Oslo: NIFU STEP.

Støren, L. A., Helland, H. & Grøgaard, J.B. (2007). *Og hvem stod igjen...? Sluttrapport fra prosjektet Gjennomstrømning i videregående opplæring blant elever som startet i videregående opplæring i årene 1999-2001* [And who was left behind...? Throughput of students in upper secondary education for classes embarking upon upper secondary education in 1999, 2000 and 2001.English Summary.] *Rapport 14/2007*. Oslo: NIFU STEP.

United Nations Educational, Scientific and Cultural Organization (2006). *Global education digest 2006. Comparing education statistics aross the world.* Montreal: UNESCO Institute for Statistics.

Wiers-Jenssen, J. & Try, S. (2005). Labour market outcomes of higher education undertaken abroad. *Studies in Higher Education 30*, 681-705.

Wiers-Jenssen, J. (2010). Norway: Mobile degree students vs. exchange students – What are the differences? In M. Saarlikallio-Torp & J. Wiers-Jenssen (2010). *Nordic students abroad. Student mobility patterns, student support systems and labour market outcomes* (pp. 84-97). Helsinki: Kela.

GABRIELA GROTKOWSKA

THE EMPLOYABILITY AND MOBILITY OF BACHELOR GRADUATES IN POLAND

STUDY STRUCTURE IN POLAND

Poland offers an example of a spectacular growth of the tertiary education popularity in recent years with the number of students growing almost fivefold in a 20-year transition period (Glowny Urzad Statystyczny [GUS], 1992, 2009a). As a result, the ratio of persons with tertiary education among the population aged 18-64 grew from 6.9 per cent in 1992 to 18 per cent in 2010 (LFS data for second quarter, Glowny Urzad Statystyczny [GUS], 1995, 2010). This significant increase was accompanied by substantial changes in the higher education system.

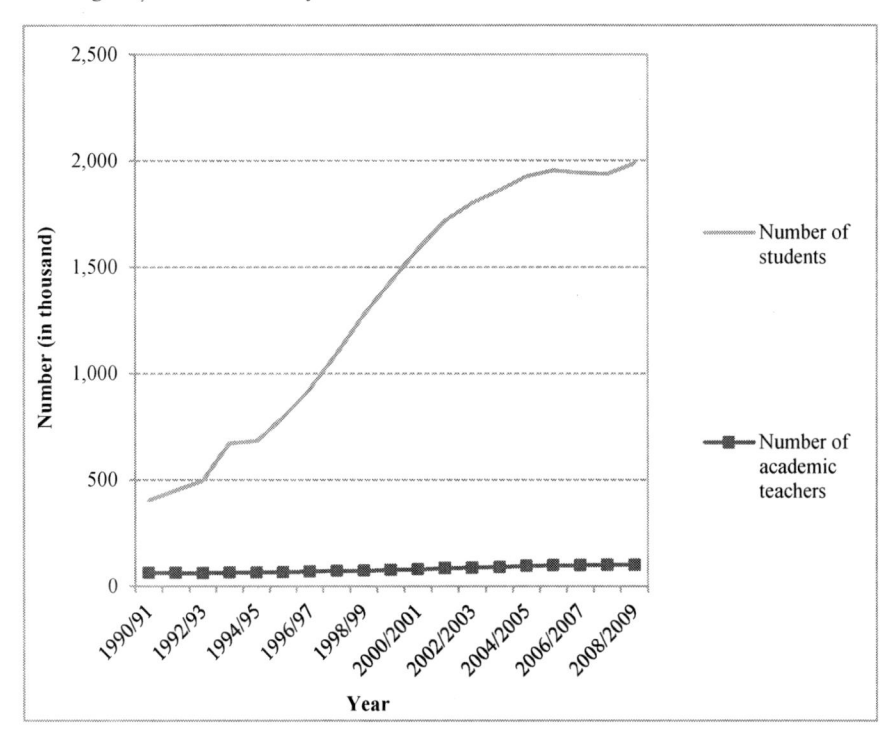

Figure 1. Total Number of Students and Academic Teachers in Poland 1990-2009

Source: GUS Statistical Yearbook, various editions

H. Schomburg and U. Teichler (eds.), *Employability and Mobility of Bachelor Graduates in Europe*, 209–227.
© 2011 *Sense Publishers. All rights reserved.*

Although the size of the Polish tertiary education system varied considerably over time, the study structure remained relatively stable up to 1990. During the post-war period, the number of higher education institutions grew from 54 (1946) to 97 (1989) and the number of students grew from 86,500 to 378,000, with 1975 being a record-breaking year (with the total number of students exceeding 468,000). In 1989, the number of students per 10,000 inhabitants equalled 75,400 (Glowny Urzad Statystyczny [GUS], 1994).

All Polish higher education institutions were state institutions. The only exception was the Catholic University of Lublin that retained a right to award the Master degree. In general, the political freedom of the Polish tertiary education system varied considerably under the socialist regime, although its situation was relatively good in comparison to other Soviet Bloc countries (with universities participating in the international exchange of scientist and fellowship programmes with Western Europe and the U.S.).

Before the beginning of the transition period, the Polish system of tertiary education offered studies leading to three kinds of degrees. Most required 5-year studies and led to the *magister* degree (Master). Concurrently, a large number of programmes, particularly in technical and agricultural domains, led to the award of an *inzynier* degree (engineer) after 3-4 years of study; often, they could be extended to a 5-year programme with graduates obtaining a "double" degree of *magister inzynier*. Polytechnics and domain-oriented academies (medical, economic, agricultural, pedagogical, musical, physical education, fine arts, etc.) and teachers' colleges offered programmes leading to a diploma. Later, they were classified as ISCED 5b level and recently equalled the *licencjat* (Bachelor) degree.

In the recent 20 years (1990-2010), the tertiary education system in Poland has undergone an in-depth transformation, both in terms of curricula and of organisation. The main features of change are:
- significant growth in the number of students in degree programmes, including Bachelor and Master degree students as well as doctoral students,
- an increasing variety of models of study programmes (different degrees, modes of education, development of part-time studies etc.),
- a dynamic development of the sector of non-public higher education institutions, operating mainly in the area of first-cycle programmes,
- a partial commercialisation of educational services provided by the public higher education institutions (with the introduction of tuition fees for some forms of study) being a response to growing demand for tertiary education and significant difficulties in the financing of public higher education, and
- growing difficulties in reconciling the growing number of students and the need to maintain quality standards, particularly (but not only) in the case of the private higher education sector.

Currently, there are four study programmes offered by Polish higher education institutions. These are: licencjat (Bachelor), inzynier (engineer), magister (Master) and doktor (Doctor). There are three levels of study programmes:

- first-cycle programmes: undergraduate programmes providing knowledge and skills in a specific area of study, preparing for work in a specific profession, and leading to the degree of *licencjat* or *inzynier*,
- second-cycle programmes: graduate programmes providing specialist knowledge in a specific area of study as well as preparing for creative work in a specific profession, and leading to the degree of *magister* or an equivalent degree,
- third-cycle programmes: doctoral programmes open to applicants holding the degree of magister or an equivalent degree, providing advanced knowledge in a specific area or discipline of science, preparing for an independent research and creative activity, and for the award of the academic degree of doctor.

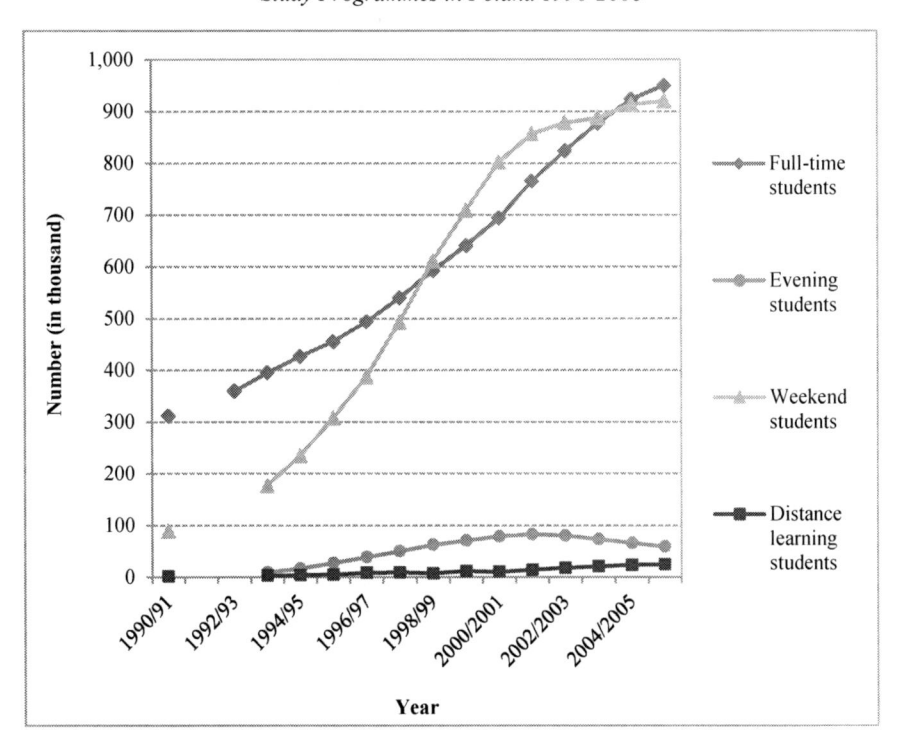

Figure 2. Number of Students according to Modes of Delivery of the Study Programmes in Poland 1990-2006

Source: GUS Statistical Yearbook, various editions

Moreover, some single-cycle programmes provide specialist knowledge in a specific area and prepare for creative work in a profession, and eventually lead to a magister or equivalent degree. They are offered mainly in the domains of medicine, law, psychology, etc.

According to the Law on Higher Education, there are five types of higher education institutions in Poland: universities, technical universities, other specialised universities, universities of technology and academies. Universities are authorised to confer the academic degree of *doktor* (PhD) in at least twelve disciplines, including at least two in humanities, social or theological sciences, mathematical, physical or engineering and technological sciences, natural sciences and in legal or economic sciences. Technical universities are authorised to confer the academic degree of *doktor* (PhD) in at least twelve disciplines, including at least eight in engineering and technological sciences. Also, these institutions may called "university" with another adjective or adjectives to define their institutional profile if they are authorised to confer the academic degree of *doktor* (PhD) in at least six disciplines, including at least four in the areas covered by the profile of the institution. Universities of technology must be authorised to confer the academic degree of *doktor* (PhD) in at least six disciplines, including four in engineering and technological sciences. Finally, academies are authorised to confer the academic degree of *doktor* (PhD) in at least two disciplines.

Major changes occurred recently in the framework of the Bologna Process. Currently, Poland may be regarded as well advanced in that process: it implemented three-year study programmes with good opportunities to continue to the next cycle of study, develop an external quality assurance system with significant student participation and implement tools to improve the recognition of higher education qualifications (diploma supplement, Lisbon Recognition Convention, ECTS). However, much remains to be done in the area of recognition of prior learning and the implementation of a national qualification framework.

THE GRADUATES' SURVEY USED FOR THE ANALYSIS

Although the implementation of the Bologna Process started in Poland around the year 2000, the system of public statistics does not reflect this change in a satisfactory way: most statistical data do not distinguish between first-cycle and second-cycle students and graduates; the same holds true for the most frequently used source of information on the labour market status and educational attainment of the labour force – the Polish Labour Force Survey (BAEL). The division between Bachelor graduates and Master graduates was not implemented in a special study on the transition from the education system to the labour market that was carried out in 2000 and 2009 under the supervision of Eurostat. The other data source is a survey on educational paths that is carried out cyclically on a representative sample of Polish households as a module survey together with a households' budgets survey. However, individual data gathered with this survey are currently unavailable. The basic data available on students and graduates are administrative data provided by higher education institutions. However, they only comprise information on the number of students and graduates by programme cycle, gender, type of higher education institution (public/private) and mode of study (full-time/part-time), some of which will be presented in the subsequent section.

More detailed data are gathered in a special graduates survey carried out in 2007, which includes information about the socio-economic characteristics of students and graduates. It was undertaken in the framework of a larger research project *"An inquiry on the labour market participation of school leavers in the context of the 'First Job' programme"* (in Polish: Badanieaktywnościzawodowejabsolwentów w kontekścierealizacji Programu "PierwszaPraca") for Ministry of Labour and Social Policy by a research consortium including team members of the Labour Market Research Centre from the Faculty of Economic Sciences, University of Warsaw. Key aims of the research project were to describe graduates' career paths with an identification of major factors shaping these, economic activities after graduation, notably the first job experience, the modes of entry into the labour market and to evaluate their effectiveness, find determinants of the economic inactivity and unemployment of graduates, study graduate mobility, assess the mismatch of graduates' qualifications and employers' requirements and identify the role and effectiveness of state institutions in the process of job intermediation.

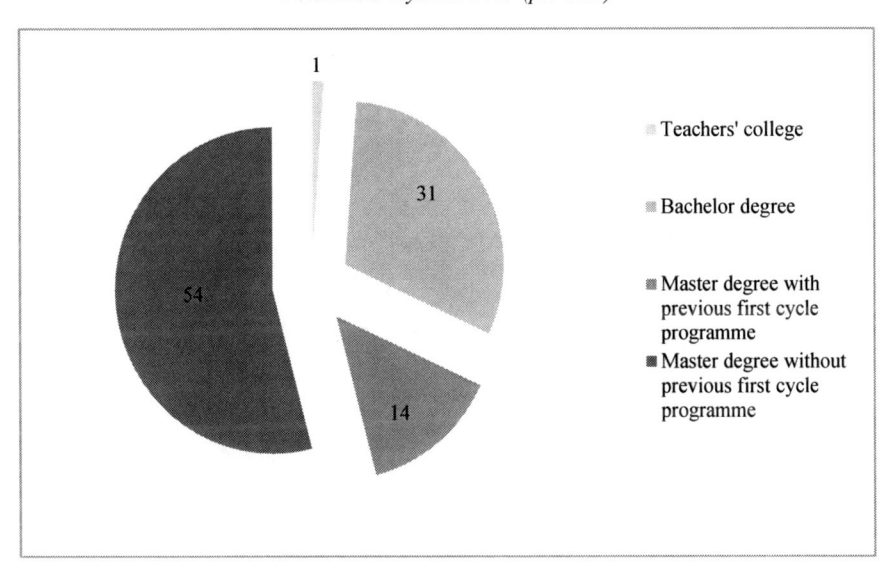

Figure 3. Types of Degree of Graduates from Tertiary Education Institutions in Poland Surveyed in 2007 (per cent)

Source: Author's calculation based on the 2007 Graduates' survey data

The data were gathered between late November 2006 and late February 2007 and the sample accounted for over 20,000 respondents selected to represent of young people in Poland. The sample consisted of persons who had completed upper secondary or higher education between January 1998 and December 2005, were under 27 years of age at the time of graduation and had not interrupted their education between the previous and the final stage for more than 12 months. The main deficiency of the dataset lies in the fact that only those who did not continue their studies were included. Therefore, it is impossible to describe the situation of Bachelor graduates who have not entered the labour market. The questionnaire addressed the educational path, job search after graduation, employment and work, impact of employment offices and spatial mobility of graduates.

A two-step sampling scheme was used with a first-step stratification according to territorial units (with the Hartley-Rao method), and a second step-sampling of households. 20,181 were surveyed, of whom 5,566 were graduates from tertiary education (ISCED 5B, 5a and VI). Of the graduates surveyed, 31 per cent graduated from a Bachelor programme, 14 per cent from Master programmes, while 54 per cent had completed a single-cycle programme and only one per cent a teacher training programme (see figure 3).

THE GRADUATES' SOCIO-BIOGRAPHIC BACKGROUND AND COURSE OF STUDY

As explained above, administrative data are available to describe the student population in Poland. Accordingly, the total number of students in higher education institutions was 1,927,762 in the academic year 2007/08. Almost 60 per cent were enrolled in first-cycle studies (of whom almost three quarters in Bachelor programmes and the others in short-cycle programmes leading to an engineer degree) about 15 per cent in second-cycle programmes and about 21 per cent in single-cycle programmes. Women constitute more than half the students in Poland, thereby having a significantly higher share in second-cycle and single-cycle programmes, but they are underrepresented in first-cycle engineering programmes. Most students in Poland study part-time (in evening or weekend classes); their share, however, is relatively small in single-cycle programmes and in first-cycle engineering programmes. Almost two thirds are enrolled in public institutions, as table 1 shows, again over-proportionally in single-cycle programmes and in first-cycle engineering programmes.

Table 1. Composition of Students in Higher Education Institutions in Poland in the Academic Year 2007/08

	Total	Women (per cent)	Full-time students (per cent)	Students in public institutions (per cent)
Total	1,927,762	57	48	65
First-cycle programmes	1,151,067	54	46	58
Among them: Bachelor programmes	831,032	64	43	50
Among them: engineering programmes	320,305	29	55	77
Second-cycle programmes	294,237	67	21	65
Single-cycle programmes	412,673	58	75	86

Source: Author's own calculations based on GUS 2009b

Those who hold a first-cycle degree represented slightly less than half the total number of graduates in the academic year 2007/08, as can be seen in table 2. Graduates from single-cycle (27 per cent) and second-cycle programmes (24 per cent) were more frequently represented among the graduates than in the overall student population. This is probably a result of the fact that the Bologna process was been implemented recently and many of the graduates who were surveyed started their study in the traditional system. However, the share of graduates from first-cycle programme who studied part-time corresponded to that among the student population.

Table 2. Composition of Graduates from Higher Education Institutions in Poland in the Academic Year 2007/08

	Total	Share of women (per cent)	Share of full-time graduates (per cent)	Share of graduates from public institutions (per cent)
Total	420,942	65	45	62
First-cycle programmes	206,744	65	38	47
Among them: Bachelor programmes	171,774	71	37	42
Among them: engineering programmes	34,970	32	44	71
Second-cycle programmes	99,180	71	19	63
Single-cycle programmes	115,018	61	80	87

Source: Author's own calculations based on GUS 2009b

The implementation of the Bologna Process progressed quickly despite the fact that some institutions introduced Bachelor programme only recently. The number of students in two-cycle programmes has increased considerably, even though the full effect of this change will be visible in a few years' time. The speed of change varies by field of study. Some (law, psychology, theology, medical domains) are excluded from this process and will remain single-cycle fields.

Table 3. Change in Graduates from Higher Education Institutions in Poland in Different Types of Study Programmes from 2003/04 to 2008/09 (2003/04 = 100 per cent)

Type of study programme	Students	Graduates
First-cycle Bachelor programmes	33	22
First-cycle engineering programmes	34	10
Second-cycle programmes	15	-6
Long-cycle programmes	-47	9

Source: Author's calculations based on GUS 2009b

Of the 2007 tertiary education graduates who were surveyed, most are women. Graduates from teachers' colleges and from second-cycle programmes subsequent to first-cycle study are over-represented. On average, graduates with a Master diploma are two years older than Bachelor graduates. Married persons, as one might expect, make up a smaller share among Bachelor graduates than among Master graduates; the same holds true with regard to those who have children. Generally, more first-cycle graduates came from rural areas than the average students (see table 4).

Table 4. Socio-biographic Background of Graduates from Tertiary Education Institutions in Poland Surveyed in 2007 (per cent*)

	Teachers' college	Bachelor degree	Master degree	Single-cycle degree	Total
Women	74	60	71	66	65
Men	26	40	29	34	35
Age					
Arithmetic mean	26.5	26.8	28.5	28.4	27.9
Median	26	26	28	28	28
Region					
Urban areas	79	72	73	76	74
Rural areas	22	29	27	25	26
Civil Status					
Single	63	59	45	52	53
Married	37	39	54	46	45
Divorced	0	2	1	1	1
Widow/er	0	0	0	0	0
With children	14	28	36	30	30
Household					
One-person	15	13	9	17	14
More than one: living together	83	84	88	81	83
More than one: living separately	2	4	3	3	3
Disability	3	1	1	1	1

* No answer included in percentages, but not documented in table 4

Source: Author's calculation based on the 2007 Graduates' survey data

Graduates from the different types of programme differ according to their family background. Bachelor graduates often come from families where only the father worked, while the mother was engaged in housework. Relatively often, they were brought up outside their families. More Master graduates than Bachelor graduates come from households where either both parents are economically active or mothers are employed, while the father was engaged in the household. Moreover, more graduates whose parents have a low level of educational attainment discontinue their studies after the Master degree (see table 5).

Table 5. *Family Background of Graduates from Tertiary Education Institutions in Poland Surveyed in 2007 (per cent*)*

	Teachers' college	Bachelor degree	Master degree	Single-cycle degree	Total
Working father, mother engaged in housework	2	36	13	48	100
Both parents' contributing to professional work and housework	1	30	15	54	100
Both parents worked professionally, mother responsible for housework	1	29	13	57	100
Working mother, father engaged in housework	0	21	23	56	100
Other model	0	36	14	50	100
Respondents brought up outside family	0	39	22	39	100
Mother					
Primary education	2	32	20	46	100
Basic vocational education	1	36	16	47	100
General secondary education	1	32	10	57	100
Vocational secondary education	1	30	14	55	100
Post-secondary education	4	33	12	51	100
Tertiary education	1	21	13	65	100
Father					
Primary education	1	38	19	42	100
Basic vocational education	1	38	16	46	100
General secondary education	1	32	11	56	100
Vocational secondary education	1	31	16	53	100
Post-secondary education	2	28	11	59	100
Tertiary education	2	23	14	62	100
Total	1	31	14	54	100

* No answer included in percentages, but not documented in table 5

Source: Author's calculation based on the 2007 Graduates' survey data

The share of Bachelor graduates and Master graduates differ according to field of study, as is seen in figure 4. Many single-cycle Master graduates had studied law, physics, health, humanities and arts. Master graduates had often studied management, economics and administration – three of the most popular fields of tertiary education in Poland. Bachelor graduates who do not continue their studies had often studied in services, security, military, engineering, administration and general programmes.

GABRIELA GROTKOWSKA

As already pointed out, the role of full-time studies declined in recent years, other modes of delivery (evening classes, weekend classes or distance education) had been at the Master stage of study (60 per cent) as well as among students who had come from vocational schools (50 per cent). In contrast, they were least frequent in teacher education (11 per cent) and in single-cycle programmes (20 per cent).

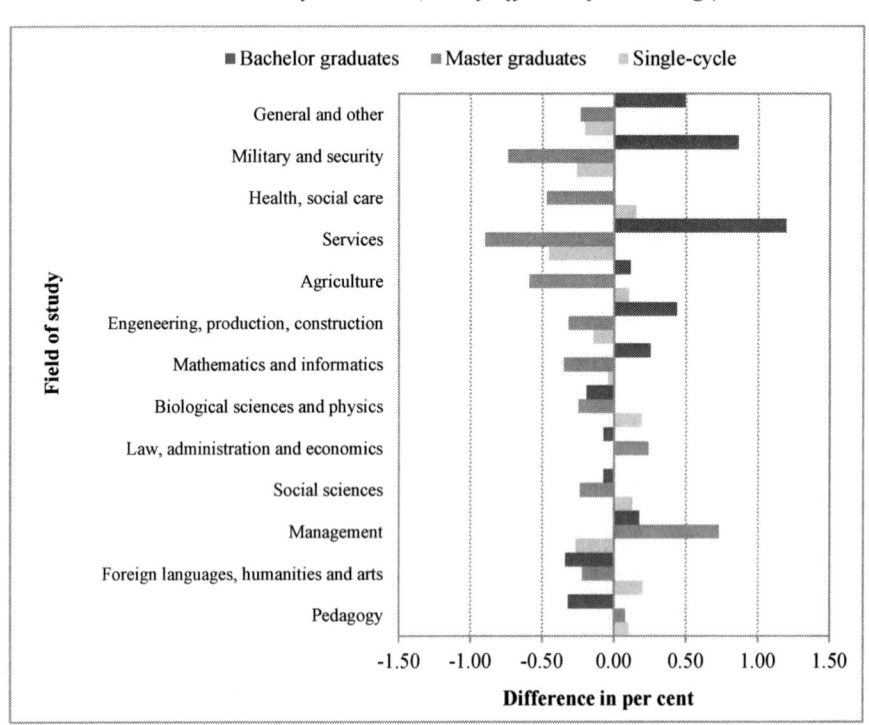

Figure 4. Field of Study of Graduates from Tertiary Education Institutions in Poland Surveyed in 2007 (rate of difference from average)

Source: Author's calculation based on the 2007 Graduates' survey data

Private higher education programmes were most strongly represented among Bachelors and Masters who had come from vocational schools (43 per cent and 42 per cent respectively). This rate was about 20 per cent among other Bachelors and Masters and 12 per cent among those studying at teachers' colleges and 9 per cent of those studying in single-cycle programmes.

GRADUATES' INTERNATIONAL MOBILITY

One of the most important goals of the implementation of the Bologna Process was to facilitate student mobility, both at national and international level. Table 6 shows the incidence of graduates' international mobility during the course of study, and table 7 informs about mobility after graduation. Almost 12 per cent of the tertiary education graduates who were surveyed report that they spent at least two weeks abroad. This percentage is slightly higher among graduates from single-cycle programmes than among those from Master programmes; one could have expected the opposite result, because the break between the Bachelor programme and the Master programme offers an additional opportunity for mobility.

It is interesting to note that about two thirds of the sojourns during the course of study are job-related and less than one third study-related. Thereby, most of the work abroad is not linked to study; this proportion is especially low among Bachelor students. Most students state that they organised the stay abroad individually. This is more often the case among Bachelor students than among those of other programmes. Overall, the sojourns abroad are not assessed very positively. The largest share of graduates believes that it did not make a difference for their development and career, while more graduates rated it as harmful.

Only about 7 per cent of the graduates travelled abroad after graduation (tourist trips excluded). The rate is slightly higher among Bachelor graduates than among those with higher degrees. Most worked abroad, but, surprisingly, this is in most cases viewed as not being related to their study. The most frequent purpose was earning money (see table 7).

48 per cent considered their work abroad as beneficial for their development and careers and 42 per as different. In contrast to the assessment of the sojourn abroad during the course of study, hardly any graduates considered the sojourn abroad after graduation as harmful for their development and career (only 8 per cent).

Table 6. Mobility during the Course of Study of Graduates from Tertiary Education Institutions in Poland Surveyed in 2007 (per cent*)

	Teachers' college	Bachelor graduates	Master graduates	Single-cycle graduates	Total
Period of at least two weeks abroad	15	8	12	14	12
Period of at least one semester abroad	3	2	3	3	3
Main aim of going abroad					
Course/training	20	14	11	10	11
Fellowship	-	4	11	11	9
Job-related stay (on organised basis)	20	15	19	16	16
Job-related stay (on individual basis)	40	56	44	47	49
Student exchange	10	7	6	8	8
Other goals	10	4	5	8	7
Total	100	100	100	100	100
Were you working whilst abroad?					
Not working	10	24	20	24	23
Working in accordance with study profile	10	7	14	18	15
Working not in accordance with study profile	70	67	62	57	60
Total	100	100	100	100	100
Organisation of the trip					
Au pair	-	2	1	2	2
Leonardo Programme	-	-	2	1	1
Socrates Erasmus Programme	-	7	5	7	7
Work experience	-	-	-	0	0
Work and travel	-	3	6	7	6
Other programme	30	18	26	21	21
Individual trip	70	71	54	61	62
Total	100	100	100	100	100
Was it beneficial for your development and career?					
Very beneficial	10	18	16	25	22
Rather beneficial	-	2	8	6	5
Didn't make any difference	20	53	38	39	41
Was rather harmful	70	27	34	30	30
Total	100	100	100	100	100

* Percentage of those spending at least two weeks abroad

Source: Author's calculation based on the 2007 Graduates' survey data

Table 7. Mobility after Graduation of Graduates from Tertiary Education Institutions in Poland Surveyed in 2007 (per cent*)

	Teachers' college	Bachelor graduates	Master graduates	Single-cycle graduates	Total
One trip abroad after graduation	5	6	3	5	5
More than one trip abroad after graduation	5	3	2	2	2
Main aim of going abroad					
For work	50	84	72	69	75
For internship	0	1	5	5	4
For course/training	50	6	9	15	11
For other purposes	0	6	12	7	7
Did you work whilst abroad?					
Worked not related to study	33	73	63	63	66
Work related to study	17	16	14	17	16
Did not work – could not find job	33	4	12	7	7
Did not work because I did not want to work	17	6	9	8	7
What was main benefit of the stay abroad?					
Gaining experience	17	2	7	7	5
Gaining knowledge	17	2	5	4	3
Earning money	0	71	67	60	64
Learning language	67	15	2	9	11
Raising qualifications	0	4	5	7	5
Contacts with other culture	0	1	9	7	5
Adventure	0	3	2	3	3
Was it beneficial for your development and career?					
Very beneficial	67	18	19	20	20
Rather beneficial	33	29	30	27	28
Indifferent for my career	0	49	33	40	42
Rather harmful	0	1	9	5	4
Very harmful	0	2	7	5	4

* Those not responding to the additional questions are included in the percentages

Source: Author's calculation based on the 2007 Graduates' survey data

THE EMPLOYMENT AND FURTHER STUDY OF BACHELOR GRADUATES

The graduate survey undertaken in 2007 does not provide information about the proportion of those continuing their studies, because it addressed only persons who did not go on to further study. However, the statistics presented above on the student population (tables 1-3) allow us to draw conclusions on the determinants for further study after the Bachelor award by comparing the composition of students studying at the Master level to the Bachelor graduates who do not continue their studies. Accordingly, there is a higher proportion of women, of students in management, economics and administration and of persons who studied in their Bachelor programme on a full-time basis at a university or at another institutions of higher education. In contrast, fewer Masters students are enrolled in fields such as services, security, engineering and IT.

80 per cent of the graduates surveyed in 2007 were professionally active. The rate ranged from 69 per cent among Bachelor graduates to 84 per cent among graduates from single-cycle programmes. In reverse, the unemployment rate was 14 per cent among Bachelor graduates, but only 8 per cent among single-cycle graduates. The proportion of those not on the labour market varied only between 8 per cent and 11 per cent according to type of degree.

Table 8. Employment Status of Graduates from Tertiary Education Institutions in Poland Surveyed in 2007 (per cent)

	Teachers' college	Bachelor graduates	Master graduates	Single-cycle graduates	Total
Employed	69	74	81	84	80
Unemployed	20	14	10	8	10
Inactive	11	13	9	8	10

Source: Author's own calculation based on the 2007 Graduates' survey data

PROFESSIONAL SUCCESS OF BACHELOR GRADUATES

The professional success of graduates can be measured in terms of employment conditions, but also of its quality (see Costrell, 1990; Champlin, 1995; de Grip & Wolbers, 2006; Green, 2006) and of the links between study and the nature of work. In looking at the employment conditions, table 9 suggests – not surprisingly – that the situation for Bachelor graduates in Poland is less favourable than for Master graduates and single-cycle graduates. They are less often permanently employed (45 per cent as compared to 52 per cent each) and more often employed in a family business (8 per cent as compared to 6 per cent and 4 per cent).

Table 9. *Employment Conditions of Employed Graduates from Tertiary Education Institutions in Poland when Surveyed in 2007 (per cent)*

	Teachers' college	Bachelor graduates	Master graduates	Single-cycle graduates	Total
Self-employed in agriculture	5	2	1	1	1
Self-employed in other sectors	3	7	5	6	6
Contributing to family farm	0	1	1	0	1
Contributing to other family business	0	0	0	0	0
Permanently employed	55	45	52	52	50
Fixed-term employed up to one year	8	16	15	14	15
Fixed-term employment for more than one year	20	19	19	17	18
Fixed-term civil contract	5	4	3	3	3
Employed without any formal contract	0	2	0	1	1
Apprenticeship contract or training	0	2	1	2	2
Total	100	100	100	100	100

Source: Author's calculation based on the 2007 Graduates' survey data

There are also differences according to economic sector, as can be seen in figure 5. Bachelor graduates are less often represented in sectors offering a relatively high degree of employment security, e.g. education, health care, public administration, etc. or offering high wages, e.g. financial intermediation. Rather, they work relatively frequently in industry (energy supply and mining in particular) and agriculture.

Figure 5. Economic Sector (NACE Section) of Employed Graduates from Tertiary Education Institutions in Poland when Surveyed in 2007 (rate of difference from average)

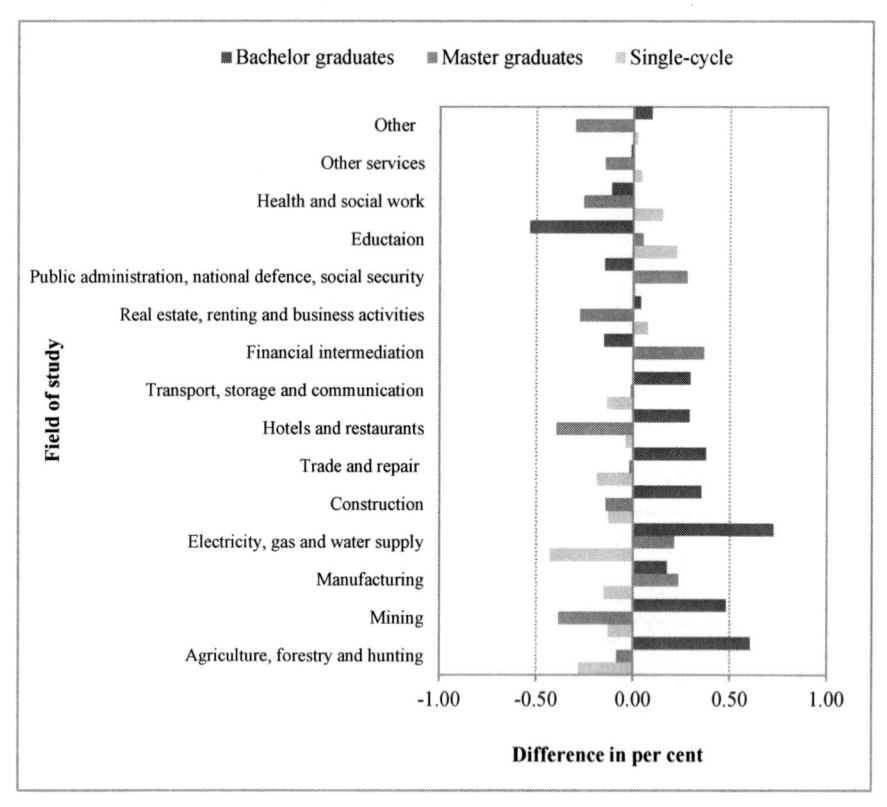

[Bar chart: Bachelor graduates, Master graduates, Single-cycle. Field of study categories (from top): Other, Other services, Health and social work, Eductaion, Public administration national defence social security, Real estate renting and business activities, Financial intermediation, Transport storage and communication, Hotels and restaurants, Trade and repair, Construction, Electricity gas and water supply, Manufacturing, Mining, Agriculture forestry and hunting. X-axis: Difference in per cent, -1.00 to 1.00.]

Source: Author's calculation based on the 2007 Graduates' survey data

As for work conditions, table 10 suggests that the situation for Bachelor graduates in Poland is less favourable than that for Master and single-cycle graduates. On the one hand, Bachelor graduates work somewhat more often on shifts, at night and at weekend. One the other hand, they report less often that their work is related to their study (60 per cent as compared to 72 per cent and 73 per cent) and that they have good promotion prospects (58 per cent as compared to 62 per cent and 64 per cent).

Table 10. Quality of Work and Links between Study and Work on the Part of Employed Graduates from Tertiary Education Institutions in Poland when Surveyed in 2007 (per cent)

	Teachers college	Bachelor graduates	Master graduates	Single-cycle degree graduates	Total
Working on shift	33	36	27	28	30
Working at night	11	18	12	15	15
Working at weekends	50	58	44	47	49
Work related to study	75	60	72	73	69
Promotion perspectives	60	58	62	64	62

Source: Author's calculation based on the 2007 Graduates' survey data

Compared to the links between study and work presented in table 10, the ratings hardly vary by type of degree, as far as the professional use of knowledge which has been acquired during the course of study is concerned. As can be seen in table 11, 82 per cent of Bachelor graduates believe that it is "very useful" or "rather useful". The respective share is 83 per cent for Master graduates and 83 per cent for single-cycle graduates.

Table 11. Professional Usefulness of Knowledge Acquired during the Course of Study according to Employed Graduates from Tertiary Education Institutions in Poland Surveyed in 2007 (per cent)

	Teachers college	Bachelor graduates	Master graduates	Single-cycle degree graduates	Total
Very useful	44	28	32	35	32
Rather useful	47	53	51	48	50
Not too useful	8	16	14	14	15
Not useful	2	3	3	4	3

Source: Author's calculation based on the 2007 Graduates' survey data

Finally, the income of Bachelor graduates in Poland is only slightly lower than that of graduates from advanced degrees. According to the 2007 survey, the net hourly wage is 8.59 PLN for Bachelor graduates, 9.24 PLN for Master graduates and 9.18 PLN for single-cycle graduates. Thus, Bachelor graduates earn only 7 per cent less per hour than Master graduates and per cent 6 per cent less than single-cycle graduates – a small difference given by the difference in the level of educational attainment.

CONCLUSION

Higher education in Poland is relatively advanced in the implementation of the Bologna Process, but most institutions have only recently introduced the three-cycle structure of study programmes. Therefore, it is too early to assess the consequences of the Bologna Process for graduate employment comprehensively. Relevant statistical data in Poland are scarce, but even if the data were better, the number of Bachelor graduates and notably of Master graduates in the new system is still too small to draw any final conclusions on their labour market advantages or disadvantages.

However, in a graduate survey undertaken in 2007, almost one third of respondents in Poland are Bachelor graduates and almost one sixth Master graduates. Therefore, it is possible to analyse and interpret some characteristics of the employment situation of Bachelor graduates.

The findings as regards international mobility could be summarised as follows:
- The share of graduates from tertiary education institutions in Poland having spent at least one semester abroad during the course of study is quite low (3 per cent). It is 2 per cent among Master graduates, 3 per cent among Master graduates and 3 per cent among graduates from single-cycle programmes.
- The information on international mobility after graduation in Poland is not comparable to that available for other countries, because the graduate survey undertaken in Poland is not comparable to that of other country, because the graduates were asked to quote the number of trips abroad for work and study purposes.

According to this definition, the employed Bachelor graduates are the most mobile (9 per cent at least one trip, as compared to 7 per cent of the Master graduates and 7 per cent of graduates from single-cycle programmes).

No accurate information is available in Poland about the whereabouts of Bachelor graduates, because the major graduate survey addresses only employed Bachelor graduates and because the general statistics do not identify their whereabouts. Statistics show that the number of Master degrees in 2007/08 corresponded to 47 per cent of the number of Bachelor degrees. As both figures grew significantly and the cohort of Master graduates could only be compared to that of the Bachelor degrees two or three years earlier, one can infer that substantially more than half the Bachelor graduates continue their studies.

The employed Bachelor graduates in Poland are in various respects in a less favourable employment situation than the Master graduates and the graduates from single-cycle programmes:
- The unemployment rate at the time of the survey is 14 per cent among Bachelor graduates as compared to 10 per cent among Master graduates and 8 per cent among single-cycle graduates.
- The Bachelor graduates are less often permanently employed (45 per cent as compared to 52 per cent each), and, in reverse, more often active in family business (8 per cent as compared to 6 per cent and 4 per cent).
- Bachelor graduates report less often that their work is related to their studies (60 per cent as compared to 72 per cent and 73 per cent) and that they have good promotion prospects (58 per cent as compared to 62 per cent and 64 per cent).

However, there are hardly any differences in the assessment that the knowledge acquired in the course of study is useful for their work (81 per cent as compared to 83 per cent and 82 per cent respectively).
- Finally, the net wage per hour of Bachelor graduates is only 7 per cent lower than that of Master graduates and 6 per cent lower than that of graduates from single-cycle programmes.

In sum, Bachelor graduates in Poland are in a more unfavourable situation in some respects, in a similar situation with regard to the use of knowledge and in a good situation as regards income, because a lower rate of 6 per cent or 7 per cent is less than one would expect given the lower level of educational attainment.

Some preliminary multivariate analyses suggest that – with control of other socio-economic characteristics (gender, age, civil status, field of education, class of settlement unit, region, disability, average grade, family background) – the probability of employment of men with a Bachelor degree is lower than for men with basic or vocational education, while only the Master degrees and the single-cycle degrees provide slightly better chances of finding a job compared to men with basic vocational education. In the case of women, the impact of a Bachelor degree is statistically negligible but very strong with the award of a Master degree. These potentially very meaningful results require further investigation with more appropriate and representative data.

REFERENCES

Champlin, D. (1995). Understanding job quality in an era of structural change: What can economics learn from industrial relations? *Journal of Economic Issues*, 29, 829-841.

Costrell, R. (1990). Methodology in the 'job quality' debate. *Industrial Relation: A Journal of Economics and Society*, 29, 94-110.

De Grip, A. & Wolbers, M. H. J. (2006). Cross-national differences in job quality among low-skilled young workers in Europe. *International Journal of Manpower*, 27, 420-433.

Glowny Urzad Statystyczny (1992). *Rocznik Statystyczny Rzeczpospolitej Polskiej 1992* [Statistical yearbook of the Republic of Poland]. Warszawa: GUS.

Glowny Urzad Statystyczny (1994). *Rocznik Statystyczny Szkolnictwa 1993/94* [Education statistical yearbook 1993/94 period]. Warszawa: GUS.

Glowny Urzad Statystyczny (1995). *Aktywnośćekonomicznaludności Polski 1992-1994* [Economic activity of Poland's population 1992-1994]. Warszawa: GUS.

Glowny Urzad Statystyczny (2009a). *Rocznik Statystyczny Rzeczpospolitej Polskiej 2009* [Statistical yearbook of the Republic of Poland]. Warszawa: GUS.

Glowny Urzad Statystyczny (2009b). *Szkoły wyższe i ichfinanse w 2008 roku* [Higher education institutions and their finances in 2008]. Warszawa: GUS.

Glowny Urzad Statystyczny (2010). *Aktywnośćzawodowaludności Polski w II kwartale 2010* [Economic activity of Poland's population in the second quarter 2010]. Warszawa: GUS.

Green, F. (2006). *Demanding work: The paradox of job quality in the affluent economy*. Princeton, NJ: Princeton University Press.

BRENDA LITTLE

THE UK BACHELORS DEGREE – A SOUND BASIS FOR FLEXIBLE ENGAGEMENT WITH AN UNREGULATED LABOUR MARKET?

THE STUDY STRUCTURE IN THE UK

The higher education system in the United Kingdom has *traditionally* consisted of a *two-cycle structure* for taught programmes, leading to two main qualifications: the Bachelor's degree at undergraduate level, which is normally awarded "with honours" and is often termed the first degree; and the Master's degree at postgraduate level. These are equivalent to first and second cycle qualifications respectively in the framework for qualifications of the European Higher Education Area (FQ-EHEA). The doctorate degree (equivalent to a third cycle qualification in the FQ-EHEA) is a research-focussed higher degree, and follows on from studies at the undergraduate level plus research training (often provided through a Masters degree). Of the 2.4 million students in UK higher education in 2008/09 over half (56 per cent) were studying at Bachelors (first) degree level; a further 21 per cent were studying at "other undergraduate level" (equivalent to short cycle qualifications in the FQ-EHEA); and the remaining fifth (22 per cent) were studying at postgraduate level. Some 670,000 higher education qualifications are awarded every year: half of these are Bachelor's/first degrees; a fifth are "other undergradduate" qualifications, and the remaining 30 per cent are postgraduate awards.

Within the United Kingdom, a distinction is made between *full-time and part-time modes of study*, with the former generally defined as studying an average of at least 21 hours per week, for at least 24 weeks/year. Overall, in 2008/09 almost two thirds of higher education students were studying on a full-time basis, and just over a third on a part-time basis. Of the 1,352,000 students on first degrees, three quarters were classified as full-time students.

Most full-time first degree students (69 per cent) are registered on three-year programmes, but there is considerable variation in *length of programmes* between fields of study; programmes longer than four years are mainly linked to professional training in veterinary science and medicine and dentistry, and to a much smaller extent to engineering and technology, and architecture, building and planning). In 2008/09, only four per cent of first year, full-time first degree students were on such programmes. Most complete their studies within the "set" duration. Because of the differently structured compulsory education system in Scotland and the slightly lower minimum entry age to first degrees in (17 years of age instead of 18 in the rest of the United Kingdom), honours degree programmes are four years long (instead of the more usual three years elsewhere in the United Kingdom).

A further 508,000 students were on *"other undergraduate" programmes,* leading to certificates, diplomas or foundation degrees, and in contrast to first degree

H. Schomburg and U. Teichler (eds.), Employability and Mobility of Bachelor Graduates in Europe, 229–251.
© 2011 *Sense Publishers. All rights reserved.*

students. 75 per cent were studying on a part-time basis. The foundation degree is a new qualification introduced in 2001 to meet employers" demands for intermediate level skills. Currently, they represent around 14 per cent of the "other undergraduate" student population.

Just over a fifth of the student population (22 per cent) studies at *post-graduate level*, with numbers evenly split between full-time and part-time modes of study. In 2008/09, some 320,000 postgraduate students were following Master's programmes, and accounted for 60 per cent of the postgraduate student population. These programmes normally require one or two years of full-time study, but are often studied part-time for mid-career professional training purposes. In this respect, we should note that in the United Kingdom, new first degree graduates do not move straight on to Master's programmes. Almost half of all Masters degree students study on a part-time basis and they are likely to be older and more experienced in the labour market than their full-time counterparts (Higher Education Careers Services Unit, 2009). A further 136,000 students were on other postgraduate (taught) courses, accounting for a quarter of the postgraduate population. Over 80,000 were on doctorate degrees, accounting for 15 per cent of the postgraduate population. Full-time doctorate studies normally comprise three or four years (depending on candidate's prior research methods training) of supervised research, culminating in a substantial thesis based on original research. Since the 1990s, "professional" doctorates have been developed within the United Kingdom. They have a higher "taught" component than traditional doctorates, frequently involve work-based research, and are aimed at enhancing professional practice by making a contribution to professional knowledge.

Higher education is offered primarily by *universities*, but also by *other higher education institutions*. There are currently over 160 higher education institutions in the United Kingdom, of which 116 are universities. Universities have their own degree awarding powers and are very diverse in terms of size, mission, subject spread and history. Higher education is also provided by colleges, some with their own degree-awarding powers and in others, the qualifications are validated (approved) by a university (or a national accrediting body). Higher education provision is also offered in some Further education (FE) colleges. These colleges provide continuing education and training for young people (aged 16+) who have chosen not to remain in the school system, and for adults. FE provision includes academic, vocational, leisure and personal development courses usually below higher education level. But within England, around ten per cent of higher education provision is through further education colleges, and in Scotland the proportion is rather higher – at around 17 per cent (The Scottish Government, 2010).

Prior to 1992, there was binary system of higher education in the UK, comprising universities on the one hand and polytechnics (and central institutions, in Scotland) on the other. But since the Further and Higher Education Act of 1992 granted university status to the polytechnics, the binary divide has been abolished and in theory the United Kingdom now has a unitary higher education system. Though "unitary" in name, there is a quite steep reputational hierarchy differentiating institutions.

85 per cent of students in United Kingdom higher education are UK-domiciled. Among *the internationally mobile students*, just five per cent are from other member countries of the European Union, and ten per cent are from non-EU countries. Almost half the non-UK students are on postgraduate programmes, and whilst most UK postgraduates study on a part-time basis, most non-UK postgraduates are full-time. It should be noted that British educational statistics do not indicate the students" citizen ship, but rather the country of domicile.

Within the United Kingdom there has been a long-standing tradition of young people moving "away" from home to study for their first degree on a full-time basis, although with the more diverse student population the balance between *"residential" students* (who have moved away to study) and *"commuting" students* (who attend their local university) is changing. A recent report by the Higher Education Funding Council for England (HEFCE) concerned with the term-time accommodation of young, full-time, first degree entrants to higher education in England and Wales notes that in 1984-85 only around eight per cent of young entrants were living at home with their parents (Higher Education Funding Council for England [HEFCE], 2009a). But during the 1990s, this proportion rose steadily so that, by 2000-01, around 20 per cent of young entrants to first degrees were living at home; and this proportion has remained steady over the period 2001-02 to 2006-07. HEFCE notes certain associations between rates of living at home and certain groups of students, but is careful to avoid ascribing such variation to any particular variable. So, for example, female students are more likely to live at home in their first year of study than their male counterparts; Bangladeshi and Pakistani students are more likely to live at home than students from other ethnic groups; students whose parents are from higher socio-economic groups are less likely to live at home.

Generally, first degree students in the United Kingdom tend to be both *younger and older* than the European average. In 2008/09, four in ten first year (UK) entrants to full-time first degrees were aged 18 or under, a further fifth were aged 19, and seven per cent were aged 20; so, overall, two thirds were aged 20 or under. Only one in five (21 per cent) were aged 25 or over. However, the age distribution of entrants to part-time first degrees is rather different, with just seven per cent of first year entrants being aged 20 or under, and three quarters (77 per cent) aged 25 or over (Higher Education Statistics Agency [HESA], 2009c). This age on entry to full-time first degrees, coupled with the fact that most students who complete do so within the "set" duration for the programme means that the vast majority of Bachelor graduates in the United Kingdom (who studied full-time) are aged 24 or less when they first leave higher education.

GRADUATE SURVEYS USED IN THIS ANALYSIS

The main system-wide data used in this chapter is drawn from national *Higher Education Statistics Agency (HESA)* publications. HESA produces a series of reference volumes annually, including: reports on students in higher education institutions, based on data returns made by *all* publicly-funded higher education institutions in the United Kingdom; and the destinations of graduates from higher education institutions (DLHE) survey. In standard HESA publications, data relating to qualification level tend to concern two main levels of study, undergraduate and postgraduate; the former is broken down into "first degrees" and "other undergraduate" and the latter (postgraduate) is split between higher degrees (doctorates; other higher degrees) and "other postgraduate" (Post Graduate Certificate in Education; other postgraduate qualifications). As such, discrete data relating to "just" Master's degree students and qualifiers are not necessarily readily available in the public domain. In keeping with the overall thrust of individual chapters in this book, and in particular comparisons between Bachelor graduates and Master graduates in this chapter on higher education in the United Kingdom, we do present some comparisons between Bachelor degree students and Master degree students where such data are readily available. However, in other instances such specific comparisons cannot be made, and rather broader categories of "other higher degrees", or "postgraduate qualifications" have had to be used instead.

The DLHE survey is now carried out in two stages. The first stage, the *"early survey"*, is a *census* of individuals who have completed higher education courses in the United Kingdom and is undertaken *six months after students complete their studies*. The survey covers full-time and part-time students, and since 2000 has been limited to UK- and EU-domiciled students. The "early survey" is undertaken by all higher education institutions with the procedure for data capture prescribed by HESA. The target response rates set for the DLHE survey vary by mode of study and by domicile. Table 1 shows the target and response rates for the 2007/08 DLHE survey.

Table 1. Response Rates of Destinations of Graduates from Higher Education Institutions Surveyed in the United Kingdom in 2007/08, by Domicile and Mode of Study (per cent)

Mode of study and domicile of graduates	Actual rate	Target rate
Full-time UK	79	80
Full-time other EU	55	50
Part-time UK	71	70
Part-time other EU	50	50

Source: Higher Education Statistics Agency (2009a), table i

In 2007/08, there were almost half a million qualifiers (474,455) and 344,715 valid responses received, giving a survey-wide response rate of 73 per cent (Higher Education Statistics Agency [HESA], 2009a). The vast majority of responses (98 per cent) came from UK-domiciled students. HESA notes that DLHE response rates vary greatly between institutions and are dependent in part on the amount of resources committed by the institution to the various stages of the process.

The second stage of the DLHE analysis is a *follow-up survey* which explores the destinations of leavers up to *three and a half years after* they qualified (HESA, 2009c), and is referred to as the "longitudinal survey". It is based on a *sample* of leavers from a previous "early survey". The 2004/05 DLHE *longitudinal survey*, undertaken during winter 2008/09 obtained a response rate of 25.7 per cent (i.e. 41,000 responses from 161,000 graduates from higher education in 2004/05).

The system-wide national data are useful to describe the overall shape and size of higher education in the United Kingdom, and overall patterns of destinations after completing higher education. More fine-grained descriptions of particular facets (for example, graduates" success in finding suitable employment after graduation; the nature of such employment, including the extent to which graduates" perceive they are using their knowledge and skills) may also be found in specific one-off studies. In this chapter we draw on system-wide national data, findings from other studies of certain aspects of higher education in the United Kingdom, and the findings of a recent Europe-wide study of graduates five years after graduation, namely the REFLEX study[1]. The target population for the 2004/05 REFLEX survey was those who had completed their initial higher education in 1999/2000; UK graduates in this sample had completed a Bachelor degree (though some subsequently obtained a Master degree within the time frame of the survey) whereas most other respondents had obtained a Master-equivalent qualification. The sample in the United Kingdom was drawn from 43 higher education institutions covering a range of types of institutions and locations. The sample was broadly representative of the first degree graduating population of 1999/2000, and comprised 1,578 valid responses (a response rate of 23 per cent). Given that the REFLEX study was comparative in nature, we are able to use the data to highlight some particular similarities and differences between United Kingdom graduates and mainland Europe graduates.

---

[1] The REFLEX study – full title "The flexible professional in the knowledge society: New demands on higher education in Europe" was a European Commission Framework VI project which examined how graduates in different European countries were prepared for the labour market.

GRADUATES' SOCIO-BIOGRAPHIC BACKGROUND AND COURSE OF STUDY

In 2008/09, the age *participation rate* for English-domiciled first time participants in higher education was 45 per cent (up from 43 per cent in 2007/08) (Department for Business, Innovation and Skills, 2010). But within the United Kingdom, social class remains a strong determinant of participation in higher education, and, despite various government initiatives, the gap between participation rates of those from higher social classes and those from lower social classes has not lessened in the last 40-50 years (The Panel on Fair Access to the Professions, 2009). Government figures show that participation rates in higher education for young people from socio-economic groups I and II have risen from 28 per cent in 1960 to 48 per cent in 2000; over the same period, participation rates from socio-economic groups III, IV and V have also risen, but from a much lower base of five per cent in 1960 to 18 per cent in 2000. Despite some progress in narrowing the gap between *participation rates for certain socio-economic groups*, almost three times as many young people with parents in professional occupations attend university as those with parents in routine occupations (ibid, p. 88). Despite the fact that over half of all young people in England come from lower socio-economic backgrounds, only 29 per cent of university students are from this group. Thus we see that participation rates vary considerably when based on parental background; moreover, the more selective universities remain "over-populated by students from wealthier backgrounds, often privately educated" (ibid., p. 88). Much of this "over-population" can be explained by differential levels of attainment (pre-higher education) but application rates to the more selective institutions are also a large factor (Harris, 2010). More generally within the United Kingdom, the report from the National Equality Panel (set-up to examine how inequalities in people's economic outcomes are related to their characteristics and circumstances) finds that differences in "school readiness" by parental resources and social class are already apparent in children's early years, and widen through compulsory schooling, i.e. pre-higher education (National Equality Panel, 2010).

The distribution of higher education students by socio-economic background and programme of study is not readily available from HESA publications. In the following sub-section, we look at the distribution of students by field[2] and level of study. The table below shows the "top five" field of study areas by level of study.

---

[2] HESA uses a 19-subject area categorisation in its published reference volumes

Table 2. "Top Five" Field of Study Areas of all Students at Higher Education Institutions in the United Kingdom 2008/09, by Level of Study (per cent in brackets)

	Other Undergraduate (21 per cent of all students)	First degree (56 per cent of all students)	Higher degree (taught) (13 per cent of all students)	Higher degree (research) (4 per cent of all students)	Other postgraduate (6 per cent of all students)
1	Subjects allied to medicine (25)	Business and admin. studies (13)	Business and admin. studies (28)	Biological sciences (12)	Education (50)
2	Combined (18)	Biological sciences (10)	Social studies (9)	Engineering and technology (12)	Subjects allied to medicine (14)
3	Education (12)	Social studies (10)	Education (9)	Physical sciences (11)	Business and admin. studies (11)
4	Business and admin. studies (10)	Creative arts and design (9)	Subjects allied to medicine (8)	Social studies (9)	Law (5)
5	Social studies (7)	Subjects allied to medicine (9)	Engineering and technology (8)	Medicine and dentistry (8)	Social studies (5)

Source: Higher Education Statistics Agency (2009c), table E

As can be seen in table 2, certain fields of study dominate certain levels of study; for example at "other undergraduate" level, a quarter of all students are studying subjects allied to medicine, yet at taught higher degree level (i.e. Master's level) business and administrative studies is the main subject studied, accounting for over a quarter of students. The field of study distribution also reflects the specific functions of certain qualifications in the UK labour market. Thus, almost half of all students on "other postgraduate" programmes are studying education – the Postgraduate Certificate in Education which is one of the main routes by which graduates train to become school teachers.

At first degree level, no single field of study area dominates and students are more evenly spread among a range of fields, although as with Masters degrees, business and administrative studies is the most popular subject. Within the UK, the first degree has tended to provide a broad educational base, rather than an occupation-specific programme culminating automatically in professional recognition. Thus, UK graduates' professional formation is likely to take place after completion of the relatively short first degree – either through further study or through supervised work experiences gained in employment (or a mixture of both). Only a small proportion of first degree programmes lead to both an academic qualification and a "licence to practise" as a professional in a specific occupation (for example, nursing; primary school teaching).

Analyses of patterns of student enrolments in full-time first degree courses by field of study over a period of more than ten years show:
- consistent increases in enrolments in subjects allied to medicine, biological sciences, and creative arts and design;
- reduction in enrolments in physical sciences, engineering and technology, computer science, and agricultural subjects;
- some indications in growth in enrolments in languages, after a period of decline (Ramsden, 2009).

FIRST DEGREE GRADUATES' INTERNATIONAL MOBILITY DURING THE COURSE OF STUDY

As noted in section 1, the vast majority of the higher education student population in the United Kingdom is UK-domiciled (85 per cent). Of the 15 per cent of non-UK students, almost half are on postgraduate programmes. But at undergraduate level, only 10 per cent are from outside the United Kingdom.

First degree students in the United Kingdom are not very internationally mobile, compared to some of their mainland European counterparts. In the REFLEX study, only 15 per cent of graduates from institutions of higher education in the United Kingdom had spent some time abroad for study or study-related activities, compared to 20 per cent of European graduates (and almost 30 per cent of Austrian and German graduates); and an even smaller proportion of graduates from institutions of higher education in the United Kingdom (five per cent) had spent time abroad during higher education for work-related purposes.

A recent analysis of national student data linked to periods of *study abroad quotes* figures as low as four per cent of a cohort of full-time first degree students having spent up to one year abroad for study purposes (Higher Education Funding Council for England [HEFCE], 2009b). The analysis of a single cohort of students entering first degrees in 2002-03 and subsequently qualifying (some 200,000 students in all) was concerned with students undertaking a study period abroad through the ERASMUS scheme or other arrangements. Over half studying abroad via Erasmus did so for the whole academic year; and the majority of others studying abroad also did a whole academic year.

The student profile of those four per cent of the cohort who had studied abroad was slightly different from the whole cohort of first degree students in 2002-03; in particular, they were:
- more likely to be female; be younger; be from higher socio-economic classes (82 per cent from managerial, professional, intermediate occupations family background, compared to 74 per cent of all young students); have higher than average entry qualifications; and
- less likely to be from an ethnic minority group; to come from low participation neighbourhoods (14 per cent did so, compared to 22 per cent overall).

The HEFCE analysis also found that those who studied abroad had a better profile of (first) degree results, and six months after graduation they were more likely to be doing further study; also, those in employment were more likely to be employed abroad and have above-average salaries. A more recent (2010) review of international mobility (commissioned by HEFCE) once again points to the low rates of UK student mobility compared to other European countries. The review also notes that the international mobility of UK students is more buoyant in research-intensive, pre-1992 universities, and is constrained by individual-scale factors "such as language competence, desire for adventure and employability" (King, Findlay & Ahrens, 2010, p. 2).

In terms of *mobility after graduation*, the national longitudinal destinations of leavers survey provides some data. The 2007/08 DLHE longitudinal survey found that some three and a half years after graduating (in 2004/05), less than seven per cent of "leavers" who were in employment were working outside the United Kingdom (Higher Education Statistics Agency [HESA], 2009b). Not surprisingly, UK domiciled respondents were much less likely to do so (less than four per cent) than those domiciled outside the United Kingdom (71 per cent). Of the UK-domiciled leavers working abroad there was some slight variation by level of higher education qualification: those with postgraduate qualifications, including Master degrees (4 per cent), and Bachelors degrees (4 per cent) were more likely to be working abroad than those with other undergraduate qualifications (2 per cent).

EMPLOYMENT AND FURTHER STUDY OF BACHELOR AND MASTER GRADUATES

Students on *Bachelor* (first degree) programmes in the United Kingdom tend to be both younger and older than their European counterparts (Brennan & Tang, 2008). This *age pattern*, coupled with the shorter first cycle degrees (which most students complete in the "set" time of three years) means that graduates from institutions of higher education in the United Kingdom tend to be younger than their European counterparts when they leave higher education for the first time. Data from the Reflex study shows that almost three quarters of students in the United Kingdom were aged 24 or under on graduation, compared to less than half (44 per cent) of all European graduates (Little & Tang, 2008).

As noted above, national aggregate data on graduate employment are provided by the annual destinations of leavers from higher education institutions (DLHE) surveys ("early stage" and longitudinal survey). The DLHE is limited to UK and other European domiciled students. Table 3 presents the details for UK-domiciled students six months after graduation ("early stage" DLHE).

Table 3. *Destinations of UK-Domiciled Graduates from Higher Education Institutions in the United Kingdom Six Months after Graduation in 2007/08, by Level of Degree and Mode of Study (per cent)*

Destination	Bachelors Full-time	Bachelors Part-time	Masters* Full-time	Masters* Part-time
Employment only (paid, unpaid)	63	67	69	81
Further study only	15	6	13	3
Further study + work	8	15	7	10
Assumed unemployed	8	5	6	2
Other (including not available for employment)	5	7	4	4
Total	101	100	99	100
Total student numbers (N)	191,740	21,530	16,565	14,520

* HESA data refers to "other higher degrees" (so refers primarily to Masters graduates)

Source: Higher Education Statistics Agency (2009a)

As we can see, some 90 per cent of Bachelor qualifiers in 2007/08 had graduated from full-time programmes. Six months after graduating with a first degree in 2007/08, 63 per cent of full-time Bachelor graduates from higher education institutions in the United Kingdom were employed, and a further 23 per cent were doing further study, either on its own or combined with work (67 per cent and 21 per cent respectively for part-time students). Of those Bachelor graduates doing further study, 56 per cent were aiming for a postgraduate qualification, and 17 per cent were doing professional qualifications (HESA, 2009a).

Qualifiers from *Master* programmes were evenly spread between full-time and part-time. Figures for full-time graduates were very similar to first degree outcomes; 69 per cent were in employment and a further 20 per cent were doing further study, either on its own or combined with work; the figures for part-time graduates were a little different with a higher percentage in employment (81 per cent) and only 13 per cent engaged in further study (only or combined with work). Given the propensity of those already in employment to use part-time Master's programmes for early- or mid-career professional training purposes, such differences in employment rates are not surprising.

The overall figures for Bachelor graduates conceal some wide variations by field of study; over 80 per cent of graduates from full-time first degrees in medicine and dentistry, veterinary science, subjects allied to medicine, and education were employed six months after graduation. At the same time, those full-time students who had studied computer science were most likely to be unemployed (15 per cent), and unemployment rates for mass communications and documentation, creative arts and design, engineering and technology, architecture, building and planning, and historical and philosophical studies were all above 10 per cent.

Patterns of further study after graduating with a first (Bachelor) degree also show variations by field of study. Overall, around 15 per cent go on to further study only, but over half the full-time students who had studied law at first degree level were doing further study (as would be necessary if they were intending to enter the legal profession). Those who had graduated in mathematical sciences, physical sciences and historical and philosophical studies were also more likely than the average to be studying further (30 per cent were doing so). Such variation is likely to reflect specific requirements for entry to particular professions as well as a more general desire on students' behalf to continue studying (possibly in the field of study of their first degree) as a way of enhancing their progress in to the labour market.

Table 4. Occupational Group of UK-Domiciled Graduates from First Degree Study Programmes at Higher Education Institutions in the United Kingdom Employed Six Months after Graduation in 2007/08, by Mode of Study (per cent)

Occupational group	Full-time	Part-time
Managers and senior officials	8	14
Professional occupations	28	27
Associate professional & technical occupations	30	37
Administrative & secretarial occupations	12	9
Sales & customer service	11	3
Other	11	10
Total	100	100
Total student numbers (N)	135,440	17,595

Source: Higher Education Statistics Agency (2009a), table Ei, Eii

Of those full-time first degree qualifiers who were employed six months after graduation, two thirds were in managerial, professional, or associate professional *occupations*. The comparable figure for part-time students was rather higher, at just over three-quarters (78 per cent). Since a large proportion of part-time students will already have been employed whilst undertaking higher education, it is not surprising that the proportion employed in managerial, professional and associate professional occupations is higher than for full-time graduates. Table 4 provides more details for full-time and part-time first degree qualifiers.

Further, given the rather loose *link between higher education and the labour market* in the United Kingdom (especially compared to some other mainland European countries) we could expect that only six months after completing their first degree, graduates from institutions of higher education in the United Kingdom (particularly full-time graduates) may still be looking for employment that "fits" well with their aspirations and career goals.

Turning to the question of Master graduates, the published HESA data on first destinations of qualifiers from postgraduate studies provides some information about postgraduates' type of employment. But the data do not distinguish between the different types of postgraduate study, other than "doctorates" and "other postgraduate degrees' (Master's, postgraduate certificates and diplomas). Table 5 provides the details for those leaving higher education institutions in 2007/08.

Table 5. *Occupational Group of UK-Domiciled Graduates from "Other Postgraduate" Study Programmes at Institutions of Higher Education in the United Kingdom Employed Six Months after Graduation in 2007/08, by Mode of Study (per cent)*

Occupational group	Full-time	Part-time
Managers and senior officials	5	23
Professional occupations	68	48
Associate professional & technical occupations	18	24
Administrative & secretarial occupations	5	3
Sales & customer service	2	1
Other	3	2
Total	100	100
Total student numbers (N)	29,725	23,390

Source: Higher Education Statistics Agency (2009a), table Ei, Eii

Compared with the occupations of Bachelor graduates (see table 4), we see that those with "other postgraduate degrees' were much more likely to be employed in professional occupations. Given that a postgraduate qualification is one of the main routes into certain occupations in the UK labour market (e.g. secondary school teaching and law), it is perhaps not so surprising that this is the case. From table 5 we also see that those who had studied at postgraduate level on a part-time basis were much more likely to be in managerial and senior positions six months after completion than those who had studied on a full-time basis (23 per cent compared to only five per cent of full-timers). This is likely to reflect the fact that those already in employment often study part-time at postgraduate level for mid-career training purposes.

The DLHE "early survey" provides a snapshot of graduates' situation six months after completing higher education, but the longitudinal survey can provide a slightly longer-term perspective. For example, the longitudinal survey of 2004/05 leavers undertaken *three and a half years after* they completed higher education found that 82 per cent of first degree graduates were now working (compared to 63 per cent six months after graduation); around 14 per cent were doing further study (either on its own or combined with working) compared to 23 per cent six months after graduating, and three per cent were assumed to be unemployed (far fewer than the eight per cent quoted for six months after graduation).

Once again, these overall figures for leavers from first degrees mask some quite wide variations by field of study and some of these are rather different from the variations prevalent just six months after graduation (HESA, 2009b). Now, three and a half years after graduation, employment was most likely among those who had studied medicine and dentistry, engineering and technology, and business and administrative studies (with rates of 93 per cent or higher), and the lowest rates were found among graduates in physical sciences and biological sciences (78 per cent and 80 per cent respectively). So we see that whereas six months after graduation, engineering and technology Bachelor degree holders did not seem to be faring well in the labour market, with ten per cent unemployed, three years later they had one of the highest rates of employment. At the same time, those who had studied first degrees in mass communications and documentation, creative arts and design, and computer science were still most likely to be unemployed three and a half years after graduation (around four or five per cent), although these are very small percentages.

Table 6. *Occupational Group of UK-Domiciled Graduates from First Degree Study Programmes at Institutions of Higher Education in the United Kingdom UK Employed Three and a Half Years after Graduation in 2004/05, by and Mode of Study (per cent)*

Occupational group	Full-time	Part-time
Managers and senior officials	13	19
Professional occupations	37	28
Associate professional & technical occupations	29	37
Administrative & secretarial occupations	12	8
Sales & customer service	3	2
Other	6	6
Total	100	100

Source: Higher Education Statistics Agency (2009b)

In terms of type of occupational groups, we can see that of those full-time first degree qualifiers who were employed three and a half years after graduating in 2004/05, 79 per cent are now in managerial, professional, or associate professional occupations. The comparable figure for part-time students is slightly higher (84 per cent). Table 6 provides the details.

Further, whereas six months after graduation, graduates with a first degree in law were most likely to be undertaking further study, three and a half years after graduation it was those who had graduated in biological sciences, physical sciences and mathematical science who were most likely to be continuing their studies (around a fifth to a quarter).

The DLHE "longitudinal survey" also provides a retrospective look at what further qualifications these Bachelor graduates have obtained in the period between initial graduation and some three and a half years later.

As noted above, the DLHE 2004/05 "early survey" found that 23 per cent of first degree graduates were doing further study six months after gaining their first degree – 15 per cent doing only further study, and a further eight per cent studying and working. Data from the DLHE longitudinal survey undertaken three and a half years later (in November 2008) found that four in ten of the UK-domiciled first degree graduates of 2004/05 had now gained a *further qualification*. As we can see from table 7, the most likely further qualifications were a postgraduate certificate/-diploma (accounting for a quarter); professional qualifications (accounting for a fifth), or a "taught" higher degree, most probably a Master degree (also accounting for a fifth).

Table 7. Level of Highest Qualification of UK-Domiciled 2004/05 Graduates from First Degrees Programmes at Institutions of Higher Education in the United Kingdom Three and a Half Years Later (per cent of those achieving further qualifications)

Level of highest qualification	Percentage
Higher degree, mainly by research	2
Higher degree, mainly taught	22
Postgraduate certificate/diploma	25
First degree	3
Other diploma/certificate	17
Professional qualification	23
Other qualification	9
Total	101

Source: Higher Education Statistics Agency (2009b)

The DLHE longitudinal survey also provides data on postgraduate qualifiers, some three and a half years after graduation; irrespective of the mode of study, the vast majority of those who completed postgraduate studies in 2004/05 were, by 2008, in employment (over 85 per cent in each case). Table 8 shows the type of occupation for these postgraduates.

For postgraduate qualifiers, there is little variation in occupational classification between the initial "snapshot" data six months after completion and the longer-term perspective of three and a half years; and as noted in the "early survey" data, those who had studied at postgraduate level part-time were more likely to be in managerial posts than those who had studied full-time.

Table 8. Occupational Group of UK-Domiciled 2004/05 Graduates from Postgraduate Programmes at Institutions of Higher Education in the United Kingdom Employed Three and a Half Years after Graduation, by Mode of Study (per cent)

	Full-time	Part-time
Managers and senior officials	9	30
Professional occupations	71	45
Associate professional & technical occupations	14	18
Administrative & secretarial occupations	3	4
Sales & customer service	1	1
Other	2	3
Total	100	101

Source: Higher Education Statistics Agency (2009b)

PROFESSIONAL SUCCESS OF BACHELOR GRADUATES

In many European countries, there tends to be separately structured vocational and higher educational pathways into the labour market, with tighter links between credentials and jobs obtained; by way of contrast, in the United Kingdom there are no such clearly demarcated pathways. This situation in many European countries has a number of consequences for the links between education and the world of work, including: the greater specificity of employment outcomes means that students and teachers alike have a much clearer sense of the kind of employment situations that students are destined for, and hence greater preparation for such jobs can be attempted; the traditionally longer first degrees (leading to Master's qualifications) have allowed the inclusion of a greater volume of occupationally-relevant preparation than on the shorter Bachelor first degrees in the United Kingdom (Arthur, Brennan & de Weert, 2007). On the other hand, it may be argued that the Anglo-Saxon tradition of offering first degrees which in the main provide a broad educational base as a foundation for subsequent professional education and training might actually enhance graduates' capacity to be flexible in the workplace, and provide more scope for graduates and employers to approach the job allocation process in a flexible manner (Arthur & Little, 2010). More generally, it is recognised that the labour market in the United Kingdom is one of the least regulated and hence most flexible in the developed world, and such flexibility is sometimes viewed as providing the United Kingdom with a real competitive advantage (Keep & James, 2010). Such contexts need to be borne in mind when talking about the "professional success" of Bachelor graduates and considering what, for example, should count as a measure of success.

Period from graduation from Bachelor degrees to first employment

The published data in the national Destinations of Leavers from Higher Education Institutions do not contain information about the period between graduation and first employment. However, findings from the REFLEX study seem to suggest that, in general, graduates from universities in the United Kingdom start searching for jobs rather sooner than their counterparts in most other European countries: nearly four in ten (38 per cent) started searching for jobs prior to their graduation in 2000, compared to the European average of a quarter. As Brennan and Tang (2008) note, this earlier job search start probably reflects a number of factors, including the more developed careers services in higher education institutions in the United Kingdom; and possibly a greater perception among UK graduates of the difficulty in finding a job (which, in turn, could reflect the higher proportion of non-vocational courses and the "looser link" between credentials and job allocation found in liberal market economies generally.) However, on average, graduates from universities in the United Kingdom tended to spend a little more time before (1.6 months) and a little less time after graduation (2.2 months) in their job search than European graduates overall (1.2 months and 2.7 months respectively).

Income levels for Bachelor graduates

The DLHE "early" survey and the longitudinal survey both contain data on salary levels. The mean salary of first degree students who had graduated in 2008/09 and were employed six months later was £20,500; for those who had studied part-time, the mean salary of £27,500 was considerably higher than that of those who had studied full-time (£19,500), probably because many of those graduating from part-time study were already in employment during study and continued in that employment on graduation (Higher Education Statistics Agency [HESA], 2010).

Table 9. *Mean Annual Salaries of Full-time Employed 2002/03 Graduates from Institutions of Higher Education in the United Kingdom according to Fields of Study Showing "Top Three" Highest Earners and "Bottom Three" Lowest Earners Six Months and Three a Half Years after Graduation)*

Six months after graduation		Three and a half years after graduation	
Top three			
Medicine	£29,260	Medicine	£40,078
Nursing	£19,052	Pharmacy and pharmacology	£28,683
Engineering	£17,981	Architecture, building and planning	£26,873
Bottom three			
Media Studies	£13,358	Psychology	£21,391
Psychology	£13,345	Biosciences	£21,382
Design and creative arts	£13,151	Media studies	£21,187

Source: Higher Education Funding Council for England (2008), tables 17, 18

But UK data on first degree graduates' annual salary levels six months and three and a half years after graduation show wide variations by subject of study, with the highest earning subjects being those related towards a specific career (Higher Education Funding Council for England [HEFCE], 2008, 26). Table 9 shows the top three highest earning subjects and bottom three lowest earning subjects for full-time first degree qualifiers who graduated in 2002-03 and were in full-time employment at the time of the "early" survey (six months after graduation), and the longitudinal survey (three and a half years after graduation).

Studying medicine carries the highest rewards in terms of salary levels, both immediately after graduation and some three and a half years later. However, whereas those who had studied nursing or engineering were among the highest earners straight after graduation, some three and a half years later their "place" had been taken by pharmacy, and architecture (for which mean salaries at six months were at a modest level of £15,162 and £16,965 respectively). In fact, though salary levels for medicine graduates had increased by 37 per cent in this period, those of pharmacy graduates had increased by a massive 90 per cent in the same period. At the other end of the scale, those studying media studies or psychology were most likely to be low earners both straight after graduation and some three and a half years later, even though, for each of these subjects, salary levels had increased by around 60 per cent during this period.

Employment matching level of educational attainment

National data from the DLHE "early survey" show that 60 per cent of Bachelor graduates who completed their studies in 2002-03 and were employed six months later were in jobs which required a first degree; but 40 per cent were in jobs that someone without a first degree could obtain (HEFCE, 2008, p. 23). However, three and a half years after graduation, 79 per cent were in jobs requiring a first degree. Not surprisingly, these overall figures conceal some quite wide variations by field of study, as can be seen in table 10.

Data on the "fit" between levels of education attainment and Bachelor graduates' initial employment (six months after graduation) may not compare favourably with the situation in some other European countries. But we should note the earlier comments about the low levels of regulation in the labour market of the United Kingdom, which means that access to many jobs is not restricted to those holding specific qualifications; further, data from broader skills surveys within the UK indicate that 40 per cent consider that they hold qualifications at levels above those needed to obtain or undertake their current job. This proportion has increased in recent years (Felstead et al., 1997 quoted in Keep & James, 2010).

Table 10. *Employment in Jobs Requiring a First Degree of 2002/03 First Degree Graduates from Higher Education Institutions in the United Kingdom Six Months and Three and a Half Years after Graduation, by Fields of Study with Highest and Lowest Proportions (per cent)*

Six months after graduation		Three and a half years after graduation	
Subjects with 85% or more graduates in graduate-level job			
Medicine	100	Medicine	98
Nursing	98	Nursing	97
Architecture, building and planning	88	Pharmacy and pharmacology	95
Pharmacy and pharmacology	88	Architecture, building and planning	92
		Chemistry	91
		Health studies	91
		Education	89
Subjects with 50% or less graduates in graduate-level job			
Design and creative arts	50	None	
Humanities and language-based studies	49		
Psychology	43		
Media studies	42		

Source: Higher Education Funding Council for England (2008), table 14, 15

Using knowledge and skills

According to the REFLEX study, first degree graduates from universities in the United Kingdom were most likely to indicate that their first job did not require higher education (38 per cent, compared to an average of 15 European countries of only 18 per cent). The same study found that graduates from universities in the United Kingdom were more likely to say that their first job did not require a particular field of study (35 per cent compared to 13 per cent overall); and a third of graduates from universities in the United Kingdom considered that they hardly used their knowledge and skills or not at all (compared to a European average of 19 per cent) in their first jobs. So it seems that, in comparison with graduates from various European countries, graduates from universities in the United Kingdom were more likely to consider they were over-qualified for their first employment after graduation.

However, REFLEX data on graduates' situations some five years after graduation present a rather different picture (see table 11). By now, almost three quarters of graduates from universities in the United Kingdom (72 per cent) felt that their current highest level of education matched their current job requirements – the same proportion as European graduates overall; only a fifth of graduates from universities in the United Kingdom felt that their current job did not require a particular field of study – this was still higher than the European average of nine per cent, but much less than the third of graduates from universities in the United

Kingdom who felt this in relation to their first job; and only 14 per cent of graduates from universities in the United Kingdom considered that they hardly used their knowledge and skills in their current job (compared to around a third in relation to their first job).

Table 11. The Relationships between Higher Education and Job of 1999/2000 Graduates from First Degree Programmes at Institutions of Higher Education in the United Kingdom and in European Countries Five Years after Graduation (per cent)

	Europe	UK
Required an education level below tertiary	10	15
Did not require particular field	9	20
Did not/hardly used knowledge and skills	9	14

Source: Brennan and Tang (2008) (based on REFLEX data)

Certain characteristics of graduates' jobs five years after graduation have been explored above. But were these graduates satisfied with their jobs? Clearly, the notion of satisfaction with a job embraces a number of aspects of the job and relates to an individual's values and aspirations. The REFLEX study explored notions of satisfaction by seeking graduates' views about the importance of certain job characteristics (ten in all) and the extent to which they applied in their current jobs (see table 12).

Table 12. Job Characteristics of 1999/2000 Graduates from Institutions of Higher Education in the United Kingdom Five YearsLlater (per cent*)

Rank	Importance to work		Applicable to current work	
1	Opportunity to learn new things	89	Job security	66
2	New challenges	85	Opportunity to learn new things	64
3	Job security	79	New challenges	61
4	Enough time for leisure activities	78	Work autonomy	60
5	Good career prospects	78	Good career prospects	51
6	Work autonomy	70	Enough time for leisure activities	48
7	Chance of doing something useful for society	63	Chance of doing something useful for society	48
8	High earnings	61	High earnings	32
9	Good chance to combine work with family tasks	45	Social status	32
10	Social status	34	Good chance to combine work with family tasks	30

*Importance of work: per cent very important/important; applicability: per cent to a very great/great extent

Source: Brennan and Tang (2008) (based on REFLEX data)

As we can see from the REFLEX data presented in table 12, for many job characteristics, there was a considerable gap between their importance and the extent to which they applied in UK graduates' current jobs. However, overall, it seemed that UK graduates' current jobs matched their values to a reasonable extent (in terms of rank ordering), and so in that sense one could conclude that the graduates were fairly satisfied with their current work.

CONCLUSIONS

In higher education in the United Kingdom, the Bachelors/first degree is still the dominant study programme. In 2008/09, Bachelor programmes accounted for over half of all student enrolments and half of all higher education qualifications awarded. Overall, almost two thirds of students at institutions of higher education in the United Kingdom study full-time, but the balance between full- and part-time modes of study varies by level of qualification. At first degree/Bachelor level, three quarters study on a full-time basis; at postgraduate level, student numbers are more evenly split between full-time and part-time.

Six months after graduation, there is little variation in the employment rates for full-time and part-time Bachelor graduates, and full-time Master graduates; around two thirds are employed. But part-time Master graduates have higher employment rates (around 80 per cent). This difference can be explained, at least in part, by the fact that rather than first degree students moving straight on to a Master programmes, those already in employment often enrol in these programmes for mid-career professional training purposes and study on a part-time basis. In fact, data relating to the cohort of Bachelor graduates graduating from higher education in 2004/05 show that only a quarter of students had gone straight on to further study (either full-time, or combined with working). But some three years after graduation, around four in ten had obtained a further qualification. These qualifications were most likely to be a postgraduate certificate/diploma (accounting for a quarter) and probably linked to entry to specific occupations; professional qualifications and taught higher degrees (most likely Master degrees) each accounted for a further fifth.

In terms of type of occupation, we see some differences between Bachelor graduates and Master graduates, and within that, by mode of study. Thus, shortly after graduation, around two thirds of full-time Bachelor graduates are in managerial, professional or associate professional jobs, compared to three quarters of those who studied part-time. At the postgraduate level, data for graduates from "other postgraduate" programmes (including Master programmes) show that over 90 per cent are working in managerial, professional or associate professional jobs, irrespective of mode of study.

Within these overall figures for employment rates and type of occupation and incidence of further study beyond graduation, there are variations by subject of study. Much of this variation is likely to reflect, in part, the rather low level of labour market regulation in the United Kingdom, compared to most European countries and the fact that traditionally, first degrees programmes in the United

Kingdom have, with the exception of certain vocationally-oriented subjects, been seen as providing a broad educational base for subsequent professional education and training, which in itself may be a mix of on-the-job experience and further study (possibly through Master programmes, but also other postgraduate certificates/diploma programmes, and professional body qualifications). Thus we should not necessarily expect to see a close alignment between first degrees and Bachelor graduates' type of occupation shortly after graduation. Data presented in this chapter relating to graduates' employment situations some three or more years after graduating from higher education arguably show a closer alignment to level of occupation, with the vast majority (around 80 per cent) now in managerial, professional or associate professional jobs.

Various recent government initiatives have been directed at actions to increase and widen access to higher education in the United Kingdom. But social class still remains a strong determinant of whether or not an individual progresses to higher education, and higher education participation rates vary considerably by parental background, whereby the more selective universities remain over-populated by students from wealthier backgrounds. Much of this bias can be explained by different levels of attainment before higher education.

Graduates from institutions of higher education have not been very internationally mobile during the course of study compared to some of their counterparts in many other European countries, and the profile of those (few) who study abroad as part of their degree differs slightly from their fellow (non-mobile) students, being more likely to be female, younger, from higher socio-economic backgrounds, and having higher entry qualifications. Once they have graduated, very few UK-domiciled students work abroad – some three or more years after graduation less than five per cent are doing so and there is little variation between Master graduates' and Bachelor graduates' mobility.

The above represents the current situation – but some rather broad changes are planned which could change the higher education landscape of the United Kingdom in significant ways in the next few years. Essentially, the underlying rationale for the changes being proposed by the government is that central funding for higher education should follow student choice, and in the future most support for higher education will be in the form of student financial aid rather than directly funding most of the costs of tuition (through teaching grants to higher education institutions), as is currently the case. The main changes (for England) relate to the range and level of financial support available to higher education students, irrespective of whether they study on a full-time or part-time basis; the level of tuition fees such students will have to pay for their studies (after completing study and earning a certain level of salary) with the possibility of fees rising almost threefold from the current level of £3,250 per year to £9,000 in the academic year 2012/13; and the complete removal of teaching funds/grants to higher education institutions (except for certain priority subjects) in 2013/14. Of course, the detail of much of these proposals has yet to be worked out, and relevant legislation must be drafted and approved through Parliament during spring/summer 2011. Further, it is likely that tuition fees and funding regimes will increasingly diverge across the four nations of the United Kingdom (England, Scotland, Wales and Northern Ireland). But taken together, the measures herald a much larger role for student choice and the markets to determine the future size and shape of higher education in the United Kingdom. It remains to be seen just what the effects of such marketisation will be on higher education students, their choices of subjects, the ways in which they study, the levels at which they choose to study, be it at undergraduate or postgraduate level, and the sort of occupations they seek to enter once they have graduated.

REFERENCES

Arthur, L., Brennan, J. & de Weert, E. (2007). *Employer and higher education perspectives on graduates in the knowledge society.* London: Centre for Higher Education Research and Information, the Open University and the Netherlands, Center for Higher Education Policy Studies, University of Twente.

Arthur, L. & Little, B. (2010). The Reflex study: exploring graduates' views on the relationship between higher education and employment. In J. Brennan, L. Arthur, B. Little, A. Cochrane, R. Williams, M. David, T. Kim & R. King (Eds.), *Higher education and society: a research report.* London: CHERI, 13-19.

Brennan, J. & Tang, W. (2008). *The employment of UK graduates: comparisons with Europe. Report to HEFCE by the Centre for Higher Education Research and Information, the Open University.* Retrieved October, 2010, http://www.hefce.ac.uk/pubs/rdreports/2008/rd22_08_1.pdf

Department for Business, Innovation and Skills (2010). *Participation rates in higher education: Academic Years 2006/07 to 2008/09 (Provisional).* Retrieved November, 2010, http://stats.bis.gov.uk/he/participation_rates_in_HE_2008-09.pdf

Harris, M. (2010). *What more can be done to widen access to highly selective universities? A report from Sir Martin Harris, Director of Fair Access.* Retrieved June, 7, 2010, from http://www.offa.org.uk/wp-content/uploads/2010/05/Report-on-access-to-highly-selective-universities.pdf

Higher Education Career Services Unit (2009). *What do masters graduates do? 2010.* Retrieved February 18, 2010, from http://www.hecsu.ac.uk/research_reports_what_do_graduates_do_november_2010.htm

Higher Education Funding Council for England (2008). *Graduates and their early careers.* Bristol: HEFCE. Retrieved February, 2010, from http://www.hefce.ac.uk/pubs/hefce/2009/09_44/09_44.pdf

Higher Education Funding Council for England (2009a). *Patterns of higher education: living at home.* Bristol: HEFCE. Retrieved October, 2010, from http://www.hefce.ac.uk/pubs/hefce/2009/09_20/09_20.pdf.

Higher Education Funding Council for England (2009b). *Attainment in higher education: Erasmus and placement students.* Bristol: HEFCE.

Higher Education Statistics Agency (2009a). *Destinations of leavers from Higher Education Institutions 2007/08.* Cheltenham: HESA.

Higher Education Statistics Agency (2009b). *Destinations of leavers from Higher Education Institutions Longitudinal Survey of the 2004/05 cohort. Key Findings Report Published 2009.* Cheltenham: HESA. Retrieved February, 2010, from http://www.hesa.ac.uk/dox/dlhe_longitudinal/0405/Long_DLHE_0405_WEB.pdf

Higher Education Statistics Agency (2009c). *Students in Higher Education Institutions 2008/09.* Cheltenham: HESA.

Higher Education Statistics Agency (2010). *Destinations of leavers from higher education in the United Kingdom for the academic year 2007/08* (Statistical First Release 137). Retrieved November, 2010, from http://www.hesa.ac.uk/index.php?option=com_content&task=view&id=1479&Itemid=161

Keep, E. & James, S. (2010). "What incentives to learn at the bottom end of the labour market?" *SKOPE Research Paper,* No. 94. Cardiff: Oxford and Cardiff University.

King, R., Findlay, A. & Ahrens, J. (2010). *International student mobility literature review. Report to HEFCE, and co-funded by the British Council, UK National Agency for Erasmus.* Bristol: Higher Education Funding Council for England. Retrieved November, 2010, from http://www.hefce.ac.uk/pubs/rdreports/2010/rd20_10/rd20_10.pdf

Little, B. & Tang, W. (2008). *Age differences in graduate employment across Europe. Report to HEFCE by the Centre for Higher Education Research and Information, the Open University.* Retrieved February, 2010, from http://www.hefce.ac.uk/pubs/rdreports/2008/rd22_08_5.pdf

National Equality Panel (2010). *An anatomy of economic inequality in the UK. Report of the National Equality Panel.* London: Centre for Analysis of Social Exclusion, London School of Economics, and Government Equalities Office. Retrieved November, 2010, from http://www.equalities.gov.uk/pdf/NEP%20Report%20bookmarkedfinal.pdf

Ramsden, B. (2009). *Patterns of higher education institutions in the UK: Ninth report.* London: Universities UK.

The Panel on Fair Access to the Professions (2009). *Unleashing aspiration: the final report of the Panel on Fair Access to the Professions.* Retrieved November 2010, from http://www.bis.gov.uk/assets/biscore/corporate/migratedd/publications/p/panel-fair-access-to-professions-finalreport21july09.pdf

The Scottish Government (2010). *Statistics publication notice lifelong learning series: Students in higher education at scottish institutions.* Retrieved November 2010, from http://www.scotland.gov.uk/publications/2010/03/18144043/4

HARALD SCHOMBURG

EMPLOYABILITY AND MOBILITY OF BACHELOR GRADUATES: THE FINDINGS OF GRADUATE SURVEYS IN TEN EUROPEAN COUNTRIES ON THE ASSESSMENT OF THE IMPACT OF THE BOLOGNA REFORM

INTRODUCTION

In this analysis of graduate surveys undertaken in recent years in ten European countries, we examine the findings which can be considered as valuable for the response to key questions regarding the impact of the Bologna reform: What is the situation of "mobility" and "employability" after some ten years of efforts to establish a convergent system of study programmes and degrees?

In the introductory chapter of this volume, it was pointed out that surveys of recent graduates are most useful to provide information regarding four respects of mobility and graduate employment and work in Europe with respect to the Bologna Process. They are formulated here as questions:

– What share of students in each country have had the *experience of studying a least for some period in another country* or of other study-related experience in their course of study up to graduation and possibly transition to employment?
– What share of students has been professionally mobile across borders in their early professional career?
– What rate of Bachelor graduates – all Bachelors or possibly those from university programmes as compared to those from other programmes and institutions – *transfers to employment* after the award of the Bachelor degree, and how many *continue their studies*?
– How far is the *professional success* of Bachelor graduates – again possibly from different types of programmes and institutions – soon after graduation similar, or how far does it differ from that of Master graduates and of graduates from old and new single-cycle programmes? How far do the differences observed correspond the levels of educational attainments, or indicate a different degree of "success"?

Obviously, graduate surveys are a valuable tool to examine certain aspects of mobility and graduate employment and work in the Bologna Process. However, as it was pointed out in the introductory chapter of this volume, an overview of the findings of recent graduate surveys has its *limitations* as far as an overall assessment of the "mobility" and "employability" impact of the Bologna Reform is concerned:

– First, only a *time series-analysis* would help to analyse changes with regard to mobility and graduate employment. However, as most country reports in this comparative study only provide detailed information about recent graduates, changes over time were taken up only in passing.

H. Schomburg and U. Teichler (eds.), *Employability and Mobility of Bachelor Graduates in Europe*, 253–273.
© 2011 *Sense Publishers. All rights reserved.*

- Second, graduate surveys are the best way of measuring temporary outward mobility. Other approaches are more suitable to measure *outward diploma mobility* (i.e. mobility for the whole study programme up to a diploma or a degree) and mobility from other continents.
- Third, graduate surveys that analyse the mobility and employment of former students can measure both mobility and employment at certain points in time, but they provide only limited information on the *causes*.
- Fourth, graduate surveys have some *endemic methodological weaknesses*, e.g. limited response rates and possible differences in the composition of findings between the respondents and non-respondents. They do not take into account the impact of the new study programmes on students who discontinue their studies before graduation. Standardised questionnaires comprise questions and categories of responses which do not mirror the complexity of facts and views.

Finally, it was pointed out in the introductory chapter that there was no recent comparative graduate survey that comprised a large number of European countries. The two major comparative surveys addressed graduates from the mid-1990s and thus only reflect the impact of study provisions and conditions prior to the Bologna Reform. Therefore, this comparative analysis had to draw from national graduate surveys. 10 European countries were considered where conditions were fulfilled: national studies were available and the Bologna reform had progressed considerably. Thus, one of its major challenges is to identify similarities and differences amidst the diversity of themes addressed and methods employed in the surveys and the stages of progression of the Bologna Process. It should be stressed that this study primarily addresses Bachelor graduates and that comparisons are often made with Master graduates and with those of other programmes leading to Master-equivalent degrees. No reference is made to the employment of doctoral degree holders.

THE INFORMATION PROVIDED BY THE GRADUATE SURVEYS IN THE 10 COUNTRIES

Surveys were conducted between 2007 and 2010 in all 10 countries; hence, some analyse results from earlier surveys. Most country reports *comprise graduate cohorts* between the academic year 2006/07 and the calendar year 2009; only the French country report is based on an earlier cohort, i.e. those graduating in 2004 (see table 1). The surveys vary substantially *concerning the graduation year*:
- six months after graduation in Norway and the United Kingdom,
- between one and two years after graduation in Austria, Germany, Hungary, Italy and the Netherlands,
- between three and five years after graduation in France, in two older surveys in the Czech Republic, and in the second, follow-up survey in the United Kingdom, and
- over various years in the most recent survey in the Czech Republic.

In some countries, *more than a single cohort of graduates* was addressed for different reasons. There were cases where a data set comprised more than a single cohort; this method was used to increase the absolute number of graduates within the data set (Austria, Germany and the Netherlands); in other cases, some relevant thematic areas were in other surveys than the key survey presented in the country report (Austria, Czech Republic and Italy); in other cases, reference to surveys from different years provided the opportunity to undertake a time-series analysis in selected thematic areas (Czech Republic, France and the United Kingdom).

Table 1. Graduate Surveys in Selected European Countries

Country	Conducted in Year(s)	Graduation Year(s)	Timing (After graduation)
AT Austria	2010	2007-2008	1½ – 2½ years
CZ Czech Republic I	2006	2001-2002	4-5 years
CZ Czech Republic II	2010	2005-2006	4-5 years
CZ Czech Republic III	2007-2008	•	(up to 59 years old)
DE Germany	2009-2010	2007-2008	1½ years
FR France	2007	2004	3 years
HU Hungary	2009	2008	1 year
IT Italy	2008 (2009)	2007 (2008)	1 year
NL The Netherlands	2004-2008	2002/03-2006/07	1-2 years
NO Norway	2007	2007	6 months
PL Poland	2007	1998-2005	2-9 years
UK United Kingdom I	2008	2007/2008	6 months
UK United Kingdom II	2008	2004/05	3½ years

Figures are based on country reports of this volume.

All authors of the country reports selected surveys which provide information on a relatively *recent cohort of Bachelor graduates*. All ten country reports provide information on *university Bachelor graduates*. But there are problems in comparing their whereabouts and professional success:
– The surveys on graduates in Italy and the United Kingdom address only Bachelor graduates whose degree was awarded by a university. In Italy, nearly all Bachelor titles are awarded by universities, and in the United Kingdom, few are awarded by other institutions.
– For the Czech Republic, Hungary and Poland, the surveys present findings for all Bachelor graduates and therefore do not make a distinction between those graduating from universities and those graduating from other higher education institutions; this is based on the assumption that differences according to institutional type no longer play an important role.
– In the report on graduates from institutions in Norway, Bachelor graduates from universities are included, but only some from other higher education institutions.
– In the country reports on France and the Netherlands, information on all themes addressed is provided as regards Bachelor graduates from the vocational sector

(vocational Bachelors and HBO Bachelors respectively), but only limited information as regards Bachelors from the general university sector.

Finally, the Bachelor graduates are consistently sub-divided in three country reports: in the Austrian and German country reports between graduates from universities on the one hand and those from Fachhochschulen (universities of applied sciences) on the other, and in the country report on the United Kingdom between those graduating from full-time programmes and those graduating from part-time programmes.

The definitions of *other degrees comprised in the analysis* vary between countries. Information on Master graduates is provided in almost all country reports; yet, there are limits as far as comparability is concerned: in some cases, information on all Master graduates is provided, whereas in others they are subdivided according to type of higher education institution. In the case of France and partly of the Czech Republic, there is no clear separation between Master-type degrees and traditional single-cycle degrees. Most countries provide information on graduates from single-cycle degrees; they are differentiated in some cases between traditional degrees (divided into traditional university degrees and degrees from other higher education institutions) and new single-cycle degrees, whereas this distinction is not made in other cases; moreover, some country reports address special disciplinary groups (notably engineering). Finally, reference is made in exceptional cases to short-cycle diploma holders or even secondary school leavers.

Even if information is provided on graduates from Bachelor, Master and – new and old – single-cycle programmes, a comparison of their professional success is difficult: the composition of graduates by field of study tends to vary between these groups – notably because the introduction of the two-cycle structure varied in some countries by field of study and because study programmes in some fields of study with favourable employment opportunities – e.g. medicine – are not transformed into two-cycle programmes.

It must also be pointed out that *not all the surveys* addressed in the country reports of this volume *are based on a representative sample* of all those graduating in the respective country at Bachelor and Master level:
– In France and the Netherlands, Bachelors who continue their studies are not included.
– In Germany, Hungary and Italy, the survey addressed a large number of higher education institutions that were willing to cooperate in the survey and were not selected through a stratified sampling.
– In France and the United Kingdom, foreign graduates or graduates living abroad were not surveyed.
– In some cases, some small sub-groups (e.g. graduates from private institutions, from teacher colleges) were either excluded from the survey or were included in the survey but disregarded in the analysis.
– In most country reports, however, such limitations do not call into question the validity of the data.

Finally, it should be pointed out that, although the purpose of the comparative analysis was not to compare the changes in graduates' mobility and employment over time, a *time series analysis* was sometimes undertaken regarding some thematic areas. This held true for the reports on the Czech Republic, France, Italy and the United Kingdom.

THE BOLOGNA CHALLENGE FOR CHANGE IN THE DEGREE STRUCTURE

As already pointed out in the introductory chapters, we note *five different types of structural changes or structural continuity of study programmes* that may be linked differently to types of higher education institutions – i.e. five types in ten countries:
(1) Substitution of a more or less unitary system (only universities, almost only long study programmes) by a two-cycle system within a single institutional type: Italy.
(2) Substitution of a two-institution type system with single-cycle study programmes (longer programmes at universities and shorter programmes at other higher education institutions) by a two-cycle system with Master programmes in both institutional types: Austria, Germany, Hungary and the Czech Republic, where first steps towards a two-cycle structure were already undertaken prior to the Bologna Declaration.
(3) Substitution of the same model as above (two-institution type system by single-cycle study programmes of different lengths) by a two-cycle (Bachelor-Master) system by Master programmes at one type of institution (universities) and only Bachelor programmes at other higher education institutions: the Netherlands.
(4) Substitution of a system of long study programmes at universities in a broad range of fields and short study programmes at universities as well as in a limited number of fields by a two-cycle system in a broad range of fields: France, Norway and Poland. In the case of France, a new vocational bachelor degree was added to which most students move after the award of a two-year diploma programme to a third-year vocational Bachelor programme. In Norway, two types of short study programmes existed previously: programmes for certain fields of study (notably humanities and natural sciences) at universities and study programmes in most fields of study provided by other higher education institutions.
(5) Continuation of a traditional two-cycle structure: United Kingdom.

As a consequence of varied structures before the Bologna Declaration and varied approaches within the Bologna Process, we note now a variety of patterns of study *programmes and degrees*:
(1) As regards (first-cycle) Bachelor programmes, a single type of Bachelor graduates seems to have emerged de jure or de facto in Italy, Poland and the United Kingdom. In contrast, two types have been created de jure or de facto in Austria, the Czech Republic, France, Germany, Hungary, the Netherlands and Norway. Hence, the university Bachelor graduates are viewed as a partly new or completely new type of graduate and the other Bachelor graduates are viewed as successors of the graduates from the previous short study programmes at other higher education institutions.
(2) As regards (second-cycle) Master programmes, the country reports on Austria and Germany present a division by institutional type, although more refined and

overlapping typologies exist in these countries. The presentation of this "division" by institution is based on the observation that university Master graduates are sometimes seen by the labour market as successors of those from traditional university programmes, whereas the Master graduates from the other higher education institutions tend to be viewed as new type of graduates.

(3) As regards long single-cycle programmes, we see that the two-cycle structure was not established in all fields of study. There are single-cycle long study programmes in all countries in which the two-cycle structure was introduced in the framework of the Bologna Process as the dominant pattern. In some instances, traditional programmes persist which will probably be phased out over time. But in all countries, efforts often led to decisions to keep single-cycle programmes in selected fields of study: most frequently in medical fields, but also in some other fields. Most country reports do not delineate traditional and new single-cycle programmes; the terms "traditional study programmes" and "single-cycle programmes" are not clearly distinguished in the country reports.

The authors of the Bologna Declaration of 1999 had obviously expected complications in the implementation of Bachelor programmes in universities and therefore had stressed that: "The degree awarded after the first cycle shall also be relevant to the European labour market".

In comparing the ten country reports, we note that the introduction of the university degree posed the *strongest challenge* in those countries where no short programmes existed previously in universities but did in other higher education institutions and where now, as a consequence of the Bologna reform, Bachelor programmes in universities co-exist with Bachelor programmes in other types of higher education institutions. This holds true most clearly in *Austria and Germany*. Here, the central questions are: Do university Bachelor graduates continue to study after the award of the Bachelor degree more often than other Bachelors, and are they less successful professionally? And: How does the professional success of university Bachelor graduates differ from that of Master graduates?

The *challenge is less striking* if some short programmes had already existed and/or if there is no clear division between university Bachelor programmes and Bachelor programmes from other types of higher education institutions (or in the case of France between general and vocational Bachelors). This can be observed for seven of the ten countries addressed in this comparative analysis. Here, the question is: What share of Bachelor graduates continues their studies? But either this share cannot be compared with respective shares of other Bachelor graduates because such a comparison group does not exist, or the difference between the professional success of university Bachelor graduates and other Bachelor graduates is likely to be smaller because there was already a tradition of transfer to employment on the part of university short-programme graduates prior to the Bologna Process. Therefore, more attention or at least the same degree of attention is paid to the second question.

MOBILITY

Graduate surveys in nine of the ten countries addressed in this comparative analysis provided some information on the share of graduates who had been *outward mobile* to another country or other countries *during their course of study*. There are problems, though, in the comparability of data because some countries report mobility for the purpose of study, others mobility for the purpose of study and other study-related activities, and others make a distinction between study and other study-related activities. Moreover, definitions of study abroad vary according to the minimum duration between two weeks and a whole semester. These differences have enormous implications: for example, it seems justified to assume that the share of those going abroad for a period of study and/or other study-related activities is about twice as high as that of those going abroad only for the purpose of study.

Table 2 provides an overview of the share that had been temporarily outward mobile for the purpose of study, whereby as a rule study abroad for at least one semester is referred to. Three findings are worth mentioning:

- The share of those studying temporarily abroad during the course of study *varies substantially by country*. In three countries – the Netherlands, Austria and Norway – the target set in the Bologna Process in 2009 – i.e. a quota of 20 per cent in the year 2020 – is already reached or exceeded for Bachelor graduates. In Germany, it is about 15 per cent. One can argue that the 20 per cent target is already reached in Germany if one takes into consideration the transition from Bachelor to Master programmes and those German graduates who had studied abroad for their whole study period. In the other countries – Czech Republic, France, Italy, Poland and the United Kingdom – the share of Bachelor graduates having spent a study period abroad is only about 5 per cent or less. Even if one takes into consideration the factor above with respect to Germany, the share of mobile students is still clearly below the Bologna target for the year 2020.
- In most countries where information is available for university Bachelors and Bachelors from other institutions and programmes, mobility among university Bachelor is higher, but the difference is remarkably small.
- The data provided in the country reports do not allow us to establish whether mobility in the framework of the new Bachelor-Master system is higher than in the long single-cycle system. This is not only because there are differences in the composition of fields, but also because it is not specified whether the data refer only to the Master stage or to the whole study period.

Table 2. Periods Abroad during the Course of Study of Graduates from selected European Countries (per cent)

Country	Bachelor graduates Univ.	Bachelor graduates Other HEIs	Bachelor graduates All	Master graduates Univ.	Master graduates Other HEIs	Master graduates All	Single-cycle/ traditional degrees Univ.	Single-cycle/ traditional degrees Other HEIs	Single-cycle/ traditional degrees All
AT Austria									
Study	16	22	18	•	•	•	22	23	22
Various activities	24	33	27	•	•	•	37	40	37
CZ Czech Republic									
Study	•	•	6	•	•	18	•	•	•
Work	•	•	6	•	•	15	•	•	•
DE Germany									
Study	16	14	•	17	9	•	19	9	•
Various activities	28	27	•	35	22	•	37	20	•
FR France									
Study	6	2	•	12	22	•	11	•	•
Various activities	20	22	•	29	54	•	32	•	•
IT Italy									
Study	5	•	5	15	•	15	10	•	10
NL The Netherlands									
Study	28	21	•	28	•	28	35	16	•
NO Norway									
Study	20	•	•	25	•	•	•	•	•
PL Poland									
Study	•	•	2	•	•	3	•	•	3
UK United Kingdom									
Study	4	•	•	•	•	•	•	•	•

Univ. = University
Other HEIs = Other Higher Education Institutions (e.g. Fachhochschulen, Grandes Écoles etc.)

Figures are based on country reports of this volume.

Information on *employment abroad after graduation* provided in the country reports is less comprehensive (e.g. only on six countries) and less homogeneous than that on mobility during the course of study. Table 3 shows that the share of those working abroad at the time of the survey ranged from less than five per cent to less than ten per cent among Bachelor graduates; the respective share is slightly higher among Master graduates. Altogether, the number of persons graduating in the framework of the Bachelor-Master structure who work abroad after graduation seems to be higher than that of persons graduating from long single-cycle programmes. Among the six countries, international graduate mobility is least frequent in Poland.

Table 3. Employment Abroad after Graduation of Graduates from selected European Countries (per cent)

	Bachelor graduates			Master graduates			Single-cycle/ traditional degrees		
	Univ.	Other HEIs	All	Univ.	Other HEIs	All	Univ.	Other HEIs	All
AT Austria									
Since Graduation	12	12	12	•	•	•	20	22	20
Currently	9	9	9	•	•	•	11	8	11
CZ Czech Republic									
Not specified	•	•	10	•	•	11	•	•	•
DE Germany									
Since graduation	6	13	•	20	23	•	12	12	•
Currently	7	8	•	11	8	•	5	4	•
NL The Netherlands									
Currently	5	3	•	7	•	7	4	2	•
PL Poland									
More than one trip abroad	•	•	3	•	•	2	•	•	2
UK United Kingdom									
Currently	7	•	•	•	•	•	•	•	•

Univ. = University
Other HEIs = Other Higher Education Institutions (e.g. Fachhochschulen, Grandes Écoles etc.)

Figures are based on country reports of this volume.

GRADUATES' WHEREABOUTS

When the new cycle-structure of study programmes was agreed upon in the Bologna Declaration as a target for Europe, most actors and experts assumed that less than half of all Bachelor graduates would continue their studies. This reflected the experience of countries with a long tradition of Bachelor programmes and degrees (e.g. United Kingdom, the U.S. and Australia) where no more than about 40 per cent of Bachelor graduates obtain a Master or another corresponding degree. However, one assumed from the beginning that the transition rate to Master study would be higher among Bachelor graduates from universities/academic programmes than among those from other higher education institutions/vocational programmes.

The most recent data show that only slightly less than 20 per cent of Bachelor graduates in the United Kingdom continue their studies immediately after graduation. Almost the same proportion embarks on further study or on programmes of professional training within the subsequent years; the overall rate within the first four years after graduation is about 40 per cent. This comparative study shows (see table 4) that the *rate of further study and training* of university Bachelor graduates is very high in a number of countries: about three quarters in France (estimate of general Bachelors), Germany (university Bachelors), Norway (university Bachelors), the Czech Republic (even among all Bachelor graduates) and Austria (68 per cent university Bachelors). This seems to be true for the Netherlands as well, although no precise data are available.

Table 4. Whereabouts of Bachelor Graduates from selected European Countries

Country	Total Employment	Solely Employment	Employment + Study	Solely Study	Total Study
AT Austria					
University	56	26	28	40	68
Fachhochschule	66	42	23	31	54
CZ Czech Republic-2008					
(6-12 months after)	•	•	•	•	72
DE Germany					
University	45	18	24	51	75
Fachhochschule	71	52	17	24	41
HU Hungary	65	39	16	28	44
IT Italy	46	31	15	42	57
NL The Netherlands					
HBO	89	73	16	7	23
NO Norway					
University	62	23	39	34	73
UK United Kingdom					
Full-time study	71	63	8	15	23
Part-time study	82	67	15	6	21

Figures are based on country reports of this volume.

But there are countries where the percentage of university graduates who continue their studies is lower: 57 per cent in Italy and 44 per cent in Hungary (all Bachelors). Obviously, this rate is lower among Bachelors from other higher education institutions or vocational Bachelor programmes. The graduate surveys provide rates for Dutch HBO Bachelor graduates (23 per cent), German Fachhochschule Bachelor graduates (41 per cent) and Austrian Fachhochschule Bachelor graduates (54 per cent).

It is very difficult, however, to estimate the rate of Master graduates at this historical time for four reasons:
– In most countries, it is not feasible to compare current numbers of Master graduates with the number of Bachelor graduates a few years before because the share of persons having gone through the new Bachelor-structure from the first

year of study up to Master degree is still very small (e.g. persons of the 2002/03 or 2003/04 beginner student cohorts or even earlier).
- Some Bachelor graduates embark on further study only a few years after graduation. They are therefore not counted as embarking on further study in graduate surveys undertaken soon after graduation.
- The graduate surveys comprise Bachelor graduates as continuing study, some of whom have chosen a type of study or training which does not lead to an advanced level such as a Master.
- The information for the respective rate of Master awards is valid only years after the award of Bachelor degrees because some Master students may drop out.
- We do not yet know the share of Bachelor graduates who are employed and embark on further study concurrently that will continue study up to a Master degree.

One major surprising finding is the high number of Bachelor graduates in some countries who choose *concurrent employment and further study*. This holds true for almost 40 per cent of university Bachelor graduates in Norway, more than a quarter in Austria, about a quarter in Germany and almost one fifth in some other countries. There is little information about their motives and prospects: How many enrol while being primarily interested in a job search? How many want to study and see employment as a means of funding their studies? How many have opted for both in order to delay the choice between studying up to a higher level and transfer to employment? Other options might also play a role.

As expected, the *overall employment rate* (i.e. including concurrent study) is highest among Bachelor graduates from other higher education institutions (82 per cent in the Netherlands). But there are variations: The employment rates of Bachelor graduates from these institutions and from universities differ moderately in Austria, but more strongly in Germany and even more strongly in the Netherlands. The overall employment rate of university Bachelor graduates is between 40 per cent and 50 per cent in these three countries, hence the share of those solely employed varies by between about one third and two-thirds, and more than 60 per cent in Norway, where almost two-thirds study alongside their job. In comparison, over 70 per cent of university graduates begin to work, while only a small minority study at the same time.

The risk of *being unemployed* after graduation cannot be well established with this comparative study on university graduates. Surveys undertaken six months or one year after graduation quote unemployment rates ranging from 5 per cent in Norway to 14 per cent in Poland and 15 per cent in Hungary. But these figures refer predominantly to unemployment during the first year. This can be illustrated by time series data available in the Czech Republic: The unemployment rate of 2007 Bachelor graduates was 10 per cent six months after graduation, 4 per cent one year after graduation and 2 per cent two years after graduation. As many surveys addressed in this comparative study were undertaken quite soon after graduation, it is not possible to estimate unemployment rates of Bachelor graduates in Europe beyond the search stage.

There were hardly any data on differences in employment rates soon after graduation between Bachelor graduates from universities and those from other higher education institutions: In Germany, the unemployment rate among university Bachelor graduates surveyed about 1½ years after graduation (2 per cent) was lower than among those from other higher education institutions (4 per cent); in Austria, the situation was the opposite about 1½ to 2½ years after graduation: 2 per cent as compared to 1 per cent.

EMPLOYMENT CONDITIONS AND LINKS BETWEEN STUDY AND WORK

In various countries included in this comparative analysis, four themes of employment and work success are addressed for which the criteria of success are the same for Bachelor and Master graduates: whether they have an unlimited contract, whether they are employed full-time or part-time and the links between study and work both vertically and horizontally.

One must bear in mind that the data are likely to give a less favourable impression of the professional success of Bachelor graduates from the outset. First, the Bachelor has not been introduced – varying by country – in some fields where graduates' professional success tends to be high (notably medicine). Second, the data on Bachelor graduates in some countries include those who both study and are employed; many of those have only opted for temporary employment (in other countries only those Bachelor graduates who study solely in order to avoid such a distortion are included). Third, a comparison between Bachelor graduates from universities and those from other higher education institutions must take into account that there are more graduates from universities than from other higher education institutions whose field of study is not geared to certain professional areas.

Information on *full-time versus part-time employment* is available for five countries (see table 5). In Norway, the data are distorted by the fact that university Bachelors who study and work are included. Among the other countries, the full-time ratio among university Bachelor graduates is 8 per cent lower on average than among Bachelors from other types of higher education institutions or from vocational programmes. It is also 7 per cent lower on average than among university Masters and 4 per cent lower than among graduates from long single-cycle programmes. The Bachelor graduates from other higher education institutions, in contrast, are not employed full-time to a lesser extent than those from their reference groups.

Table 5. Full-time Employment of Graduates from selected European Countries
(per cent of employed graduates)

	Bachelor graduates			Master graduates			Single-cycle/traditional degrees		
	Univ.	Other HEIs	All	Univ.	Other HEIs	All	Univ.	Other HEIs	All
AT Austria	65	83	73	•	•	•	79	91	82
DE Germany	85	90	•	91	91	•	85	92	•
FR France	79	96	•	90	98	•	85	•	•
NL The Netherlands	78	65	•	81	•	81	76	59	•
NO Norway	30	•	•	•	•	85	•	•	•

Univ. = University
Other HEIs = Other Higher Education Institutions (e.g. Fachhochschulen, Grandes Écoles etc.)

Figures are based on country reports of this volume.

According to the information provided for seven countries, there is no difference between the university Bachelors and their reference groups as far as the share of those employed on *unlimited contracts* is concerned. In some countries, it is similar, as is shown in table 6. In Germany, we note more short-term employment both of university Bachelor graduates and other Bachelor graduates both in comparison to their reference groups at Master level and to those with traditional degrees. In contrast, university Bachelor graduates in the Netherlands are more often permanently employed than university Master graduates and single-cycle university graduates.

Table 6. Unlimited-term Contracts of Graduates from selected European Countries
(per cent of employed graduates)

	Bachelor graduates			Master graduates			Single-cycle/traditional degrees		
	Univ.	Other HEIs	All	Univ.	Other HEIs	All	Univ.	Other HEIs	All
AT Austria	80	86	82	•	•	•	77	90	80
DE Germany	55	66	•	68	85	•	65	75	•
FR France	70	80	•	77	91	•	71	•	•
IT Italy	49	•	49	•	•	•	•	•	•
NL The Netherlands	63	63	•	52	•	52	50	66	•
NO Norway	50	•	•	•	•	60	•	•	•
PL Poland	•	•	45	•	•	52	•	•	52

Univ. = University
Other HEIs = Other Higher Education Institutions (e.g. Fachhochschulen, Grandes Écoles etc.)

Figures are based on country reports of this volume.

Concerning the *links between the level of education and the position of the graduates*, we note a relatively high number of graduates who state that their position matches their level of educational attainment or is even higher. This proportion is about three quarters among university Bachelor graduates and higher among Bachelor graduates from other higher education institutions where only those graduates who are employed full-time are included. In those cases, the share of university Bachelor graduates who consider themselves as appropriately employed is almost identical to the respective quota among university Master graduates, but almost 10 per cent lower on average than among university graduates from single-cycle long programmes. Among the Bachelor graduates from other higher education institutions or from vocational programmes, the proportion of those who consider themselves as appropriately employed is slightly higher in most cases than among university Bachelor graduates, and it only slightly lower on average than among graduates from traditional programme at other higher education institutions (see table 7).

Table 7. Strong Vertical Link between Level of Educational Attainment and Position among Graduates from selected European Countries (per cent of employed graduates)

	Bachelor graduates			Master graduates			Single-cycle/ traditional degrees		
	Univ.	Other HEIs	All	Univ.	Other HEIs	All	Univ.	Other HEIs	All
AT Austria	77	83	80	•	•	•	86	88	87
CZ Czech Republic	•	•	84	•	•	87	•	•	•
DE Germany	75	81	•	78	85	•	82	86	•
FR France	55	40	•	82	88	•	97	•	•
IT Italy	80	•	80	•	•	•	•	•	•
NL The Netherlands	47	81	•	64	•	64	64	78	•
NO Norway	37	•	•	•	•	58	•	•	•
PL Poland	60	•	•	•	•	•	•	•	•

Univ. = University
Other HEIs = Other Higher Education Institutions (e.g. Fachhochschulen, Grandes Écoles etc.)

Figures are based on country reports of this volume.

In order to identify the horizontal links between study and work, graduates in various countries were asked to state the extent to which they use the competences they have acquired during their studies in their job. Considerable use is stated on average by more than half the employed Bachelors, but the respective percentage varies between only 35 per cent of solely employed university Bachelor graduates in Germany and 81 per cent of all Bachelor graduates in Poland. In some countries, the rate of strong horizontal links between study and work is similar between Bachelor graduates and those from Master programmes and traditional programmes: in Austria, the Czech Republic, Italy and Poland as well as in the case of Bachelor graduates from other higher education institutions in the Netherlands. In other countries, Bachelor graduates more rarely perceive a close link between study and work than graduates from Master programmes and traditional programmes: in Germany and Hungary as well as university Bachelor graduates in Norway and the Netherlands (see table 8).

Table 8. Strong Horizontal Link between Study and Work Assignments among Graduates from selected European Countries (per cent of employed graduates)

	Bachelor graduates			Master graduates			Single-cycle/ traditional degrees		
	Univ.	Other HEIs	All	Univ.	Other HEIs	All	Univ.	Other HEIs	All
AT Austria	48	51	49	•	•	•	47	54	49
CZ Czech Republic	•	•	65	•	•	67	•	•	•
DE Germany	35	48	•	56	64	•	50	51	•
HU Hungary	•	•	61	•	•	•	76	59	•
IT Italy	40	•	40	•	•	•	•	•	•
NL The Netherlands	54	62	•	66	•	66	66	64	•
NO Norway	65	•	•	•	•	87	•	•	•
PL Poland	•	•	82	•	•	83	•	•	83

Univ. = University
Other HEIs = Other Higher Education Institutions (e.g. Fachhochschulen, Grandes Écoles etc.)

Figures are based on country reports of this volume.

INCOME AND OCCUPATIONAL GROUP

Given the general conditions of an educational meritocracy, we can expect that those who graduate with a higher degree transfer more often to the highest categories of the occupational hierarchy and have a higher income than those who transfer to employment with a lower level degree. In this respect, occupation and income of graduates systematically differ from the four categories of professional success discussed above. However, all the issues of a possible over-estimation of the employment problems of Bachelor graduates or notably university Bachelor graduates stated above hold true here as well.

It does not come as a surprise to note that in most of the six countries for which the respective information is available a substantially higher share of Master graduates and graduates from traditional university programmes is employed in *managerial and professional occupations* and, a substantially lower share is employed as *associate professionals*. To illustrate this with the example of France: Only about one sixth of Bachelor graduates (both from general and vocational programmes) is employed as managers and professionals, compared to about 60 per cent and about 90 per cent of the graduates from the different categories of Master and single-cycle long programmes. In contrast, about two-thirds of the former but less than one third of the latter are semi-professionals. The respective figures for the UK are 36 per cent and 73 per cent (see table 9). In Hungary, bachelor graduates are even as frequently active as managers and professionals as graduates from traditional university programmes (62 per cent each).

Table 9. Graduates in Managerial/Professional Position and in Associate Professional Position among Graduates from selected European Countries (per cent of employed graduates)

	Bachelor graduates			Master graduates			Single-cycle/ traditional degrees		
	Univ.	Other HEIs	All	Univ.	Other HEIs	All	Univ.	Other HEIs	All
CZ Czech Republic									
Managerial/Prof. Position	•	•	31	•	•	60	•	•	•
Associate Prof. Position	•	•	52	•	•	34	•	•	•
FR France									
Managerial/Prof. Position	17	15	•	63	81	•	91	•	•
Associate Prof. Position	64	67	•	29	15	•	7	•	•
HU Hungary									
Managerial/Prof. Position	•	•	62	•	•	•	62	58	•
Associate Prof. Position	•	•	29	•	•	•	31	34	•
NL The Netherlands									
Managerial/Prof. Position	57	52	•	71	•	71	71	52	•
Associate Prof. Position	11	22	•	10	•	10	9	23	•
NO Norway									
Managerial/Prof. Position	27	•	•	•	•	75	•	•	•
Associate Prof. Position	11	•	•	•	•	13	•	•	•
UK United Kingdom									
Managerial/Prof. Position	36	•	•	73	•	•	•	•	•
Associate Prof. Position	30	•	•	18	•	•	•	•	•

Prof. = Professional
Univ. = University
Other HEIs = Other Higher Education Institutions (e.g. Fachhochschulen, Grandes Écoles etc.)

Figures are based on country reports of this volume.

Two cases that are distinct from most countries must be cited. In the Netherlands, Bachelor graduates are also less often employed as managers and professionals than graduates from Master programmes and traditional university programmes, but even among the former more than half are managers or professionals (57 per cent of university Bachelor graduates and 52 per cent of Bachelor graduates from other higher education institutions). In Hungary, Bachelor graduates are as frequently employed as managers and professionals as those from traditional university programmes (62 per cent each).

In six of the eight countries for which respective information is available university Bachelor graduates or all Bachelors (if no distinction is made according to institutional types) have a clearly lower *income* on average than Master graduates and graduates from long single-cycle programmes. But this difference varies strikingly from about 10 per cent less (in Austria and Poland) to about 30 per cent less (in France and Hungary). In contrast, university Bachelor graduates in Italy and the Netherlands earn as much or even slightly more on average than their reference groups with a higher degree (see table 10).

Table 10. Gross Income of Graduates from selected European Countries (in Euro; arithmetic mean of employed graduates)

	Bachelor graduates			Master graduates			Single-cycle/ traditional degrees		
	Univ.	Other HEIs	All	Univ.	Other HEIs	All	Univ.	Other HEIs	All
AT Austria (monthly)	2,358	2,748	2,532	•	•	•	2,641	2,888	2,705
DE Germany (monthly)	2,448	2,817	2,718	3,012	3,743	3,346	3,070	3,037	3,053
FR France (net monthly)	1,368	1,575	•	1,904	2,313	•	2,383	•	•
HU Hungary (annual)	•	•	8,884	•	•	•	11,958	9,327	•
IT Italy (net monthly)	1,109	•	1,109	1,057	•	1,057	1,110	•	1,110
NL The Netherlands	2,589	2,040	•	2,439	•	2,439	2,476	1,938	•
NO Norway (annual)	38,259	45,228	•	•	•	46,012	•	•	
PL Poland (net hourly)	•	•	2,23	•	•	2,40	•	•	2,38

Univ. = University
Other HEIs = Other Higher Education Institutions (e.g. Fachhochschulen, Grandes Écoles etc.)

Figures are based on country reports of this volume.

In four countries a distinction is made between the income of university Bachelor graduates and that of Bachelor graduates from other higher education institutions or vocational programmes. In three of these countries (Austria, Germany and France), university Bachelor graduates earn more than 10 per cent less on average than other Bachelor graduates (mainly because of the different compositions of fields of study), but in the Netherlands, the other Bachelor graduates earn about 20 per cent less than university Bachelor graduates.

Information on the income of graduates from other higher education institutions both with a Bachelor degree and a traditional degree is available for only three countries. In Austria and the Netherlands, the average income between these two groups does not differ substantially. In Germany, however, Bachelor graduates from other higher education institutions earn 7 per cent less on average than those from traditional programmes of these institutions because most Bachelor programmes are about one year shorter than the traditional programmes at Fachhochschulen.

SATISFACTION

Finally, the proportion of those who are globally satisfied with their job is quite high. There are differences by countries, with an average rate of satisfaction above 80 per cent in France and Hungary, above 70 per cent in Austria and the Czech Republic, and above 60 per cent in Germany and the Netherlands (see table 11).

Table 11. High Overall Job Satisfaction of Graduates from selected European Countries (per cent of employed graduates)

	Bachelor graduates			Master graduates			Single-cycle/ traditional degrees		
	Univ.	Other HEIs	All	Univ.	Other HEIs	All	Univ.	Other HEIs	All
AT Austria	71	73	72	•	•	•	73	78	74
CZ Czech Republic	•	•	73	•	•	71	•	•	•
DE Germany	63	69	•	66	65	•	66	67	•
FR France	76	82	•	82	88	•	97	•	•
HU Hungary	•	•	81	•	•	•	84	79	•
NL The Netherlands	63	65	•	70	•	70	69	64	•
NO Norway	48	•	•	•	•	74	•	•	•

Univ. = University
Other HEIs = Other Higher Education Institutions (e.g. Fachhochschulen, Grandes Écoles etc.)

Figures are based on country reports of this volume.

Altogether, the rates of satisfaction do not vary substantially according to level of degree and type of institutions. The clearly higher rate of satisfied Master graduates as compared to Bachelor graduates in Norway could be due to the fact that the figure for Bachelor graduates includes those who study and work and therefore take on temporary jobs to fund their subsequent study.

CONCLUSION

This comparative analysis of the professional situation of Bachelor graduates from 10 European countries can be viewed as an early, almost premature snapshot. It refers on average to 2007 graduates and to their first two years after graduation. If we wanted to have information on cohorts where most students have already started their studies in a Bachelor-Master system and if we wanted to include graduates who had moved to Master studies a few years after the award of the Bachelor degree, we would have to wait until about the year 2015. But this account in the year 2010 also provides very interesting information.

In looking at countries with a long tradition of Bachelor and Master degrees one could have expected that only a minority of Bachelor graduates would opt for further study. But this comparative study shows that most Bachelor graduates in the countries that have recently introduced a cycle-system of study programmes and degrees continue to study after the award of the Bachelor degree. In various countries, this rate is about three quarters among university Bachelor graduates. Certainly, a mix of warnings by university professors about an incompleteness of Bachelor study at universities, half-hearted curricular reforms, cautious views by employers and uncertainties and high aspirations by students has led to such high rates of further study.

A look at the transition from Bachelor study to employment, however, shows that employment after the Bachelor award is by no means rare even among university Bachelor graduates: about half on average are employed. As one might expect, this proportion is higher among Bachelor graduates from other institutions of higher education, but the difference between Bachelors of the two types of institutions (where they exist) is great in some countries and small in others. How can high rates of further study and high rates of transition to employment among university Master graduates co-exist? The interesting answer to this question is: varying by country between about one third and about two-thirds of those who are employed study concurrently. We do not know the extent to which Bachelor graduates postpone their decision to make a choice, work to fund their studies or intend to be both professionally active in an appropriate position and with a close link to study, competences and work tasks as well as pursuing study to a higher degree level.

In order to compare the professional success of Bachelor graduates with that of Master graduates and those from single-cycle programmes, it is appropriate to include only those professionally active Bachelor graduates who do not study concurrently. In fact, some country reports analyse the professional success of those Bachelor graduates who are only employed.

Given the usual relationships between level of educational attainment and level of employment in economically advanced countries shaped by principles of education meritocracy, one could expect from the outset that most Bachelor graduates would be employed as associate professionals while most Master graduates would be employed as managers and professionals. Also one could have expected that the Bachelor graduates earned about 10-20 per cent less than the Master graduates.

Actually, the average across the nine European countries in which the Bachelor-Master structure of study programmes and degrees was recently introduced fits this expectation. Most striking, however, is the enormous variety between countries. The difference in income of Bachelor graduates and graduates from university Master programmes and long single-cycle programmes ranges from about 30 per cent less to a slightly higher income. There are cases where employment in professional and managerial positions varies dramatically according the level of degree. And there are cases where the many graduates from Master programmes or long single-cycle programmes work as associate professionals or where most Bachelor graduates are employed as managers and professionals.

Altogether, we note that the professional success of Bachelor graduates in the Central and Eastern European countries – the Czech Republic, Hungary and Poland – differs to a lesser extent from that of the Master graduates and the graduates from long single-cycle programmes than in Western European countries. This might be a consequence of the fact that rates of highly qualified persons among the labour force have been lower in the former countries for a long time and that the Bachelor graduates fill a gap caused by traditional shortage. However, as the enrolment rates have increased substantially in these countries in recent years, this favourable situation of Bachelor graduates in Central and Eastern European countries might fade in the near future.

If the new Bachelor-Master system was fully accepted by all groups of actors involved, one could expect that Bachelor graduates would not differ much from Master graduates or graduates from long single-cycle programmes with respect to employments conditions such as full-time study and permanent employment. Also, one would not expect any difference in the extent to which they perceive holding a position that matches their degree level and the extent to which they note a close link between the substance of their study and their competences and job requirements .

Actually, we note again an enormous diversity by country and the patterns are not consistent according to these four measures of professional success. We note many instances where university Bachelor graduates perceive professional success as frequently as graduates from higher-level programmes. But some differences underscore problems on the part of the university Bachelor graduates: For example, only 35 per cent of the Bachelor graduates from German universities report a high use on the job of their competences acquired in the course of study, compared to about 50 per cent or more of the other categories of graduates. The data show even more striking differences of this kind in some respects in Norway, but this might be due in some cases to the fact that some of Norwegian findings include all employed Bachelor graduates (i.e. including those who are employed and studying). On average, the data for university Bachelors seem 5-10 per cent less favourable than those for graduates with higher degrees. This difference shows that the university Bachelor has not become a fully normal phenomenon in the labour market. But the professional success of Bachelor graduates and among them university Bachelor graduates is more favourable than one can assume on the basis of the public discourse where negative assessments are widespread.

The employed Bachelor graduates obviously do note rate the situation negatively. A high degree of overall job satisfaction varies between countries by about 60 per cent and more than 80 per cent, whereby the ratings of the Bachelor graduates and of university Bachelor graduates hardly differ from those of other categories of graduates in their respective country.

As pointed out in the introduction, educational statistics are the most frequently employed sources to discuss mobility in framework of the Bologna Process. This holds true, even though the available statistics for students have enormous weaknesses: Often attention is paid to nationality rather than to mobility for the purpose of study. Moreover, the available international statistical data are almost useless with respect to temporary mobility – the most important issue of intra-European mobility in the Bologna Process.

Graduate surveys, however, are the best possible source to measure the fulfilment of a mobility target set in the Bologna Process; graduate surveys can establish what proportion of (eventually graduating) students have been abroad at least once for a period of study. Actually, this comparative analysis has shown an enormous range in this respect: In some countries the Bologna target for the year 2020 – that 20 per cent have studied abroad during their course of study – had already been surpassed more than 10 years earlier. In other countries, this rate is still below five per cent.

Finally, graduate surveys can gather information about professional mobility abroad after graduation. This is not explicitly expressed in the Bologna Process, but it has played a substantial role in the context of EU policies. Past analyses of labour market statistics have suggested that less than five per cent of degree holders in Europe are employed abroad. This comparative study does not suggest that these rates have substantially increased in recent years.

All these findings must be reported with caution. This study addresses only ten countries because the number of European countries where conceptually and methodologically satisfying national graduate surveys have been undertaken recently is limited. Also multi-country surveys have not been undertaken for recent graduate cohorts. The surveys undertaken in the 10 countries differ so much from each other that comparability was quite a challenge for this comparative study. As this comparative study demonstrates both the potentials of comparative graduate surveys and the current limitations, we can hope that it will have a mobilising effect for methodological improvement, for increasing the similarity among the national graduate surveys, for establishing national graduate surveys in more European countries or to move – surveys of that kind in the past have addressed those graduating around the mid-1990s and around the year 2000 – towards the establishment of a regular European graduate survey. We hope that better surveys will enable experts to undertake a more solid comparative analysis around 2015 when the impact of the Bologna Reform on graduate employment and work as well as on mobility during the course of study and after graduation can be fully explored.

THE AUTHORS

AUSTRIA

Helmut Guggenberger, Department of Sociology, University of Klagenfurt

Maria Keplinger, Austrian Federal Ministry for Science and Research (bmwf), Vienna

Martin Unger, Institute for Advanced Studies, Vienna

CZECH REPUBLIC

Radim Ryška, Faculty of Education, Charles University in Prague

Martin Zelenka, Faculty of Education, Charles University in Prague

FRANCE

Jean-François Giret, Institute of Research in Education: Sociology and Economics of Education (IREDU), National Centre for Scientific Research (CNRS), University of Burgundy, Dijon

Christine Guegnard, Centre for Research on Education, Training and Employment, Institute of Research in Education: Sociology and Economics of Education (IREDU), National Centre for Scientific Research (CNRS), University of Burgundy, Dijon.

Claire Michot, Institute of Research in Education: Sociology and Economics of Education (IREDU), National Centre for Scientific Research (CNRS), University of Burgundy, Dijon

GERMANY

Harald Schomburg, International Centre for Higher Education Research (INCHER-Kassel), University of Kassel

Ulrich Teichler, International Centre for Higher Education Research (INCHER-Kassel), University of Kassel

HUNGARY

László Kiss, Educatio Public Services Nonprofit LLC, Budapest

Zsuzsanna Veroszta, Educatio Public Services Nonprofit LLC, Budapest

---

H. Schomburg and U. Teichler (eds.), Employability and Mobility of Bachelor Graduates in Europe, 275–276.
© 2011 *Sense Publishers. All rights reserved.*

THE AUTHORS

ITALY

Gilberto Antonelli, Faculty of Law, Alma Mater Studiorum-University of Bologna; Coordinator of the Scientific Committee of the AlmaLaurea Inter-University Consortium

Andrea Cammelli, Faculty of Statistical Sciences, Alma Mater Studiorum-University of Bologna; AlmaLaurea Inter-University Consortium

Angelo di Francia, Scientific Director at the AlmaLaurea Inter-University Consortium

Giancarlo Gasperoni, Department Communication Disciplines, Alma Mater Studiorum-University of Bologna; AlmaLaurea Inter-University Consortium

Matteo Sgarzi, AlmaLaurea Inter-University Consortium

NORWAY

Clara Åse Arnesen, Nordic Institute for Studies in Innovation, Research and Education (NIFU)

Liv Anne Støren, Nordic Institute for Studies in Innovation, Research and Education (NIFU)

Jannecke Wiers-Jenssen, Nordic Institute for Studies in Innovation, Research and Education (NIFU)

POLAND

Gabriela Grotkowska, Faculty of Economics Sciences, University of Warsaw

THE NETHERLANDS

Jim Allen, Research Center for Higher Education and the Labour Market (ROA), Maastricht University

Johan Coenen, Top Institute for Evidence Based Education Research (TIER), Maastricht University

UNITED KINGDOM

Brenda Little, Center for Higher Education Research and Information (CHERI), Open University